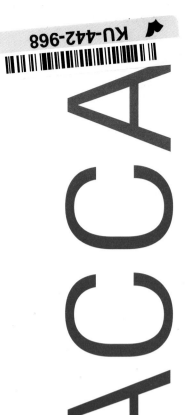

Paper 2.3

BUSINESS TAXATION
(FINANCE ACTS 2005)

For exams in June and December 2006

Study Text

In this August 2005 new edition

- A new **user-friendly format** for easy navigation

- **Exam-centred topic coverage**, directly linked to ACCA's syllabus and study guide

- **Exam focus points** showing you what the examiner will want you to do

- Regular **fast forward** summaries emphasising the key points in each chapter

- **Questions** and **quick quizzes** to test your understanding

- **Exam question bank** containing exam standard questions with answers

- A full index

BPP's **i-Learn** and **i-Pass** products also support this paper.

FOR EXAMS IN JUNE AND DECEMBER 2006

PROFESSIONAL EDUCATION

First edition February 2001
Sixth edition August 2005

ISBN 0 7517 2355 X (Previous edition 0 7517 1720 7)

British Library Cataloguing-in-Publication Data
A catalogue record for this book
is available from the British Library

Published by

BPP Professional Education
Aldine House, Aldine Place
London W12 8AW

www.bpp.com

Printed in Great Britain by Ashford Colour Press

We are grateful to the Association of Chartered
Certified Accountants for permission to reproduce past
examination questions. The suggested solutions in the
exam answer bank have been prepared by BPP
Professional Education.

Contents

Computer-based learning products from BPP

If you want to reinforce your studies by **interactive** learning, try BPP's **i-Learn** product, covering major syllabus areas in an interactive format. For **self-testing**, try **i-Pass**, which offers a large number of **objective test questions**, particularly useful where objective test questions form part of the exam.

See the order form at the back of this text for details of these innovative learning tools.

Learn Online

Learn Online uses BPP's wealth of teaching experience to produce a fully **interactive** e-learning resource **delivered via the Internet**. The site offers comprehensive **tutor support** and features areas such as **study**, **practice**, **email service**, **revision** and **useful resources**.

Visit our website www.bpp.com/acca/learnonline to sample aspects of Learn Online free of charge.

Learning to Learn Accountancy

BPP's ground-breaking **Learning to Learn Accountancy** book is designed to be used both at the outset of your ACCA studies and throughout the process of learning accountancy. It challenges you to consider how you study and gives you helpful hints about how to approach the various types of paper which you will encounter. It can help you **focus your studies on the subject and exam**, enabling you to **acquire knowledge**, **practise and revise efficiently and effectively**.

The BPP Study Text

Aims of this Study Text

> To provide you with the knowledge and understanding, skills and application techniques that you need if you are to be successful in your exams

This Study Text has been written around the **Business Taxation** syllabus.

- It is **comprehensive**. It covers the syllabus content. No more, no less.

- It is written at the **right level**. Each chapter is written with ACCA's syllabus and study guide in mind

- It is targeted to the **exam**. We have taken account of the pilot paper, guidance the examiner has given and the assessment methodology.

- It is fully up to date for **Finance Acts 2005**. These will be examined in June 2006 and December 2006.

> To allow you to study in the way that best suits your learning style and the time you have available, by following your personal Study Plan (see page (viii))

You may be studying at home on your own until the date of the exam, or you may be attending a full-time course. You may like to (and have time to) read every word, or you may prefer to (or only have time to) skim-read and devote the remainder of your time to question practice. Wherever you fall in the spectrum, you will find the BPP Study Text meets your needs in designing and following your personal Study Plan.

> To tie in with the other components of the BPP Effective Study Package to ensure you have the best possible chance of passing the exam (see page (vi))

The BPP Effective Study Package

Recommended period of use	The BPP Effective Study Package
From the outset and throughout	**Learning to Learn Accountancy** Read this invaluable book as you begin your studies and refer to it as you work through the various elements of the BPP Effective Study Package. It will help you to acquire knowledge, practise and revise, efficiently and effectively.
Three to twelve months before the exam	**Study Text and i-Learn** Use the Study Text to acquire knowledge, understanding, skills and the ability to apply techniques. Use BPP's **i-Learn** product to reinforce your learning.
Throughout	**Learn Online** Study, practise, revise and take advantage of other useful resources with BPP's fully interactive e-learning site with comprehensive tutor support.
Throughout	**i-Pass** **i-Pass**, our computer-based testing package, provides objective test questions in a variety of formats and is ideal for self-assessment.
One to six months before the exam	**Practice & Revision Kit** Try the numerous examination-format questions, for which there are realistic suggested solutions prepared by BPP's own authors. Then attempt the two mock exams.
From three months before the exam until the last minute	**Passcards** Work through these short, memorable notes which are focused on what is most likely to come up in the exam you will be sitting.
One to six months before the exam	**Success CDs** The CDs cover the vital elements of your syllabus in less than 90 minutes per subject. They also contain exam hints to help you fine tune your strategy.

Help yourself study for your ACCA exams

Exams for professional bodies such as ACCA are very different from those you have taken at college or university. You will be under **greater time pressure before** the exam – as you may be combining your study with work. There are many different ways of learning and so the BPP Study Text offers you a number of different tools to help you through. Here are some hints and tips: they are not plucked out of the air, but **based on research and experience**. (You don't need to know that long-term memory is in the same part of the brain as emotions and feelings - but it's a fact anyway.)

The right approach

1   The right attitude

Believe in yourself	Yes, there is a lot to learn. Yes, it is a challenge. But thousands have succeeded before and you can too.
Remember why you're doing it	Studying might seem a grind at times, but you are doing it for a reason: to advance your career.

2   The right focus

Read through the Syllabus and learning outcomes	These tell you what you are expected to know and are supplemented by Exam focus points in the text.
Study the Exam Paper section	Past papers are likely to be good guides to what you should expect in the exam.

3   The right method

The whole picture	You need to grasp the detail - but keeping in mind how everything fits into the whole picture will help you understand better.
	• The **Introduction** of each chapter puts the material in context.
	• The **Syllabus content**, **Study guide** and **Exam focus points** show you what you need to **grasp**.
In your own words	To absorb the information (and to practise your written communication skills), it helps to **put it into your own words**.
	• **Take notes.**
	• Answer the **questions** in each chapter. You will practise your written communication skills, which become increasingly important as you progress through your ACCA exams.
	• Draw **mindmaps**. We have an example for the whole syllabus.
	• Try **'teaching' a subject** to a colleague or friend.
Give yourself cues to jog your memory	The BPP Study Text uses **bold** to **highlight key points**.
	• Try **colour coding** with a highlighter pen.
	• Write **key points** on cards.

4   **The right review**

Review, review, review	It is a **fact** that regularly reviewing a topic in summary form can **fix it in your memory**. Because **review** is so important, the BPP Study Text helps you to do so in many ways.
	• **Chapter roundups** summarise the 'Fast forward' key points in each chapter. Use them to recap each study session.
	• The **Quick quiz** is another review technique you can use to ensure that you have grasped the essentials.
	• Go through the **Examples** in each chapter a second or third time.

Developing your personal Study Plan

BPP's **Learning to Learn Accountancy** book emphasises the need to prepare (and use) a study plan. Planning and sticking to the plan are key elements of learning success.
There are four steps you should work through.

Step 1   **How do you learn?**

First you need to be aware of your style of learning. The BPP **Learning to Learn Accountancy** book commits a chapter to this **self-discovery**. What types of intelligence do you display when learning? You might be advised to brush up on certain study skills before launching into this Study Text.

BPP's **Learning to Learn Accountancy** book helps you to identify what intelligences you show more strongly and then details how you can tailor your study process to your preferences. It also includes handy hints on how to develop intelligences you exhibit less strongly, but which might be needed as you study accountancy.

Are you a **theorist** or are you more **practical**? If you would rather get to grips with a theory before trying to apply it in practice, you should follow the study sequence on page (ix). If the reverse is true (you like to know why you are learning theory before you do so), you might be advised to flick through Study Text chapters and look at examples and questions (Steps 7 and 8 in the **suggested study sequence**) before reading through the detailed theory.

Step 2   **How much time do you have?**

Work out the time you have available per week, given the following.

- The standard you have set yourself
- The time you need to set aside later for work on the Practice & Revision Kit and Passcards
- The other exam(s) you are sitting
- Very importantly, practical matters such as work, travel, exercise, sleep and social life

Hours

Note your time available in box A.   A   [   ]

Step 3   Allocate your time

- Take the time you have available per week for this Study Text shown in box A, multiply it by the number of weeks available and insert the result in box B.

  B ☐

- Divide the figure in box B by the number of chapters in this text and insert the result in box C.

  C ☐

Remember that this is only a rough guide. Some of the chapters in this book are longer and more complicated than others, and you will find some subjects easier to understand than others.

Step 4   Implement

Set about studying each chapter in the time shown in box C, following the key study steps in the order suggested by your particular learning style.

This is your personal **Study Plan**. You should try and combine it with the study sequence outlined below. You may want to modify the sequence a little (as has been suggested above) to adapt it to your **personal style**.

BPP's **Learning to Learn Accountancy** gives further guidance on developing a study plan, and deciding where and when to study.

Suggested study sequence

It is likely that the best way to approach this Study Text is to tackle the chapters in the order in which you find them. Taking into account your individual learning style, you could follow this sequence.

Key study steps	Activity
Step 1 **Topic list**	Each numbered topic is a numbered section in the chapter.
Step 2 **Introduction**	This gives you the big picture in terms of the context of the chapter. The content is referenced to the Study Guide, and Exam Guidance shows how the topic is likely to be examined. In other words, it sets your objectives for study.
Step 3 **Fast forward**	Fast forward boxes give you a quick summary of the content of each of the main chapter sections. They are listed together in the roundup at the end of each chapter to provide you with an overview of the contents of the whole chapter.
Step 4 **Explanations**	Proceed methodically through the chapter, reading each section thoroughly and making sure you understand.
Step 5 **Key terms and Exam focus points**	- Key terms can often earn you *easy marks* if you state them clearly and correctly in an appropriate exam answer (and they are highlighted in the index at the back of the text). - Exam focus points state how we think the examiner intends to examine certain topics.
Step 6 **Note taking**	Take brief notes, if you wish. Avoid the temptation to copy out too much. Remember that being able to put something into your own words is a sign of being able to understand it. If you find you cannot explain something you have read, read it again before you make the notes.
Step 7 **Examples**	Follow each through to its solution very carefully.

Key study steps	Activity
Step 8 **Questions**	Make a very good attempt at each one.
Step 9 **Answers**	Check yours against ours, and make sure you understand any discrepancies.
Step 10 **Chapter roundup**	Work through it carefully, to make sure you have grasped the significance of all the fast forward points.
Step 11 **Quick quiz**	When you are happy that you have covered the chapter, use the Quick quiz to check how much you have remembered of the topics covered and to practise questions in a variety of formats.
Step 12 **Question practice**	Either at this point, or later when you are thinking about revising, make a full attempt at the Question(s) suggested at the very end of the chapter. You can find these in the Exam Question Bank at the end of the Study Text, along with the answers so you can see how you did. We highlight those that are introductory, and those which are of the standard you would expect to find in an exam. If you have bought i-Pass, use this too.

Short of time: Skim study technique?

You may find you simply do not have the time available to follow all the key study steps for each chapter, however you adapt them for your particular learning style. If this is the case, follow the **skim study** technique below.

- Study the chapters in the order you find them in the Study Text.
- For each chapter:
  - Follow the key study steps 1-3
  - Skim-read through step 5
  - Jump to step 10
  - Go back to step 5
  - Follow through step 7
  - Prepare outline answers to questions (steps 8/9)
  - Try the Quick quiz (step 11), following up any items you can't answer
  - Do a plan for the Question (step 12), comparing it against our answers
  - You should probably still follow step 6 (note-taking), although you may decide simply to rely on the BPP Passcards for this.

Moving on...

However you study, when you are ready to embark on the practice and revision phase of the BPP Effective Study Package, you should still refer back to this Study Text, both as a source of **reference** (you should find the index particularly helpful for this) and as a way to **review** (the Fast forwards, Exam focus points, Chapter roundups and Quick quizzes help you here).

And remember to keep careful hold of this Study Text – you will find it invaluable in your work.

More advice on Study Skills can be found in BPP's **Learning to Learn Accountancy** book.

Syllabus

Aim

To develop knowledge and understanding in the core areas of tax related to businesses and their employees.

Objectives

On completion of this paper, candidates should be able to:

- explain the operation of the UK tax system

- prepare computations of the corporation tax liability for individual companies and groups of companies

- prepare computations of the income tax liability for employees, sole traders and partnerships

- prepare computations of the chargeable gains arising on incorporated and unincorporated businesses

- explain and apply the principles and scope of Value Added Tax

- explain the impact of National Insurance Contributions on employees, employers and the self-employed

- explain the use of exemptions and reliefs in deferring or minimising tax liabilities

- demonstrate the skills expected at Part 2

Position of the paper in the overall syllabus

An understanding of the formats of accounts used for sole traders, partnerships and companies from Paper 1.1 Preparing Financial Statements is assumed. There is no substantial integration with other papers in Part 2.

The coverage in Paper 2.3 will provide the grounding for the study of the optional Paper 3.2 Advanced Taxation.

Paper 3.2 develops the topics by applying the tax knowledge to problems encountered in practice, by giving more emphasis to planning to minimise or defer tax and by examining the interaction of taxes.

1 **Corporate business**

(a) Scope of corporation tax

(b) Residence

(c) Profits chargeable to corporation tax

    (i) Trading income
    (ii) Capital allowances
    (iii) Relief for trading losses
    (iv) Property income
    (v) Interest
    (vi) Charges on income

(d) Chargeable gains

    (i) Principles and scope
    (ii) The basis of calculation
    (iii) The identification and application of relevant exemptions and reliefs

(e) Calculation of the corporation tax liability

(f) Overseas aspects

    (i) Trading overseas via a subsidiary or a branch
    (ii) Double taxation relief
    (iii) Transfer pricing

(g) Groups of companies

(h) Self assessment system

(i) Value added tax

2 **Unincorporated businesses**

(a) Basic income tax computation

(b) Self assessment system

(c) Trading income

    (i) Badges of trade
    (ii) Computation of assessable profit
    (iii) Basis of assessment
    (iv) Change of accounting date
    (v) Capital allowances
    (vi) Relief for trading losses
    (vii) Partnerships and limited liability partnerships
    (viii) Personal pensions

(d) Capital gains tax

    (i) Principles and scope (restricted to business assets)
    (ii) The basis of calculation
    (iii) The identification and application of relevant exemptions and reliefs

(e) Value added tax

(f) Class 2 and Class 4 NIC

3   **Employees**

    (a)   Employment income

        (i)   Basis of assessment
        (ii)   Allowable deductions
        (iii) PAYE system
        (iv)   Benefits

    (b)   Occupational pension schemes

    (c)   Class 1 and Class 1A NIC

4   **Tax planning**

    (a)   Employment v self-employment
    (b)   Remuneration packages
    (c)   Choice of business medium
    (d)   Incorporation of a business
    (e)   Disposal of a business
    (f)   Directors and shareholders

Excluded topics

The following topics are specifically excluded from Paper 2.3.

1   **Corporate business**

    (a)   Scope of corporation tax

        (i)   Investment companies
        (ii)   Close companies
        (iii)   Companies in receivership and liquidation
        (iv)   Anti-avoidance legislation
        (v)   Reorganisations
        (vi)   Purchase by a company of its own shares
        (vii)   Personal service companies

    (c)   Profits chargeable to corporation tax

        (i)   Research and development expenditure

        (ii)   The 100% first year allowance for flats above shops

        (iii)   The 100% first year allowance for water technologies

        (iv)   Capital allowances for agricultural buildings, patents, scientific research and know how

        (iv)   In respect of industrial buildings allowance: enterprise zones, initial allowances, and the sale of an industrial building at less than original cost following a period of non-industrial use (note that sales for more than original cost are examinable)

        (v)   Furnished holiday lettings

        (vi)   Non-trading deficits on loan relationships

        (vii)   Trade charges on income

        (viii) Relief for intangible assets

        (ix)   The corporate venturing scheme

(d) Chargeable gains

   (i) Assets held at 31 March 1982

   (ii) Part disposals

   (iii) Negligible value chains

   (iv) Leases, chattels and wasting assets

   (v) A detailed question on the pooling provisions for shares

   (vi) The same day and nine day matching rules for shares and securities applicable to corporate businesses

   (vii) Substantial shareholdings

(e) Calculation of the corporation tax liability

   (i) In relation to the minimum corporation tax rate of 19% where profits are paid out as a dividend, an accounting period spanning 31 March 2004, dividends paid to corporate shareholders and groups of companies.

(f) Overseas aspects

   (i) Controlled foreign companies

   (ii) Foreign companies trading in the UK

   (iii) Expense relief in respect of overseas tax

   (iv) The restriction of double taxation relief for underlying tax to the full rate of corporation tax

   (v) The carry back and carry forward of unrelieved foreign tax

(g) Groups of companies

   (i) Consortia

   (ii) 51% groups and group income elections

   (iii) Pre-entry gains and losses

   (iv) The anti-avoidance provisions where arrangements exist for a company to leave a group

   (v) The tax charge that applies where a company leaves a group within six years of receiving an asset by way of a no gain/no loss transfer

(h) Self assessment system

   (i) Form CT61 and quarterly accounting for income tax

(i) Value added tax

   (i) Group registration

   (ii) Imports, exports and trading within the European Community

   (iii) Partial exemption

   (iv) Second-hand goods scheme

   (v) The capital goods scheme

   (vi) In respect of property and land: leases and do-it-yourself builders, and the landlord's option to tax

(vii) Penalties apart from the default surcharge, serious misdeclarations (but not repeated misdeclarations) and default interest

(viii) Special schemes for retailers

2 Unincorporated businesses

(a) Basic income tax computation

(i) Personal allowances other than the personal allowance for people aged under 65
(ii) Tax credits
(iii) Non-trade charges on income
(iv) Joint property of husbands and wives, maintenance payments and minor children
(v) Property income
(vi) Investment and miscellaneous income
(vii) Individual savings accounts (ISAs)
(viii) The enterprise investment scheme and venture capital trusts
(ix) Foreign income, non-residents and double taxation relief
(x) Income from trusts and settlements
(xi) Anti-avoidance legislation

(c) Trading income

(i) As for corporate businesses

(ii) Farmers averaging of profits

(iii) The averaging of profits for authors and creative artists

(iv) Loss relief for shares in unquoted trading companies

(v) Investment income and charges of a partnership

(vi) The allocation of notional profits and losses for a partnership

(vii) The simplification of pensions that is to take place from 6 April 2006. This topic will not be examinable until the June 2007 diet.

(d) Capital gains tax

(i) As for corporate businesses
(ii) Calculation of the indexation allowance
(iii) EIS deferral relief
(iv) Principal private residence
(v) Partnership capital gains
(vi) Overseas aspects
(vii) Losses in the year of death
(viii) The transfer of assets between a husband and wife
(ix) The exemption of gilt edged securities and qualifying corporate bonds
(x) The payment of CGT by annual instalments
(xi) Capital sums received in respect of the loss, destruction or damage of an asset
(xii) Relief for losses incurred on loans made to traders

(e) Value added tax

(i) As for corporate businesses

(f) Class 2 and Class 4 NIC

(i) The offset of trading losses against non-trading income (for Class 4 NIC)

3   **Employees**

    (a)   Employment income

        (i)   The calculation of car benefit where emission figures are not available

        (ii)   Share and share option incentive schemes for employees

        (iii)   Payments on the termination of employment, and other lump sums received by employees

    (b)   Occupational pension schemes

        (i)   A detailed knowledge of the conditions that must be met to obtain HMRC approval for an occupational pension scheme

        (ii)   The option for certain occupational pension schemes to apply to be subject to the personal pension scheme rules

    (c)   Class 1 and Class 1A NIC

        (i)   The calculation of directors' NIC on a month by month basis

Key areas of the syllabus

The key topic areas, taken directly from the syllabus content list, are as follows.

1   **Corporate business**

    (a)   Scope of corporation tax
    (c)   Profits chargeable to corporation tax
    (e)   Calculation of the corporation tax liability
    (h)   Self assessment system

2   **Unincorporated business**

    (a)   Basic income tax computation
    (b)   Self assessment system
    (c)   Trading income

3   **Employees**

    (a)   Employment income

Paper 2.3

Business Taxation FAs 2005
(United Kingdom)

Study Guide

1 CORPORATE BUSINESSES

(a) **Scope of corporation tax**

- Define the terms 'period of account', 'accounting period' and 'financial year'.

- Explain when an accounting period starts and finishes.

(b) **Residence**

- Explain how the residence of a company is determined.

(c) **Profits chargeable to corporation tax**

(i) Trading income

- State the expenditure that is allowable in calculating the tax-adjusted profit.

- Explain how relief can be obtained for pre-trading expenditure.

(ii) Capital allowances

- Define plant and machinery for capital allowances purposes.

- Calculate writing down allowances and first year allowances.

- Explain the treatment of motor cars.

- Compute balancing allowances and charges.

- Explain the treatment of short life assets and long life assets.

- Define an industrial building for industrial buildings allowance purposes.

- Calculate industrial buildings allowance for new and second-hand buildings.

- Compute the balancing adjustment on the disposal of an industrial building.

(iii) Relief for trading losses

- Explain how trading losses can be carried forward.

- Explain how trading losses can be claimed against income of the current or previous accounting periods.

- State the factors that will influence the choice of loss relief claim.

(iv) Property income

- Compute the property business profit.

- Explain the treatment of a premium received for the grant of a short lease.

- Explain how relief for a property business loss is given.

(v) Investment income

- Explain how profits from loan relationships and interest received are assessed.

(vi) Charges on income

- Explain the treatment of charges on income.

(d) **Chargeable gains**

(i) Principles and scope

- Prepare a basic capital gains computation.

- State the allowable deductions.

- Calculate the indexation allowance.

(ii) The basis of calculation

- Explain the treatment of capital losses.

- Explain the identification rules for disposals of shares and securities.

- Apply the pooling provisions for shares and securities.

- Explain the treatment following a bonus issue, rights issue or takeover.

As a result of the chargeable gain part disposal rules not being examinable, any question on the takeover of shares or securities will involve a paper for paper transaction.

Reorganisations are not mentioned in the Study Guide. This is because all the relevant rules can be examined by way of a takeover (for example, where shareholders receive two different classes of share in exchange for their existing shareholding).

(iii) The identification and application of relevant exemptions and reliefs

- Explain and apply rollover relief.

(e) **Calculation of the corporation tax liability**

- Prepare a basic corporation tax computation.
- Explain the implications of receiving franked investment income.
- Calculate the corporation tax liability at the starting rate, small company rate and full rate, and apply tapering relief.

- Explain how the payment of a dividend can impact on the amount of corporation tax payable.

(f) **Overseas aspects**

(i) Trading overseas via a subsidiary or a branch

- Compare the UK tax treatment of an overseas branch to an overseas subsidiary.

(ii) Double taxation relief

- Calculate double taxation relief for withholding tax and underlying tax.

(iii) Transfer pricing

- Explain and apply the transfer pricing rules.

(g) **Groups of companies**

- Define an associated company.
- Define a 75% group.
- Explain and apply the reliefs available to members of a 75% group.
- Define a 75% capital gains group.
- Explain and apply the reliefs available to members of a 75% capital gains group.

(h) **Self assessment system**

- Describe the features of self-assessment.
- Explain how HMRC can enquire into a self-assessment return.

- Calculate interest on overdue tax.
- Explain how large companies are required to account for corporation tax on a quarterly basis.

(i) **Value Added Tax**

- Describe the scope of VAT.
- State the circumstances in which a person must register for VAT, and explain the advantages of voluntary VAT registration.
- State the circumstances in which pre-registration input VAT can be recovered.
- Explain how a person can deregister for VAT.
- Explain how VAT is accounted for and administered.
- Explain how the tax point is determined.
- List the information that must be given on a VAT invoice.
- Describe the principles that apply to the valuation of supplies.
- State the circumstances in which input VAT is non-deductible.
- Describe the relief that is available for bad debts.
- List the principal zero-rated and exempt supplies.
- Describe the cash accounting, the annual accounting and the flat rate schemes.

- State the circumstances in which the default surcharge, a serious misdeclaration penalty, and default interest will be applied.

2 UNINCORPORATED BUSINESSES

(a) Basic income tax computation

- Prepare a basic income tax computation.
- Explain the treatment of savings income and dividends.
- Explain the treatment of business charges on income.

(b) Self assessment system

- Describe the features of self-assessment
- Calculate payments on account and balancing payments/ repayments
- Calculate interest on overdue tax and state the penalties that can be charged.
- Explain how HMRC can enquire into a self-assessment return.

(c) Trading income

(i) Badges of trade

- Describe and apply the badges of trade.

(ii) Computation of assessable profit

- As for corporate business.

(iii) Basis of assessment

- Explain the basis of assessment.
- Compute the assessable profits on commencement and cessation.

(iv) Change of accounting date

- State the factors that will influence the choice of accounting date.
- State the conditions that must be met for a change of accounting date to be valid.
- Compute the assessable profits on a change of accounting date.

(v) Capital allowances

- As for corporate businesses.

(vi) Relief for trading losses

- Explain how trading losses can be carried forward (although only trade charges are examinable, the impact of non-trade charges where trade charges are carried forward is examinable.

In any examination question on this area, a figure for non-trade charges will simply be given. The carry forward of losses on incorporation is examinable).

- Explain how trading losses can be claimed against total income and chargeable gains.
- Explain the relief for trading losses in the early years of a trade.
- Explain terminal loss relief.

(vii) Partnerships and Limited Liability Partnerships

- Explain how a partnership is assessed to tax.
- Allocate assessable profits between the partners following a change in the profit sharing ratio or a change in the members of the partnership.
- Describe the alternative loss relief claims that are available to partners.
- Explain the loss relief restriction that applies to the partners of a limited liability partnership.

(viii) Personal pensions

- Explain the relief given for contributions to a personal pension scheme.

(d) Capital gains tax

(i) Principles and scope (restricted to business assets)

- As for corporate businesses.

- Define a business asset for the purposes of taper relief.

- Compute taper relief (including non-business assets).

(ii) The basis of calculation

- As for corporate businesses. Quoted shares and securities including the valuation rules are examinable since certain quoted shareholdings will qualify for business asset taper relief. The indexation allowance is not examinable for individual taxpayers. Therefore, any question involving shares and securities will simply give a figure for the value of the 1985 pool as at 5 April 1998.

(iii) The identification and application of relevant exemptions and reliefs

- As for corporate businesses.

- Explain and apply holdover relief for the gift of business assets.

- Explain and apply the relief available when a business is transferred to a limited company.

(e) Value Added Tax

- As for corporate businesses.

(f) Class 2 and Class 4 NIC

- Calculate Class 2 NIC.
- Calculate Class 4 NIC.

3 EMPLOYEES

(a) Employment income

(i) Basis of assessment

- State the factors that determine whether an engagement is treated as employment or self-employment.

- Explain the basis of assessment.

- Describe the income assessable.

(ii) Allowable deductions

- List the allowable deductions, including travelling expenses.

- Explain the use of the authorised mileage allowance.

(iii) PAYE system

- Explain the PAYE system.

(iv) Benefits

- Identify PIID employees.

- Explain how benefits are assessed.

(b) Occupational pension schemes

- State the main features of an occupational pension scheme.

- Explain the significance of an occupational pension scheme being approved by HMRC.

(c) Class 1 and Class 1A NIC

- Calculate Class 1 NIC.
- Calculate Class 1A NIC.

4 TAX PLANNING

(a) Employment v self-employment

- Compare the tax implications of employment as compared to self-employment.

(b) Remuneration packages

- Compare alternative remuneration packages.

(c) Choice of business medium

- Compare the tax position of a director/shareholder with that of a sole trader.

(d) Incorporation of a business

- Explain the factors that must be considered when incorporating a business.

(e) Disposal of a business

- Explain the tax implications arising on the disposal of a business.

(f) Directors and shareholders

- Compute whether remuneration or a dividend is the most tax effective way to extract profit from a company.

The exam paper

Approach to examining the syllabus

The examination is a **three hour paper** divided into **two sections**.

Only core topics will be examined in Section A. A non-core topic may form part of a question (such as a chargeable gain in a corporation tax computation), but this will account for a maximum of ten marks. At least 40 of the 55 available marks in Section A will be of a computational nature.

- Question 1 will be on a corporate business (for approximately 30 marks).
- Question 2 will be on an unincorporated business and/or employees (for approximately 25 marks).

The questions in Section B will be a mix of computational and written, and include the minimisation or deferment of tax liability by the identification and application of relevant exemptions and reliefs.

- Question 3 will be on VAT (either for an incorporated business or an unincorporated business).

- Question 4 will be on capital gains (either for an incorporated business or an unincorporated business).

- Questions 5, 6 and 7 will be on any area of the syllabus.

		Number of Marks
Section A:	2 compulsory questions	55
Section B:	Choice of 3 from 5 questions (15 marks each)	45
		100

Tax rates, allowances and benefits will be given in the examination paper.

Additional information

The ACCA applies a six-month rule in that questions requiring an understanding of new legislation will not be set until at least six calendar months after the last day of the month in which the legislation received Royal Assent. The same rule applies to the effective date of the provisions of an Act introduced by Statutory Instruments. It would, however, be considered inappropriate to examine legislation it is proposed to repeal or substantially alter.

Knowledge of section numbers will not be needed to understand questions in this paper, nor will students be expected to use them in their answers. If students wish to refer to section numbers in their answers they may do so and will not be penalised if old, or even incorrect, section numbers are used.

Names of cases or a detailed knowledge of the judgement are not required but knowledge of the principles decided in leading cases is required.

Analysis of past papers

The analysis below shows the topics which have been examined in all sittings of the current syllabus so far and in the Pilot Paper.

June 2005

Section A

1   Corporation tax. Adjustment of profits. PCTCT. Capital allowances, group relief, rollover relief. (30 marks)
2   Employment followed by self employment. Trading loss. Loss reliefs. (25 marks)

Section B

3   VAT default surcharge. VAT errors. Bad debt relief.
4   CGT for individual. Gift relief.
5   Self assessment for individual. Payments on account. Enquiries and discovery.
6   Choice of business medium – sole trade or limited company.
7   Payment of corporation tax for 15 month period of account.

December 2004

Section A

1   Corporation tax – capital allowances on plant and machinery; industrial buildings, adjustment of profits, Schedule A. Payment of CT by instalments. Calculation of CT with and without associated companies. (30 marks)

2   Partnership. Adjustment of profits. Income tax assessments on partners. IT and CGT due. (25 marks)

Section B

3   VAT registration. VAT payable. Use of flat rate scheme. Effect of VAT registration on net profit.
4   Capital gain for company. Rollover relief. Depreciating asset.
5   Residence of companies. Double taxation relief. Transfer pricing.
6   Remuneration packages for employees. IT and NIC implications.
7   Trading loss for sole trader. Use of loss against income and gains.

June 2004

Section A

1   Corporation tax – short period of account, capital allowances on industrial buildings and plant & machinery, property business profits, loan relationships, capital gain, CT liability, submission of CT return, correction for error or mistake by company. (30 marks)

2   Sole trader. Adjustment of profit. IT and CGT liabilities. Self assessment (25 marks)

Section B

3   VAT: tax point, issue of VAT invoice, calculation of VAT payable for quarter
4   Computation of capital gains tax for individual
5   Group relief
6   Employed vs self employed
7   Personal pension schemes

December 2003

Section A

1   Corporation tax – short period of account, adjustment of profit, capital allowances, loan relationships, use of losses. (30 marks)

2   Employees. P11D employees – definition and calculation of benefits. (25 marks)

Section B

3 VAT: registration, recovery of input tax, control visits, serious misdeclaration penalty
4 Capital gains for individual and company
5 Overseas operations for company
6 Choice of business medium
7 Change of accounting date

June 2003

Section A

1 Corporation tax – long period of account, computation of CT liability, due date for submission of CT return. (30 marks)

2 Computation of income tax liability and NICs. Pension contributions. (25 marks)

Section B

3 VAT: annual accounting scheme, flat rate scheme, VAT cash accounting
4 Computation of chargeable gains
5 Group relief groups
6 Sale of business
7 Badges of trade

December 2002

Section A

1 Computation of trading profits. Computation of corporation tax liability and explanation of due date for payment of corporation tax. (30 marks)

2 Capital allowances computation. Income tax computation and income tax self assessment. (25 marks)

Section B

3 VAT: registration, correction of errors, cessation of trading
4 CGT: computations of liability and statement of due date
5 Chargeable gains groups
6 Employment v self employment
7 Corporation tax losses

June 2002

Section A

1 Corporation tax losses (30 marks)

2 Calculation of trading profits. Calculation of income tax/NIC, personal pensions (25 marks)

Section B

3 VAT: calculation, default surcharge, cash accounting
4 Computation of chargeable gains
5 Corporate overseas matters: DTR, transfer pricing
6 Employment packages
7 Partnerships

December 2001

Section A

1   Quarterly accounting for income tax (no longer examinable). Adjustment of trading profits. Calculation of corporation tax payable. (30 marks)

2   Calculation of trading loss. Relief for loss. (25 marks)

Section B

3   VAT: registration, pre-registration VAT, sales invoices, tax point
4   Chargeable gains: rollover relief
5   Corporation tax: groups
6   Trading as a sole trader. Incorporation relief.

Pilot paper

Section A

1   Calculation of CT payable. Quarterly payments of CT. (30 marks)
2   IT for employee/sole trader. Payment of IT. (25 marks)

Section B

3   VAT registration. Input tax. Deregistrations
4   Business asset taper relief. Gains on shares
5   Group relief. CT liability
6   Employee/self employed distinction. NICs. IT for employee or self employed individual
7   Partnership profit allocation. Losses

Examiner's guidance

Relief for research and development expenditure

This is not examinable.

Income tax and Form CT61

The quarterly basis by which income tax is accounted for using Form CT61 is not examinable.

You should assume that any figures for patent royalties paid/received by a company are gross.

Double tax relief

The following are not examinable:

(a)   The restriction on the set off of underlying tax relief
(b)   The carry back/forward of unrelieved foreign tax.

Averaging of profits for authors and creative artists

This is not examinable.

100% FYAs for low emission cars

In examination questions you should only treat cars as low emission if they are specifically described as such. You are not expected to know the 120g/km limit.

VAT flat rate scheme

The percentage needed for this purpose will be given to you in the examination.

Substantial shareholdings

The chargeable gains exemption for substantial shareholdings is not examinable.

100% FYA for water technologies

These are not examinable.

Minimum rate of tax on distributed profits

There are special rules where an accounting period spans 31 March 2004, where dividends are paid to non corporate shareholders and for groups of companies. These are not examinable.

Pension simplification

The taxation of pensions is to be simplified by replacing the existing pension schemes with just one new scheme. The simplification will not take effect until 6 April 2006 and this change will not be examinable until the June 2007 sitting.

Oxford Brookes BSc (Hons) in Applied Accounting

The standard required of candidates completing Part 2 is that required in the final year of a UK degree. Students completing Parts 1 and 2 will have satisfied the examination requirement for an honours degree in Applied Accounting, awarded by Oxford Brookes University.

To achieve the degree, you must also submit two pieces of work based on a **Research and Analysis Project.**

- A 5,000 word **Report** on your chosen topic, which demonstrates that you have acquired the necessary research, analytical and IT skills.

- A 1,500 word **Key Skills Statement**, indicating how you have developed your interpersonal and communication skills.

BPP was selected by the ACCA and Oxford Brookes University to produce the official text *Success in your Research and Analysis Project* to support students in this task. The book pays particular attention to key skills not covered in the professional examinations.

BPP also offers courses and mentoring services.

The Oxford Brookes project text can be ordered using the form at the end of this study text.

Oxford Institute of International Finance MBA

The Oxford Institute of International Finance (OXIIF), a joint venture between the ACCA and Oxford Brookes University, offers an MBA for finance professionals.

For this MBA, credits are awarded for your ACCA studies, and entry to the MBA course is available to those who have completed their ACCA professional stage studies. The MBA was launched in 2002 and has attracted participants from all over the world.

The qualification features an introductory module (*Foundations of Management*). Other modules include *Global Business Strategy, Managing Self Development,* and *Organisational Change & Transformation.*

Research Methods are also taught, as they underpin the **research dissertation**.

The MBA programme is delivered through the use of targeted paper study materials, developed by BPP, and taught over the Internet by OXIIF personnel using BPP's virtual campus software.

For further information, please see the Oxford Institute's website: www.oxfordinstitute.org.

Continuing professional development

ACCA introduced a new continuing professional development requirement for members from 1 January 2005. Members will be required to complete and record 40 units of CPD annually, of which 21 units must be verifiable learning or training activity.

BPP has an established professional development department which offers a range of relevant, professional courses to reflect the needs of professionals working in both industry and practice. To find out more, visit the website: www.bpp.com/pd or call the client care team on 0845 226 2422.

Tax rates and allowances

A   INCOME TAX

1   *Rates*

	2005/06	
	£	%
Starting rate	1 – 2,090	10
Basic rate	2,091 – 32,400	22
Higher rate	32,401 and above	40

2   *Personal allowance*

	2004/05
	£
Personal allowance	4,895

3   *Cars – 2005/06*

Base level of CO_2 emissions – 140g/km

4   *Car fuel charge – 2005/06*

Base figure £14,400

5   *Personal pension contribution limits*

Age	Maximum percentage %
Up to 35	17.5
36 – 45	20.0
46 – 50	25.0
51 – 55	30.0
56 – 60	35.0
61 or more	40.0

Subject to earnings cap of £105,600 for 2005/06.

Maximum contribution without evidence of earnings £3,600.

6   *Capital allowances*

	%
Plant and machinery	
Writing down allowance*	25
First year allowance**	40
First year allowance: low emission cars (CO_2 emissions of less than 120 g/km)	100
Industrial buildings allowance	
Writing down allowance	4

* 6% reducing balance for certain long life assets

** 50% for small enterprises between 1.4.04 – 31.3.05 (6.4.04 – 5.4.05 for unincorporated businesses)

B   CORPORATION TAX

   1   *Rates*

Financial year	*2003*	*2004*	*2005*
Starting rate	Nil	Nil	Nil
Small companies rate	19%	19%	19%
Full rate	30%	30%	30%
	£	£	£
Starting rate lower limit	10,000	10,000	10,000
Starting rate upper limit	50,000	50,000	50,000
Small companies rate lower limit	300,000	300,000	300,000
Small companies rate upper limit	1,500,000	1,500,000	1,500,000
Taper relief fraction			
Starting rate	19/400	19/400	19/400
Small companies rate	11/400	11/400	11/400

   From 1.4.04 profits paid out as dividends are subject to minimum rate of CT of 19%

   2   *Marginal relief*

   $(M - P) \times I/P \times$ Marginal relief fraction

C   VALUE ADDED TAX

   Registration and deregistration limits

Registration limit	£60,000
Deregistration limit	£58,000
VAT on private petrol – quarterly scale charge	
CC of car: 1400cc or less	246
Over 1400cc up to 2000cc	311
Over 2000cc	457

D   RATES OF INTEREST

   Official rate of interest: 5% (assumed)
   Rate of interest on unpaid tax: 7.5% (assumed)
   Rate of interest on overpaid tax: 3.5% (assumed)

E   CAPITAL GAINS TAX

   1   *Annual exemption (individuals)*

   2005/06   £8,500

   2   *Taper relief*

Complete years after 5.4.98 for which asset held	*Gains on business assets*	*Gains on non business assets*
1	50	100
2	25	100
3	25	95
4	25	90
5	25	85
6	25	80
7	25	75
8	25	70
9	25	65
10	25	60

F NATIONAL INSURANCE (NOT CONTRACTED OUT RATES) 2005/06

Class 1 contributions

		%
Class 1 Employee	£1–£4,895 per year	Nil
	£4,896–£32,760 per year	11.0
	£32,761 and above per year	1.0
Class 1 Employer	£1–£4,895 per year	Nil
	£4,896 and above per year	12.8

Class 2 contributions

Rate   £2.05 pw

Class 4 contributions

	%
£1–£4,895 per year	Nil
£4,896–£32,760 per year	8.0
£32,761 and above per year	1.0

Syllabus mindmap

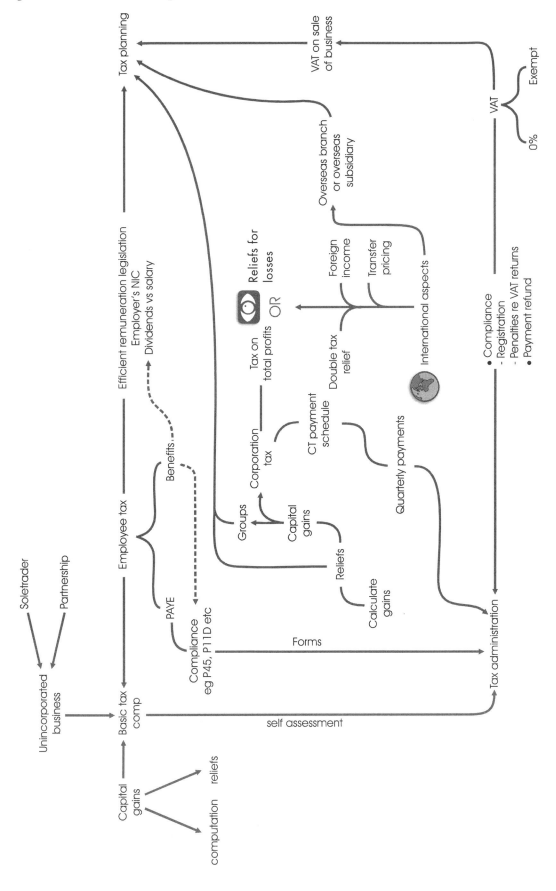

Part A

Corporate businesses

An outline of corporation tax

Topic list	Syllabus reference
1 Introduction to the UK tax system	
2 The scope of corporation tax	1(a), 1(b)
3 Profits chargeable to corporation tax	1(a), 1(d)
4 Accounting periods	1(a)
5 Charge to corporation tax	1(e)
6 Non corporate distributions	1(e)

Introduction

We start our study of tax with an introduction to the UK tax system.

As the taxation of companies is a vitally important part of the Business Taxation syllabus we then look at corporation tax (CT). This is the tax that a company must pay on its profits.

In this chapter you will learn both how to compute the profits on which a company must pay tax and how to compute the corporation tax liability on those profits.

1 Introduction to the UK tax system

There are a number of different taxes in the UK. Administration of taxation in the UK is undertaken by HM Revenue and Customs (HMRC).

1.1 Taxes in the UK

Central government raises revenue through a wide range of taxes. Tax law is made by **statute** and as this can be notoriously ambiguous and difficult to understand, there is a project to rewrite it in simpler more user-friendly language. The following Acts have resulted from the tax law rewrite project:

- the **Capital Allowances Act 2001**
- the **Income Tax (Earnings and Pensions) Act 2003**
- the **Income Tax (Trading and Other Income) Act 2005**

Statute is interpreted and amplified by **case law**. HM Revenue and Customs also issue:

(a) **Statements of practice**, setting out how they intend to apply the law

(b) **Extra-statutory concessions**, setting out circumstances in which they will not apply the strict letter of the law

(c) A wide range of **explanatory leaflets**

(d) **Business economic notes**. These are notes on particular types of business, which are used as background information by the Revenue and are also published

(e) The **Tax Bulletin**. This is a newsletter giving the Revenue's view on specific points. It is published every two months

(f) The **Internal Guidance**, a series of manuals used by Revenue staff

However, none of these Revenue publications has the force of law.

A great deal of information and the Revenue publications can be found on the HM Revenue and Custom's Internet site (www.hmrc.gov.UK).

The main taxes, their incidence and their sources, are set out in the table below.

Tax	Suffered by	Source
Income tax	**Individuals** **Partnerships**	Income and Corporation Taxes Act 1988 (ICTA 1988) and subsequent Finance Acts; Capital Allowances Act 2001 (CAA 2001); Income Tax (Earnings and Pensions) Act 2003 (ITEPA 2003), Income Tax (Trading and Other Income) Act 2005 (ITTOIA 2005)
Corporation tax	**Companies**	ICTA 1988, Finance Acts and CAA 2001 as above
Capital gains tax	**Individuals** **Partnerships** **Companies** (which pay tax on capital gains in the form of corporation tax)	Taxation of Chargeable Gains Act 1992 (TCGA 1992) and subsequent Finance Acts
Value added tax	**Businesses**, both incorporated and unincorporated	Value Added Tax Act 1994 (VATA 1994) and subsequent Finance Acts

Finance Acts are passed each year, incorporating proposals set out in the **Budget**. They make changes which apply mainly to the tax year ahead. In 2005, we have two Finance Acts because of the dissolution of Parliament in April 2005, in preparation for the general election in May 2005. **This Study Text includes the provisions of both the Finance Act 2005 and the Finance (No. 2) Act 2005.** These are examinable in June 2006 and December 2006.

1.2 The administration of taxation

The **Treasury** formally imposes and collects taxation. The management of the Treasury is the responsibility of the Chancellor of the Exchequer. **The administrative function for the collection of tax is undertaken by Her Majesty's Revenue and Customs (HMRC).** Previously there were two separate bodies called the Inland Revenue (responsible for direct taxes such as income tax and corporation tax) and HM Customs and Excise (responsible for indirect taxes such as VAT). In relation to matters which used to be dealt with by the Inland Revenue we will refer to the HMRC as "the Revenue". Rules on administration of these taxes are contained in the **Taxes Management Act 1970 (TMA 1970)**.

HMRC consists of the Commissioners for Her Majesty's Revenue and Customs and staff known **as Officers of Revenue and Customs.**

The UK has historically been divided into **tax districts**. These are being merged into larger **areas**, with the separate offices in each area being responsible for different aspects of the Revenue's work. For example, one office may be designated to deal with taxpayer's queries, another to deal with the PAYE procedures for joiners and leavers, whilst end of year PAYE returns may be dealt with by a third office. Some offices also act as **enquiry offices**, where taxpayers can visit the office and see a member of the Revenue staff in person without an appointment.

Each area is headed by an area director. The Revenue staff were historically described as **'Inspectors'** and 'Collectors'. The legislation now refers to an **'Officer of the Revenue and Customs'** when setting out the Revenue's powers. They are responsible for supervising the self-assessment system and agreeing tax liabilities. Collectors may be referred to as **receivable management officers**, and are local officers who are responsible for following up amounts of unpaid tax referred to them by the **HMRC Accounts Office.**

The structure of offices is also being changed. **Taxpayer service offices** are being set up to do routine checking, computation *and* collection work, while **Taxpayer district offices** investigate selected accounts, deal with corporation tax and enforce the payment of tax when it is not paid willingly. **Taxpayer assistance offices** handle enquiries and arrange specialist help for taxpayers.

The **General Commissioners** (not to be confused with the Commissioners for HMRC) are appointed (at the moment) by the Lord Chancellor to hear **appeals** against Revenue decisions. They are part-time and unpaid. They are appointed for a local area (a **division**). They appoint a clerk who is often a lawyer or accountant and who is paid for his services.

The **Special Commissioners** are also appointed by the Lord Chancellor. They are full-time paid professionals. They generally hear the more complex appeals.

Many taxpayers arrange for their accountants to prepare and submit their tax returns. The taxpayer is still the person responsible for submitting the return and for paying whatever tax becomes due: the accountant is only acting as the taxpayer's agent.

2 The scope of corporation tax

FAST FORWARD

Companies pay corporation tax. A company is UK resident if it is incorporated in the UK or if it is incorporated abroad and its central management and control are exercised in the UK.

2.1 Companies

Companies must pay corporation tax on their **profits chargeable to corporation tax** for each **accounting period**. We look at the meaning of these terms below.

> A '**company**' is any corporate body (limited or unlimited) or unincorporated association, eg sports club.

2.2 The residence of companies

A company incorporated in the UK is resident in the UK. A company incorporated abroad is resident in the UK if its central management and control are exercised here. Central management and control are usually treated as exercised where the board of directors meet.

3 Profits chargeable to corporation tax

FAST FORWARD

> A company pays corporation tax on its profits chargeable to corporation tax (PCTCT).

3.1 Taxable income and gains

A company may have both income and gains. As a general rule income arises from receipts which are expected to recur regularly (such as the profits from a trade) whereas chargeable gains arise on the sale of capital assets which have been owned for several years (such as the sale of a factory used in the trade).

A company may receive income from various sources. All income received must be classified according to the nature of the income as different computational rules apply to different types of income. The main types of income for a company are:

- Profits of a trade
- Profits of a property business
- Investment income
- Miscellaneous income

For unincorporated businesses and all other income tax purposes (see later in this Text) these classes of income have replaced the old classification system under which the different types of income were known as **Schedules**, some of which were divided into **Cases**. These old rules still apply for corporation tax purposes, for example trading profits are strictly known as Schedule D Case I profits and the profits of a property business are called Schedule A profits. However, the plain English terminology above will also be used for corporation tax purposes in your exam and therefore only this new terminology is used in this Text.

Each of the types of income that a company might receive is considered in detail later in this text.

UK companies receive interest gross from banks and building societies. Interest paid by other UK companies is also received gross.

> The examiner has stated that any figures for interest paid or received by a company will be gross.

A company's profits chargeable to corporation tax are arrived at by aggregating its various sources of income and chargeable gains and then deducting charges on income. Here is a pro forma computation. All items are explained later in this text.

	£
Trading profits	X
Investment income	X
Foreign income	X
Miscellaneous income	X
Property business profits	X
Chargeable gains	X
Total profits	X
Less charges on income (gross)	(X)
Profits chargeable to corporation tax (PCTCT) for an accounting period	X

Exam focus point

> It would be of great help in the exam if you could learn the above proforma. Then when answering a corporation tax question you could immediately reproduce the proforma and insert the appropriate numbers as you are given the information in the question.

Dividends received from UK resident companies are not included in the profits chargeable to corporation tax. The one exception to this rule is where shares are held as trading assets, and not as investments, any dividends on those shares will be treated for tax purposes as trading profits.

3.2 Charges on income

Having arrived at a company's total profits, charges on income are deducted to arrive at the profits chargeable to corporation tax (PCTCT). A **charge on income** is a payment which tax law allows as a deduction.

Exam focus point

> The only charge on income examinable at paper 2.3 is a charitable gift aid donation. As gift aid donations are not paid for trade purposes you may often see them referred to as non-trade charges on income.

Almost all donations of money to charity can be made under the **gift aid scheme** whether they are one off donations or are regular donations. **Gift aid donations are paid gross**.

Donations to charities which are incurred wholly and exclusively for the purposes of a trade are deducted in the calculation of the tax adjusted trading profits instead of as charges on income. We will look at the calculation of trading profits later in this text.

4 Accounting periods

FAST FORWARD

> Companies pay corporation tax on their PCTCT of each accounting period. An accounting period cannot exceed 12 months in length so a long period of account must be split into two accounting periods. The first accounting period is always twelve months in length.

Corporation tax is chargeable in respect of accounting periods. It is important to understand the difference between an accounting period and a period of account. A period of account is any period for which a company prepares accounts; usually this will be 12 months in length but it may be longer or shorter than this. An accounting period starts when a company starts to trade, or otherwise becomes liable to corporation tax, or immediately after the previous accounting period finishes. An accounting period finishes on the earliest of:

- 12 months after its start
- the end of the company's period of account
- the commencement of the company's winding up
- the company's ceasing to be resident in the UK
- the company's ceasing to be liable to corporation tax

If a company has a period of account, exceeding 12 months (a long period), it is split into two accounting periods: the first 12 months and the remainder. For example, if a company prepares accounts for the sixteen months to 30 April 2005, the two accounting periods for which the company will pay corporation tax will be the twelve months to 31 December 2004 and the four months to 30 April 2005.

Where the period of account differs from the corporation tax accounting periods, profits are **allocated to the relevant periods** as follows:

- **Trading income** before capital allowances is apportioned on a **time basis.**

- **Capital allowances** and balancing charges are **calculated for each accounting period.**

- **Other income is allocated to the period to which it relates** (eg rents to the period when accrued). Miscellaneous income, however, is apportioned on a time basis.

- **Chargeable gains and losses** are allocated to the **period in which they are realised.**

- **Charges on income (ie gift aid donations)** are deducted in the accounting **period in which they are paid.**

Question	Long period of account

Xenon Ltd makes up an 18 month set of accounts to 30 June 2006 with the following results.

	£
Trading profits	180,000
Property business profits	
18 months @ £500 accruing per month	9,000
Capital gain (1 May 2006 disposal)	250,000
Less: Gift aid donation (paid 31.12.05)	(50,000)
	389,000

What are the profits chargeable to corporation tax for each of the accounting periods based on the above accounts?

Answer

The 18 month period of account is divided into:

Year ending 31 December 2005
6 months to 30 June 2006

Results are allocated:

	Y/e 31.12.05 £	6m to 30.6.06 £
Trading profits 12:6	120,000	60,000
Property income		
12 × £500	6,000	
6 × £500		3,000
Capital gain (1.5.06)		250,000
Less: Charge on income	(50,000)	
PCTCT (profits chargeable to corporation tax)	76,000	313,000

5 Charge to corporation tax

Tax rates are set for financial years. The rate of tax will depend on the level of a company's 'profits' (PCTCT plus grossed up dividends received) in the financial year. The PCTCT are income plus gains minus charges.

5.1 The full rate

The rates of corporation tax are fixed for financial years. A financial year runs from 1 April to the following 31 March and is identified by the calendar year in which it begins. For example, the year ended 31 March 2006 is the financial year 2005 (FY 2005). This should not be confused with a tax year, which runs from 6 April to the following 5 April.

The full rate of corporation tax is 30% for FY 1999 to FY 2005.

5.2 The small companies rate (SCR)

Companies may be entitled to the starting rate, the small companies rate or to marginal relief, depending on their 'profits'.

The SCR of corporation tax (19% for FY 2002 to FY 2005 and 20% for FY 1999 to FY 2001) applies to the profits chargeable to corporation tax of UK resident companies whose 'profits' are more than £50,000 but not more than £300,000.

'Profits' means profits chargeable to corporation tax plus the grossed-up amount of dividends received from UK companies (or from unit trusts where treated like company dividends) **other than those in the same group.** The grossed-up amount of UK dividends is the net dividend plus the tax credit which an individual investor would receive. We gross up by multiplying by 100/90. You may see the grossed up amount of dividend received referred to as franked investment income.

Question	The small companies rate

B Ltd had the following results for the year ended 31 March 2006.

	£
Trading profits	42,000
Dividend received 1 May 2005	9,000

Compute the corporation tax payable.

Answer

Trading profits	42,000
Dividend plus tax credit £9,000 × 100/90	10,000
'Profits' (between £50,000 and £300,000 limit)	52,000
Corporation tax payable	
£42,000 × 19%	£7,980

5.3 The starting rate

A starting rate of corporation tax of 0% applies to companies with 'profits' of up to £10,000 for FY 2002 to FY 2005. The starting rate in FY2000 and in FY2001 was 10%.

Companies with 'profits' in the starting rate band may be subject to extra tax if they make distributions to non corporate shareholders (see later in this text).

Question   The starting rate of corporation tax

Dexter Limited has the following income for the year ended 31 March 2006.

(a)   Trading profits of £9,500, and
(b)   Franked investment income of £300.

Calculate the corporation tax liability for the year. Assume all profits are retained in the company.

Answer

	£
Trading profits	9,500
Franked investment income	300
'Profits'	9,800
Corporation tax on PCTCT £9,500 × 0%	£nil

5.4 Marginal relief

FAST FORWARD

The marginal rate of tax between the starting rate limits is 23.75%. The marginal rate between the small companies' limits is 32.75%. These marginal tax rates are effective rates; they are never actually used in working out corporation tax.

Small companies marginal relief (sometimes called taper relief) applies where the 'profits' of an accounting period of a UK resident company are over £300,000 but under £1,500,000. We first calculate the corporation tax at the full rate and then deduct:

(M – P) × I/P × marginal relief fraction

where M = upper limit (currently £1,500,000)
**   P = 'profits' (see above Paragraph)**
**   I = PCTCT**

The marginal relief fraction is 11/400 for FY2002 to FY 2005 inclusive (and was 1/40 for FY 1997 to FY 2001).

Question   Small companies marginal relief

Lenox Ltd has the following results for the year ended 31 March 2006.

	£
PCTCT	296,000
Dividend received 1 December 2005	12,600

Calculate the corporation tax liability, if all profits are retained for future use in the business.

Answer

	£
PCTCT	296,000
Dividend plus tax credit £12,600 × 100/90	14,000
'Profits'	310,000

'Profits' are above £300,000 but below £1,500,000, so marginal relief applies.

	£
Corporation tax on PCTCT £296,000 × 30%	88,800
Less small companies' marginal relief	
£(1,500,000 – 310,000) × 296,000/310,000 × 11/400	(31,247)
	57,553

In exam questions you often need to be aware that there is a **marginal rate of 32.75 %** which applies to any PCTCT that lies in between the small companies' limits.

This is calculated as follows;

	£				£
Upper limit	1,500,000	@	30%		450,000
Lower limit	(300,000)	@	19%		(57,000)
Difference	1,200,000				393,000

$$\frac{393,000}{1,200,000} = 32.75\%$$

Effectively the band of profits (here £1,200,000) falling between the upper and lower limits are taxed at a rate of 32.75%

5.5 Example

A Ltd has PCTCT of £350,000 for the year ended 31 March 2006. Its corporation tax liability is

	£
£350,000 × 30%	105,000
Less: small companies' marginal relief	
11/400 (1,500,000 – 350,000)	(31,625)
	73,375

This is the same as calculating tax at 19% × £300,000 + 32.75% × £50,000 = £57,000 + £16,375 = £73,375.

Consequently tax is charged at an effective rate of 32.75% on PCTCT that exceeds the small companies' lower limit.

Note that although there is an effective corporation tax charge of 32.75%, this rate of tax is never used in actually calculating corporation tax. The rate is just an effective marginal rate that you must be aware of.

For companies with 'profits' between £10,001 and £50,000, the small companies rate less a starting rate marginal relief applies. The formula for calculating this marginal relief is the same as that given above except that 'M' is the upper limit for starting rate purposes. (£50,000 – FY 2000 to FY 2005). However the fraction used here is 19/400 for FY 2002 to FY 2005 and was 1/40 in FY 2001. The small companies' rate only applies in full when 'profits' exceed £50,000.

Companies with profits in the starting rate marginal relief band will be subject to additional tax if they distribute their profits to non-corporate shareholders (see later in this text).

Question

Armstrong Ltd has the following income for its year ended 31 March 2006:

		£
(a)	Trading profits	29,500
(b)	Franked investment income	3,000

Calculate the corporation tax liability, if all profits are retained in the company for future use in the business.

Answer

	£
Trading profits	29,500
Franked investment income	3,000
Profits	32,500

	£
Corporation tax at small companies rate:	
£29,500 × 19%	5,605
Less: starting rate marginal relief –	
19/400 × ((£50,000 – £32,500) × £29,500/£32,500)	(755)
Corporation tax payable	4,850

The effective marginal rate of tax when PCTCT falls between the starting rate limits is 23.75%. Again, this is an effective marginal rate of tax that you need to be aware of but it is a rate that is never actually used in working out the CT charge. It is calculated as;

£			£
50,000	@	19%	9,500
(10,000)	@	0%	Nil
40,000			9,500

$$\frac{9{,}500}{40{,}000} = 23.75\ \%$$

PCTCT falling into the band (here £40,000) suffers tax at an effective rate of 23.75%.

5.6 Changes in the rate – Accounting periods straddling 31 March

If there is a change in the corporation tax rate, and a company's accounting period does not fall entirely within one financial year, the profits of the accounting period are apportioned to the two financial years on a time basis. Note that the profits as a whole are apportioned. We do not look at components of the profit individually, unlike apportionment of profits of a long period of account to two accounting periods.

Question

Frances Ltd makes up accounts to 31 December each year. For the year ended 31 December 2002 its profit and loss account was as follows.

	£
PCTCT	40,000
Dividends plus tax credits	2,500
'Profits'	42,500

Calculate the corporation tax liability for the year.

Answer

	FY 2001 3 months to 31 March 2002 £	FY 2002 9 months to 31 December 2002 £
PCTCT (divided 3:9)	10,000	30,000
'Profits' (divided 3:9)	10,625	31,875
Lower limit for starting rate		
FY 2001 £10,000 × 3/12	2,500	
FY 2002 £10,000 × 9/12		7,500
Upper limit for starting rate		
FY 2001 £50,000 × 3/12	12,500	
FY 2002 £50,000 × 9/12		37,500
FY 2001: £10,000 × 20%		2,000
Less starting rate marginal relief		
£(12,500 − 10,625) × 10,000/10,625 × 1/40		(44)
		1,956
FY 2002: £30,000 × 19%	5,700	
Less starting rate marginal relief		
£(37,500 − 31,875) × 30,000/31,875 × 19/400	(252)	
		5,448
Corporation tax payable		7,404

The 'profits' falling into each financial year determines the rate of corporation tax that applies to the PCTCT of that year. This could be the full rate, the small companies' rate or the starting rate.

Question

Henson Ltd had the following results for its year ended 30 September 2002.

Trading profits	£9,500
Franked investment income	£300

Calculate the corporation tax liability for the year.

Answer

	FY 2001 6 months to 31.3.02 £	FY 2002 6 months to 30.9.02 £
'Profits' (£9,800)	4,900	4,900
Profit chargeable to corporation tax	4,750	4,750
Lower limit for starting rate (6m : 6m)	5,000	5,000
Lower limit for SCR (6m : 6m)	150,000	150,000
Corporation tax payable		
£4,750 × 10%		475
£4,750 × 0%		Nil
Total corporation tax payable for 12 months APE 30.9.02		475

5.7 Associated companies and short accounting periods

FAST FORWARD

> The upper and lower limits which are used to determine tax rates are divided by the number of associated companies. The limits are also pro-rated in short accounting periods.

Key term

> The expression **'associated companies'** in tax has no connection with financial accounting. For tax purposes a company is associated with another company if either controls the other or if both are under the control of the same person or persons (individuals, partnerships or companies). Whether such a company is UK resident or not is irrelevant (even though non-UK resident companies cannot benefit from the starting rate, small companies rate or from marginal relief). Control is given by holding over 50% of the share capital or the voting power or being entitled to over 50% of the distributable income or of the net assets in a winding up.

If a company has one or more 'associated companies', then the profit limits for starting rate and small companies rate purposes are divided by the number of associated companies + 1 (for the company itself).

Companies which have only been associated for part of an accounting period are deemed to have been associated for the whole period for the purpose of determining the profit limits.

An associated company is ignored for these purposes if it has not carried on any trade or business at any time in the accounting period (or the part of the period during which it was associated). A holding company counts as not carrying on any trade or business so long as:

- Its only assets are shares in subsidiaries

- It is not entitled to deduct any outgoings as charges or management expenses, and

- Its only profits are dividends from subsidiaries, which are distributed in full to its shareholders.

The profit limits are reduced proportionately if an accounting period lasts for less than 12 months.

Question   Associated companies and short accounting periods

For the nine months to 31 January 2006 a company with two other associated companies had PCTCT of £78,000 and no dividends paid for or received. Compute the corporation tax payable.

(a) Division of the lower limit for the starting rate by the number of associated companies + 1

£10,000 × $^1/_3$ = £3,333

(b) Reduction in the lower limit for the starting rate as the accounting period is only nine months long

£3,333 × $^9/_{12}$ = £2,500

(c) Reduction in the upper limit for the starting rate

£50,000 × $^1/_3$ × $^9/_{12}$ = £12,500

(d) Reduction in the lower limit for SCR

£300,000 × $^1/_3$ × $^9/_{12}$ = £75,000

(e) Reduction in the upper limit for SCR

£1,500,000 × $^1/_3$ × $^9/_{12}$ = £375,000

(f) 'Profits' = £78,000

As 'profits' fall between the lower and upper limits for SCR purposes, the full rate less small companies' marginal relief applies:

(g) Corporation tax

	£
£78,000 × 30%	23,400
Less small companies' marginal relief £(375,000 − 78,000) × 11/400	(8,168)
Corporation tax	15,232

6 Non corporate distributions

FAST FORWARD

Companies with profits chargeable to corporation tax below the threshold for starting rate marginal relief which make distributions to individual shareholders are subject to special rules when calculating the tax payable on their profits.

6.1 Minimum rate of tax

There is special legislation that applies to non-corporate distributions that impact on the corporation tax payable by 'small' companies.

This change affects companies which pay tax at 19% or lower, ie including those which pay at the starting rate of 0% and the starting rate marginal relief. In summary, companies which have an UNDERLYING rate of tax of less than 19%.

It will only affect these 'small' companies if, in any given accounting period, **profits are distributed after 1 April 2004 to non-corporate shareholders – ie dividends paid to individuals**. Companies which pay dividends to corporate shareholders or which retain their profits are not caught by these rules.

In effect, the purpose of these rules is to ensure that **any distributions to non-corporate shareholders are taxed at a minimum of 19%.**

The **underlying rate of corporation tax** is calculated as $\dfrac{CT \times 100}{PCTCT}$. CT is after starting rate marginal relief but before any other deductions, such as DTR (see later in this text).

6.2 Example

Assume that PCTCT for an accounting period are £9,000. These profits are distributed by way of a dividend to individuals. The tax computation would be:

Step 1   **Workout CT using normal rules**

PCTCT £9,000 @ 0% =	£nil
Corporation Tax due =	£nil

Step 2   **Calculate the underlying rate**

The underlying rate:	
(tax/PCTCT × 100) = 0.000/9,000×100 =	0%

Step 3   **Tax PCTCT up to the amount of the non corporate distribution at 19%**

Non corporate distribution £9,000 @ 19% =	£1,710

Step 4   **Tax remaining PCTCT at the underlying rate**

Remaining PCTCT	Nil
Total CT due	£1,710

6.3 Example

Assume that the PCTCT for an accounting period is £38,000. The distributions made during the accounting period totalled £30,000, all payable to individuals. The tax calculation will be:

Step 1   **Workout CT using normal rules**

		£
PCTCT	£38,000 @ 19% =	7,220
Less Starting rate marginal relief	£(50,000 − 38,000) × 19/400 =	(570)
Corporation tax due on PCTCT		6,650

Step 2   **Calculate the underlying rate**

The underlying rate is	6,650/38,000 × 100 =17.5%

Step 3   **Tax PCTCT up to the amount of the non corporate distribution at 19%**

£30,000 @ 19% =	5,700

Step 4   **Tax remaining PCTCT at the underlying rate**

(£38,000 – £30,000) @ 17.5%	£8,000 @ 17.5% =	1,400
Total CT due		7,100

The **tax due using these rules is reported on the Corporation Tax Self Assessment return of the company in the normal way**. (See later in this text).

The normal due date for the payment of corporation tax for small companies applies, which is nine months day after the end of the accounting period. (See later in this text).

Where non-corporate distributions exceed PCTCT for the accounting period, the excess is taken forward to the next accounting period. It is then treated as a non-corporate distribution made in that period (in addition to any actual non-corporate distribution in next period).

There is no carry back of excess distributions and the normal rules apply to losses. (See later in this Text)

Question
Excess distribution

R Ltd has a year end of 31 March. For the year to 31 March 2006 it has PCTCT of £30,000. The company made a non corporate distribution of £35,000 on 31 December 2005, partly out of retained profits. For the year to 31 March 2007, R Ltd has PCTCT of £25,000. It paid a dividend of £15,000 to non-corporate shareholders on 31 December 2006.

Calculate the corporation tax liabilities for both years.

Answer

Y/e 31/03/06

As the dividend exceeds PCTCT, the CT liability is solely based on the amount of dividend up to PCTCT ie:

£30,000 × 19%	£5,700
Excess dividend c/f (£35,000 − 30,000)	£5,000

Y/e 31/03/07 £

Step 1   **Workout CT using normal rules**

PCTCT £25,000 × 19%	4,750
Less: marginal rate relief £(50,000 − 25,000) × 19/400	(1,188)
Corporation tax due on PCTCT	3,562

Step 2   **Calculate the underlying rate**

Underlying rate 3,562/25,000×100	14.248%

Step 3   **Tax PCTCT up to the amount of the non corporate distribution at 19%**

£(5,000 b/f + 15,000) = £20,000 × 19%	3,800

Step 4   **Tax remaining PCTCT at the underlying rate**

£(25,000−5,000−15,000) = £5,000 × 14.248%	712
Corporation tax	4,512

Chapter roundup

- There are a number of different taxes in the UK. Administration of taxation in the UK is undertaken by HM Revenue and Customs (HMRC).

- Companies pay corporation tax. A company is UK resident if it is incorporated in the UK or if it is incorporated abroad and its central management and control are exercised in the UK.

- A company pays corporation tax on its profits chargeable to corporation tax (PCTCT).

- Companies pay corporation tax on their PCTCT of each accounting period. An accounting period cannot exceed 12 months in length so a long period of account must be split into two accounting periods. The first accounting period is always twelve months in length.

- Tax rates are set for financial years. The rate of tax will depend on the level of a company's 'profits' (PCTCT plus grossed up dividends received) in the financial year. The PCTCT are income plus gains minus charges.

- Companies may be entitled to the starting rate, the small companies rate or to marginal relief, depending on their 'profits'.

- The marginal rate of tax between the starting rate limits is 23.75%. The marginal rate between the small companies' limits is 32.75%. These marginal tax rates are effective rates; they are never actually used in working out corporation tax.

- The upper and lower limits which are used to determine tax rates are divided by the number of associated companies. The limits are also pro-rated in short accounting periods.

- Companies with profits chargeable to corporation tax below the threshold for starting rate marginal relief which make distributions to individual shareholders are subject to special rules when calculating the tax payable on their profits.

Quick quiz

1   When does an accounting period end?

2   How are trading profits (before capital allowances) of a long period of account divided between accounting periods?

3   Which companies are entitled to the starting rate of corporation tax?

4   What is the marginal relief formula?

5   What is an associated company?

6   What is the minimum rate of tax that must be paid by a company that makes distributions to non corporate shareholders?

Answers to quick quiz

1   An accounting period ends on the earliest of:

    (a)   12 months after its start
    (b)   the end of the company's period of account
    (c)   the commencement of the company's winding up
    (d)   the company ceasing to be resident in the UK
    (e)   the company ceasing to be liable to corporation tax

2   Trading income (before capital allowances) is apportioned on a time basis.

3   Companies with profits of up to £10,000

4   $(M - P) \times I/P \times$ marginal relief fraction

where:

M = upper limit
P = 'profits'
I = PCTCT

5   A company is associated with another company if either controls the other or if both are under the control of the same person or persons (Individual, partnership or companies).

6   19%

Now try the question below from the Exam Question Bank			
Number	**Level**	**Marks**	**Time**
Q1	Examination	15	27 mins

Trading profits

Topic list	Syllabus reference
1 The adjustment of profits	1(c)(i)
2 Deductible and non-deductible expenditure	1(c)(i)
3 Income not taxable as trading profits	1(c)(i)
4 Deductible expenditure not charged in the accounts	1(c)(i)
5 The cessation of trades	1(c)(i)

Introduction

We have seen how to compute a company's total profits. In this chapter we see how to compute one particular type of a company's profits, namely its taxable trading profits.

Your starting point in computing the taxable trading profits is always the net profits in a company's accounts but this must be adjusted to arrive at the taxable trading profits. For tax purposes, standard rules on the computation of profits are used instead of individual company accounting policies, so as to ensure fairness.

1 The adjustment of profits

The net profit in the company's accounts must be adjusted to find the taxable trading profit.

1.1 Illustrative adjustment

Although the net profit before taxation shown in the accounts is the starting point in computing the taxable trading profit, many adjustments may be required to find the taxable trading profits.

Here is an illustrative adjustment.

	£	£
Net profit per accounts		140,000
Add: expenditure charged in the accounts which is not deductible from trading profits	50,000	
income taxable as trading profits which has not been included in the accounts	30,000	
		80,000
		220,000
Less: profits included in the accounts but which are not taxable trading profits	40,000	
expenditure which is deductible from trading profits but has not been charged in the accounts	20,000	
		60,000
Profit adjusted for tax purposes		160,000

You may refer to deductible and non-deductible expenditure as allowable and disallowable expenditure respectively. The two sets of terms are interchangeable.

1.2 Accounting policies

As a rule, accounts drawn up on normal accepted accounting principles are acceptable for tax purposes. Two special points are worth noting.

- If there is a legal action in progress, the best estimate of the cost should be debited, not the most prudent estimate.

- Under SSAP 9, a loss on a long-term contract is recognised as soon as it is foreseen. Anticipating a loss in this way is not acceptable for tax purposes, so the debit to profit and loss must be added back.

The taxable profits of a trade, profession or vocation must normally be computed on a basis which gives a true and fair view, subject to adjustments permitted or required by tax law.

2 Deductible and non-deductible expenditure

Disallowable expenditure must be added back to the accounts profit in the computation of the taxable trading profit. Any item not deducted wholly and exclusively for trade purposes is disallowable expenditure. Certain other items, such as depreciation, are specifically disallowable.

2.1 Payments contrary to public policy and illegal payments

Fines and penalties are not deductible. However, **the Revenue usually allow employees' parking fines incurred in parking their employer's cars while on their employer's business. Fines relating to directors, however, are never allowed.**

A payment is not deductible if making it constitutes an offence by the payer. This covers protection money paid to terrorists and bribes. Statute also prevents any deduction for payments made in response to blackmail or extortion.

2.2 Capital expenditure

Capital expenditure is not deductible. The most contentious items of expenditure will often be repairs (revenue expenditure) **and improvements** (capital expenditure).

(a)   The cost of restoration of an asset by, for instance, replacing a subsidiary part of the asset is revenue expenditure. Expenditure on a new factory chimney replacement was allowable since the chimney was a subsidiary part of the factory (*Samuel Jones & Co (Devondale) Ltd v CIR 1951*). However, in another case a football club demolished a spectators' stand and replaced it with a modern equivalent. This was held not to be repair, since repair is the restoration by renewal or replacement of subsidiary parts of a larger entity, and the stand formed a distinct and *separate* part of the club (*Brown v Burnley Football and Athletic Co Ltd 1980*).

(b)   The cost of initial repairs to improve an asset recently acquired to make it fit to earn profits is disallowable capital expenditure. In *Law Shipping Co Ltd v CIR 1923* the taxpayer failed to obtain relief for expenditure on making a newly bought ship seaworthy prior to using it.

(c)   The cost of initial repairs to remedy normal wear and tear of recently acquired assets is allowable. *Odeon Associated Theatres Ltd v Jones 1971* can be contrasted with the *Law Shipping* judgement. Odeon were allowed to charge expenditure incurred on improving the state of recently acquired cinemas.

Other examples to note include:

(a)   A one-off payment made by a hotel owner to terminate an agreement for the management of a hotel was held to be revenue rather than capital expenditure in *Croydon Hotel & Leisure Co v Bowen 1996*. The payment did not affect the whole structure of the taxpayer's business; it merely enabled it to be run more efficiently.

(b)   A one-off payment to remove a threat to the taxpayer's business was also held to be revenue rather than capital expenditure in *Lawson v Johnson Matthey plc 1992*.

(c)   An initial payment for a franchise (as opposed to regular fees) is capital and not deductible.

The costs of **registering patents and trade marks** are deductible.

2.3 Appropriations

Depreciation, amortisation and general provisions are not deductible. A specific provision against a particular trade debt is deductible if it is a reasonable estimate of the likely loss.

Where the payments are to or on behalf of employees, the full amounts are deductible but the employees are taxed on benefits if the payment has a private element.

Gift aid payments are added back in the calculation of the taxable trading profit. They are deducted instead as a charge on income from profits chargeable to corporation tax. Gifts aid payments are deducted on a paid basis.

2.4 Entertaining and gifts

Entertaining for and gifts to employees are normally deductible. Where gifts are made, or the entertainment is excessive, a charge to tax may arise on the employee under the benefits legislation.

Gifts to customers not costing more than £50 per donee per year are allowed if they carry a conspicuous advertisement for the business and are not food, drink, tobacco or vouchers exchangeable for goods.

Gifts to charities may also be allowed although many will fall foul of the 'wholly and exclusively' rule below. If a gift aid declaration is made in respect of a gift, tax relief will be given under the gift aid scheme. This means that the gift will be treated as a charge on income, not as a trading deduction.

Tax relief is available for certain donations of trading stock and equipment (see below). All other expenditure on entertaining and gifts is non-deductible.

2.5 Lease charges for expensive cars

Although leasing costs will normally be an allowable expense, there is a restriction for costs relating to expensive cars. **If the retail price of the car when new exceeds £12,000 the deductible part of any leasing charge is reduced by multiplying it by the fraction (£12,000 + RP) / 2RP, where RP is the retail price of the car.**

Thus for a car with a retail price of £20,000 and an annual leasing charge of £5,000 the allowable deduction is £5,000 x [(12,000 + 20,000) / 2 x 20,000] = £4,000, so £1,000 of the charge is added back.

This restriction does not apply to low emission cars, ie those with carbon dioxide emissions not exceeding 120 g/km and electrically propelled cars.

2.6 Expenditure not wholly and exclusively for the purposes of the trade

Expenditure is not deductible if it is not for trade purposes (the remoteness test), or if it reflects more than one purpose (the duality test).

The remoteness test is illustrated by the following cases.

- *Strong & Co of Romsey Ltd v Woodifield 1906*

  A customer injured by a falling chimney when sleeping in an inn owned by a brewery claimed compensation from the company. The compensation was not deductible: 'the loss sustained by the appellant was not really incidental to their trade as innkeepers and fell upon them in their character not of innkeepers but of householders'.

- *Bamford v ATA Advertising Ltd 1972*

  A director misappropriated £15,000. The loss was not allowable: 'the loss is not, as in the case of a dishonest shop assistant, an incident of the company's trading activities. It arises altogether outside such activities'.

- Expenditure which is wholly and exclusively to benefit the trades of several companies (for example in a group) but is not wholly and exclusively to benefit the trade of one specific company is not deductible *(Vodafone Cellular Ltd and others v Shaw 1995)*.

- *McKnight (HMIT) v Sheppard (1999)* concerned expenses incurred by a stockbroker in defending allegations of infringements of Stock Exchange regulations. It was found that the expenditure was incurred to prevent the destruction of the taxpayer's business and that as the expenditure was incurred for business purposes it was deductible. It was also found that although the expenditure had the effect of preserving the taxpayer's reputation, that was not its purpose, so there was no duality of purpose.

The **duality test** is illustrated by the following cases.

- *Mallalieu v Drummond 1983*

  Expenditure by a lady barrister on black clothing to be worn in court (and on its cleaning and repair) was not deductible. The expenditure was for the dual purpose of enabling the barrister to be warmly and properly clad as well as meeting her professional requirements.

2.7 Subscriptions and donations

The general 'wholly and exclusively' rule determines the deductibility of expenses. Subscriptions and donations are not deductible unless the expenditure is for the benefit of the trade. The following are the main types of subscriptions and donations you may meet and their correct treatments.

(a) Trade subscriptions (such as to a professional or trade association) are generally deductible.

(b) Charitable donations are deductible only if they are small and to local charities. Tax relief may be available for donations under the gift aid scheme. In the latter case they are not a deductible trading expense.

(c) Political subscriptions and donations are generally not deductible. However, if it can be shown that political expenditure is incurred for the survival of the trade then it may be deducted. This follows a case in which it was held that expenditure incurred in resisting nationalisation was allowable on the grounds that it affected the survival of the business (*Morgan v Tate and Lyle Ltd 1954*).

(d) When a business makes a gift of equipment manufactured, sold or used in the course of its trade to an educational establishment or for a charitable purpose, nothing need be brought into account as a trading receipt or (if capital allowances had been obtained on the asset) as disposal proceeds, so full relief is obtained for the cost. The donor must claim the relief. The donor company must claim relief within two years of the end of the accounting period of the gift. The value of any benefit to the donor from the gift is taxable.

(e) Where a donation represents the most effective commercial way of disposing of stock (for example, where it would not be commercially effective to sell surplus perishable food), the donation can be treated as for the benefit of the trade and the disposal proceeds taken as £Nil. In other cases, the amount credited to the accounts in respect of a donation of stock should be its market value.

2.8 Legal and professional charges

Legal and professional charges relating to capital or non-trading items are not deductible. These include charges incurred in acquiring new capital assets or legal rights, issuing shares, drawing up partnership agreements and litigating disputes over the terms of a partnership agreement.

Charges are deductible if they relate directly to trading. Deductible items include:

- Legal and professional charges incurred defending the taxpayer's title to fixed assets
- Charges connected with an action for breach of contract
- Expenses of the **renewal** (not the original grant) of a lease for less than 50 years
- Charges for trade debt collection
- Normal charges for preparing accounts/assisting with the self assessment of tax liabilities

Accountancy expenses arising out of an enquiry into the accounts information in a particular year's return are not allowed where the enquiry reveals discrepancies and additional liabilities for the year of enquiry, or any earlier year, which arise as a result of negligent or fraudulent conduct.

Where, however, the enquiry results in no addition to profits, or an adjustment to the profits for the year of enquiry only and that assessment does not arise as a result of negligent or fraudulent conduct, the additional accountancy expenses are allowable.

2.9 Irrecoverable and doubtful debts

Only irrecoverable debts incurred in the course of a business are deductible for taxation purposes. Thus loans to employees written off are not deductible unless the business is that of making loans, or it can be shown that the writing-off of the loan was earnings paid out for the benefit of the trade. If a trade debt is released as part of a voluntary arrangement under the Insolvency Act 1986, or a compromise or arrangement under s 425 Companies Act 1985, the amount released is deductible as an irrecoverable debt.

Allowances for debtors are not deductible, although specific allowances and write-offs against individual debts are deductible. The only adjustment needed to the accounts profit is to add back an increase (or deduct a decrease) in any allowance for debtors that is not specific.

2.10 Interest

Interest paid on a loan taken out for trade purposes (a trading loan relationship) is a deductible trading expense. Similarly interest received on a trading loan relationship is included within trading profits. This means that no adjustment to the accounts profit is required for such interest.

Interest paid and received on loans not taken out for trade purposes (non trading loan relationships) is deductible/ taxable to calculate the investment income. This means that the accounts profit must be adjusted to exclude such interest.

Loan relationships will be looked at in more detail later in this text.

2.11 Miscellaneous deductions

The **costs of seconding employees to charities or educational establishments are deductible.**

Expenditure incurred before the commencement of trade (**pre-trading expenditure**) is deductible, if it is incurred within seven years of the start of trade and it is of a type that would have been deductible had the trade already started. It is treated as a trading expense incurred on the first day of trading.

If earnings for employees are charged in the accounts but are not paid within nine months of the end of the period of account, the cost is only deductible for the period of account in which the earnings are paid. When a tax computation is made within the nine month period, it is initially assumed that unpaid earnings will not be paid within that period. The computation is adjusted if they are so paid.

Earnings are treated as paid at the same time as they are treated as received for employment income purposes.

Redundancy payments made when a trade ends are deductible on the earlier of the day of payment and the last day of trading. If the trade does not end, they can be deducted as soon as they are provided for, so long as the redundancy was decided on within the period of account, the provision is accurately calculated and the payments are made within nine months of the end of the period of account.

Here is a list of various other items that you may meet.

Item	Treatment	Comment
Educational courses for staff	Allow	
Removal expenses (to new business premises)	Allow	Only if not an expansionary move
Contribution to expenses of agents under the payroll deduction scheme	Allow	
Redundancy pay in excess of the statutory amount	Allow	If the trade ceases, the limit on allowability is 3 × the statutory amount (in addition to the statutory amount)
Compensation for loss of office and ex gratia payments	Allow	If for benefit of trade: *Mitchell v B W Noble Ltd 1927*
Counselling services for employees leaving employment	Allow	If qualify for exemption from for specific employment income charge on employees
Contributions to any of: 　Local enterprise agencies 　Training and enterprise councils 　Local enterprise companies 　Business link organisations	Allow	
Pension contributions 　(to schemes for employees and company directors)	Allow	If paid, not if only provided for; special contributions may be spread over the year of payment and future years
Premiums for insurance: 　against an employee's death or illness 　to cover locum costs or fixed overheads whilst the policyholder is ill	Allow	Receipts are taxable
Payments to employees for restrictive undertakings	Allow	Taxable on employee
Damages paid	Allow	If not too remote from trade: *Strong and Co v Woodifield 1906*
Preparation and restoration of waste disposal sites	Allow	Spread preparation expenditure over period of use of site. Pre-trading expenditure is treated as incurred on the first day of trading. Allow restoration expenditure in period of expenditure

Exam focus point

In the exam you could be given a profit and loss account and asked to calculate 'taxable profit'. You must look at every expense in the accounts to decide if it is (or isn't) 'tax deductible'. This means that you must become familiar with the many expenses you may see and the correct tax treatment. Look at the above paragraphs again noting what expenses are (and are not) allowable for tax purposes.

3 Income not taxable as trading profits

Receipts not taxable as trading profit must be deducted from the accounts profit. For example, rental income, interest on non trading loan relationships and dividends received from other UK companies are not taxable as trading profit. The rental income is taxed as property business income, whilst the interest is taxed as investment income.

There are three types of receipts which may be found in the accounting profits but which must be excluded from the taxable trading profit computation. These are:

(a)   **Capital receipts**
(b)   **Income taxed in another way** (at source or as another type of income)
(c)   **Income specifically exempt from tax**

However, compensation received in one lump sum for the loss of income is likely to be treated as income (*Donald Fisher (Ealing) Ltd v Spencer 1989*).

Income taxed as another type of income, for example property business income, is excluded from the computation of taxable trading profits but it is brought in again further down in the computation of profits chargeable to corporation tax. Similarly capital receipts are excluded from the computation of taxable trading profits income but they may be included in the computation of chargeable gains.

In some trades, (eg petrol stations and public houses), a wholesaler may pay a lump sum to a retailer in return for the retailer's only supplying that wholesaler's products for several years (an **exclusivity agreement**). If the payment must be used for a specific capital purpose, it is a capital receipt. If that is not the case, it is a revenue receipt. If the sum is repayable to the wholesaler but the requirement to repay is waived in tranches over the term of the agreement, each tranche is a separate revenue receipt when the requirement is waived.

4 Deductible expenditure not charged in the accounts

Amounts not charged in the accounts that are deductible from trading profits must be deducted when computing the taxable trading income. An example is capital allowances.

Capital allowances (see the next chapter) **are** an example of **deductible expenditure not charged in the accounts.**

A second example is **an annual sum** which can be deducted by a company that has paid **a lease premium to a landlord who is taxable on the premium as property business income** (see later in this text). Normally, the amortisation of the lease will have been deducted in the accounts and must be added back as an appropriation of profit.

Question — Calculation of taxable trading profit

Here is the profit and loss account of Pring Ltd, a trading company.

	£	£
Gross operating profit		30,860
Wages and salaries	7,000	
Rent and rates	2,000	
Depreciation	1,500	
Bad debts written off	150	
Allowance for fall in the price of raw materials	5,000	
Entertainment expenses	750	
Gift aid donation (amount paid)	1,200	
Bank interest (paid for trade purposes)	300	
Legal expenses on acquisition of new factory	250	
		(18,150)
Net profit		12,710

(a) No staff were entertained.
(b) The provision of £5,000 is charged because of an anticipated trade recession.

Compute the taxable trading profit.

Answer

	£	£
Profit per accounts		12,710
Add: Depreciation	1,500	
Allowance for fall in raw material prices	5,000	
Entertainment expenses	750	
Gift aid donation paid (to treat as a charge)	1,200	
Legal expenses	250	
		8,700
Adjusted taxable trading profits		21,410

5 The cessation of trades

 FAST FORWARD

Special rules ensure that post-cessation receipts are taxable and post-cessation expenses are tax deductible.

5.1 Post cessation receipts and expenses

Post-cessation receipts (including any releases of debts incurred by the company) **are taxable as miscellaneous income**.

Post-cessation expenses can be deducted so long as they would have been deductible had the trade continued, and they did not arise as a result of the cessation. Capital allowances which the company was entitled to immediately before the discontinuance but which remain unrelieved can also be deducted.

5.2 Valuing trading stock on cessation

When a trade ceases, the closing stock must be valued. The higher the value, the higher the profit for the final period of trading will be.

If the stock is sold to a UK trader who will deduct its cost in computing his taxable profits, it is valued under the following rules.

(a)   If the seller and the buyer are unconnected, take the actual price.

(b)   If the seller and the buyer are connected, take what would have been the price in an arm's length sale.

(c)   However, if the seller and the buyer are connected, the arm's length price exceeds both the original cost of the stock and the actual transfer price, and both the seller and the buyer make an election, then take the greater of the original cost of the stock and the transfer price. The time limit for election is two years after the end of the accounting period of cessation.

In all cases covered above, the value used for the seller's computation of profit is also used as the buyer's cost.

Key term

> Companies are **connected** with anyone controlling them, with other companies under common control and with partnerships under common control.

If the stock is not transferred to a UK trader who will be able to deduct its cost in computing his profits, then it is valued at its open market value as at the cessation of trade.

Chapter roundup

- The net profit in the company's accounts must be adjusted to find the taxable trading profit.

- Disallowable expenditure must be added back to the accounts profit in the computation of the taxable trading profit. Any item not deducted wholly and exclusively for trade purposes is disallowable expenditure. Certain other items, such as depreciation, are specifically disallowable.

- Receipts not taxable as trading profit must be deducted from the accounts profit. For example, rental income, interest on non trading loan relationships and dividends received from other UK companies are not taxable as trading profit. The rental income is taxed instead as property business income, whilst the interest is taxed as investment income.

- Amounts not charged in the accounts that are deductible from trading profits must be deducted when computing the taxable trading income. An example is capital allowances.

- Special rules ensure that post-cessation receipts are taxable and post-cessation expenses are tax deductible.

Quick quiz

1   What are the remoteness test and the duality test?

2   What pre-trading expenditure is deductible?

3   In which period of account are emoluments paid 12 months after the end of the period for which they are charged deductible?

4   What is the maximum allowable amount of redundancy pay on the cessation of a trade?

Answers to quick quiz

1 Expenditure is not deductible if it is not for trade purposes (the remoteness test), or if it reflects more than one purpose (the duality test)

2 Pre-trading expenditure is deductible if it is incurred within seven years of the start of the trade and is of a type that would have been deductible if the trade had already started.

3 In the period in which they are paid

4 3 × statutory amount

Now try the question below from the Exam Question Bank

Number	Level	Marks	Time
Q2	Examination	15	27 mins

3

Capital allowances

Topic list	Syllabus references
1 Capital allowances in general	1(c)(ii)
2 Plant and machinery – qualifying expenditure	1(c)(ii)
3 Allowances on plant and machinery	1(c)(ii)
4 Short-life assets	1(c)(ii)
5 Hire purchase and leasing	1(c)(ii)
6 Successions	1(c)(ii)
7 Industrial buildings – types	1(c)(ii)
8 Allowances on industrial buildings	1(c)(ii)

Introduction

Depreciation cannot be deducted in computing taxable trade profits. Instead, capital allowances are given. In this chapter, we look at capital allowances, starting with plant and machinery.

Our study of plant and machinery falls into three parts. Firstly, we look at what qualifies for allowances: many business assets get no allowances at all. Secondly, we see how to compute the allowances and lastly, we look at special rules for assets with short lives, for assets which the taxpayer does not buy outright and for transfers of whole businesses.

We then look at industrial buildings. Again, we start off by looking at what qualifies for the allowances and then how to compute the allowances.

1 Capital allowances in general

FAST FORWARD ➤➤ Capital allowances are available to give tax relief for certain capital expenditure.

Capital expenditure cannot be deducted in computing taxable trading profits, but it *may* attract capital allowances. Capital allowances are treated as a trading expense and are deducted in arriving at taxable trading profits. Balancing charges, effectively negative allowances, are added in arriving at those profits.

Capital allowances are calculated for accounting periods.

For capital allowances purposes, expenditure is generally deemed to be incurred when the obligation to pay becomes unconditional. This will often be the date of a contract, but if for example payment is due a month after delivery of a machine, it would be the date of delivery. However, amounts due more than four months after the obligation becomes unconditional are deemed to be incurred when they fall due.

2 Plant and machinery – qualifying expenditure

FAST FORWARD ➤➤ Statutory rules generally exclude specified items from treatment as plant, rather than include specified items as plant.

2.1 Definition of plant and machinery

Capital expenditure on plant and machinery qualifies for capital allowances if the plant or machinery is used for a qualifying activity, such as a trade. "Plant" is not defined by the legislation, although some specific exclusions and inclusions are given. The word "machinery" may be taken to have its normal everyday meaning.

2.2 The statutory exclusions

2.2.1 Buildings

Expenditure on a building and on any asset which is incorporated in a building or is of a kind normally incorporated into buildings does not qualify as expenditure on plant, but see below for exceptions.

In addition to complete buildings, **the following assets count as 'buildings', and are therefore not plant**.

- Walls, floors, ceilings, doors, gates, shutters, windows and stairs
- Mains services, and systems, of water, electricity and gas
- Waste disposal, sewerage and drainage systems
- Shafts or other structures for lifts etc.

2.2.2 Structures

Expenditure on structures and on works involving the alteration of land **does not qualify as expenditure on plant**, but see below for exceptions.

A 'structure' is a fixed structure of any kind, other than a building.

2.2.3 Exceptions

Over the years a large body of case law has been built up under which plant and machinery allowances have been given on certain types of expenditure which might be thought to be expenditure on a building or structure. Statute therefore gives a list of various assets which *may* still be plant. These are:

- Any machinery not within any other item in this list

- Electrical (including lighting), cold water, gas and sewerage systems:

    (i)   Provided mainly to meet the particular requirements of the trade, or

    (ii)   Provided mainly to serve particular machinery or plant used for the purposes of the trade

- Space or water heating systems and powered systems of ventilation

- Manufacturing and display equipment

- Cookers, washing machines, refrigeration or cooling equipment, sanitary ware and furniture and furnishings

- Lifts etc

- Sound insulation provided mainly to meet the particular requirements of the trade

- Computer, telecommunication and surveillance systems

- Sprinkler equipment, fire alarm and burglar alarm systems

- Strong rooms in bank or building society premises; safes

- Partition walls, where movable and intended to be moved

- Decorative assets provided for the enjoyment of the public in the hotel, restaurant or similar trades; advertising hoardings

- Glasshouses which have, as an integral part of their structure, devices which control the plant growing environment automatically

- Swimming pools (including diving boards, slides) and structures for rides at amusement parks.

- Caravans provided mainly for holiday lettings

- Movable buildings intended to be moved in the course of the trade

- Expenditure on altering land for the purpose only of installing machinery or plant

- Dry docks and jetties

- Pipelines, and also underground ducts or tunnels with a primary purpose of carrying utility conduits

- Silos provided for temporary storage and storage tanks, slurry pits and silage clamps

- Fish tanks, fish ponds and fixed zoo cages

- A railway or tramway

Items falling within the above list of exclusions will only qualify as plant if they fall within the meaning of plant as established by case law. This is discussed below.

2.2.4 Land

Land or an interest in land does not qualify as plant and machinery. For this purpose 'land' excludes buildings, structures and assets which are installed or fixed to land in such a way as to become part of the land for general legal purposes.

2.3 The statutory inclusions

Certain expenditure is specifically deemed to be expenditure on plant and machinery.

The following are deemed to be on plant and machinery.

- Expenditure incurred by a trader in complying with fire regulations for a building which he occupies

- Expenditure by a trader on thermal insulation of an industrial building

- Expenditure by a trader in meeting statutory safety requirements for sports ground

- Expenditure (by an individual or a partnership, not by a company) on *security assets* provided to meet a special threat to an individual's security that arises wholly or mainly due to the particular trade concerned. Cars, ships, aircraft and dwellings are specifically excluded from the definition of a security asset

On disposal, the sale proceeds for the above are deemed to be zero, so no balancing charge (see below) can arise.

Capital expenditure on computer software (both programs and data) **qualifies as expenditure on plant and machinery**:

(a)   Regardless of whether the software is supplied in a tangible form (such as a disk) or transmitted electronically, and

(b)   Regardless of whether the purchaser acquires the software or only a licence to use it.

Disposal proceeds are brought into account in the normal way, except that if the fee for the grant of a licence is taxed as income of the licensor, no disposal proceeds are taken into account in computing the licensee's capital allowances.

Where someone has incurred expenditure qualifying for capital allowances on computer software (or the right to use software), and receives a capital sum in exchange for allowing someone else to use the software, that sum is brought into account as disposal proceeds. However, the cumulative total of disposal proceeds is not allowed to exceed the original cost of the software, and any proceeds above this limit are ignored for capital allowances purposes (although they may lead to chargeable gains).

If software is expected to have a useful economic life of less than two years, its cost may be treated as revenue expenditure.

For companies the rules for computer software are overridden by the rules for intangible fixed assets unless the company elects otherwise.

2.4 Case law

FAST FORWARD

There are several cases on the definition of plant. To help you to absorb them, try to see the function/setting theme running through them.

The original case law **definition of plant** (applied in this case to a horse) is **'whatever apparatus is used by a businessman for carrying on his business: not his stock in trade which he buys or makes for sale; but all goods and chattels, fixed or movable, live or dead, which he keeps for permanent employment in the business'** (*Yarmouth v France 1887*).

Subsequent cases have refined the original definition and have largely been concerned with the **distinction between plant actively used in the business (qualifying) and the setting in which the business is carried on (non-qualifying). This is the 'functional' test**. Some of the decisions have now been enacted as part of statute law, but they are still relevant as examples of the principles involved.

The whole cost of excavating and installing a swimming pool was allowed to the owners of a caravan park. *CIR v Barclay Curle & Co 1969* was followed: the pool performed **the function** of giving 'buoyancy and enjoyment' to the persons using the pool (*Cooke v Beach Station Caravans Ltd 1974*) (actual item now covered by statute).

A barrister succeeded in his claim for his law library: 'Plant includes a man's tools of his trade. It extends to what he uses day by day in the course of his profession. It is not confined to physical things like the dentist's chair or the architect's table' (*Munby v Furlong 1977*).

Office partitioning was allowed. Because it was movable it was not regarded as part of the setting in which the business was carried on (*Jarrold v John Good and Sons Ltd 1963*) (actual item now covered by statute).

A ship used as a floating restaurant was regarded as a 'structure in which the business was carried on rather than apparatus employed ... ' (Buckley LJ). No capital allowances could be obtained *(Benson v Yard Arm Club 1978)*. The same decision was made in relation to a football club's spectator stand. The stand performed no function in the actual carrying out of the club's trade (*Brown v Burnley Football and Athletic Co Ltd 1980*).

At a motorway service station, false ceilings contained conduits, ducts and lighting apparatus. **They did not qualify because they did not perform a function in the business. They were merely part of the setting in which the business was conducted** (*Hampton v Fortes Autogrill Ltd 1979*).

Light fittings, decor and murals can be plant. A company carried on business as hoteliers and operators of licensed premises. The function of the items was the creation of an atmosphere conducive to the comfort and well being of its customers (*CIR v Scottish and Newcastle Breweries Ltd 1982*) (decorative assets used in hotels etc, now covered by statute).

On the other hand, it has been held that when an attractive floor is provided in a restaurant, the fact that the floor performs the function of making the restaurant attractive to customers is not enough to make it plant. It functions as premises, and the cost therefore does not qualify for capital allowances (*Wimpy International Ltd v Warland 1988*).

General lighting in a department store is not plant, as it is merely setting. Special display lighting, however, can be plant (*Cole Brothers Ltd v Phillips 1982*).

Free-standing decorative screens installed in the windows of a branch of a building society qualified as plant. Their function was not to act a part of the setting in which the society's business was carried on; it was to attract local custom, and accordingly the screens formed part of the apparatus with which the society carried on its business (*Leeds Permanent Building Society v Proctor 1982*).

In *Bradley v London Electricity plc 1996* an electricity substation was held not to be plant because it functioned as premises in which London Electricity carried on a trading activity rather than apparatus with which the activity was carried out.

3 Allowances on plant and machinery

FAST FORWARD

With capital allowances computations, the main thing is to get the layout right. Having done that, you will find that the figures tend to drop into place.

3.1 Pooling expenditure

Most expenditure on plant and machinery is put into a pool of expenditure on which capital allowances may be claimed. An addition increases the pool whilst a disposal decreases it.

Exceptionally the following items are not pooled.

  (i)   cars costing more than £12,000
  (ii)   short life assets where an election has been made.

Each of these items is dealt with in further detail below.

3.2 Writing down allowances

> Most expenditure on plant and machinery qualifies for a WDA at 25% every 12 months.

Key term

> A **writing down allowance (WDA)** is given on pooled expenditure **at the rate of 25% a year** (on a reducing balance basis). The WDA is calculated on the written down value (WDV) of pooled plant, after adding the current period's additions and taking out the current period's disposals.

When plant is sold, proceeds (but **limited to a maximum of the original cost**) are taken out of the pool. Provided that the trade is still being carried on, the pool balance remaining is written down in the future by WDAs, even if there are no assets left.

3.3 Example

E Ltd has a balance of unrelieved expenditure on its general pool of plant and machinery of £16,000 on 1.4.05. In the year to 31.3.06 the company bought a car for £8,000 and disposed of plant which originally cost £4,000 for £6,000.

Calculate the capital allowances available for the year.

	£
Pool value b/f	16,000
Addition	8,000
Less: Disposal (Limited to cost)	(4,000)
	20,000
WDA @ 25%	(5,000)
TWDV c/f	15,000

WDAs are 25% × months/12 where the accounting period is shorter than 12 months (a company's accounting period for tax purposes is never longer than 12 months), or where the trade concerned started in the accounting period and was therefore carried on for fewer than 12 months.

Expenditure on plant and machinery by a person about to begin a trade is treated as incurred on the first day of trading. Assets previously owned by a trader and then brought into the trade (at the start of trading or later) are treated as bought for their market values at the times when they are brought in.

3.4 First year allowances

> First year allowances (FYA) may be available for certain expenditure. FYAs are never pro-rated in short or long periods of account.

3.4.1 Spending by medium sized enterprises

Expenditure incurred on plant and machinery (other than leased assets, cars, sea going ships, railway assets or long life assets) by **medium sized enterprises qualifies for a first year allowance (FYA) of 40%.**

Exam focus point

> The rates of FYAs will be given to you on the exam paper.

A **medium sized enterprise** is a company that either satisfies at least two of the following conditions in the chargeable period/financial year in which the expenditure is incurred.

(a) **Turnover not more than £22.8 million**
(b) **Assets not more than £11.4 million**
(c) **Not more than 250 employees**

or which was medium sized in the previous year. A company must not be a member of a large group when the expenditure is incurred.

3.4.2 Spending by small sized enterprises

Expenditure incurred on plant and machinery by small sized enterprises **qualifies for a FYA of 40%** in the same way as for medium sized enterprises. This rate was increased from 40% to 50% for expenditure on or after 1 April 2004 for one year.

The examiner has said that a question could still be set where 50% first year allowance was available on expenditure incurred between 1 April 2004 and 31 March 2005.

A **small enterprise** is a company which satisfies at least two of the following conditions in the chargeable period/financial year in which the expenditure is incurred:

(a) **Turnover not more than £5.6 million**
(b) **Assets not more than £2.8 million**
(c) **Not more than 50 employees**

or which was small in the previous year. If a company is a member of a group, the group must also be small when the expenditure is incurred.

3.4.3 100% FYAs

A 100% FYA is available to all businesses for expenditure incurred on designated energy saving technologies and on plant and equipment meeting strict water saving or efficiency criteria (eg water meters, flow controllers, efficient toilets!). The equipment must be used in the person's business.

A car registered between 17 April 2002 and 31 March 2008 qualifies for 100% FYAs if it either:

- **emits not more than 120 gm/km CO_2 ; or**
- **it is electrically propelled**

In addition, the special rules for expensive cars (see below), which restrict the availability of capital allowances and the deductibility of lease rental payments, do not apply to low emission cars.

A 100% FYA is available to all businesses in respect of expenditure incurred on plant to refuel vehicles with compressed natural gas or hydrogen (in this case on expenditure between 17 April 2002 and 31 March 2008).

Equipment acquired for leasing does not normally qualify for the 100% FYA. Exceptionally, leased low emission and electric cars, natural gas/hydrogen refuelling equipment and certain energy and water saving equipment all do qualify for FYAs.

In exam questions you should only treat motor cars as low emission cars if they are specifically described as such. You are not expected to know the 120g/km limit.

3.4.4 Calculation

For FYA purposes, the provisions which treat capital expenditure incurred prior to the commencement of trading as incurred on the first day of trading do not apply except insofar as they require the FYAs to be given in the first period of account (or accounting period for companies).

First year allowances are given in the place of writing down allowances. For subsequent years a WDA is given on the balance of expenditure at the normal rate. You should therefore transfer the balance of the expenditure to the pool at the end of the first period.

FYAs are given for incurring expenditure. It is irrelevant whether the basis period of expenditure is twelve months or not. FYAs are not scaled up or down by reference to the length of the period.

Question   Calculation of taxable profits

Walton Ltd starts a trade on 1 March 2002, and has the following results (before capital allowances).

Period of account	Profits
	£
1.3.02 - 31.7.03	42,500
1.8.03 - 31.7.04	36,800
1.8.04 - 31.7.05	32,000

Plant (none of which is information or communication technology equipment or energy saving plant) is bought as follows.

Date	Cost
	£
1.3.02	13,000
1.6.02	9,603
1.9.03	5,000
1.12.04	1,600

On 1 May 2004, plant which cost £7,000 is sold for £4,000. Walton Ltd's business is a small sized enterprise for FYA purposes. Show the taxable trading profits arising in the above periods of account.

Answer

The seventeen month period of account must be split into two accounting periods for corporation tax purposes. The first period is the twelve months to 28.2.03 and the second period is the five months to 31.7.03.

The capital allowances are as follows.

FYA	£	Pool £	Allowances £
1.3.02 – 28.2.03			
Additions (1.3.02 and 1.6.02)	22,603		
FYA 40%	(9,041)		9,041
		13,562	
1.3.03 – 31.7.03			
WDA @ 25% x 5/12		(1,413)	1,413
		12,149	
1.8.03 – 31.7.04			
Disposals (1.5.04)		(4,000)	
		8,149	
WDA 25%		(2,037)	2,037
		6,112	
Addition (1.9.03)	5,000		
FYA 40%	(2,000)		2,000
		3,000	4,037
		9,112	
1.8.04 – 31.7.05			
WDA 25%		(2,278)	2,278
		6,834	
Addition (1.12.04)	1,600		
FYA 50%	(800)		800
		800	
TWDV c/f		7,634	
			3,078

The profits of the first three periods of account are as follows:

Period of account	Working	Profits £
1.3.02 – 28.2.03	£(42,500 x 12/17 - 9,041)	20,959
1.3.03 – 31.7.03	£(42,500 x 5/17 – 1,413)	11,087
1.8.03– 31.7.04	£(36,800 – 4,037)	32,763
1.8.04– 31.7.05	£(32,000 – 3,078)	28,922

Exam focus point

> Note the tax planning opportunities available. It may be important to buy plant just before an accounting date, so that allowances become available as soon as possible. On the other hand, it may be worthwhile to claim less than the maximum allowances so as to even out the annual assessments and avoid higher rate tax.

3.5 The disposal value of assets

The most common disposal value at which assets are entered in a capital allowances computation is the sale proceeds. But there are a number of less common situations.

Where the asset is sold at below market value (or is given away) the market value is used instead of the actual sale proceeds. This general rule has two exceptions. The actual proceeds of sale are used:

(a) Where the buyer will be able to claim capital allowances on the expenditure

(b) Where an employee acquires an asset from his employer at undervalue (or as a gift) and so faces a charge under the employment income benefit rules

If the asset is demolished, destroyed or otherwise lost, the disposal value is taken to be the actual sale proceeds from any resulting scrap, plus any insurance or other compensation moneys.

With all these rules, there is an overriding rule that the capital allowances **disposal value cannot exceed the original purchase price.**

When a building is sold, the vendor and purchaser can make a joint election to determine how the sale proceeds are apportioned between the building and its fixtures. There are anti-avoidance provisions that ensure capital allowances given overall on a fixture do not exceed the original cost of the fixture.

3.6 Balancing charges and allowances

Balancing charges occur when the disposal value deducted exceeds the balance remaining in the pool. The charge equals the excess and is effectively a negative capital allowance, increasing profits. Most commonly this happens when the trade ceases and the remaining assets are sold. It may also occur, however, whilst the trade is still in progress.

Balancing allowances on the capital allowance pools of expenditure arise only when the trade ceases. The balancing allowance is equal to the remaining unrelieved expenditure after deducting the disposal value of all the assets. Balancing allowances also arise on items which are not pooled (see below) whenever those items are disposed of.

3.7 Long life assets

Key term

> **Long life assets** are assets with an expected working life of 25 years or more.

The writing down allowance available on such assets is 6% per annum on a reducing balance basis. Expenditure on such assets must be kept in a pool that is separate from the general pool.

The following are not **treated as long life assets** (and therefore (with the exception of expensive cars: see below) still qualify for writing down allowances of 25% per annum):

(a)   **Plant and machinery in dwelling houses, retail shops, showrooms, hotels and offices**
(b)   **Motor cars**
(c)   **Ships and railways assets** bought before 1 January 2011
(d)   **Second-hand machinery in respect of which the vendor obtained allowances at 25%**

The **long life asset rules do not apply to companies whose total expenditure on long life assets in a chargeable period is £100,000**, or less. If the expenditure exceeds £100,000, the whole of the expenditure qualifies for allowances at 6% per annum only. For this purpose all expenditure incurred under a contract is treated as incurred in the first chargeable period to which that contract relates.

The £100,000 limit is reduced or increased proportionately in the case of a chargeable period of less or more than 12 months. In the case of groups of companies, the limit must be divided between the number of associated companies in the group (see later in this text).

The £100,000 exclusion is not available in respect of leased assets, second-hand assets where the vendor was only able to claim allowances of 6%, or assets where the trader has only bought a share.

3.8 Assets which are not pooled

A separate record of allowances and WDV must be kept for each asset which is not pooled and when it is sold a balancing allowance or charge emerges.

Motor cars costing more than £12,000 are not pooled. The maximum WDA is £3,000 a year. The limit is £3,000 × months/12 in short accounting periods.

FYAs are not available on cars (except for certain low emission or electric cars – see above).

Short life assets are not pooled (see below).

3.9 The cessation of a trade

When a business ceases to trade no FYAs or WDAs are given in the final accounting period. Each asset is deemed to be disposed of on the date the trade ceased (usually at the then market value). Additions in the relevant period are brought in and then the disposal proceeds (limited to cost) are deducted from the balance of qualifying expenditure. If the proceeds exceed the balance then a balancing charge arises. If the balance of qualifying expenditure exceeds the proceeds then a balancing allowance is given.

4 Short-life assets

FAST FORWARD

Short life asset elections can bring forward the allowances due on an asset.

A trader can elect that specific items of plant be kept separately from the general pool. The election is irrevocable. For a company, the time limit for electing is two years after the end of the accounting period of the expenditure. (For an unincorporated business, the time limit for electing is the 31 January which is 22 months after the end of the tax year in which the period of account of the expenditure ends.) **Any asset subject to this election is known as a 'short-life asset', and the election is known as a 'de-pooling election'.**

Key term

> Provided that the asset is disposed of within four years of the end of the period of account or accounting period in which it was bought (ie before 5 WDAs have been claimed), it is a **short life asset** and a balancing charge or allowance is made on its disposal.

The receipt of a capital sum in return for the right to use computer software does not count as a disposal for this purpose. If the asset is not disposed of in the correct time period, its tax written down value is added to the general pool at the end of that time.

The election should be made for assets likely to be sold within four years for less than their tax written down values. It should not be made for assets likely to be sold within four years for more than their tax written down values. (These are, of course, only general guidelines based on the assumption that a trader will want to obtain allowances as quickly as possible. There may be other considerations, such as a desire to even out annual taxable profits.)

Question   Short life assets

Caithlin Ltd bought an asset on 1 May 2001 for £12,000 and made a de-pooling election. Its accounting year end is 30 April. Calculate the capital allowances due if:

(a)   The asset is scrapped for £300 in August 2005.
(b)   The asset is scrapped for £200 in August 2006.

Assume that first year allowances were not available.

Answer

(a)   *Year to 30.4.02*

		£
Cost		12,000
WDA 25%		(3,000)
		9,000

Year to 30.4.03

WDA 25%		(2,250)
		6,750

Year to 30.4.04

WDA 25%		(1,688)
		5,062

Year to 30.4.05

WDA 25%		(1,266)
		3,796

Year to 30.4.06

Disposal proceeds		(300)
Balancing allowance		3,496

(b)   If the asset is still in use at 30 April 2006, a WDA of 25% × £3,796 = £949 would be claimable in the year to 30 April 2006. The tax written down value of £3,796 – £949 = £2,847 would be added to the general pool at the beginning of the next period of account. The disposal proceeds of £200 would be deducted from the general pool in that period's capital allowances computation.

Short-life asset treatment cannot be claimed for:

- Motor cars
- Plant used partly for non-trade purposes
- Plant brought into use for the trade following non-business use
- Plant received by way of gift
- Plant in respect of which a subsidy is received
- Long life assets

Where a short-life asset is disposed of within the four year period to a connected person (see below):

(a)   The original owner receives a balancing allowance calculated as normal and the new owner receives WDAs on the cost to him, but

(b)   **If both parties so elect, the asset is treated as being sold for its tax written down value at the start of the chargeable period in which the transfer takes place, so there is no balancing charge or allowance for the vendor.**

In both situations, the acquiring party will continue to 'de-pool' the asset up to the same date as the original owner would have done.

Companies are connected with anyone controlling them, with other companies under common control and with partnerships under common control.

5 Hire purchase and leasing

FAST FORWARD   There are special rules for capital allowances on hired or leased assets.

5.1 Assets on hire purchase

Any asset (including a car) bought on hire purchase (HP) is treated as if purchased outright for the cash price. Therefore:

(a) The buyer normally obtains **capital allowances on the cash price** when the agreement begins.

(b) He may write off the **finance charge as a trade expense** over the term of the HP contract.

5.2 Leased assets

Under a lease, the lessee merely hires the asset over a period. The hire charge can normally be deducted in computing trade profits.

An expensive car (one costing over £12,000) will attract WDAs limited to £3,000 a year if bought. If it is leased instead, the maximum allowable deduction from trading profits for lease rentals is limited as described earlier in this text.

A lessor of plant normally obtains the benefit of capital allowances although there are anti-avoidance provisions which deny or restrict capital allowances on certain finance leases. Leasing is thus an activity which attracts tax allowances and which can be used to defer tax liabilities where the capital allowances given exceed the rental income. For individuals, any losses arising from leasing are available for offset against other income only if the individual devotes substantially all of his time to the conduct of a leasing business.

6 Successions

> **FAST FORWARD**
>
> Balancing adjustments which usually arise on the cessation of a business can be avoided where the business is being taken over by a connected person.

Balancing adjustments arise on the cessation of a business. No writing down allowances are given, but the final proceeds (limited to cost) on sales of plant are compared with the tax WDV to calculate balancing allowances or charges.

Balancing charges may be avoided where the trade passes from one connected person to another. If a succession occurs both parties must elect if the avoidance of the balancing adjustments is required. **An election will result in the plant being transferred at its tax written down value for capital allowances purposes**. The predecessor can write down the plant for the period prior to cessation and the successor can write it down from the date of commencement. The election must be made within two years of the date of the succession.

If no election is made on a transfer of business to a connected person, assets are deemed to be sold at their market values.

If an election is made, the limit on proceeds to be brought into account on a later sale of an asset is the original cost of the asset, not the deemed transfer price.

7 Industrial buildings – types

> **FAST FORWARD**
>
> The computations for industrial buildings are a little more complicated than those for plant and machinery, but there is less case law to learn. Basically allowances equal to the fall in value of the building whilst it was being used industrially are available to the trader.

7.1 General definition

A special type of capital allowance (an **industrial buildings allowance** or IBA) is available in respect of **expenditure on industrial buildings**.

The allowance is available to:

- Trading companies (with taxable trading profits)
- Companies that let qualifying buildings to traders.

Traders can choose whether to segregate expenditure on long life assets in buildings and claim plant and machinery allowances (see above) or whether to claim industrial buildings allowances on the expenditure.

Key term

> **Industrial buildings** include:
>
> (a) All factories and ancillary premises used in:
>
>   (i) A manufacturing business
>   (ii) A trade in which goods and materials are subject to any process
>   (iii) A trade in which goods or raw materials are stored
>
> (b) Staff welfare buildings (such as workplace nurseries and canteens, but not directors' restaurants) where the trade is qualifying
>
> (c) Sports pavilions in any trade
>
> (d) Buildings in use for a transport undertaking, agricultural contracting, mining or fishing
>
> (e) Roads operated under highway concessions. The operation of such roads is treated as a trade for capital allowances purposes. The operator is treated as occupying the roads.

The key term in (a) (ii) above is 'the subjection of goods to any process'.

- The unpacking, repacking and relabelling of goods in a wholesale cash and carry supermarket did not amount to a 'process' but was a mere preliminary to sale (*Bestway Holdings Ltd v Luff 1998*).

- The mechanical processing of cheques and other banking documents was a process but pieces of paper carrying information were not 'goods' and thus the building housing the machinery did not qualify (*Girobank plc v Clarke 1998*).

Estate roads on industrial estates qualify, provided that the estate buildings are used wholly or mainly for a qualifying purpose.

Dwelling houses, retail shops, showrooms and offices are not industrial buildings.

Warehouses used for storage often cause problems in practice. A warehouse used for storage which is merely a transitory and necessary incident of the conduct of the business is not an industrial building. Storage is only a qualifying purpose if it is an end in itself.

Any building is an industrial building if it is constructed for the welfare of employees of a trader whose trade is a qualifying one (that is, the premises in which the trade is carried on are industrial buildings).

Sports pavilions provided for the welfare of employees qualify as industrial buildings. In this case, it does not matter whether the taxpayer is carrying on a trade in a qualifying building or not. Thus a retailer's sports pavilion would qualify for IBAs.

Drawing offices which serve an industrial building are regarded as industrial buildings themselves (*CIR v Lambhill Ironworks Ltd 1950*).

7.2 Hotels

Allowances on hotels are given as though they were industrial buildings.

Key term

> For a building to qualify as a '**hotel**' for industrial buildings allowance purposes:
>
> (a) It must have at least ten letting bedrooms
>
> (b) It must have letting bedrooms as the whole or main part of the sleeping accommodation
>
> (c) It must offer ancillary services including at least:
>
> > (i) Breakfast
> > (ii) Evening meals
> > (iii) The cleaning of rooms
> > (iv) The making of beds
>
> (d) It must be open for at least four months during the April to October season.

7.3 Eligible expenditure

Capital allowances are computed on the amount of eligible expenditure incurred on qualifying buildings. The eligible expenditure is:

- The original cost of a building if built by the trader, or
- The purchase price if the building was acquired from a person trading as a builder.

If the building was acquired other than from a person trading as a builder, the eligible expenditure is the lower of the purchase price and the original cost incurred by the person incurring the construction expenditure.

If a building is sold more than once before being brought into use, the last buyer before the building is brought into use obtains the allowances. If, in such cases, the building was first sold by someone trading as a builder, the eligible expenditure is the lower of the price paid by the first buyer and the price paid by the last buyer.

In all cases where a building is sold before use and artificial arrangements have increased the purchase price, it is reduced to what it would have been without those arrangements.

Where part of a building qualifies as an industrial building and part does not, the whole cost qualifies for IBAs, provided that the cost of the non-qualifying part is not more than 25% of the total expenditure. If the non-qualifying part of the building does cost more than 25% of the total, its cost must be excluded from the capital allowances computation.

Difficulties arise where non-qualifying buildings (particularly offices and administration blocks) are joined to manufacturing areas. In *Abbott Laboratories Ltd v Carmody 1968* a covered walkway linking manufacturing and administrative areas was not regarded as creating a single building. The administrative area was treated as a separate, non-qualifying building.

The cost of land is disallowed but expenditure incurred in preparing land for building does qualify. The cost of items which would not be included in a normal commercial lease (such as rental guarantees) also does not qualify.

Professional fees, for example architects' fees, incurred in connection with the construction of an industrial building qualify. The cost of repairs to industrial buildings also qualifies, provided that the expenditure is not deductible as a trading expense.

8 Allowances on industrial buildings

FAST FORWARD

> An allowance, normally at the rate of 4% per annum, is given if a building is in industrial use on the last day of the period of account concerned. If the building is in non industrial use a notional allowance will be given.

8.1 Writing down allowances

A writing down allowance (WDA) is given to the person holding the 'relevant interest'. Broadly, the relevant interest is the interest of the first acquirer of the industrial building and may be a freehold or leasehold interest.

Where a long lease (more than 50 years) has been granted on an industrial building, the grant may be treated as a sale so that allowances may be claimed by the lessee rather than the lessor. A claim must be made by the lessor and lessee jointly, within two years of the start of the lease. The election allows allowances to be claimed on industrial buildings where the lessor is not subject to tax (as with local authorities).

The WDA is given for a period provided that the industrial building was in use as such on the last day of the period concerned.

If the building was not in use as an industrial building at the end of the relevant period it may have been:

- **Unused** for any purpose, or
- **Used for a non-industrial purpose.**

The distinction is important in ascertaining whether WDAs are due to the taxpayer. **If any disuse is temporary and previously the building had been in industrial use, WDAs may be claimed in exactly the same way as if the building were in industrial use.** The legislation does not define 'temporary' but in practice, any subsequent qualifying use of the building will usually enable the period of disuse to be regarded as temporary.

Non-industrial use has different consequences. If this occurs a notional WDA is deducted from the balance of unrelieved expenditure but no WDA may be claimed by the taxpayer.

The WDA is 4% of the eligible expenditure incurred by the taxpayer.

The allowance is calculated on a straight line basis (in contrast to WDAs on plant and machinery which are calculated on the reducing balance), starting when the building is brought into use.

The WDA is 4% × months/12 if the period concerned is not 12 months long.

Buildings always have a **separate computation for each building**. They are never pooled.

8.2 Balancing adjustments on sale

8.2.1 The tax life

The 'tax life' of an industrial building is 25 years (hence the 4% straight line WDA) after it is first used. Balancing adjustments apply *only* if a building is sold within its tax life of 25 years.

On a sale between connected persons, the parties may jointly elect that the transfer price for IBAs purposes should be the lower of the market value and the residue of unallowed expenditure before the sale. This avoids a balancing charge unless there has been non-industrial use.

8.2.2 Sales without non-industrial use

The seller's calculation is quite straightforward providing the building has not been put to non-industrial use at any time during his ownership. It takes the following form.

	£
Cost	X
Less allowances previously given	(X)
Residue (ie WDV) before sale	X
Less proceeds (limited to cost)	(X)
Balancing (charge)/allowance	(X)

The buyer obtains annual straight line WDAs for the remainder of the building's tax life. This life is calculated to the nearest month. The allowances are granted on the residue after sale which is computed thus.

	£
Residue before sale	X
Plus balancing charge **or** less balancing allowance	X
Residue after sale	X

This means that **the second owner will write off the lower of its cost or the original cost**.

Question	Calculation of IBAs

Frankie Ltd, which started to trade in 2000 preparing accounts to 31 December, bought an industrial building for £100,000 (excluding land) on 1 October 2001. The company brought it into use as a factory immediately. On 1 September 2005 it sold it for £120,000 to Holly Ltd, whose accounting date is 30 September and who brought the building into industrial use immediately. Show the IBAs available to Frankie Ltd and to Holly Ltd.

Answer

Frankie Ltd	£
Cost 1.10.01	100,000
Y/e 31.12.01 to y/e 31.12.04 WDA 4 × 4%	(16,000)
Residue before sale	84,000
Y/e 31.12.05 Proceeds (limited to cost)	(100,000)
Balancing charge	(16,000)
Holly Ltd	
Residue before sale	84,000
Balancing charge	16,000
Residue after sale	100,000

The tax life of the building ends on 1.10.01 + 25 years = 30.9.2026
The date of Holly Ltd's purchase is 1.9.05
The unexpired life is therefore 21 years 1 month

	£
Y/e 30.9.05 WDA £100,000/21.083333	4,743
Next 20 accounting periods at £4,743 a year	94,860
Y/e 30.9.26 (balance)	397
	100,000

The Revenue allow IBAs equal to the fall in value of a building over the trader's use of that building. As a general rule if an industrial building is sold for more than its original cost a balancing charge equal to the allowances given to date will arise. This is because there was no fall in value so no allowances are actually due.

If it is sold for less than original cost we could calculate the fall in value of the building and that would equal the allowances available for this building. If we compare this to the allowances already given, the difference would be the balancing adjustment due on the sale.

In the above question if Frankie Ltd sold the building Holly Ltd for £90,000:

	£
Fall in value (£100,000 – £90,000) = allowances due	10,000
Less: allowances already given to Frankie Ltd	16,000
Balancing adjustment = Balancing charge	6,000

Over the use of the building by Frankie Ltd £16,000 of IBAs were claimed. On the sale of the building the fall in value is calculated as £10,000. Thus Frankie Ltd should only have received £10,000 of allowances not £16,000. So £6,000 is paid back as a balancing charge.

Businesses are denied a balancing allowance where disposal proceeds are less than they would have been as a result of a tax avoidance scheme.

8.3 Sales after non-industrial use

If at the end of a period, an industrial building was in non-industrial use, then the owner will not have been able to claim WDAs, but the building will have been written down by notional WDAs.

If, following a period of non-industrial use, an industrial building is sold for more than its original cost, the balancing charge is the actual allowances given. The residue after sale is the original cost minus the notional allowances.

Sales for less than original cost after a period of non industrial use will not be examined.

Question   Non-industrial use

The facts are as in the above question except that on 1 October 2002 Frankie Ltd ceases manufacturing in the building, letting it out as a theatrical rehearsal studio. On 1 June 2004 it recommences manufacturing in the building and, as before, sells it to Holly Ltd for £120,000 on 1 September 2005. Show the IBAs available to Frankie Ltd and to Holly Ltd.

Answer

Frankie Ltd	£
Cost 1.10.01	100,000
Y/e 31.12.01 WDA 4%	(4,000)
	96,000
Y/e 31.12.02 and y/e 31.12.03 No WDA since not in industrial use at the ends of the accounting periods, but deduct notional allowances 2 × 4%	(8,000)
	88,000
Y/e 31.12.04 WDA 4%	(4,000)
Residue before sale	84,000
Balancing charge for y/e 31.12.05: real (not notional) allowances £(4,000 + 4,000)	£(8,000)

Holly Ltd	£
Residue before sale	84,000
Add: balancing charge	8,000
Residue after sale	92,000

	£
Y/e 30.9.05 WDA £92,000/21.083333	4,364
Next 20 account periods at £4,364 a year	87,280
Y/e 30.9.26 (balance)	356
	92,000

Chapter roundup

- Capital allowances are available to give tax relief for certain capital expenditure.

- Statutory rules generally exclude specified items from treatment as plant, rather than include specified items as plant.

- There are several cases on the definition of plant. To help you to absorb them, try to see the function/setting theme running through them.

- With capital allowances computations, the main thing is to get the layout right. Having done that, you will find that the figures tend to drop into place.

- Most expenditure on plant and machinery qualifies for a WDA at 25% every 12 months.

- First year allowances (FYA) may be available for certain expenditure. FYAs are never pro-rated in short or long periods of account.

- Short life asset elections can bring forward the allowances due on an asset.

- There are special rules for capital allowances on hired or leased assets.

- Balancing adjustments which usually arise on the cessation of a business can be avoided where the business is being taken over by a connected person.

- The computations for industrial buildings are a little more complicated than those for plant and machinery, but there is less case law to learn.   Basically allowances equal to the fall in value of the building whilst it was being used industrially are available to the trader.

- An allowance, normally at the rate of 4% per annum, is given if a building is in industrial use on the last day of the period of account concerned. If the building is in non industrial use a notional allowance may be given.

Quick quiz

1   For what periods are capital allowances for unincorporated businesses calculated?

2   Are writing down allowances pro-rated in a six month period of account?

3   Are first year allowances pro-rated in a six month period of account?

4   When may balancing allowances arise?

5   Within what period must an asset be disposed of if it is to be treated as a short life asset?

6   List four types of building which do not usually qualify for industrial buildings allowance.

7   When are drawing offices industrial buildings?

8   What are the conditions for a hotel to qualify for allowances?

9   When must a 'notional allowance' be deducted from the qualifying cost of an industrial building?

10   What is the amount of the balancing charge on a sale where there been non-industrial use?

Answers to quick quiz

1   Periods of account

2   Yes. In a six month period, writing down allowance are pro-rated by multiplying by 6/12.

3   No. First year allowances are given in full in a short period of account.

4   Balancing allowances may arise in respect of pooled expenditure only when the trade ceases. Balancing allowances may arise on non-pooled items whenever those items are disposed of.

5   Within four years of the end of the period of account (or accounting period) in which it was bought

6   Dwelling houses, retail shops, showrooms and offices

7   Drawing offices which serve an industrial building are industrial buildings

8   (a)   It must have ten letting bedrooms

     (b)   It must have letting bedrooms as the whole or main part of the sleeping accommodation

     (c)   It must offer ancillary services including at least

          (i)   Breakfast
          (ii)   Evening meals
          (iii)   The cleaning of rooms
          (iv)   The making of beds

     (d)   It must be open for at least four months during the April to October letting season.

9   A notional allowance will be given if a building was in non-industrial use at the end of the period of account (accounting period) concerned

10   The balancing charge is equal to the industrial buildings allowances actually given

Now try the questions below from the Exam Question Bank			
Number	Level	Marks	Time
Q3	Examination	15	27 mins
Q4	Examination	15	27 mins

4

Loan relationships/ property business income

Topic list	Syllabus reference
1 Loan relationships (borrowing and lending)	1(c)(v)
2 Property business income	1(c)(v)

Introduction

When a company borrows or lends money it has a loan relationship. In this chapter we see how loan relationships affect a company's CT liability. We also see how to compute the property business income that we must include in calculating a company's PCTCT and how relief is given for property business losses.

1 Loan relationships (borrowing and lending)

Interest arising on a non-trading loan relationship is taxable, normally on an accruals basis, as investment income. Bank and building society accounts held for investment purposes are an example of a non-trading loan relationship.

1.1 Introduction

If a company borrows or lends money, including issuing or investing in debentures or buying gilts, it **has a loan relationship. This can be a creditor relationship** (where the company lends or invests money) **or a debtor relationship** (where the company borrows money or issues securities).

1.2 Treatment of trading loan relationships

If the company is a party to a **loan relationship for trade purposes, any debits – ie interest paid or other debt costs – charged through its accounts are allowed as a trading expense** and are therefore deductible in computing taxable trading profits.

Similarly **if any credits – ie interest income or other debt returns – arise on a trading loan these are treated as a trading receipt and are taxable as trading profits.** This is not likely to arise unless the trade is one of money lending eg a bank.

1.3 Treatment of non-trading loan relationships

If a loan relationship is not one to which the company is a party for trade purposes any debits or credits must be pooled. A net credit on the pool is chargeable as investment income. This means that any interest received by a company on its non-trading loan relationships is taxable as investment income. A net deficit on the pool may be relieved in certain ways, but this is not in your syllabus.

Bank and building society accounts held for investment purposes are an example of investment income.

1.4 Accounting methods

Debits and credits must be brought into account using UK generally accepted accounting practice (UK GAAP) or, from 1 January 2005, using International Accounting Standards (IAS). Under UK GAAP this will generally be either:

    (a)   The amortised cost basis of accounting, or

    (b)   The fair value basis.

Under the amortised cost basis the cost of the asset or liability must be included in the accounts at cost less cumulative amortisation. The debit or credit brought into account will be the amortisation for the period, together with any interest for the period. This method is effectively the accruals basis, and will be used in this text.

1.5 Incidental costs of loan finance

Under the loan relationship rules expenses ('debits') are allowed if incurred directly:

    (a)   in bringing a loan relationship into existence

    (b)   entering into or giving effect to any related transactions

    (c)   making payment under a loan relationship or related transactions

(d)   taking steps to ensure the receipt of payments under the loan relationship or related transaction

A related transaction means 'any disposal or acquisition (in whole or in part) of rights or liabilities under the relationship, including any arising from a security issue in relation to the money debt in question'.

The above categories of incidental costs are also allowable even if the company does not enter into the loan relationship (ie abortive costs). Cost directly incurred in varying the terms of a loan relationship are also allowed.

1.6 Other matters

It is not only the interest costs of borrowing that are allowable or taxable. The capital costs are treated similarly. Thus if a company issues a loan at a discount and repays it eventually at par, the capital cost is allowed either on redemption (if the accruals basis is adopted) or period by period (if it is accounted for on a mark to market basis).

Relief for pre-trading expenditure extends to expenses incurred on trading loan relationships in accounting periods ending within seven years of the company starting to trade. An expense that would have been a trading debit if it was incurred after the trade had commenced, is treated as a trading debit of the first trading period. An election has to be made within two years of the end of the first trading period.

Payments of interest between UK companies are paid gross. Short interest or interest to a UK bank is payable gross while yearly interest is payable net of 20% tax if not paid to a corporate recipient.

Interest charged on underpaid tax is allowable and interest received on overpaid tax is assessable under the loan relationship rules as investment income.

2 Property business income

FAST FORWARD

Income from land is taxed as property business income. Property business profits are computed on an accruals basis in the same way as trading profits. A 10% wear and tear allowance may be available when property is let furnished.

2.1 Income taxable as property business income

Income from land and buildings in the UK, including caravans and houseboats which are not moved, is taxed as property business income.

A company with rental income is treated as running a property business. All the rents and expenses for all properties are pooled, to give a single profit or loss. Profits and losses are computed in the same way as trading profits, on an accruals basis (see Chapter 2). The trading profit rules on post-cessation receipts and expenses apply.

Interest paid on a loan taken out to buy a property is dealt with under the loan relationship rules (see above). It is not deducted in computing property business income.

Capital allowances are given on plant and machinery used in the property business and on industrial buildings, in the same way as they are given for a normal trade. Capital allowances are not normally available on plant or machinery used in a dwelling (although in certain cases, they may exceptionally be available on radiators and boilers). A company that lets property furnished cannot claim capital allowances on the furniture. However, it can choose instead between the renewals basis and the 10% wear and tear allowance.

- Under the *renewals* basis, there is no deduction for the cost of the first furniture provided, but the cost of replacement furniture is treated as a revenue expense. However, the part of the cost attributable to improvement, as opposed to simple replacement, is not deductible.

- Under the *10% wear and tear* basis, the actual cost of furniture is ignored. Instead, an annual deduction is given of 10% of rents. The rents are first reduced by amounts which are paid by the landlord but are normally a tenant's burden. These amounts include any water rates and council tax paid by the landlord.

If plant and machinery is used partly in a dwelling house and partly for other purposes a just and reasonable apportionment of the expenditure can be made.

Rent for furniture supplied with premises is taxed as part of the rent for the premises, unless there is a separate trade of renting furniture.

2.2 Loss relief

FAST FORWARD

Property business losses may be relieved against other profits of the current period, carried forward or surrendered as group relief.

Property business losses are first set off against non-property business income and gains of the company for the current period and any excess is:

(a)   carried forward as a property business loss of the following accounting period provided that the property business has not ceased; or

(b)   available for surrender as group relief (see later in this text).

2.3 Premiums on leases

FAST FORWARD

The premium payable on the grant of a lease is partly treated as a receipt of income taxable as property income.

When a premium or similar consideration is received on the grant (that is, by a landlord to a tenant) **of a short lease (50 years or less), part of the premium is treated as rent received in the year of grant**. A lease is considered to end on the date when it is most likely to terminate.

The premium taxed as property business income is the whole premium, less 2% of the premium for each complete year of the lease, except the first year.

This rule does not apply on the *assignment* of a lease (one tenant selling his entire interest in the property to another).

2.3.1 Premiums paid

Where a trading company pays a premium for a lease it may deduct an amount from his taxable profits in each year of the lease. The amount deductible is the figure treated as rent received by the landlord divided by the number of years of the lease. For example, suppose that B Ltd, pays A Ltd a premium of £30,000 for a ten year lease. A Ltd is treated as receiving £30,000 − (£30,000 × (10 − 1) × 2%) = £24,600. B Ltd can therefore deduct £24,600/10 = £2,460 in each of the ten years. The company starts with the accounting period in which the lease starts and apportions the relief to the nearest month.

2.3.2 Premiums for granting subleases

A tenant may decide to sublet property and to charge a premium on the grant of a lease to the subtenant. This premium is treated as rent received in the normal way (because this is a grant and not an assignment, the original tenant retaining an interest in the property). **Where the tenant originally paid a premium for his own head lease, this deemed rent is reduced by:**

$$\text{Rent part of premium for head lease} \times \frac{\text{duration of sublease}}{\text{duration of head lease}}$$

If the relief exceeds the part of the premium for the sub-lease treated as rent (including cases where there is a sub-lease with no premium), the balance of the relief is treated as rent payable by the head tenant, spread evenly over the period of the sub-lease. This rent payable is an expense, reducing the overall property business profit.

Question	Taxable premium received

C Ltd granted a lease to D Ltd on 1 March 1995 for a period of 40 years. D Ltd paid a premium of £16,000. On 1 June 2005 D Ltd granted a sublease to E Ltd for a period of ten years. E Ltd paid a premium of £30,000. Calculate the amount treated as rent out of the premium received by D Ltd.

Answer

	£
Premium received by D Ltd	30,000
Less £30,000 × 2% × (10-1)	(5,400)
	24,600
Less allowance for premium paid	
(£16,000 - (£16,000 × 39 × 2%)) × 10/40	(880)
Premium treated as rent	23,720

Chapter roundup

- Interest arising on a non-trading loan relationship is taxable, normally on an accruals basis, as investment income. Bank and building society accounts held for investment purposes are an example of a non-trading loan relationship.

- Income from land is taxed as property business income. Property business profits are computed on an accruals basis in the same way as trading profits. A 10% wear and tear allowance may be available when property is let furnished.

- Property business losses may be relieved against other profits of the current period, carried forward or surrendered as group relief.

- The premium payable on the grant of a lease is partly treated as a receipt of income taxable as property income.

Quick quiz

1 How is interest paid on a non-trading loan relationship treated for tax purposes?

2 What interest income is received gross by companies?

3 How are property business profits computed?

4 What relief is given when a lessee who paid a premium grants a sublease for a premium?

Answers to quick quiz

1 Non trading credits and debits are pooled. Net credit taxed as investment income. Net deficit may be relieved.

2 Gross interest receipts by company from:

- Banks/building societies
- UK companies
- Gilts (in most cases)

3 All profits/losses pooled to calculate income from property business.

4 Deemed rent reduced by:

$$\text{Rent part of premium for head lease} \times \frac{\text{duration of sub - lease}}{\text{duration of head lease}}$$

Now try the question below from the Exam Question Bank

Number	Level	Marks	Time
Q5	Introductory	11	20 mins

Chargeable gains

Topic list	Syllabus reference
1 Taxing a company's chargeable gains	1(d)(i)
2 Chargeable persons, disposals and assets	1(d)(i)
3 Computing a gain or loss	1(d)(ii)
4 The indexation allowance	1(d)(ii)
5 Share matching rules for companies	1(d)(ii)
6 The FA 1985 pool	1(d)(ii)
7 Alterations of share capital	1(d)(ii)
8 Rollover relief	1(d)(iii)

Introduction

Companies can have both income and capital gains. If, for example, a company buys a factory for £10,000, uses the factory for 20 years and then sells it for £200,000, it will have a capital gain. In this chapter we see when a chargeable gain will arise and how to compute a chargeable gain.

We then look at shares and securities. Shares and securities need a special treatment because a company may hold several shares or securities in the same company, bought at different times for different prices but otherwise identical.

Finally, we consider how a company may defer a gain when it sells a business asset.

1 Taxing a company's chargeable gains

A company pays corporation tax on its taxable gains.

1.1 History of taxing gains

Since its introduction by the Finance Act 1965, the taxation of chargeable gains has undergone significant amendment. As some knowledge of the history of taxing gains may help you understand the present rules, we summarise the main changes below:

1965	The taxation of chargeable gains was introduced.
1982	An indexation allowance was introduced to give some relief in respect of gains due to inflation.
1985	There were major amendments to the calculation of the indexation allowance.
1988	The base date for taxing gains was generally moved from 1965 to 1982, the tax charge being confined to gains accruing from 31 March 1982. You will not have to deal with gains or losses on assets acquired before 31 March 1982.
1992	Legislation concerning the taxation of gains was consolidated into the Taxation of Chargeable Gains Act 1992 (TCGA 1992).
1993	The use of the indexation allowance to create or increase a loss ended.

1.2 Losses

A company's net chargeable gains (gains less losses) for an accounting period are included within the computation of profits chargeable to corporation tax. A company, therefore, pays CT on its net chargeable gains. Any overall allowable loss in an accounting period is carried forward to set against the first chargeable gains arising in future accounting periods. Capital losses cannot be set against income.

1.3 Timing of disposals

From a tax planning point of view it is important to realise that a badly timed disposal (near the end of the accounting period) can raise the 'profits' of a company into a higher rate band of CT. In addition, from a cash flow point of view, by delaying a disposal into the next accounting period the payment date for CT on the gain is delayed for twelve months.

2 Chargeable persons, disposals and assets

Key term

For a chargeable gain to arise there must be:

- A **chargeable person**; and
- A **chargeable disposal**; and
- A **chargeable asset**

otherwise no charge to tax occurs.

For a charge to tax to arise on a gain, there must be a chargeable person who has made a chargeable disposal of a chargeable asset.

2.1 Chargeable persons

A company is a chargeable person.

2.2 Chargeable disposals

The following are chargeable disposals.

- Sales of assets or parts of assets
- Gifts of assets or parts of assets
- Receipts of capital sums following the surrender of rights to assets
- Receipts of capital sums following the loss or destruction of assets
- The appropriation of assets as trading stock

A chargeable disposal occurs on the date of the contract (where there is one, whether written or oral), or the date of a conditional contract becoming unconditional. This may differ from the date of transfer of the asset. However, when a capital sum is received on a surrender of rights or the loss or destruction of an asset, the disposal takes place on the day the sum is received.

Where a disposal involves an acquisition by someone else, the date of acquisition is the same as the date of disposal.

2.3 Transfers to and from trading stock

When a company acquires an asset other than as trading stock and then uses it as trading stock, the appropriation to trading stock normally leads to an immediate chargeable gain or allowable loss, based on the asset's market value at the date of appropriation. The asset's cost for trading profits purposes is that market value.

Alternatively, the company can elect to have no chargeable gain or allowable loss: if it does so, the cost for trading profit purposes is reduced by the gain or increased by the loss. The time limit for the election is two years after the end of the accounting period of appropriation.

When an asset which is trading stock is appropriated to other purposes, the company is treated for trading profit purposes as selling it for its market value, and for those other purposes as having bought it at the time of the appropriation for the same value.

2.4 Chargeable assets

All forms of property, wherever in the world they are situated, are chargeable assets unless they are specifically designated as exempt.

The following are exempt assets (thus gains are not taxable and losses on their disposal are not in general allowable losses).

- Motor vehicles suitable for private use
- Certain chattels (eg racehorses)
- Debts (except debts on a security)

3 Computing a gain or loss

FAST FORWARD

A chargeable gain is computed by taking the proceeds and deducting both the cost and the indexation allowance. Incidental costs of acquisition and disposal may be deducted together with any enhancement expenditure reflected in the state and nature of the asset at the date of disposal.

3.1 Basic calculation

A chargeable gain (or an allowable loss) is generally calculated as follows.

	£
Disposal consideration (or market value)	45,000
Less incidental costs of disposal	(400)
Net proceeds	44,600
Less allowable costs	(21,000)
Unindexed gain	23,600
Less indexation allowance	(8,500)
Indexed gain	15,100

Incidental costs of disposal may include:

- valuation fees (but not the cost of an appeal against the Revenue's valuation)
- estate agency fees
- advertising costs
- legal costs

These costs should be deducted separately from any other allowable costs (because they do not qualify for any indexation allowance if it was available on that disposal).

Allowable costs include:

- the original cost of acquisition
- incidental costs of acquisition
- capital expenditure incurred in enhancing the asset

Incidental costs of acquisition may include the types of cost listed above as incidental costs of disposal, but acquisition costs do qualify for indexation allowance (from the month of acquisition) if it is available on the disposal.

Enhancement expenditure is capital expenditure which enhances the value of the asset and is reflected in the state or nature of the asset at the time of disposal, or expenditure incurred in establishing, preserving or defending title to, or a right over, the asset. Excluded from this category are:

- costs of repairs and maintenance
- costs of insurance
- any expenditure deductible from trading profits
- any expenditure met by public funds (for example council grants)

Enhancement expenditure may qualify for indexation allowance from the month in which it becomes due and payable.

3.2 The consideration for a disposal

Usually the disposal consideration is the proceeds of sale of the asset, but a disposal is deemed to take place at market value:

- where the disposal is **not a bargain at arm's length**
- where the disposal is made for a **consideration which cannot be valued**
- where the disposal is by way of a **gift**.

3.3 Valuing assets

Quoted shares and securities are valued using prices in The Stock Exchange Daily Official List, taking the lower of:

- lower quoted price + ¼ × (higher quoted price - lower quoted price) ('quarter-up' rule)
- the average of the highest and lowest marked bargains (ignoring bargains marked at special prices)

Question

Shares in A plc are quoted at 100-110p. The highest and lowest marked bargains were 99p and 110p. What would be the market value for CGT purposes?

Answer

The value will be the lower of:

(a) $100 + ¼ × (110 − 100) = 102.5$;

(b) $\dfrac{110 + 99}{2} = 104.5$.

The market value for CGT purposes will therefore be 102.5p per share.

Unquoted shares are harder to value than quoted shares. The Revenue have a special office, the Shares Valuation Division, to deal with the valuation of unquoted shares.

Where market value is used in a chargeable gains computation, the value to be used is the price which the assets in question might reasonably be expected to fetch on a sale in the open market.

4 The indexation allowance

FAST FORWARD
The indexation allowance gives relief for the inflationary element of a gain.

4.1 Purpose of indexation allowance

The purpose of having an indexation allowance is to remove the inflationary element of a gain from taxation.

Companies are entitled to an indexation allowance from the date of acquisition until the date of disposal of an asset.

4.2 Example: indexation allowance

J Ltd bought a painting on 2 January 1987 and sold it on 19 November 2005.

Indexation allowance is available from January 1987 until November 2005.

Exam formula

The indexation factor is:

$$\frac{\text{RPI for month of disposal} - \text{RPI for month of acquisition}}{\text{RPI for month of acquisition}}$$

The calculation is expressed as a decimal and is rounded to three decimal places.

The indexation factor is multiplied by the cost of the asset to calculate the indexation allowance. If the RPI has fallen, the indexation allowance is zero: it is not negative.

Question The indexation allowance

An asset is acquired by a company on 15 February 1983 (RPI = 83.0) at a cost of £5,000. Enhancement expenditure of £2,000 is incurred on 10 April 1984 (RPI = 88.6). The asset is sold for £25,500 on 20 December 2005 (RPI = 191.6). Incidental costs of sale are £500. Calculate the chargeable gain arising.

Answer

The indexation allowance is available until December 2005 and is computed as follows.

	£
$\dfrac{191.6 - 83.0}{83.0} = 1.308 \times £5,000$	6,540
$\dfrac{191.6 - 88.6}{88.6} = 1.163 \times £2,000$	2,326
	8,866

The computation of the chargeable gain is as follows.

	£
Proceeds	25,500
Less incidental costs of sale	(500)
Net proceeds	25,000
Less allowable costs £(5,000 + 2,000)	(7,000)
Unindexed gain	18,000
Less indexation allowance (see above)	(8,866)
Chargeable gain	9,134

4.3 Indexation and losses

The indexation allowance cannot create or increase an allowable loss. If there is a gain before the indexation allowance, the allowance can reduce that gain to zero, but no further. If there is a loss before the indexation allowance, there is no indexation allowance.

5 Share matching rules for companies

FAST FORWARD

Matching rules are required to determine which shares are disposed of where the company has made multiple acquisitions of shares in another company.

Quoted and unquoted shares and securities, and units in a unit trust present special problems when attempting to compute gains or losses on disposal. For instance, suppose that a company buys some quoted shares in X plc as follows.

Date	Number of shares	Cost
		£
5 May 1983	100	150
17 January 1985	100	375
10 June 2005	50	300

On 15 June 2005, it sells 120 of its shares for £1,450. To determine its chargeable gain, we need to be able to work out which shares were actually sold.

We therefore need **matching rules**. These **allow us to decide which shares have been sold and so work out what the allowable cost on disposal should be.**

At any one time, we will only be concerned with shares or securities of the same class in the same company. If a company owns both ordinary shares and preference shares in X plc, we will deal with the two classes of share entirely separately, because they are distinguishable.

In what follows, we will use 'shares' to refer to both shares and securities.

For companies the matching of shares sold is in the following order.

(a) Shares acquired on the **same day**
(b) Shares acquired in the **previous nine days**, taking earlier acquisitions first
(c) Shares from the **FA 1985 pool**

If a company owns 2% or more of another company, disposals are matched (after same day acquisitions) with shares acquired within one month before or after the disposal (for Stock Exchange transactions) or six months (in other cases) before being matched with shares from the FA 1985 pool.

Where shares are disposed of within nine days of acquisition, **no indexation allowance is available** even if the acquisition and the disposal fall in different months. Acquisitions matched with disposals under the nine day rule never enter the FA 1985 pool.

The composition of the FA 1985 pool is explained below.

6 The FA 1985 pool

 When dealing with shares held by companies, we usually need to set up a FA 1985 pool.

6.1 What is in the FA 1985 pool?

For companies we treat shares as a 'pool' which grows as new shares are acquired and shrinks as they are sold. **The FA 1985 pool** (so called because it was introduced by rules in the Finance Act 1985) **comprises the following shares of the same class in the same company.**

- **Shares held by a company on 1 April 1985 and acquired by that company on or after 1 April 1982.**

- **Shares acquired by that company on or after 1 April 1985.**

In making computations which use the FA 1985 pool, we must keep track of:

(a) the **number** of shares
(b) the **cost** of the shares ignoring indexation
(b) the **indexed cost** of the shares

Each FA 1985 **pool is started by aggregating the cost and number of shares acquired between 1 April 1982 and 1 April 1985** inclusive. In order to calculate the indexed cost of these shares, an indexation allowance, computed from the relevant date of acquisition of the shares to April 1985, is added to the cost.

6.2 Example: the FA 1985 pool

Oliver Ltd bought 1,000 shares in Judith plc for £2,750 in August 1984 and another 1,000 for £3,250 in December 1984. RPIs are August 1984 = 89.9, December 1984 = 90.9 and April 1985 = 94.8. The FA 1985 pool at 1 April 1985 is as follows.

Solution

	No of shares	Cost £	Indexed cost £
August 1984 (a)	1,000	2,750	2,750
December 1984 (b)	1,000	3,250	3,250
	2,000	6,000	6,000
Indexation allowance			
$\dfrac{94.8 - 89.9}{89.9} = 0.055 \times £2,750$			151
$\dfrac{94.8 - 90.9}{90.9} = 0.043 \times £3,250$			140
Indexed cost of the pool at 1 April 1985			6,291

Disposals and acquisitions of shares which affect the indexed value of the FA 1985 pool are termed **'operative events'. Prior to reflecting each such operative event within the FA 1985 share pool, a further indexation allowance (described as an indexed rise) must be computed up to the date of the operative event concerned from the date of the last such operative event** (or from the later of the first acquisition and April 1985 if the operative event in question is the first one).

Indexation calculations within the FA 1985 pool (after its April 1985 value has been calculated) **are not rounded to three decimal places**. This is because rounding errors would accumulate and have a serious effect after several operative events.

If there are several operative events between 1 April 1985 and the date of a disposal, the indexation procedure described above will have to be performed several times over.

Question	Value of FA 1985 pool

Following on from the above example, assume that Oliver Ltd acquired 2,000 more shares on 10 July 1986 at a cost of £4,000. Recalculate the value of the FA 1985 pool on 10 July 1986 following the acquisition. Assume the RPI in July 1986 = 97.5.

Answer

	No of shares	Cost £	Indexed cost £
Value at 1.4.85	2,000	6,000	6,291
Indexed rise			
$\dfrac{97.5 - 94.8}{94.8} \times £6,291$			179
	2,000	6,000	6,470
Acquisition	2,000	4,000	4,000
Value at 10.7.86	4,000	10,000	10,470

In the case of a disposal, following the calculation of the indexed rise to the date of disposal, the cost and the indexed cost attributable to the shares disposed of are deducted from the amounts within the

FA 1985 pool. The proportions of the cost and indexed cost to take out of the pool should be computed by using the proportion of cost that the shares disposed of bear to the total number of share held.

The indexation allowance is the indexed cost taken out of the pool minus the cost taken out. As usual, the indexation allowance cannot create or increase a loss.

Question
The FA 1985 pool

Continuing the above exercise, suppose that Oliver Ltd sold 3,000 shares on 10 July 2005 for £17,000. Compute the gain, and the value of the FA 1985 pool following the disposal. Assume RPI July 2005 = 190.6.

Answer

	No of shares	Cost £	Indexed cost £
Value at 10.7.86	4,000	10,000	10,470
Indexed rise			
$\dfrac{190.6 - 97.5}{97.5} \times £10,470$			9,998
	4,000	10,000	20,468
Disposal	(3,000)		
Cost and indexed cost $\dfrac{3,000}{4,000} \times £10,000$ and £20,468		(7,500)	(15,351)
Value at 10.7.05	1,000	2,500	5,117

The gain is computed as follows:

	£
Proceeds	17,000
Less cost	(7,500)
	9,500
Less indexation allowance £(15,351 − 7,500)	(7,851)
Chargeable gain	1,649

When shares are transferred on a no gain no/loss basis between group companies, thereby creating or adding to an FA 1985 pool belonging to the acquiring company, the usual rules on no gain/no loss disposals and later disposals set out in Chapter 7 do not apply. The disposing company still has no gain and no loss, but the acquiring company takes the shares into their FA 1985 pool at original cost to the disposing company plus (in the indexed cost column) indexation up to the date of transfer.

Exam focus point

The examiner has said that a question will not be set which requires a detailed calculation of the 1985 pool.

7 Alterations of share capital

FAST FORWARD

On an alteration of share capital the pooled base cost of the original shares needs to be apportioned, if more than one type of share is acquired.

7.1 Bonus issues (scrip issues)

When a company issues bonus shares all that happens is that the size of the original holding is increased. Since bonus shares are issued at no cost there is no need to adjust the original cost. Instead the numbers purchased at particular times are increased by the bonus.

7.2 Rights issues

The difference between a bonus issue and a rights issue is that in a rights issue the new shares are paid for and this results in an adjustment to the original cost. For the purposes of calculating the indexation allowance, expenditure on a rights issue is taken as being incurred on the date of the issue and not on the date of acquisition of the original holding.

As with bonus issues, rights shares derived from the 1985 pool shares go into that pool rather than being treated as a new acquisition. This would be important if shares are sold within nine days of the rights issue as the usual '9 day' rule would not apply to the rights issue shares.

In an **open offer** shareholders have a right to subscribe for a minimum number of shares based on their existing holdings and may buy additional shares. Subscriptions up to the minimum entitlement are treated as a rights issue. Additional subscriptions are treated as new purchases of shares.

Question	Rights issues

J Ltd had the following transactions in the shares of T plc.

July 1985   Purchased 1,000 shares for £3,000
May 1986   Took up one for four rights issue at £4.20 per share
October 2005   Sold 1,250 shares for £10,000

Compute the chargeable gain or allowable loss arising on the sale in October 2005. RPI July 1985 = 95.2, May 1986 = 97.8, October 2005 = 191.2.

Answer

The FA 1985 pool	No of shares	Cost £	Indexed cost £
July 1985	1,000	3,000	3,000
Indexed rise to May 1986			
$\frac{97.8 - 95.2}{95.2} \times £3,000$			82
May 1986 one for four rights	250	1,050	1,050
	1,250	4,050	4,132
Indexed rise to October 2005			
$\frac{191.2 - 97.8}{97.8} \times £4,132$			3,946
	1,250	4,050	8,078
Disposal in October 2005	(1,250)	(4,050)	(8,078)

The chargeable gain	£
Proceeds	10,000
Less cost	(4,050)
	5,950
Less indexation allowance £(8,078 – 4,050)	(4,028)
Chargeable gain	1,922

7.3 Reorganisations

A reorganisation takes place where new shares or a mixture of new shares and debentures (ie loan notes) are issued in exchange for the original shareholdings. The new shares take the place of the old shares. The problem is how to apportion the original cost between the different types of capital issued on the reorganisation.

If the new shares and securities are quoted, then the cost is apportioned by reference to the market values of the new types of capital on the first day of quotation after the reorganisation. No amendment to the indexation process occurs unless further consideration is contributed, when indexation will be computed as for rights issues; indexation on new consideration will run from the time when it is contributed.

Question   Reorganisations

An original quoted shareholding is made up of 3,000 ordinary shares purchased in 1985 for £13,250.

In 2005 there is a reorganisation whereby each ordinary share is exchanged for two 'A' ordinary shares (quoted at £2 each) and one preference share (quoted at £1 each). Show how the original costs will be apportioned.

Answer

The new holding will be as follows.

	Value £
6,000 new 'A' ordinary shares at £2	12,000
3,000 preference shares at £1	3,000
	15,000

The costs will be apportioned between the new 'A' ordinary shares and the preference shares in the ratio of 12,000:3,000 = 4:1 as follows.

FA 1985 pools

	£
6,000 new 'A' ordinary shares, deemed acquired in 1985 ($^4/_5$ x £13,250)	10,600
3,000 preference shares, deemed acquired in 1985 ($^1/_5$ x £13,250)	2,650
	13,250

Where a reorganisation takes place and the new shares and securities are unquoted, the cost of the original holding is apportioned using the values of the new shares and securities when they come to be disposed of. Further consideration is treated in the same way as for quoted shares.

For both quoted and unquoted shares and securities, any incidental costs (such as professional fees) are treated as additional consideration for the new shares and securities.

7.4 Takeovers

A chargeable gain does not arise on a 'paper for paper' takeover, that is, one where shares or securities in the old company are exchanged for shares or securities in the new company which has taken over the old company. **The cost of the original holding is passed on to the new holding** which takes the place of the original holding. The same rules apply as for reorganisations (above) in relation to the apportionment of the original base costs.

The takeover rules apply where the company issuing the new shares ends up with more than 25% of the ordinary share capital of the old company or the majority of the voting power in the old company, or the company issuing the new shares makes a general offer to shareholders in the other company which is initially made subject to a condition which, if satisfied, would give the first company control of the second company.

Question   Takeovers

Le Bon Ltd held 20,000 £1 shares out of a total number of issued shares of one million bought for £2 each in Duran plc. In 2005 the board of Duran plc agreed to a takeover bid by Spandau plc under which shareholders in Duran received three ordinary Spandau shares plus one preference share for every four shares held in Duran plc. Immediately following the takeover, the ordinary shares in Spandau plc were quoted at £5 each and the preferences shares at 90p. Show the unindexed base costs of the ordinary shares and the preference shares.

Answer

The total value due to Le Bon Ltd on the takeover is as follows.

		£
Ordinary	20,000 × 3/4 × £5	75,000
Preference	20,000 × 1/4 × 90p	4,500
		79,500

The base costs are therefore:

	£
Ordinary shares: 75,000/79,500 × 20,000 × £2	37,736
Preference shares: 4,500/79,500 × 20,000 × £2	2,264
	40,000

8 Rollover relief

FAST FORWARD

When 'qualifying' assets are sold and the proceeds are reinvested in other such assets, it is possible to 'rollover' the gains on the assets sold. The reinvestment in qualifying assets must take place in the period starting one year before and ending three years after disposal. If any proceeds are not reinvested a gain equal to the amount of the proceeds not reinvested is chargeable immediately.

8.1 Conditions for relief

A gain may be 'rolled over' (deferred) where it arises on the disposal of a business asset which is replaced. This is **rollover relief**. A claim cannot specify that only part of a gain is to be rolled over.

All the following conditions must be met.

- **The old asset sold and the new asset bought are both used only in the trade** or trades carried on **by the company claiming rollover relief**. Where part of a building is in non-trade use for all or a substantial part of the period of ownership, the building (and the land on which it stands) can be treated as two separate assets, the trade part (qualifying) and the non-trade part (non-qualifying). This split cannot be made for other assets.

- **The old asset and the new asset both fall within one** (but not necessarily the same one) **of the following classes**.

    (i)   Land and buildings (including parts of buildings) occupied as well as used only for the purpose of the trade

    (ii)   Fixed (that is, immovable) plant and machinery

(iii) Ships, aircraft and hovercraft

(iv) Satellites, space stations and spacecraft

- **Reinvestment of the proceeds of the old asset takes place in a period beginning one year before and ending three years after the date of the disposal.**

- **The new asset is brought into use in the trade on its acquisition** (not necessarily immediately, but not after any significant and unnecessary delay).

The new asset can be for use in a different trade from the old asset.

A rollover claim is not allowed when a company buys premises, sells part of the premises at a profit and then claims to roll over the gain into the part retained *(Watton v Tippet 1997)*. However, a rollover claim is allowed (by concession) when the proceeds of the old asset are spent on improving a qualifying asset which the company already owns. The improved asset must already be in use for a trade, or be brought into trade use immediately the improvement work is finished.

8.2 Method of obtaining relief

 FAST FORWARD

A rolled over gain is deducted from the base cost of the asset acquired.

Deferral is obtained by deducting the chargeable gain from the cost of the new asset. For full relief, the whole of the consideration for the disposal must be reinvested. Where only part is reinvested, a part of the gain equal to the lower of the full gain and the amount not reinvested will be liable to tax immediately.

The new asset will have a base 'cost' for chargeable gains purposes, of its purchase price less the gain rolled over into its acquisition.

If a company expects to buy new assets, it can make a provisional rollover claim on its tax return which includes the gain on the old asset. The gain is reduced accordingly. If new assets are not actually acquired, the Revenue collect the tax saved by the provisional claim.

Question   Rollover relief

A freehold factory was purchased by X Ltd in August 1998. It was sold in December 2005 for £70,000, giving rise to an indexed gain of £17,950. A replacement factory was purchased in June 2006 for £60,000. Compute the base cost of the replacement factory, taking into account any possible rollover gain from the disposal in December 2005.

Answer

	£
Total gain	17,950
Less: amount not reinvested, immediately chargeable £(70,000 – 60,000)	(10,000)
Rollover gain	7,950
Cost of new factory	60,000
Less rolled over gain	(7,950)
Base cost of new factory	52,050

Where an old asset has not been used in the trade for a fraction of its period of ownership, the amount of the gain that can be rolled over is reduced by the same fraction. If the proceeds are not fully reinvested the restriction on rollover by the amount not reinvested is also calculated by considering only the proportion of proceeds relating to the part of the asset used in the trade or the proportion relating to the period of trade use.

Y Ltd bought a factory in July 1992 for £100,000. It sold the factory in November 2005 for £215,000. The company let out a quarter of the factory on commercial terms for the entire period of ownership.
Y Ltd bought a replacement factory in August 2005 for £165,000, which was used wholly for its trade.

Calculate the chargeable gain on the first factory and the base cost of the second factory. Assume RPIs: July 1992 = 138.8, November 2005 = 191.4.

Answer

Gain on 1st factory

	Business (75%) £	Non business (25%) £
Proceeds	161,250	53,750
Less: cost	(75,000)	(25,000)
	86,250	28,750
Less: indexation allowance $\frac{191.4 - 138.8}{138.8}$ (= 0.379) × £75,000/25,000	(28,425)	(9,475)
Indexed gain	57,825	19,275

The gain of £19,275 is chargeable.

Base cost of 2nd factory

All of business proceeds (£161,250) are reinvested so full relief is available.

	£
Cost	165,000
Less: rolled over gain	(57,825)
Base cost	107,175

8.3 Depreciating assets

FAST FORWARD

When the replacement asset is a depreciating asset, the gain on the old asset is 'frozen' rather than rolled over.

Where the replacement asset is a depreciating asset, the gain is not rolled over by reducing the cost of the replacement asset. Rather it is 'frozen' until it crystallises on the earliest of:

- the disposal of the replacement asset
- ten years after the acquisition of the replacement asset
- the date the replacement asset ceases to be used in the trade

Key term

An asset is a **depreciating asset** if it is, or within the next ten years will become, a wasting asset (one with a useful life of 50 years or less). Thus, any asset with an expected life of 60 years or less is covered by this definition. Plant and machinery (including ships, aircraft, hovercraft, satellites, space stations and spacecraft) is always treated as depreciating unless it becomes part of a building: in that case, it will only be depreciating if the building is held on a lease with 60 years or less to run.

Question — Frozen gain on investment into depreciating asset

N Ltd bought a factory for use in its business in June 2001 for £125,000. The factory was sold for £140,000 on 1 August 2005. On 10 July 2005, N Ltd bought some fixed plant and machinery for use in its business, costing £150,000. The company sold the plant and machinery for £167,000 on 19 November 2006. Show N Ltd's chargeable gains position. Assume RPIs:

June 2001 = 174.4
July 2005 = 190.6
August 2005 = 190.8
November 2006 = 193.8

Answer

Gain deferred

	£
Proceeds of factory	140,000
Less cost	(125,000)
Gain	15,000
Less indexation $\frac{190.8-174.4}{174.4} = 0.094 \times £125,000$	(11,750)
	3,250

This gain is deferred in relation to the purchase of the plant and machinery. Sale of plant and machinery

	£
Proceeds	167,000
Less cost	(150,000)
Gain	17,000
Less indexation $\frac{193.8-190.6}{190.6} = 0.017 \times £150,000$	(2,550)
	14,450

Total gain chargeable on sale (gain on plant and machinery plus deferred gain)
£(3,250 + 14,450) — £17,700

Where a gain on disposal is deferred against a replacement depreciating asset it is possible to transfer the deferred gain to a non-depreciating asset provided the non-depreciating asset is bought before the deferred gain has crystallised.

Question — Transfer of deferred gain into non-depreciating asset

In July 1995, Julius Ltd sold a warehouse used in its trade, realising a gain of £30,000. The company invested the whole of the proceeds of sale of £95,000 into fixed plant and machinery in January 1996 and made a claim to defer the gain on the warehouse.

In August 2005, Julius Ltd bought a freehold shop for use in its business costing £100,000. Julius Ltd has not bought any other assets for use in the business and wishes to minimise chargeable gains arising in its accounting period to 31.3.06. What advice would you give Julius Ltd?

Answer

Julius Ltd should claim to transfer the deferred gain of £30,000 to the purchase of the shop. If it does not do so, the deferred gain will be chargeable in January 2006, at the latest (10 years after the acquisition of the plant and machinery).

The effect of the claim will be to reduce the base cost of the shop to £(100,000 - 30,000) = £70,000.

73

Chapter roundup

- A company pays corporation tax on its taxable gains.

- For a charge to tax to arise on a gain, there must be a chargeable person who has made a chargeable disposal of a chargeable asset.

- A chargeable gain is computed by taking the proceeds and deducting both the cost and the indexation allowance. Incidental costs of acquisition and disposal may be deducted together with any enhancement expenditure reflected in the state and nature of the asset at the date of disposal.

- The indexation allowance gives relief for the inflationary element of a gain.

- Matching rules are required to determine which shares are disposed of where the company has made multiple acquisitions of shares in another company.

- When dealing with shares held by companies, we usually need to set up a FA 1985 pool.

- On an alteration of share capital the pooled base cost of the original shares needs to be apportioned, if more than one type of share is acquired.

- When 'qualifying' assets are sold and the proceeds are reinvested in other such assets, it is possible to 'rollover' the gains on the assets sold. The reinvestment in qualifying assets must take place in the period starting one year before and ending three years after disposal. If any proceeds are not reinvested a gain equal to the amount of the proceeds not reinvested is chargeable immediately.

- A rolled over gain is deducted from the base cost of the asset acquired.

- When the replacement asset is a depreciating asset, the gain on the old asset is 'frozen' rather than rolled over.

Quick quiz

1 What is enhancement expenditure?

2 How are quoted shares valued?

3 In what order are acquisitions of shares matched with disposals?

4 What shares are included in the FA 1985 pool?

5 A Ltd sells a factory for £500,000 realising a gain of £100,000. It acquires a factory two months later for £480,000. How much rollover relief is available?

6 What deferral of a gain is available when a business asset is replaced with a depreciating business asset?

Answers to quick quiz

1   Enhancement expenditure is capital expenditure enhancing the value of the asset and reflected in the state/nature of the asset at disposal, or expenditure incurred in establishing, preserving or defending title to asset.

2   Quoted shares are lower of:
   - lower quoted price + $\frac{1}{4} \times$ (higher quoted price – lower quoted price)
   - average of highest and lowest marked bargains

3   Share matching rules:
   - same day acquisitions
   - previous nine days acquisitions (earlier acquisitions first)
   - FA 1985 pool

4   FA 1985 pool has shares held by company on 1 April 1985 acquired on or after 1 April 1982 and shares acquired on or after 1 April 1985.

5   Amount not reinvested £(500,000 – 480,000) = £20,000. Rollover relief £(100,000 – 20,000) = £80,000.

6   Gain is frozen on acquisition of depreciating asset until earlier of disposal of that asset; cessation of use of asset in trade; 10 years after acquisition of replacement asset.

Now try the questions below from the Exam Question Bank

Number	Level	Marks	Time
Q6	Introductory	5	9 mins
Q7	Examination	15	27 mins

6

Losses

Introduction

We now see how a company may obtain relief for losses.

1 Reliefs for losses

1.1 Trading losses

Trading losses may be relieved against current total profits, against total profits of earlier periods or against future trading income.

In summary, the following reliefs are available for trading losses incurred by a company.

(a)   **Set-off against current profits**
(b)   **Carry back against earlier profits**
(c)   **Carry forward against future trading profits**

Reliefs (a) and (b) must be claimed, and are given in the order shown. Relief (c) is given for any loss for which the other reliefs are not claimed.

1.2 Capital losses

Capital losses can only be set against capital gains in the same or future accounting periods, never against income (except losses suffered by an investment company on shares in a qualifying trading company). Capital losses must be set against the first available gains.

1.3 Foreign losses

In the case of a trade which is controlled outside the UK **any loss made in an accounting period can only be set against trading income from the same trade in later accounting periods.** The same rule applies to losses on overseas property businesses.

1.4 Property income losses

Property business losses are first set off against non-property business income and gains of the company for the current period. Any excess is then:

(a)   Carried forward as if a property business loss arising in the later accounting period for offset against future income (of all descriptions), or

(b)   Available for surrender as group relief (see later in this text).

1.5 Miscellaneous income losses

Where in an accounting period a company makes a loss in a transaction taxable as miscellaneous income, **the company can set the loss against any income from other transactions taxable as miscellaneous income in the same or later accounting periods.** The loss must be set against the earliest income available.

2 Loss relief against future trading income: s 393(1) ICTA 1988

Trading losses carried forward can only be set against future trading profits arising from the same trade.

A company must set off a trading loss, not otherwise relieved, against income from the same trade in future accounting periods. Relief is against the first available profits.

Question — Carrying forward losses

A Ltd has the following results for the three years to 31 March 2006.

	Year ended		
	31.3.04	31.3.05	31.3.06
	£	£	£
Trading profit/(loss)	(8,550)	3,000	6,000
Property income	0	1,000	1,000
Gift aid donation	300	1,400	1,700

Calculate the profits chargeable to corporation tax for all three years showing any losses available to carry forward at 1 April 2006.

Answer

	Year ended		
	31.3.04	31.3.05	31.3.06
	£	£	£
Trading profits	0	3,000	6,000
Less: gift aid donation		(3,000)	(5,550)
	0	0	450
Property income	0	1,000	1,000
Less: gift aid donation	0	(1,000)	(1,450)
PCTCT	0	0	0
Unrelieved gift aid donation	300	400	250

Note that the trading loss carried forward is set only against the trading profit in future years. It cannot be set against the property income.

The non-trade charges that become unrelieved remain unrelieved as they cannot be carried forward.

Loss memorandum

	£
Loss for y/e 31.3.04	8,550
Less s 393(1) relief y/e 31.3.05	(3,000)
Loss carried forward at 1.4.05	5,550
Less s 393(1) relief y/e 31.3.06	(5,550)
Loss carried forward at 1.4.06	0

3 Loss relief against total profits: s 393A(1) ICTA 1988

 S393A relief is given against total profits before charges. Gift Aid donations remain unrelieved.

A company may claim to set a trading loss (arising in a UK trade, not an overseas trade controlled abroad) **incurred in an accounting period against total profits before deducting charges (ie gift aid donations) of the same accounting period.**

 S393A relief may be given against current period profits and against profits of the previous 12 months (or previous 36 months if the trade is ceasing).

Such a loss may then be carried back and set against total profits before deducting gift aid donations of an accounting period falling wholly or partly within the 12 months of the start of the period in which the loss was incurred.

If a period falls partly outside the 12 months, loss relief is limited to the proportion of the period's profits (before gift aid donations) equal to the proportion of the period which falls within the 12 months.

> **FAST FORWARD**
>
> A claim for current period S393A relief can be made without a claim for carryback. However, if a loss is to be carried back a claim for current period relief must have been made first.

Any possible s 393A(1) claim for the period of the loss must be made before any excess loss can be carried back to a previous period.

Any carry-back is to more recent periods before earlier periods. Relief for earlier losses is given before relief for later losses.

A claim for relief against current or prior period profits must be made within two years of the end of the accounting period in which the loss arose. Any claim must be for the *whole* loss (to the extent that profits are available to relieve it). The loss can however be reduced by not claiming full capital allowances, so that higher capital allowances are given (on higher tax written down values) in future years. Any loss remaining unrelieved may be carried forward under s 393(1) to set against future profits of the same trade.

Question   S 393A loss relief

Helix Ltd has the following results.

	Year ended		
	30.9.04	30.9.05	30.9.06
	£	£	£
Trading profit/(loss)	10,500	10,000	(35,000)
Bank interest	500	500	500
Chargeable gains	0	0	4,000
Charges on income:			
Gift Aid donation	250	250	250

Show the PCTCT for all the years affected assuming that s 393A(1) loss relief is claimed. Assume the provisions of FA 2005 continue to apply.

Answer

The loss of the year to 30.9.06 is relieved under s 393A ICTA 1988 against current year profits and against profits of the previous twelve months.

	Year ended		
	30.9.04	30.9.05	30.9.06
	£	£	£
Trading profit	10,500	10,000	0
Investment income	500	500	500
Chargeable gains	0	0	4,000
	11,000	10,500	4,500
Less s 393A current period relief	0	0	(4,500)
	11,000	10,500	0
Less s 393A carryback relief	0	(10,500)	0
	11,000	0	0
Less: gift aid donation	(250)	0	0
PCTCT	10,750	0	0
Unrelieved gift aid donation		250	250

S 393A (1) loss memorandum	£
Loss incurred in y/e 30.9.06	35,000
Less s 393A (1): y/e 30.9.06	(4,500)
y/e 30.9.05	(10,500)
Loss available to carry forward under s 393(1)	20,000

The 12 month carry back period is extended to 36 months where the trading loss arose in the 12 months immediately before the company ceased to trade.

Question   Ceasing to trade

Loser Ltd had always made up accounts to 31 December, but ceased to trade on 31 December 2005. Results had been as follows.

	Year ended			
	31.12.02	*31.12.03*	*31.12.04*	*31.12.05*
	£	£	£	£
Trading profit/(loss)	36,000	26,000	23,000	(61,200)
Investment income	2,000	2,000	2,000	0
Gift Aid donation	170	170	170	80

Show the profits chargeable to corporation tax for all years after relief for the loss.

Answer

	Year ended			
	31.12.02	*31.12.03*	*31.12.04*	*31.12.05*
	£	£	£	£
Trading profit	36,000	26,000	23,000	0
Investment income	2,000	2,000	2,000	0
	38,000	28,000	25,000	0
Less: s 393A carryback	(8,200)	(28,000)	(25,000)	0
	29,800	0	0	0
Less: gift aid donations	(170)	0	0	0
	29,630	0	0	0
Unrelieved gift aid donations		170	170	80

4 Restrictions on loss relief

FAST FORWARD

If there is a change in ownership of a company, the carry forward of losses is restricted if there is also a major change in the nature of the trade within three years of the change in ownership.

4.1 The continuity of trades

Relief under s 393(1) is only available against future profits arising from the same trade as that in which the loss arose.

The continuity of trade for this purpose was considered in a case involving a company trading as brewers: *Gordon & Blair Ltd v CIR 1962*. It ceased brewing but continued to bottle and sell beer. The company claimed that it carried on the same trade throughout so that its losses from brewing could be set off against profits from the bottling trade. The company lost their case and were prevented from obtaining any further relief for losses in the brewing trade under s 393(1).

4.2 The disallowance of loss relief following a change in ownership

No relief is available for trading losses in accounting periods on one side of (before or after) a change in ownership of a company if the loss making accounting period is on the other side of (after or before) the change in ownership and either:

- There is a major change in the nature or conduct of the trade within three years before or three years after the change in ownership, or

- After the change in ownership there is a considerable revival of the company's trading activities which at the time of the change had become small or negligible.

Examples of a major change in the nature or conduct of a trade include changes in:

- The type of property dealt in (for example a company operating a dealership in saloon cars switching to a dealership in tractors)

- The services or facilities provided (for example a company operating a public house changing to operating a discotheque)

- Customers

- Outlets or markets

However, changes to keep up to date with technology or to rationalise existing ranges of products are unlikely to be regarded as major. The Revenue consider both qualitative and quantitative issues in deciding if a change is major.

If the change in ownership occurs in (and not at the end of) an accounting period, that period is notionally divided into two periods, one up to and one after the change, for the purposes of this rule, with profits and losses being time-apportioned.

A change in ownership is disregarded for this purpose if both immediately before and immediately after the change the company is a 75% subsidiary of the same company.

4.3 Uncommercial trades

A loss made in a trade which is not conducted on a commercial basis and with a view to the realisation of gain cannot be set off against the company's profits in the same or previous accounting periods under s 393A(1). Such losses are only available to carry forward under s 393(1) against future profits of the same trade.

4.4 Farming and market gardening

A company carrying on the trade of farming or market gardening is treated in the same way as one that trades on an uncommercial basis in any accounting period if, in the five successive years immediately before that accounting period, the trade made a loss (before capital allowances).

5 Choosing loss reliefs and other planning points

FAST FORWARD

When selecting a loss relief, firstly consider the rate at which relief is obtained and, secondly, the timing of the relief.

5.1 Making the choice

Several alternative loss reliefs may be available. In making a choice consider:

- **The rate at which relief will be obtained:**

  (i)   30% at the full rate (FY 2005)
  (ii)   19% at the small companies' rate (FY 2005)
  (iii)   0% at the starting rate (FY 2005)
  (iv)   23.75% if the starting rate marginal relief applies (FY 2005)
  (v)   32.75% if the small companies' marginal relief applies (FY 2005)

  We previously outlined how the 23.75% and 32.75% marginal rates are calculated. Remember these are just marginal rates of tax; they are never actually used in computing a company's corporation tax.

  Remember that the rates of corporation tax were different in earlier financial years.

- **How quickly relief will be obtained**: s 393A(1) relief is quicker than s 393(1) relief.

- **The extent to which relief for gift aid donations might be lost.**

Exam focus point

When choosing between loss relief claims ALWAYS consider the rate of tax 'saved' by the loss first.

If in the current period the loss 'saves' 19% tax but if carried forward saves 30% tax then a carry forward is the better choice (even though the timing of loss relief is later).

If the tax saved now is 30% and in the future is the same (30%) THEN consider timing (in this example a current claim is better timing wise).

So, first – rate of tax saved, second – timing.

Question   The choice between loss reliefs

M Ltd has had the following results.

| | Year ended 31 March | | | | |
	2002	2003	2004	2005	2006
	£	£	£	£	£
Trading profit/(loss)	5,000,000	2,000	(1,000,000)	200,000	138,000
Chargeable gains	0	35,000	750,000	0	0
Gift aid donations paid	20,000	30,000	20,000	20,000	20,000

Recommend appropriate loss relief claims, and compute the mainstream corporation tax for all years based on your recommendations. Assume that future years' profits will be similar to those of the year ended 31 March 2006 and that any profits made by the company are retained for future use in the business.

Answer

A s 393A(1) claim for the year ended 31 March 2004 will save tax partly in the small companies' marginal relief band, partly at the small companies rate and partly in the starting rate marginal relief band. It will waste the gift aid donation of £20,000.

PCTCT in the previous year is £7,000 (£35,000 + £2,000 – £30,000) and falls into the starting rate band lower limit. Corporation tax at 0% would have been due in this year (FY 2002).

If no current period s 393A(1) claim is made, £200,000 of the loss will save tax at the small companies rate and in the starting rate marginal relief band in the year ended 31 March 2005, with £20,000 of gift aid donations being wasted. The remaining £800,000 of the loss, would be carried forward to the year ended 31 March 2006 and later years to save tax at the small companies rate and in the starting rate marginal relief band.

To conclude a s 393A(1) claim should be made for the year of the loss but not in the previous year. £20,000 of gift aid donations would be wasted in the current year, but much of the loss would save tax at the small companies' marginal corporation tax rate and relief would be obtained quickly.

The final computations are as follows.

| | Year ended 31 March | | | | |
	2002	2003	2004	2005	2006
	£	£	£	£	£
Trading profit	5,000,000	2,000	0	200,000	138,000
Less s393(1) relief	0	0	0	(200,000)	(50,000)
	5,000,000	2,000	0	0	88,000
Chargeable gains	0	35,000	750,000	0	0
	5,000,000	37,000	750,000	0	88,000
Less: s393A current relief		0	(750,000)	0	0
	5,000,000	37,000	0	0	88,000
Less: gift aid donations	(20,000)	(30,000)	0	0	(20,000)
Profits chargeable to corporation tax	4,980,000	7,000	0	0	68,000
MCT at 30% / 0% / 0% / 19%	1,494,000	0	0	0	12,920
Unrelieved gift aid donations	0	0	20,000	20,000	0

5.2 Other tax planning points

A company must normally claim capital allowances on its tax return. A company with losses should consider claiming less than the maximum amount of capital allowances available. This will result in a higher tax written down value to carry forward and therefore higher capital allowances in future years.

Reducing capital allowances in the current period reduces the loss available for relief under s 393A. As s393A relief, if claimed, must be claimed for all of a loss available, a reduced capital allowance claim could be advantageous where all of a loss would be relieved at a lower tax rate in the current (or previous) period than the effective rate of relief for capital allowances will be in future periods.

Chapter roundup

- Trading losses may be relieved against current total profits, against total profits of earlier periods or against future trading income.

- Trading losses carried forward can only be set against future trading profits arising from the same trade.

- S393A relief is given against total profits before charges. Gift Aid donations remain unrelieved.

- S393A relief may be given against current period profits and against profits of the previous 12 months (or, previous 36 months if the trade is ceasing).

- A claim for current period S393A relief can be made without a claim for carryback. However, if a loss is to be carried back a claim for current period relief must have been made first.

- If there is a change in ownership of a company, the carry forward of losses is restricted if there is also a major change in the nature of the trade within three years of the change in ownership.

- When selecting a loss relief, firstly consider the rate at which relief is obtained and, secondly, the timing of the relief.

Quick quiz

1   Against what profits may trading losses carried forward be set?

2   To what extent may losses in a continuing trade be carried back?

3   What relief is available in the current AP for a non-trading deficit?

4   Why might a company make a reduced capital allowances claim?

Answers to quick quiz

1   Profits from the same trade.

2   A loss may be carried back and set against total profits (before deducting gift aid donations) of the prior 12 months. The loss carried back is the trading loss left unrelieved after a claim against total profits (before deducting gift aid donations) of the loss making AP has been made.

3   A deficit on a non-trading loan relationship may be set against profit of the same AP. Relief is given after relief for any trading loss brought forward but before relief is given for a current or future trading loss.

    The deficit is also eligible for group relief.

4   Reducing capital allowances in the current AP reduces the loss available for relief under s 393A. Section 393A demands that all of the available loss is utilised. Reducing capital allowances reduces the size of the available loss.

Now try the question below from the Exam Question Bank

Number	Level	Marks	Time
Q8	Examination	15	27 mins

7

Groups

Topic list	Syllabus references
1 Types of group	1(g)
2 Group relief	1(g)
3 Chargeable gains	1(g)

Introduction

In this chapter we consider the extent to which tax law recognises group relationships between companies. Companies in a group are still separate entities with their own tax liabilities, but tax law recognises the close relationship between group companies. They can, if they meet certain conditions, share their losses and pass assets between each other without chargeable gains.

1 Types of group

1.1 Definitions of groups

A group exists for taxation purposes where one company is a subsidiary of another. The percentage shareholding involved determines the taxation consequences of the fact that there is a group.

The four types of relationship for tax purposes are:

- **Associated companies**
- **75% subsidiaries**
- **Consortia**
- **Groups for chargeable gains purposes (capital gains groups)**

1.2 Associated companies

Associated companies affect the limits for starting rate, small companies rate and marginal relief. Broadly, associated companies are worldwide trading companies under common control.

Two companies are associated with each other for taxation purposes if one is under the control of the other, or both are under the control of a third party. Control for these purposes means entitlement to more than 50% of any one of:

- The share capital
- The votes
- The income
- The net assets on a winding up

The number of associated companies determines the limits for the starting rate of corporation tax, the small companies rate and marginal relief.

2 Group relief

Within a 75% group, current period trading losses, excess property business losses and excess charges on income can be surrendered between UK companies. Profits and losses of corresponding accounting periods must be matched up. Group relief is available where the existence of a group is established through companies resident anywhere in the world.

2.1 Group relief provisions

The group relief provisions enable companies within a 75% group to transfer trading losses to other companies within the group, in order to set these against taxable profits and reduce the group's overall corporation tax liability.

Key term

For one company to be a **75% subsidiary** of another, the holding company must have:

- At least 75% of the ordinary share capital of the subsidiary
- A right to at least 75% of the distributable income of the subsidiary, and
- A right to at least 75% of the net assets of the subsidiary were it to be wound up.

Two companies are members of a group for group relief purposes where one is a 75% subsidiary of the other, or both are 75% subsidiaries of a third company. Ordinary share capital is any share capital other than fixed dividend preference shares.

Two companies are in a group only if there is a 75% effective interest. Thus an 80% subsidiary (T) of an 80% subsidiary (S) is not in a group with the holding company (H), because the effective interest is only 80% × 80% = 64%. However, S and T are in a group and can claim group relief from each other. S *cannot* claim group relief from T and pass it on to H; it can only claim group relief for its own use.

A group relief group may include non-UK resident companies. **However, losses may generally only be surrendered between UK resident companies**.

2.2 The relief

A surrendering company can surrender any amount of its loss but a claimant company can only claim an amount up to its available profits. The best option is normally to surrender losses to set against profits where the highest marginal rate of tax would otherwise be suffered.

A **claimant company** is assumed to use its own current year losses or losses brought forward in working out the profits against which it may claim group relief, even if it does not in fact claim s 393A relief for current losses. Furthermore, **group relief is against profits after all other reliefs for the current period or brought forward from earlier periods**, including non-trading deficits on loan relationships and charges. Group relief is given before relief for any amounts brought back from later periods.

A surrendering company may group relieve a loss before setting it against its own profits for the period of the loss, and may specify any amount to be surrendered. This is **important** for **tax planning as it enables the surrendering company to leave profits in its own computation to be charged to corporation tax at the small companies rate or starting rate, while surrendering its losses to other companies to cover profits which would otherwise fall into a marginal relief band or be taxed at the full rate**. Note that profits in the small companies' marginal relief band are taxed at the marginal rate of 32.75%. Profits in the starting rate marginal relief band are taxed at the marginal rate of 23.75%.

Question	Group relief of losses

In a group of four companies, the results for the year ended 31 March 2006 are as follows.

	Profit/(loss) £
A Ltd	2,000
B Ltd	212,500
C Ltd	1,000,000
D Ltd	(400,000)

How should the loss be allocated to save as much tax as possible? How much tax is saved?

Note: No dividends were paid by any group company during this year.

Answer

The upper and lower limits for small companies' marginal relief are £1,500,000/4 = £375,000 and £300,000/4 = £75,000 respectively. The upper and lower limits for starting rate marginal relief are £50,000/4 = £12,500 and £10,000/4 = £2,500 respectively.

	A Ltd £	B Ltd £	C Ltd £
Profits before group relief	2,000	212,500	1,000,000
Less group relief (note)	0	(137,500)	(262,500)
PCTCT	2,000	75,000	737,500

	A Ltd £	B Ltd £	C Ltd £
Tax saved			
£137,500 × 32.75%		45,031	
£262,500 × 30%			78,750
Total £(45,031 + 78,750) = £123,781			

Note: We wish to save the most tax possible for the group.

Since A Ltd is in the starting rate band any loss given to it will not save any tax (0% tax band)

B Ltd is in the marginal relief for small companies rate band. Therefore, any loss given to B saves the effective marginal rate of 32.75% until the profits fall to £75,000 (the small companies lower limit). After this only 19% is saved.

C Ltd is in the full rate band of 30% until profits fall to £375,000 (the small companies upper limit).

So to conclude it is best to give B Ltd £137,500 of loss and save 32.75% tax on the profits in the marginal relief band. The balance of the loss is then given to C Ltd to save 30% tax.

A company may surrender to other group companies trading losses, excess property business losses, non-trading deficits on loan relationships and excess charges on income. Charges can only be group-relieved to the extent that they exceed profits before taking account of any losses of the current period or brought forward or back from other accounting periods. **Excess management expenses of investment companies may also be surrendered.** If there are excess charges, property business losses and management expenses available for surrender then they are surrendered in that order.

Capital losses cannot be group relieved. However, see paragraph 3.3 below for details of how a group may net off its gains and losses.

Only current period losses are available for group relief. Furthermore, they must be set against profits of a corresponding accounting period. If the accounting periods of a surrendering company and a claimant company are not the same this means that both the profits and losses must be apportioned so that only the results of the period of overlap may be set off. Apportionment is on a time basis. However, in the period when a company joins or leaves a group, an alternative method may be used if the result given by time-apportionment would be unjust or unreasonable.

Question	Corresponding accounting periods

	£
S Ltd incurs a trading loss for the year to 30 September 2005	(15,000)
H Ltd makes taxable profits:	
for the year to 31 December 2004	20,000
for the year to 31 December 2005	10,000
What group relief can H Ltd claim from S Ltd?	

Answer

H Ltd can claim group relief as follows.

	£
For the year ended 31 December 2004 profits of the corresponding accounting period (1.10.04 – 31.12.04) are £20,000 × 3/12	5,000
Losses of the corresponding accounting period are £15,000 × 3/12	3,750
A claim for £3,750 of group relief may be made against H Ltd's profits	
For the year ended 31 December 2005 profits of the corresponding accounting period (1.1.05 – 30.9.05) are £10,000 × 9/12	7,500
Losses of the corresponding accounting period are £15,000 × 9/12	11,250
A claim for £7,500 of group relief may be made against H Ltd's profits	

If a claimant company claims relief for losses surrendered by more than one company, the total relief that may be claimed for a period of overlap is limited to the proportion of the claimant's profits attributable to that period. Similarly, if a company surrenders losses to more than one claimant, the total losses that may be surrendered in a period of overlap is limited to the proportion of the surrendering company's losses attributable to that period.

A claim for group relief is normally made on the claimant company's tax return. It is ineffective unless a notice of consent is also given by the surrendering company.

A claimant company may not amend a group relief claim but it may withdraw it and replace it with a new claim. The time limit for making or withdrawing a claim is the latest of:

(a)   The first anniversary of the filing date for the CT return.

(b)   30 days after the completion of an enquiry into a return.

(c)   30 days after the amendment of a self assessment by the Revenue following the completion of an enquiry.

(d)   30 days after the settlement of an appeal against an amendment to the self assessment made by the Revenue following an enquiry.

The Revenue has discretion to accept a late claim/withdrawal.

Group wide claims/surrenders can be made as one person can act for two or more companies at once.

Any payment by the claimant company for group relief, up to the amount of the loss surrendered, is ignored for all corporation tax purposes.

2.3 Anti-avoidance rules

If arrangements exist for a company to leave a group, then group relief is not available in respect of losses incurred after such arrangements are made. 'Arrangements' is a very wide term in this context and can include any form of informal agreement for the disposal of a subsidiary company, even on normal commercial terms. Also if entitlement to profits or assets could vary in the future, for example because of options, the lowest possible percentage entitlements are taken to apply now in determining whether a group exists.

Question

Group relief

C Ltd has one wholly owned subsidiary, D Ltd. The results of both companies for the four years ended 31 March 2006 are shown below.

	12 months to 31 March			
	2003	*2004*	*2005*	*2006*
	£	£	£	£
C Ltd				
Trading profit (loss)	200	(1,700)	100	(2,000)
Property business income	800	800	800	800
Gift aid donation paid	(40)		0	(60)
D Ltd				
Trading profit (loss)	(2,300)	3,260	(870)	2,400
Interest on gilts (non-trading investment) (gross)	1,800	0	1,200	1,300
Gift aid donation paid	0	(400)	(300)	(500)

Show the profits chargeable to corporation tax for both companies for all years shown, assuming that loss relief and group relief are claimed as early as possible, and no dividends are paid or received by the companies.

Answer

C Ltd

	Accounting periods to 31 March			
	2003	*2004*	*2005*	*2006*
	£	£	£	£
Trading profit	200	0	100	0
Property income	800	800	800	800
	1,000	800	900	800
Less s 393A(1) – current period relief		(800)	0	(800)
		0	900	0
Less s 393A – carry back	0	0	(900)	0
	1000	0	0	0
Less charges paid	(40)	0	0	0
	960	0	0	0
Less group relief claim	(500)	0	0	0
PCTCT	460	0	0	0

Loss memorandum

Loss		(1,700)		(2,000)
S 393A(1) claim: current year		800		800
		(900)		(1,200)
S 393A(1) claim: carry back				900
				(300)
Group relief surrender		900		300
		0		0

D Ltd

Trading income	0	3,260	0	2,400
Investment income	1,800	0	1,200	1,300
	1,800	3,260	1,200	3,700
Less s 393A(1) – current period relief	(1,800)		(870)	
	0		330	
Less charges paid	0	(400)	(300)	(500)
	0	2,860	30	3,200
Less group relief claim		(900)		(300)
PCTCT	0	1,960	30	2,900

Loss memorandum	£	£
Loss	(2,300)	(870)
S 393A(1) claim	1,800	870
	(500)	0
Group relief surrender	500	
	0	

Note. The excess charges of £60 arising in C Ltd for the year to 31.3.2006 are wasted.

2.4 Tax planning for group relief

This section outlines some tax planning points to bear in mind when dealing with a group.

Group relief should first be given in this order:

1st   To companies in the small companies marginal relief band paying 32.75% tax (but only sufficient loss to bring profits down to the SCR limit)

2nd   To companies paying the full rate of tax at 30%

3rd   To companies in the starting rate marginal relief band paying 23.75% tax (but only sufficient loss to bring profits down to the starting rate limit)

4th   To companies paying SCR at 19%

5th   To companies paying starting rate at Nil% (**not** worth doing)

Similarly, a company should make a s 393A(1) claim to use a loss itself rather than surrender the loss to other group companies if the s 393A(1) claim would lead to a tax saving at a higher rate.

Companies with profits may benefit by reducing their claims for capital allowances in a particular year. This may leave sufficient profits to take advantage of group relief which may only be available for the current year. The amount on which writing-down allowances can be claimed in later years is increased accordingly.

3 Chargeable gains

3.1 Intra-group transfers

FAST FORWARD

A capital gains group consists of the top company plus companies in which the top company has a 50% effective interest, provided there is a 75% holding at each level. Within a capital gains group, assets are transferred at no gain and no loss.

Companies are in a capital gains group if:

(a)   At each level, there is a 75% holding, and
(b)   The top company has an effective interest of over 50% in the group companies.

If A holds 75% of B, B holds 75% of C and C holds 75% of D, then A, B and C are in such a group, but D is outside the group because A's interest in D is only $75\% \times 75\% \times 75\% = 42.1875\%$. Furthermore, D is not in a group with C, because the group must include the top company (A).

Companies in a capital gains group make intra-group transfers of chargeable assets without a chargeable gain or an allowable loss arising. No election is needed, as this relief is compulsory. The assets are deemed to be transferred at such a price as will give the transferor no gain and no loss.

Non-UK resident companies are included as members of a capital gains group. Provided the assets transferred do not result in a potential leakage of UK corporation tax, no gain/no loss transfers are possible within a worldwide (global) group of companies. This means that it may be possible to make no gain/no loss transfers to non-UK resident companies with a permanent establishment in the UK.

3.2 Exceptions to the 'no gain/no loss' transfer price

FAST FORWARD ⟫

Gains and losses can be matched within a group. This can be done by electing that any asset disposed of outside the group is treated as transferred between group companies before disposal outside the group.

There are exceptions to the 'no gain no loss' transfer price for intra-group transfers of capital assets. There will be an immediate chargeable disposal:

- Where an intra-group **transfer is in satisfaction of a debt.**

- On the **disposal of an interest in shares in a group company by way of a capital distribution.**

- **Where cash or other assets are received upon the redemption of shares in another company.**

In addition, when an asset is transferred between two group companies and is trading stock for one of those companies but not for the other, it is treated as appropriated to or from trading stock by the company for which it is trading stock. This may give rise to an immediate chargeable gain, allowable loss or trading profit or loss (see earlier in this Text).

3.3 Matching group gains and losses

Capital losses cannot be included in a group relief claim. However, **two members of a capital gains group can elect that an asset that has been disposed of outside the group is treated as if it had been transferred between them immediately before disposal.** The deemed transferee company is then treated as having made the disposal. This election may be made within two years of the end of the accounting period in which the disposal took place.

From a tax planning point of view, elections(s) should be made to ensure that net taxable gains arise in the company subject to the lowest rate of corporation tax.

3.4 Rollover relief

FAST FORWARD ⟫

Rollover relief is available in a capital gains group.

If a member of a capital gains group disposes of an asset eligible for capital gains rollover or holdover relief it may treat all of the group companies as a single unit for the purpose of claiming such relief. Acquisitions by other group members within the qualifying period of one year before the disposal to three years afterwards may therefore **be matched with the disposal.** However, both the disposing company and the acquiring company must make the claim. If an asset is transferred at no gain and no loss between group members, that transfer does not count as the acquisition of an asset for rollover or holdover relief purpose.

Claims may also be made by non-trading group members which hold assets used for other group members' trades.

Exam focus point

Try to remember the following summary - it will be of great help in the exam.

Parent Co **controls** over 50% of subsidiary

- associated companies for upper and lower limits

Parent Co **owns** 75% or more of subsidiary

- surrender trading losses, property business losses, excess charges to companies with some PCTCT for same time period

Parent Co **owns** 75% or more of subsidiary and subsidiary owns 75% or more of its subsidiaries

- transfer assets between companies automatically at no gain/no loss
- capital gains and losses can be matched between group member companies
- all companies treated as one for rollover relief purposes.

Chapter roundup

- Associated companies affect the limits for starting rate, small companies rate and marginal relief. Broadly, associated companies are worldwide trading companies under common control.

- Within a 75% group, current period trading losses, excess property business losses and excess charges on income can be surrendered between UK companies. Profits and losses of corresponding accounting periods must be matched up. Group relief is available where the existence of a group is established through companies resident anywhere in the world.

- A surrendering company can surrender any amount of its loss but a claimant company can only claim an amount up to its available profits. The best option is normally to surrender losses to set against profits where the highest marginal rate of tax would otherwise be suffered.

- A capital gains group consists of the top company plus companies in which the top company has a 50% effective interest, provided there is a 75% holding at each level. Within a capital gains group, assets are transferred at no gain and no loss.

- Gains and losses can be matched within a group. This can be done by electing that any asset disposed of outside the group is treated as transferred between group companies before disposal outside the group.

- Rollover relief is available in a capital gains group.

Quick quiz

1 List the types of losses which may be group relieved.

2 When may assets be transferred intra-group at no gain and no loss?

3 How can capital gains and losses within a group be matched with each other?

Answers to quick quiz

1   Trading losses, excess property business losses and excess charges on income (gift aid donations).

2   No gain no loss asset transfers are mandatory between companies in an 'assets group' (ie a capital gains group).

3   Two member of an 'assets group' can elect that an asset which has been disposed of to a third party is treated as transferred between them prior to disposal. This election effectively allow the group to match its gains and losses in one company.

Now try the questions below from the Exam Question Bank

Number	Level	Marks	Time
Q9	Examination	15	27 mins
Q10	Examination	15	27 mins

Overseas aspects of corporate taxation

Topic list	Syllabus reference
1 Permanent establishment (PE) or subsidiary abroad	1f(i)
2 Double taxation relief (DTR)	1f(ii)
3 Transfer pricing	1f(iii)

Introduction

In this chapter we look at UK companies trading abroad. We see how relief may be given for overseas taxes suffered and how the transfer pricing legislation applies.

1 Permanent establishment (PE) or subsidiary abroad

Key term

> A **permanent establishment** (PE) is a fixed place of business through which the business of the enterprise is wholly or partly carried on. It includes a branch, office, factory, workshop, mine, oil or gas well, quarry and construction project lasting more than twelve months. It does not include use of storage facilities, maintenance of a stock of goods and delivery of them or a fixed place of business used solely for purchasing goods or any ancillary activity.

FAST FORWARD

> A UK resident company intending to do business abroad must choose between a PE and a subsidiary. A PE may be useful if losses are expected in the early years. If a subsidiary is chosen, it must bear in mind the rules on trading at artificial prices.

1.1 Taxation of foreign income and gains

A UK resident company is subject to corporation tax on its worldwide profits. It is also (unlike a non-resident company) entitled to the starting rate of corporation tax, the small companies rate and to marginal relief.

If a UK resident company makes investments abroad it will be liable to corporation tax on the profits made, the taxable amount being before the deduction of any foreign taxes. The profits may be any of the following.

(a)   Interest and dividends received through paying agents

(b)   Trading profits of an overseas PE controlled from the UK

(c)   Investment income from foreign securities, for example debentures in overseas companies

(d)   Income from other overseas possessions including:

(i)   dividends from overseas subsidiaries
(ii)   profits of an overseas PE controlled abroad

(e)   Capital gains on disposals of foreign assets

Overseas dividends and interest received by a company are taxed at normal corporation tax rates.

A company may be subject to overseas taxes as well as to UK corporation tax on the same profits. Double taxation relief (see below) is available in respect of the foreign tax suffered.

1.2 Taxation of foreign PE and foreign subsidiaries

Where a foreign country has a lower rate of company taxation than the UK, it can be beneficial for the UK company to conduct its foreign activities through a **non-UK resident subsidiary** if profits are anticipated, and through a **PE if losses are likely to arise**.

The **profits of a foreign PE** are treated as part of the profits of the UK company and are normally included in its computation of taxable trading profits. If, however, the operations of the overseas PE amount to a separate trade which is wholly carried on overseas, the profits are assessed separately as foreign trading income.

Losses of a foreign PE can be surrendered as group relief to the extent the loss cannot be relieved against profits in the overseas country. Alternatively a foreign trading loss can be carried forward to set against future profits of the same trade. A UK trading loss is first set against other UK trading profits. The usual loss reliefs are then available.

The profits of a non-resident **foreign subsidiary** are only liable to UK tax when remitted to the UK, for example in the form of dividends as foreign income. However, no relief can be obtained against the UK parent's profits for any overseas losses of a non-resident subsidiary.

1.3 Incorporation of a foreign PE

Where a foreign operation is likely to show a loss in the early years followed by a profit it may be worthwhile to trade through a foreign PE whilst losses arise (these are usually then automatically netted off against the company's UK profits) and then later to convert the PE into a non-UK resident subsidiary company (so that profits can be accumulated at potentially lower rates of foreign tax).

This conversion of a PE into a non-UK resident subsidiary has some important implications and the tax effects both in the UK and the overseas country need to be considered. Firstly, it may be necessary to secure the consent of the Treasury for the transaction. It is illegal for a UK resident company to cause or permit a non-UK resident company over which it has control to create or issue any shares or debentures. It is also illegal for a UK resident company to transfer to any person, or cause or permit to be transferred to any person, any shares or debentures of a non-UK resident company over which it has control.

The Treasury have published General Consents which permit certain intra-group transactions and third party transactions provided full consideration is given. Additionally certain movements of capital between EEA states are allowed automatically. Thus in practice specific Treasury consent may not be required for a transaction of the type presently under consideration.

Secondly, the conversion will constitute a disposal of the assets of the PE giving rise to a chargeable gain or loss in the hands of the UK company. A chargeable gain can be postponed where:

(a) the trade of the foreign PE is transferred to the non-UK resident company with all the assets used for that trade except cash; and

(b) the consideration for the transfer is wholly or partly securities (shares or shares and loan stock); and

(c) the transferring company owns at least 25% of the ordinary share capital of the non-resident company; and

(d) a claim for relief is made.

There is full postponement of the net gains arising on the transfer where the consideration is wholly securities. Where part of the consideration is in a form other than securities, eg cash, that proportion of the net gains is chargeable immediately.

The postponement may be indefinite. The gain becomes chargeable only when:

(a) the transferor company at any time disposes of any of the securities received on the transfer; or

(b) the non-UK resident company within six years of the transfer disposes of any of the assets on which a gain arose at the time of the transfer.

The 'global group' concept applies to certain intra-group transfers of assets. Such asset transfers are on a no gain/no loss basis provided the assets transferred do not result in a potential leakage of UK corporation tax.

1.4 European Community companies

If all or part of a trade carried on in the UK by a company resident in one EC state is transferred to a company resident in another EC state, then the transfer is deemed to be at a price giving no gain and no loss, if all the following conditions are fulfilled.

(a)   The transfer is wholly in exchange for shares or securities.

(b)   The company receiving the trade would be subject to UK corporation tax on any gains arising on later disposals of the assets transferred.

(c)   Both parties claim this special treatment.

(d)   The transfer is for bona fide commercial reasons. Advance clearance that this condition is satisfied may be obtained.

2 Double taxation relief (DTR)

2.1 Types of DTR

In the UK, relief for foreign tax suffered by a company is available in three ways:

(a)   **Treaty relief**

Under a treaty entered into between the UK and the overseas country, a treaty may exempt certain profits from taxation in one of the countries involved, thus completely avoiding double taxation. More usually treaties provide for credit to be given for tax suffered in one of the countries against the tax liability in the other.

(b)   **Unilateral credit relief**

Where no treaty relief is available, unilateral relief may be available in the UK giving credit for the foreign tax against the UK tax.

(c)   **Unilateral expense relief**

Not examined in your syllabus.

Exam focus point

> DTR was changed in Finance Act 2000. However the examiner has stated that these changes will not be examined.

2.2 Treaty relief

A tax treaty based on the OECD model treaty may use either the exemption method or the credit method to give relief for tax suffered on income from a business in country B by a resident of country R.

(a)   Under the **exemption method**, the income is not taxed at all in country R, or if it is dividends or interest (which the treaty allows to be taxed in country R) credit is given for any country B tax against the country R tax.

(b)   Under the **credit method**, the income is taxed in country R, but credit is given for any country B tax against the country R tax.

Under either method, any credit given is limited to the country B tax attributable to the income.

2.3 Unilateral credit relief

FAST FORWARD

> A company may obtain double taxation relief for overseas withholding tax, and also (if it owns at least 10% of the voting power) for underlying tax. Underlying tax is calculated as
>
> $$\text{Gross dividend income} \times \frac{\text{foreign tax paid}}{\text{after - tax accounting profits}}$$
>
> To calculate the taxable foreign income gross up for withholding tax and then, if appropriate for underlying tax.

Double tax relief is the lower of:

(i)   the UK tax on a source of income
(ii)   the overseas tax on that income source (withholding and underlying tax).

2.3.1 Relief for withholding tax

Relief is available for overseas tax suffered on PE profits, dividends, interest and royalties, up to the amount of the UK corporation tax (at the company's average rate) attributable to that income. The tax that is deducted overseas is usually called withholding tax. The gross income including the withholding tax is included within the profits chargeable to corporation tax.

Question

Unilateral credit relief

On 1 May 2005, AS plc receives a dividend from Bola of £80,000. This has been paid subject to 20% withholding tax. AS plc has UK trading income of £2,000,000 for the year to 31.3.06. Show that the taxable foreign income is £100,000 and compute the corporation tax payable.

Answer

	Total £	UK £	Overseas £
Trading profits	2,000,000	2,000,000	
Foreign dividend(W)	100,000		100,000
PCTCT	2,100,000	2,000,000	100,000
Corporation tax at 30%	630,000	600,000	30,000
Less DTR: lower of:			
(a) overseas tax: £20,000; or			
(b) UK tax on overseas income: £30,000	(20,000)		(20,000)
MCT	610,000	600,000	10,000

Working: foreign dividend
£80,000 × 100/(100 − 20) = £100,000.

2.3.2 Underlying tax relief

In addition to the relief available for withholding tax shown above, relief is available for underlying tax relating to a dividend received from a foreign company in which the UK company owns at least 10% of the voting power, either directly or indirectly. The underlying tax is the tax attributable to the relevant profits out of which the dividend was paid. Underlying tax is calculated as

$$\text{Gross dividend income} \times \frac{\text{foreign tax paid}}{\text{after} - \text{tax accounting profits}}$$

Relief for underlying tax is not available to individuals.

We may need to decide which accounting profits have been used to pay a dividend. If the dividend is declared for a particular year, the set of accounts for that year are used. If this information is not given, the relevant profits are those of the period of account immediately before that in which the dividend was payable.

There is an anti-avoidance provision which restricts relief for underlying tax in certain circumstances where there is a scheme the purpose, or one of the main purposes, of which is to obtain relief for underlying tax.

Question   Underlying tax relief

A Ltd, a UK company with no associated companies, holds 30,000 out of 90,000 voting ordinary shares in B Inc (resident in Lintonia).

The profit and loss account of B Inc for the year to 31 March 2006 is as follows (converted into sterling).

		£	£
Trading profit			1,000,000
Less taxation:	provided on profits	300,000	
	transfer to deferred tax account	100,000	
			(400,000)
			600,000
Less dividends:	Net	240,000	
	withholding tax (20%)	60,000	
			(300,000)
Retained profits			300,000

The actual tax paid on the profits for the year to 31 March 2006 was £270,000.

Apart from the net dividend of £80,000 received out of the above profits from B Inc on 31 May 2005 the only other taxable profit of A Ltd for its year to 31 March 2006 was £610,000 UK trading profit. A Ltd paid no dividends during the year and received no UK dividends.

Calculate A Ltd's UK corporation tax liability after double taxation relief.

Answer

A LTD: UK CORPORATION TAX LIABILITY

	£	£
Trading profit		610,000
Foreign dividend:		
Net dividend	80,000	
Withholding tax at 20%		
£80,000 × 20/80	20,000	
Gross dividend	100,000	
Underlying tax		
£100,000 × $\frac{270,000}{600,000}$	45,000	
Gross income		145,000
PCTCT		755,000

	Total £	UK £	Overseas £
Trading profit	610,000	610,000	
Foreign dividend	145,000		145,000
PCTCT	755,000	610,000	145,000
Corporation tax £755,000 × 30%			226,500
Less small companies' marginal relief £(1,500,000 − 755,000) × 11/400			(20,488)
			206,012

The average rate of corporation tax is £206,012/£755,000 = 27.28635%.

Corporation tax at the average rate	206,012	166,447	39,565

Less DTR: lower of:
(a) overseas tax £(20,000 + 45,000) = £65,000;
(b) UK tax on overseas income £39,565

	(39,565)		(39,565)
	166,447	166,447	0

Corporation tax of £166,447 is payable. £(65,000 – 39,565) = £25,435 of overseas tax is unrelieved (ie excess). It is possible to carry the unrelieved tax back or forward.

2.3.3 Allocation of losses and charges

> **FAST FORWARD**
>
> Charges and losses should initially be set against UK income. They should subsequently be set against the overseas income source that suffers the lowest rate of overseas tax.

One further factor affects the computation of UK tax on overseas income against which credit for overseas tax may be claimed. This is the allocation of charges and losses relieved against total profits under s 393A(1).

A company may allocate its charges and losses relieved under s 393A(1) in whatever manner it likes for the purpose of computing double taxation relief. It should set the maximum amount against any UK profits, thereby maximising the corporation tax attributable to the foreign profits and hence maximising the double taxation relief available.

If a company has several sources of overseas profits, then charges and losses should be allocated first to UK profits, and then to overseas sources which have suffered the **lowest** rates of overseas taxation.

Losses relieved under s 393(1) must in any case be set against the first available profits of the trade which gave rise to the loss.

A company with a choice of loss reliefs should consider the effect of its choice on double taxation relief. For example, a s 393A(1) claim might lead to there being no UK tax liability, or a very small liability, so that foreign tax would go unrelieved. S 393(1) relief might avoid this problem and still leave very little UK tax to pay for the period of the loss.

3 Transfer pricing

> **FAST FORWARD**
>
> The transfer pricing legislation restricts the freedom of a company to buy and sell goods at whatever price it wishes between associated persons. A profit on such a transfer must be computed as though the transfer had been made at an arm's length price. Note, however, that the transfer pricing legislation does not apply to transactions between two UK resident persons unless they are large enterprises.

Companies which have subsidiaries resident in countries with lower corporate tax rates than the UK may attempt to divert profits by inter-company pricing arrangements. For example, a UK company has contracted to sell goods with an invoice value of £20,000 to a foreign customer:

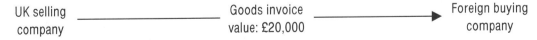

In this case all the profit on the sale arises to the UK company; alternatively the sale could be rearranged.

In this case £4,000 of the profit has been diverted to a subsidiary operating in a low-tax country (tax haven).

Although a company may buy and sell goods etc at any price it wishes there is **anti avoidance legislation** which **requires profit to be computed as if the transactions had been carried out at arms length.**

The transfer pricing rules apply to transactions between two persons if either:

(a)   one person directly or indirectly participates in the management, control or capital of the other; or

(b)   a third party directly or indirectly participates in the management, control or capital of both.

For profits arising on or after 1 April 2004, the transfer pricing regime is extended to transactions within the UK.

Small and medium-sized enterprises are from 1 April 2004 normally exempt from the transfer pricing requirements. Companies dormant at 1 April 2004 are exempt as long as they remain dormant.

There is a temporary relaxation of penalties imposed for failing to keep evidence to demonstrate that transactions have been carried out at arm's length until 31 March 2006.

Companies must self-assess their liability to tax under the transfer pricing rules and pay any corporation tax due. A statutory procedure exists for advance pricing arrangements (APAs) whereby a company can agree in advance that its transfer pricing policy is acceptable to the Revenue – ie, not requiring a self-assessment adjustment. The APA facility is voluntary but companies may feel the need to use the facility as it provides necessary advance confirmation that their approach to transfer pricing in their self-assessment is acceptable.

Chapter roundup

- A UK resident company intending to do business abroad must choose between a PE and a subsidiary. A PE may be useful if losses are expected in the early years. If a subsidiary is chosen, it must bear in mind the rules on trading at artificial prices.

- A company may obtain double taxation relief for overseas withholding tax, and also (if it owns at least 10% of the voting power) for underlying tax. Underlying tax is calculated as

$$\text{Gross dividend income} \times \frac{\text{Foreign tax paid}}{\text{after}-\text{tax accounting profits}}$$

    To calculate the taxable foreign income gross up for withholding tax and then, if appropriate for underlying tax.

    Double tax relief is the lower of:

    (i)   the UK tax on a source of income
    (ii)   the overseas tax on that income source (withholding and underlying tax).

- Charges and losses should initially be set against UK income. They should subsequently be set against the overseas income source that suffers the lowest rate of overseas tax.

- The transfer pricing legislation restricts the freedom of a company to buy and sell goods at whatever price it wishes between associated persons. A profit on such a transfer must be computed as though the transfer had been made at an arms length price. Note, however, that the transfer pricing legislation does not apply to transactions between two UK resident persons unless they are large enterprises.

Quick quiz

1   A UK company is planning to set up a new operation in Australia that will initially be loss making. Should it set up as a PE or a subsidiary of the UK company?

2   When is a company UK resident?

3   How is underlying tax calculated?

4   How best should charges be allocated in computing credit relief for foreign tax?

5   What steps can be taken against the use of artificial transfer prices?

Answers to quick quiz

1   If losses are expected to arise then a PE operation is best since losses of a foreign PE can be surrendered as group relief.

2   A company is resident in the UK if it is incorporated in the UK or if its central management and control are exercised in the UK.

3   Underlying tax is calculated as

$$\text{Dividend plus withholding tax} \times \frac{\text{foreign tax paid}}{\text{after-tax accounting profits}}$$

4   Charges should be set-off firstly from any UK profits, then from overseas income sources suffering the lowest rates of overseas taxation before those suffering at the higher rates.

5   Although a company may buy and sell goods at any price it wishes, the transfer pricing anti-avoidance legislation requires profit to be computed as if the transactions had been carried out at arms length, in certain circumstances.

Now try the question below from the Exam Question Bank

Number	Level	Marks	Time
Q11	Examination	15	27 mins

Payment of tax by companies

9

Topic list	Syllabus references
1 Returns, records, enquiries, assessments and claims	1(h)
2 Payment of corporation tax and interest	1(h)

Introduction

We have looked at the computation of a company's CT liability. In this chapter we look at the self assessment system for CT.

107

1 Returns, records, enquiries, assessments and claims

 FAST FORWARD A company must notify the Revenue within 3 months of starting to trade.

1.1 Notification to Revenue

A company must notify HMRC (the Revenue) of the beginning of its first accounting period (ie usually when it starts to trade) and the beginning of any subsequent period that does not immediately follow the end of a previous accounting period. The notice must be in the prescribed form and submitted within three months of the relevant date. Failure to comply with this requirement will mean a maximum penalty of £3,000.

1.2 Returns

FAST FORWARD CT 600 returns must, in general, be filed within twelve months of the end of an accounting period.

A company's tax return (CT 600) must include a self assessment of any tax payable.

An obligation to file a return arises only when the company receives a notice requiring a return. A return is required for each accounting period ending during or at the end of the period specified in the notice requiring a return. A company also has to file a return for certain other periods which are not accounting periods (eg for a period when the company is dormant).

A company that does not receive a notice requiring a return must, if it is chargeable to tax, **notify the Revenue within twelve months of the end of the accounting period.** Failure to do so results in a maximum penalty equal to the tax unpaid twelve months after the end of the accounting period. Tax for this purpose includes corporation tax and notional tax on loans to participators of close companies (see later in this Text).

A notice to file a return may also require other information, accounts and reports. For a UK resident company the requirement to deliver accounts normally extends only to the accounts required under the Companies Act.

A return is due on or before the filing date. This is the later of:

(a) **12 months after the end of the period to which the return relates**;

(b) **if the relevant period of account is not more than 18 months long, 12 months from the end of the period of account**;

(c) **if relevant the period of account is more than 18 months long, 30 months from the start of the period of account**; and

(d) **three months from the date on which the notice requiring the return was made**.

The relevant period of account is that in which the accounting period to which the return relates ends.

✎ **Question**   Filing date

A Ltd prepares accounts for the eighteen months to 30 June 2005. A notice requiring a return for the period ended 30 June 2005 was issued to A Ltd on 1 September 2005. State the periods for which A Ltd must file a tax return and the filing dates.

Answer

The company must file a return for the two accounting periods ending in the period specified in the notice requiring a return. The first accounting period is the twelve months to 31 December 2004 and the second is the six months to 30 June 2005. The filing date is twelve months after the end of the relevant period of account, 30 June 2006.

There is a £100 penalty for a failure to submit a return on time, rising to £200 if the delay exceeds three months. These penalties become £500 and £1,000 respectively when a return was late (or never submitted) for each of the preceding two accounting periods.

An additional tax geared penalty is applied if a return is more than six months late. The penalty is 10% of the tax unpaid six months after the return was due if the total delay is up to 12 months, and 20% of that tax if the return is over 12 months late.

There is a tax geared penalty for a fraudulent or negligent return and for failing to correct an innocent error without unreasonable delay. The maximum penalty is equal to the tax that would have been lost had the return been accepted as correct. The Revenue can mitigate this penalty. If a company is liable to more than one tax geared penalty, the total penalty is limited to the maximum single penalty that could be charged.

A company may amend a return within twelve months of the filing date. The Revenue may amend a return to correct obvious errors within nine months of the day the return was filed, or if the correction is to an amended return, within nine months of the filing of an amendment. The company may amend its return so as to reject the correction. If the time limit for amendments has expired, the company may reject the correction by giving notice within three months.

1.3 Records

Companies must keep records until the latest of:

    (a)   six years from the end of the accounting period;

    (b)   the date any enquiries are completed;

    (c)   the date after which enquiries may not be commenced.

All business records and accounts, including contracts and receipts, must be kept.

If a return is demanded more than six years after the end of the accounting period, any records which the company still has must be kept until the later of the end of any enquiry and the expiry of the right to start an enquiry.

Failure to keep records can lead to a penalty of up to £3,000 for each accounting period affected. However, this penalty does not apply when the only records which have not been kept are ones which could only have been needed for the purposes of claims, elections or notices not included in the return.

The Revenue do not generally insist on original records being kept but original records of the following must be preserved:

    (a)   Qualifying distributions and tax credits

    (b)   Gross and net payments and tax deducted for payments made net of tax

    (c)   Certificates of payments made to sub-contractors net of tax

    (d)   Details of foreign tax paid, although the Revenue will accept photocopies or foreign tax assessments when calculating underlying tax (see later in this text) on dividends from abroad

1.4 Enquiries

The Revenue can enquire into returns.

A return or an amendment need not be accepted at face value by the Revenue. **They may enquire into it, provided that they first give written notice that they are going to enquire.** The notice must be given by a year after the later of:

(a)   The filing date;

(b)   The 31 January, 30 April, 31 July or 31 October next following the actual date of delivery of the return or amendment.

Only one enquiry may be made in respect of any one return or amendment.

If a notice of an enquiry has been given, the Revenue may demand that the company produce documents for inspection and copying. However, documents relating to an appeal need not be produced and the company may appeal against a notice requiring documents to be produced.

If the Revenue demand documents, but the company does not produce them, there is a penalty of £50. There is also a daily penalty, which applies for each day from the day after the imposition of the £50 penalty until the documents are produced. The daily penalty may be imposed by the Revenue, in which case it is £30. If, however, the Revenue ask the Commissioners to impose the penalty, it is £150.

The Revenue may amend a self assessment at any time during an enquiry if they believe there might otherwise be a loss of tax. The company may appeal against such an amendment within 30 days. The company may itself make amendments during an enquiry under the normal rules for amendments. No effect will be given to such amendments during the enquiry but they may be taken into account in the enquiry.

An enquiry ends when the Revenue give notice that it has been completed and notify what they believe to be the correct amount of tax payable. Before that time, the company may ask the Commissioners to order the Revenue to notify the completion of its enquiry by a specified date. Such a direction will be given unless the Revenue can demonstrate that they have reasonable grounds for continuing the enquiry.

The company has 30 days from the end of an enquiry to amend its self assessment in accordance with the Revenue's conclusions. If the Revenue are not satisfied with the company's amendments, they have a further 30 days to amend the self assessment. The company then has another 30 days in which it may appeal against the Revenue's amendments.

1.5 Determinations and discovery assessments

If a return is not delivered by the filing date, the Revenue may issue a determination of the tax payable within the five years from the filing date. This is treated as a self assessment and there is no appeal against it. However, it is automatically replaced by any self assessment made by the company by the later of five years from the filing date and 12 months from the determination.

If the Revenue believe that not enough tax has been assessed for an accounting period they can make a discovery assessment to collect the extra tax. However, when a tax return has been delivered this power is limited as outlined below.

No discovery assessment can be made on account of an error or mistake as to the basis on which the tax liability ought to be computed, if the basis generally prevailing at the time when the return was made was applied.

A discovery assessment can only be made if either:

(a)   the loss of tax is due to fraudulent or negligent conduct by the company or by someone acting on its behalf; or

(b)   the Revenue could not reasonably be expected to have been aware of the loss of tax, given the information so far supplied to them, when their right to start an enquiry expired or when they notified the company that an enquiry had finished. The information supplied must be sufficiently detailed to draw the Revenue's attention to contentious matters such as the use of a valuation or estimate.

The time limit for raising a discovery assessment is six years from the end of the accounting period but this is extended to 21 years if there has been fraudulent or negligent conduct. The company may appeal against a discovery assessment within 30 days of issue.

1.6 Claims

Wherever possible claims must be made on a tax return or on an amendment to it and must be quantified at the time the return is made.

If a company believes that it has paid excessive tax because of an error in a return, an error or mistake claim may be made within six years from the end of the accounting period. An appeal against a decision on such a claim must be made within 30 days. An error or mistake claim may not be made if the return was made in accordance with a generally accepted practice which prevailed at the time.

Other claims must be made by six years after the end of the accounting period, unless a different time limit is specified. If an error or mistake is made in a claim, a supplementary claim may be made within the time limit for the original claim.

If the Revenue amend a self assessment or issue a discovery assessment then the company has a further period to make, vary or withdraw a claim (unless the claim is irrevocable) even if this is outside the normal time limit. The period is one year from the end of the accounting period in which the amendment or assessment was made, or one year from the end of the accounting period in which the enquiry was closed if the amendment is the result of an enquiry. The relief is limited where there has been fraudulent or negligent conduct by the company or its agent.

2 Payment of corporation tax and interest

FAST FORWARD
> In general, corporation tax is due nine months after the end of an accounting period but large companies must pay their corporation tax in four quarterly instalments.

2.1 Payment dates

Corporation tax is due for payment by small and medium sized companies **nine months after the end of the accounting period**.

Large companies, however, must pay their corporation tax in instalments. **Broadly, a large company is any company that pays corporation tax at the full rate** (profits exceed £1,500,000 where there are no associated companies).

Instalments are due on the 14th day of the month, starting in the seventh month. Provided that the accounting period is twelve months long subsequent instalments are due in the tenth month during the accounting period and in the first and fourth months after the end of the accounting period. If an accounting period is less than twelve months long subsequent instalments are due at three monthly intervals but with the final payment being due in the fourth month of the next accounting period.

2.2 Example

X Ltd is a large company with a 31 December accounting year end. Instalments of corporation tax will be due to be paid by X Ltd on:

- 14 July and 14 October in the accounting period;
- 14 January and 14 April after the accounting period ends.

Thus for the year ended 31 December 2005 instalment payments are due on 14 July 2005, 14 October 2005, 14 January 2006 and 14 April 2006.

Instalments are based on the estimated corporation tax liability for the current period (regardless of the liability in the previous period). This means that it will be extremely important for companies to forecast their tax liabilities accurately. Large companies whose directors are poor at estimating may find their company's incurring significant interest charges. The amount of each instalment is computed by:

(a)   working out $3 \times CT/n$ where CT is the amount of the estimated corporation tax liability payable in instalments for the period and n is the number of months in the period;

(b)   allocating the smaller of that amount and the total estimated corporation tax liability to the first instalment;

(c)   repeating the process for later instalments until the amount allocated is equal to the corporation tax liability. This gives four equal instalments for 12 month accounting periods and also caters for periods which end earlier than expected.

The company is therefore required to estimate its corporation tax liability before the end of the accounting period, and must revise its estimate each quarter.

Question   Short accounting period

A company has a CT liability of £880,000 for the eight month period to 30 September 2005. Accounts had previously always been prepared to 31 January. Show when the CT liability is due for payment.

Answer

£880,000 must be paid in instalments.

The amount of each instalment is $3 \times \dfrac{£880,000}{8} = £330,000$

The due dates are:

	£
14 August 2005	330,000
14 November 2005	330,000
14 January 2006	220,000 (balance)

A company is not required to pay instalments in the first year that it is 'large', unless its profits exceed £10 million. The £10 million limit is reduced proportionately if there are associated companies. For this purpose only, a company will be regarded as an associated company where it was an associated company at the START of an accounting period. (This differs from the normal approach in CT where being an associated company for any part of the AP affects the thresholds of both companies for the whole of the AP).

There is a de minimis limit in that any company whose liability does not exceed £10,000 need not pay by instalments.

Interest runs from the due date on over/underpaid instalments. The position is looked at cumulatively after the due date for each instalment. The Revenue calculate the interest position after the company submits its corporation tax return.

2.3 Example

X plc prepared accounts to 31 December 2005. The company has always prepared accounts to 31 December each year. It paid CT instalments of:

Date	Amount
	£
14.7.05	3.5m
14.10.05	8.5m
14.01.06	4.5m
14.4.06	4.5m
	21.0m

X plc's CT return showed a CT liability of £22m. The £1m balance was paid on 1.10.06. £22m should have been paid in instalments. The under(over) payments were:

Date	Paid	Correct	Under(over) paid
	£	£	£
14.7.05	3.5m	5.5m	2m
14.10.05	8.5m	5.5m	
	12.0m	11.0m	(1m)
14.1.06	4.5m	5.5m	
	16.5m	16.5m	–
14.4.06	4.5m	5.5m	
	21.0m	22.0m	1m

Interest would be charged (received) as follows.

14.7.05 – 13.10.05	Interest charged on £2m
14.10.05 – 13.1.06	Interest received on £1m
14.1.06 – 13.4.06	No interest
14.4.06 – 30.9.06	Interest charged on £1m

Interest paid/received on late payments or over payments of corporation tax is dealt with as investment income as interest paid/received on a nontrading loan relationship.

There are penalties if a company deliberately and flagrantly fails to pay instalments of sufficient size. After a company has filed its return or the Revenue has determined its liability, the Revenue may wish to establish the reason for inadequate instalment payments. It can do this by asking the company to produce relevant information or records (presumably to decide if a penalty applies). The failure to supply these will lead to an initial fixed penalty which may also be followed by a daily penalty which may continue until the information/records are produced.

Companies can have instalments repaid if they later conclude they ought not to have been paid.

Chapter roundup

- A company must notify the Revenue within 3 months of starting to trade.

- CT 600 returns must, in general, be filed within twelve months of the end of an accounting period.

- The Revenue can enquire into returns.

- In general, corporation tax is due nine months after the end of an accounting period but large companies must pay their corporation tax in four quarterly instalments.

Quick quiz

1   What are the fixed penalties for failure to deliver a corporation tax return on time?

2   What is the penalty if a company fails to keep records?

3   When must the Revenue give notice that it is going to start an enquiry if a return was filed on time?

4   State the due dates for the payment of quarterly instalments of corporation tax for a 12 month accounting period.

5   Which companies must pay quarterly instalments of their corporation tax liability?

Answers to quick quiz

1   There is a £100 penalty for failure to submit a return on time rising to £200 if the delay exceeds three months. These penalties increased to £500 and £1,000 respectively when a return was late for each of the preceding two accounting periods.

2   £3,000 for each accounting period affected.

3   Notice must be given by one year after the filing date.

4   14th day of:

    (a)   7th month in AP
    (b)   10th month in AP
    (c)   1st month after AP ends
    (d)   4th month after AP ends

5   'Large' companies ie: companies that pay corporation tax at the full rate.

Now try the questions below from the Exam Question Bank			
Number	**Level**	**Marks**	**Time**
Q12	Introductory	10	18 mins
Q29	Examination	30	54 mins

Value added tax 1

Introduction

In this and the next chapter, we study value added tax (VAT). VAT is a tax on turnover rather than on profits.

As the name of the tax suggests, it is charged (usually at 17.5%) on the value added. If someone in a chain of manufacture or distribution buys goods for £1,000 and sells them for £1,200 he has increased their value by £200. (He may have painted them, packed them or distributed them to shops to justify his mark-up, or he may simply be good at making deals to buy cheaply and sell dearly.) Because he has added value of £200, he collects VAT of £200 × 17.5% = £35 and pays this over to the government. The VAT is collected bit by bit along the chain and finally hits the consumer who does not add value, but uses up the goods.

VAT is a tax with simple computations but many detailed rules to ensure its enforcement. You may find it easier to absorb the detail if you ask yourself, in relation to each rule, exactly how it helps to enforce the tax.

1 Basic principles

VAT is charged on turnover at each stage in a production process, but in such a way that the burden is borne by the final consumer.

1.1 The nature of VAT

The legal basis of value added tax (VAT) is to be found in the Value Added Tax Act 1994 (VATA 1994), supplemented by regulations made by statutory instrument and amended by subsequent Finance Acts. VAT is administered by HM Revenue and Customs (HMRC). Previously there were two separate bodies called the Inland Revenue (responsible for direct taxes such as income tax and corporation tax) and HM Customs & Excise (responsible for indirect taxes such as VAT). In this chapter we will deal with matters which used to be dealt with by Customs and Excise and we may refer to HMRC as "Customs" in this context.

VAT is a tax on turnover, not on profits. The basic principle is that the VAT should be borne by the final consumer. Registered traders may deduct the tax which they suffer on supplies to them (input tax) from the tax which they charge to their customers (output tax) at the time this is paid to Customs. Thus, at each stage of the manufacturing or service process, the net VAT paid is on the value added at that stage.

1.2 Example: the VAT charge

A forester sells wood to a furniture maker for £100 plus VAT. The furniture maker uses this wood to make a table and sells the table to a shop for £150 plus VAT. The shop then sells the table to the final consumer for £300 plus VAT. VAT will be accounted for to Customs as follows.

	Cost	Input tax 17.5%	Net sale price	Output tax 17.5%	Payable to Customs
	£	£	£	£	£
Forester	0	0	100	17.50	17.50
Furniture maker	100	17.50	150	26.25	8.75
Shop	150	26.25	300	52.50	26.25
					52.50

Because the traders involved account to Customs for VAT charged less VAT suffered, their profits for income tax or corporation tax purposes are based on sales and purchases net of VAT.

2 The scope of VAT

VAT is chargeable on taxable supplies made by a taxable person. Supplies may be of goods or services.

2.1 Taxable supplies

VAT is charged on taxable supplies of goods and services made in the UK by a taxable person in the course or furtherance of any business carried on by him.

Key term

> A **taxable supply** is a supply of goods or services made in the UK, other than an exempt supply.

A taxable supply is either standard-rated or zero-rated. The standard rate is 17.5% (although on certain supplies, for example the supply of domestic fuel and power, a lower rate is charged of 5%) and zero-rated supplies are taxed at 0%. An exempt supply is not chargeable to VAT. The categories of zero-rated and exempt supplies are listed in the next chapter.

PROFESSIONAL EDUCATION

2.2 Supplies of goods

Goods are supplied if exclusive ownership of the goods passes to another person.

The following are treated as supplies of goods.

- The supply of any form of power, heat, refrigeration or ventilation, or of water
- The grant, assignment or surrender of a major interest (the freehold or a lease for over 21 years) in land
- Taking goods permanently out of the business for the non-business use of a taxable person or for other private purposes including the supply of goods by an employer to an employee for his private use
- Transfers under an agreement contemplating a transfer of ownership, such as a hire purchase agreement

Gifts of goods are normally treated as sales at cost (so VAT is due). **However, business gifts are not supplies of goods if**:

(a) **The total cost of gifts made to the same person does not exceed £50 in any 12 month period**. If the £50 limit is exceeded, output tax will be due in full on the total of gifts made. Once the limit has been exceeded a new £50 limit and new 12 month period begins.

(b) **The gift is a sample**. However, if two or more identical samples are given to the same person, all but one of them are treated as supplies.

2.3 Supplies of services

Apart from a few specific exceptions, **any supply which is not a supply of goods and which is done for consideration is a supply of services**. Consideration is any form of payment in money or in kind, including anything which is itself a supply.

A supply of services also takes place if:

- Goods are lent to someone for use outside the business
- Goods are hired to someone
- Services bought for business purposes are used for private purposes

The European Court of Justice has ruled that restaurants supply services rather than goods.

2.4 Taxable persons

The term 'person' includes individuals, partnerships (which are treated as single entities, ignoring the individual partners), **companies, clubs, associations and charities. If a person is in business making taxable supplies, then the value of these supplies is called the taxable turnover. If a person's taxable turnover exceeds certain limits then he is a taxable person and should be registered for VAT**.

3 Registration

FAST FORWARD

A trader becomes liable to register for VAT if the value of taxable supplies in any period up to 12 months exceeds £60,000 or if there are reasonable grounds for believing that the value of the taxable supplies will exceed £60,000 in the next 30 days. A trader may also register voluntarily.

3.1 Compulsory registration

At the end of every month a trader must calculate his cumulative turnover of taxable supplies to date. However this cumulative period does not extend beyond the previous 12 months. **The trader becomes liable to register for VAT if the value of his cumulative taxable supplies** (excluding VAT) **exceeds £60,000** (from 1 April 2005 onwards). The person is required to notify Customs within 30 days of the end of the month in which the £60,000 limit is exceeded. Customs will then register the person with effect from the end of the month following the month in which the £60,000 was exceeded, or from an earlier date if they and the trader agree.

Registration under this rule is not required if Customs are satisfied that the value of the trader's taxable supplies (excluding VAT) in the year then starting will not exceed £58,000 (from 1 April 2005 onwards).

A person is also liable to register at any time if there are reasonable grounds for believing that his taxable supplies (excluding VAT) in the following 30 days will exceed £60,000. Only taxable turnover of that 30 day period is considered **not** cumulative turnover. Customs must be notified by the end of the 30 day period and registration will be with effect from the beginning of that period.

When determining the value of a person's taxable supplies for the purposes of registration, supplies of goods and services that are *capital assets* of the business are to be disregarded, except for non zero-rated taxable supplies of interests in land.

Question	VAT registration

Fred started to trade in cutlery on 1 January 2005. Sales (excluding VAT) were £5,325 a month for the first nine months and £7,700 a month thereafter. From what date should Fred be registered for VAT?

Answer	

	£
Sales to 31 October 2005	55,625
Sales to 30 November 2005	63,325 (exceeds £60,000)

Fred must notify his liability to register by 30 December 2005 (not 31 December) and will be registered from 1 January 2006 or from an agreed earlier date.

When a person is liable to register in respect of a past period, it is his responsibility to pay VAT. If he is unable to collect it from those to whom he made taxable supplies, the VAT burden will fall on him. A person must start keeping VAT records and charging VAT to customers as soon as it is known that he is required to register. However, VAT should not be shown separately on any invoices until the registration number is known. The invoice should show the VAT inclusive price and customers should be informed that VAT invoices will be forwarded once the registration number is known. Formal VAT invoices should then be sent to such customers within 30 days of receiving the registration number.

Notification of liability to register must be made on form VAT 1. Simply writing to, or telephoning, a local VAT office is not enough. On registration the VAT office will send the trader a certificate of registration. This shows the VAT registration number, the date of registration, the end of the first VAT period and the length of later VAT periods.

If a trader makes a supply before becoming liable to register, but gets paid after registration, VAT is not due on that supply.

3.2 Voluntary registration

A person may decide to become registered even though his taxable turnover falls below the registration limit. Unless a person is registered he cannot recover the input tax he pays on purchases.

Voluntary registration is advantageous where a person wishes to recover input tax on purchases. For example, consider a trader who has one input during the year which cost £1,000 plus £175 VAT; he works on the input which becomes his sole output for the year and he decides to make a profit of £1,000.

(a)   If he is not registered he will charge £2,175 and his customer will obtain no relief for any VAT.

(b)   If he is registered he will charge £2,000 plus VAT of £350. His customer will have input tax of £350 which he will be able to recover if he, too, is registered.

If the customer is a non-taxable person he will prefer (a) as the cost to him is £2,175. If he is taxable he will prefer (b) as the net cost is £2,000. Thus, a decision whether or not to register voluntarily may depend upon the status of customers. It may also depend on the status of the outputs and the image of his business the trader wishes to project (registration may give the impression of a substantial business). The administrative burden of registration should also be considered.

3.3 Intending trader registration

Providing that a trader satisfies Customs that he is carrying on a business, and intends to make taxable supplies, he is entitled to be registered if he chooses. But, once registered, he is obliged to notify Customs within 30 days if he no longer intends to make taxable supplies.

3.4 Exemption from registration

If a person makes only zero-rated supplies, he may request exemption from registration. The trader is obliged to notify Customs of any material change in the nature of his supplies.

Customs may also allow exemption from registration if only a small proportion of supplies are standard-rated, provided that the trader would normally receive repayments of VAT if registered.

3.5 Deregistration

3.5.1 Voluntary deregistration

A person is eligible for voluntary deregistration if Customs are satisfied that the value of his taxable supplies (net of VAT and excluding supplies of capital assets) **in the following one year period will not exceed £58,000 (from 1 April 2005).** However, voluntary deregistration will not be allowed if the reason for the expected fall in value of taxable supplies is the cessation of taxable supplies or the suspension of taxable supplies for a period of 30 days or more in that following year.

Customs will cancel a person's registration from the date the request is made or from an agreed later date.

3.5.2 Compulsory deregistration

Traders may be compulsorily deregistered. Failure to notify a requirement to deregister within 30 days may lead to a penalty. Compulsory deregistration may also lead to Customs reclaiming input tax which has been wrongly recovered by the trader since the date on which he should have deregistered.

Other points to note are:

•   If Customs are misled into granting registration then the registration is treated as void from the start.

- A person may be compulsorily deregistered if Customs are satisfied that he is no longer making nor intending to make taxable supplies.

- Changes in legal status also require cancellation of registration. For example:

    (i)   A sole trader becoming a partnership
    (ii)   A partnership reverting to a sole trader
    (iii)   A business being incorporated
    (iv)   A company being replaced by an unincorporated business

3.5.3 The consequences of deregistration

On deregistration, VAT is chargeable on all stocks and capital assets in a business on which input tax was claimed, since the registered trader is in effect making a taxable supply to himself as a newly unregistered trader. If the VAT chargeable does not exceed £1,000, it need not be paid.

This special VAT charge does not apply if the business (or a separately viable part of it) **is sold as a going concern to another taxable person** (or a person who immediately becomes a taxable person as a result of the transfer). **Such transfers are outside the scope of VAT**.

If the original owner ceases to be taxable, the new owner of the business may also take over the existing VAT number. If he does so, he takes over the rights and liabilities of the transferor as at the date of transfer.

3.6 Pre-registration input tax

VAT incurred before registration can be treated as input tax and recovered from Customs subject to certain conditions.

If the claim is for input tax suffered on goods purchased prior to registration then the following conditions must be satisfied.

(a)   The goods were acquired for the purpose of the business which either was carried on or was to be carried on by him at the time of supply.

(b)   The goods have not been supplied onwards or consumed before the date of registration (although they may have been used to make other goods which are still held).

(c)   The VAT must have been incurred in the three years prior to the effective date of registration.

If the claim is for input tax suffered on the supply of services prior to registration then the following conditions must be satisfied.

(a)   The services were supplied for the purposes of a business which either was carried on or was to be carried on by him at the time of supply.

(b)   The services were supplied within the six months prior to the date of registration.

Input tax attributable to supplies made before registration is not deductible even if the input tax concerned is treated as having been incurred after registration.

4 Accounting for VAT

FAST FORWARD

VAT is accounted for on regular returns. Extensive records must be kept.

4.1 VAT periods

The VAT period (also known as the tax period) is the period covered by a VAT return. It is usually three calendar months. The return shows the total input and output tax for the tax period and must be submitted (along with any VAT due) within one month of the end of the period. (Businesses which pay VAT electronically automatically receive a seven day extension to this time limit.)

Customs allocate VAT periods according to the class of trade carried on (ending in June, September, December and March; July, October, January and April; or August, November, February and May), to spread the flow of VAT returns evenly over the year. When applying for registration a trader can ask for VAT periods which fit in with his own accounting year. It is also possible to have VAT periods to cover accounting systems not based on calendar months.

A registered person whose input tax will regularly exceed his output tax can elect for a one month VAT period, but will have to balance the inconvenience of making 12 returns a year against the advantage of obtaining more rapid repayments of VAT.

Certain small businesses may submit an annual VAT return (see the next chapter).

4.2 The tax point

FAST FORWARD

The tax point is the deemed date of supply. The basic tax point is the date on which goods are removed or made available to the customer, or the date on which services are completed. If a VAT invoice is issued or payment is received before the basic tax point, the earlier of these dates becomes the tax point. If the earlier date rule does not apply, and the VAT invoice is issued within 14 days of the basic tax point, the invoice date becomes the actual tax point.

The tax point of each supply is the deemed date of supply. The basic tax point is the date on which the goods are removed or made available to the customer, or the date on which services are completed.

The tax point determines the VAT period in which output tax must be accounted for and credit for input tax will be allowed. The tax point also determines which rate applies if the rate of VAT or a VAT category changes (for example when a supply ceases to be zero-rated and becomes standard-rated).

If a VAT invoice is issued or payment is received before the basic tax point, the earlier of these dates automatically becomes the tax point. If the earlier date rule does not apply and if the VAT invoice is issued within 14 days after the basic tax point, the invoice date becomes the tax point (although the trader can elect to use the basic tax point for all his supplies if he wishes). This 14 day period may be extended to accommodate, for example, monthly invoicing; the tax point is then the VAT invoice date or the end of the month, whichever is applied consistently.

Question
Tax point

Julia sells a sculpture to the value of £1,000 net of VAT. She receives a payment on account of £250 plus VAT on 25 March 2006. The sculpture is delivered on 28 April 2006. Julia's VAT returns are made up to calendar quarters. She issues an invoice on 4 May 2006.

Outline the tax point(s) and amount(s) due.

Answer

A separate tax point arises in respect of the £250 deposit and the £750 balance payable.

Julia should account for VAT as follows.

(a) *Deposit*

25 March 2006: tax at 17.5% × £250 = £43.75. This is accounted for in her VAT return to 31 March 2006. The charge arises on 25 March 2006 because payment is received before the basic tax point (which is 28 April 2006 – date of delivery).

(b) *Balance*

4 May 2006: tax at 17.5% £750 = £131.25. This is accounted for on the VAT return to 30 June 2006. The charge arises on 4 May because the invoice was issued within 14 days of the basic tax point of 28 April 2006 (delivery date).

Goods supplied on sale or return are treated as supplied on the earlier of adoption by the customer or 12 months after despatch.

Continuous supplies of services paid for periodically normally have tax points on the earlier of the receipt of each payment and the issue of each VAT invoice, unless one invoice covering several payments is issued in advance for up to a year. The tax point is then the earlier of each due date or date of actual payment. However, for connected businesses the tax point will be created periodically, in most cases based on 12 month periods.

4.3 The VAT return

The regular VAT return to Customs is made on form VAT 100. The boxes on a VAT return which a trader must fill in are as follows.

(a) Box 1: the VAT due on sales and other outputs

(b) Box 2: the VAT due on acquisitions from other EU member states

(c) Box 3: the total of boxes 1 and 2

(d) Box 4: the VAT reclaimed on purchases and other inputs

(e) Box 5: the net VAT to be paid or reclaimed: the difference between boxes 3 and 4

(f) Box 6: the total value (before cash discounts) of sales and all other outputs, excluding VAT but including the total in box 8

(g) Box 7: the total value (before cash discounts) of purchases and all other inputs, excluding VAT but including the total in box 9

(h) Box 8: the total value of all sales and related services to other EU member states

(i) Box 9: the total value of all purchases and related services from other EU member states

Input and output tax figures must be supported by the original or copy tax invoices, and records must be maintained for six years.

4.4 Internet filing of VAT returns

It is possible to file VAT returns electronically. The trader must enrol with Customs before using the service.

4.5 Substantial traders

If a trader does not make monthly returns, and the total VAT liability over 12 months to the end of a VAT period exceeds £2,000,000, he must make payments on account of each quarter's VAT liability during the quarter. Payments are due a month before the end of the quarter and at the end of the quarter, with the final payment due at the usual time, a month after the end of the quarter. An electronic payment system must be used, not a cheque through the post.

For a trader who exceeds the £2,000,000 limit in the 12 months to 30 September, 31 October or 30 November, the amount of each of the two payments on account is 1/24 of the total VAT liability of those 12 months. The obligation to pay on account starts with the first VAT period starting *after* 31 March.

Question | Payments on account

Large Ltd is liable to make payments on account calculated at £250,000 each for the quarter ended 31 December 2005.

What payments/repayment are due if Large Ltd's VAT liability for the quarter is calculated as:

(a)   £680,000
(b)   £480,000?

Answer

(a)   30 November 2005   – payment of £250,000
       31 December 2005   – payment of £250,000
       31 January 2006   – payment of £180,000 with submission of VAT return for quarter

(b)   30 November 2005   – payment of £250,000
       31 December 2005   – payment of £250,000
       31 January 2006   – on submission of return Customs will repay £20,000.

A trader who first exceeds the £2,000,000 limit in 12 months ending at some other time must pay 1/24 of the VAT liability for the first 12 months in which he exceeded the £2,000,000 limit. His obligation starts with the first VAT period which starts after those 12 months, unless he first went over the £2,000,000 limit in the 12 months to 31 December: in that case, his obligation starts with the VAT period starting on 1 April.

If the total VAT liability for any later 12 months is less than 80% of the total liability for the 12 months used to compute the payments on account, the trader can apply to use 1/24 of that smaller total. The smaller total can even be used if the 12 months have not ended, so long as Customs are satisfied that it will be below the 80% limit. A trader can leave the scheme if the latest 12 months' VAT liability was less than £1,600,000

If a trader's total annual liability increases to 120% or more of the amount used to calculate the payments on account, then the new higher annual liability is used to calculate new payments on account. The increase applies from the end of the 12 months with the new higher annual liability.

Once a trader is in the scheme, the payments on account are also recomputed annually, using the liability in the 12 months to 30 September, 31 October or 30 November, even if the change is less than ± 20%. The new figure first applies to the first VAT period starting after 31 March.

Traders can choose to switch from making quarterly to monthly returns instead of paying the interim amounts calculated by Customs. For example, the actual return and liability for January would be due at the end of February.

Traders can also choose to pay their actual monthly liability without having to make monthly returns. Customs can refuse to allow a trader to continue doing this if they find he has abused the facility by not paying enough. The trader will then either have to pay the interim amount or switch to making monthly returns.

A trader does have the right to appeal to a VAT tribunal if Customs refuse to allow him to make monthly payments of his actual liability.

4.6 Refunds of VAT

There is a three year time limit on the right to reclaim overpaid VAT. This time limit does not apply to input tax which a business could not have reclaimed earlier because the supplier only recently invoiced the VAT, even though it related to a purchase made some time ago. Nor does it apply to overpaid VAT penalties.

If a taxpayer has overpaid VAT and has overclaimed input tax by reason of the same mistake, Customs can set off any tax, penalty, interest or surcharge due to them against any repayment due to the taxpayer and repay only the net amount. In such cases the normal three year time limit for recovering VAT, penalties, interest, etc by assessment does not apply.

Customs can refuse to make any repayment which would unjustly enrich the claimant. They can also refuse a repayment of VAT where all or part of the tax has, for practical purposes, been borne by a person other than the taxpayer (eg by a customer of the taxpayer) except to the extent that the taxpayer can show loss or damage to any of his businesses as a result of mistaken assumptions about VAT.

5 VAT invoices and records

FAST FORWARD

A taxable person making a taxable supply to another registered person must supply a VAT invoice within 30 days.

A taxable person making a taxable supply to another person registered for VAT must supply a *VAT* invoice within 30 days of the time of supply, and must keep a copy. The invoice must show:

    (a)   The supplier's name, address and registration number.

    (b)   The date of issue, the tax point and an invoice number.

    (c)   The name and address of the customer.

    (d)   A description of the goods or services supplied, giving for each description the quantity, the unit price, the rate of VAT and the VAT exclusive amount.

    (e)   The rate of any cash discount.

    (f)   The total invoice price excluding VAT (with separate totals for zero-rated and exempt supplies).

    (g)   Each VAT rate applicable and the total amount of VAT.

If an invoice is issued, and a change in price then alters the VAT due, a credit note or debit note to adjust the VAT must be issued.

Credit notes must give the reason for the credit (such as 'returned goods'), and the number and date of the original VAT invoice. If a credit note makes no VAT adjustment, it should state this.

A less detailed VAT invoice may be issued by a retailer where the invoice is for a total including VAT of up to £250 and the supply is not to another EU member state. Such an invoice must show:

    (a)   The supplier's name, address and registration number

    (b)   The date of the supply

    (c)   A description of the goods or services supplied

    (d)   The rate of VAT chargeable

    (e)   The total amount chargeable including VAT

Zero-rated and exempt supplies must not be included in less detailed invoices.

VAT invoices are not required for payments of up to £25 including VAT which are for telephone calls or car park fees or are made through cash operated machines. In such cases, input tax can be claimed without a VAT invoice.

Every VAT registered trader must keep records for six years, although Customs may sometimes grant permission for their earlier destruction. They may be kept on paper, on microfilm or microfiche or on computer. However, there must be adequate facilities for Customs to inspect records.

All records must be kept up to date and in a way which allows:

- The calculation of VAT due
- Officers of Customs to check the figures on VAT returns

The following records are needed.

- Copies of VAT invoices, credit notes and debit notes issued
- A summary of supplies made
- VAT invoices, credit notes and debit notes received
- A summary of supplies received
- Records of goods received from and sent to other EU member states
- Documents relating to imports from and exports to countries outside the EU
- A VAT account
- Order and delivery notes, correspondence, appointment books, job books, purchases and sales books, cash books, account books, records of takings (such as till rolls), bank paying-in slips, bank statements and annual accounts
- Records of zero-rated and exempt supplies, gifts or loans of goods, taxable self-supplies and any goods taken for non-business use

6 The valuation of supplies

FAST FORWARD

In order to ascertain the amount of VAT on a supply, the supply must be valued. If a discount is offered for prompt payment, VAT is chargeable on the net amount even if the discount is not taken up.

6.1 Value of supply

The value of a supply is the VAT-exclusive price on which VAT is charged. The consideration for a supply is the amount paid in money or money's worth. Thus with a standard rate of 17.5%:

Value + VAT = consideration
£100 + £17.50 = £117.50

The VAT proportion of the consideration is known as the 'VAT fraction'. It is

$$\frac{\text{rate of tax}}{100 + \text{rate of tax}} = \frac{17.5}{100 + 17.5} = \frac{7}{47}$$

Provided the consideration for a bargain made at arm's length is paid in money, the value for VAT purposes is the VAT exclusive price charged by the trader. If it is paid in something other than money, as in a barter of some goods or services for others, it must be valued and VAT will be due on the value.

If the price of goods is effectively reduced with money off coupons, the value of the supply is the amount actually received by the taxpayer.

6.2 Mixed supplies and composite supplies

Different goods and services are sometimes invoiced together at an inclusive price (a mixed supply). Some items may be chargeable at the standard rate and some at the zero-rate. **The supplier must account for VAT separately on the standard rated and zero rated elements by splitting the total amount payable in a fair proportion between the different elements and charging VAT on each at the appropriate rate.** There is no single way of doing this: one method is to split the amount according to the cost to the supplier of each element, and another is to use the open market value of each element. Mixed supplies are also known as "multiple supplies".

If a supply cannot be split into components, there is a composite supply, to which one VAT rate must be applied. The rate depends on the nature of the supply as a whole. Composite supplies are also known as "compound supplies".

A supply of air transport including an in-flight meal has been held to be a single, composite supply of transport (zero-rated) rather than a supply of transport (zero-rated) and a supply of a meal (standard-rated). Contrast this with where catering is included in the price of leisure travel – there are two separate supplies: standard-rated catering and zero-rated passenger transport.

Broadly, a composite supply occurs when one element of the supply is merely incidental to the main element. A mixed supply occurs where different elements of the supply are the subject of separate negotiation and customer choice giving rise to identifiable obligations on the supplier.

6.3 Discounts

Where a discount is offered for prompt payment, VAT is chargeable on the net amount, regardless of whether the discount is taken up. Supplies of retailer vouchers made on contingent discount terms (for example depending on the level of purchases) must be invoiced with VAT based on the full amount, an adjustment being made when the discount is earned. When goods are sold to staff at a discount, VAT is only due on the discounted price.

Generally, the sale of a voucher is VAT free. However, intermediate suppliers of retailer vouchers (ie vouchers for which the seller provides the redemption goods or services), must account for VAT on the purchase and sale of vouchers. Input tax is recoverable by the purchaser. There are additional rules affecting vouchers sold as part of a package of goods for which the price would not be reduced if the vouchers were excluded. These rules aim to prevent the deferral of VAT on sales of vouchers until they are redeemed.

6.4 Miscellaneous

For goods supplied under a hire purchase agreement VAT is chargeable on the cash selling price at the start of the contract.

If a trader charges different prices to customers paying with credit cards and those paying by other means, the VAT due in respect of each standard-rated sale is the full amount paid by the customer × the VAT fraction.

When goods are permanently taken from a business for non-business purposes VAT must be accounted for on their market value. Where business goods are put to a private or non-business use, the value of the resulting supply of services is the cost to the taxable person of providing the services. If services bought for business purposes are used for non-business purposes (without charge), then VAT must be accounted for on their cost, but the VAT to be accounted for is not allowed to exceed the input tax deductible on the purchase of the services.

7 Administration

VAT is administered by HMRC, and the RCPO hears appeals.

7.1 HM Revenue and Customs

The administration of VAT is now dealt with by the new joint body known as HM Revenue and Customs (HMRC).

7.2 Local offices

Local offices are responsible for the local administration of VAT and for providing advice to registered persons whose principal place of business is in their area. They are controlled by regional collectors.

Completed VAT returns should be sent to the VAT Central Unit at Southend, not to a local office.

From time to time a registered person will be visited by staff from a local office (a control visit) to ensure that the law is understood and is being applied properly. If a trader disagrees with any decision as to the application of VAT given by HMRC he can ask his local office to reconsider the decision. It is not necessary to appeal formally while a case is being reviewed in this way. Where an appeal can be settled by agreement, a written settlement has the same force as a decision by the Revenue and Customs Prosecution Office.

Customs may issue assessments of VAT due to the best of their judgement if they believe that a trader has failed to make returns or if they believe those returns to be incorrect or incomplete. The time limit for making assessments is normally three years after the end of a VAT period, but this is extended to 20 years in the case of fraud, dishonest conduct, certain registration irregularities and the unauthorised issue of VAT invoices.

Customs sometimes write to traders, setting out their calculations, before issuing assessments. The traders can then query the calculations.

7.3 Appeals

The Revenue and Customs Prosecutions office (RCPO) is independent of HMRC and provides a method of dealing with disputes. Provided that VAT returns and payments shown thereon have been made, appeals can be heard.

The RCPO can waive the requirement to pay all VAT shown on returns before an appeal is heard in cases of hardship. It cannot allow an appeal against a purely administrative matter such as Customs refusal to apply an extra statutory concession.

There may be a dispute over the deductibility of input tax which hinges on the purposes for which goods or services were used, or on whether they were used to make taxable supplies. The trader must show that Customs acted unreasonably in refusing a deduction, if the goods or services are luxuries, amusements or entertainment.

7.4 Time limits

An appeal must be lodged with the RCPO (not the local office) within 30 days of the date of any decision by Customs. If, instead, the trader would like the local office to reconsider the decision he should apply within 30 days of the decision to the relevant office. The local VAT office may either:

- Confirm the original decision, in which case the taxpayer has a further 21 days from the date of that confirmation in which to lodge an appeal with the RCPO, or

- Send a revised decision, in which case the taxpayer will have a further 30 days from the date of the revised decision in which to lodge an appeal with the RCPO.

If one of the parties is dissatisfied with a decision on a point of law he may appeal to the courts. The RCPO may award costs.

7.5 The Adjudicator

The Adjudicator for the HMRC is independent of these bodies. The Adjudicator considers complaints about the way in which taxpayers' affairs are handled, for example complaints about delays or the exercise of officials' discretion. The Adjudicator does not consider complaints where there are alternative channels of appeal, such as exist for appeals against assessments.

7.6 Tax avoidance and evasion

Significant resources are deployed to tackle fraud, tax evasion and avoidance.

Avoidance is also countered by the requirement for traders to disclose to Customs any use of a notifiable VAT avoidance scheme (see later in this text).

8 Penalties

8.1 The default surcharge

FAST FORWARD

A default occurs when a trader either submits his VAT return late, or submits the return on time but pays the VAT late. A default surcharge is applied if there is a default during a default surcharge period.

A default occurs when a trader either submits his VAT return late, or submits the return on time but pays the VAT late. It also occurs when a payment on account from a substantial trader is late. **If a trader defaults, Customs will serve a surcharge liability notice on the trader. The notice specifies a surcharge period running from the date of the notice to the anniversary of the end of the period for which the trader is in default.**

If a further default occurs in respect of a return period ending during the specified surcharge period the original surcharge period will be extended to the anniversary of the end of the period to which the new default relates. In addition, if the default involves the late payment of VAT (as opposed to simply a late return) **a surcharge is levied.**

The surcharge depends on the number of defaults involving late payment of VAT which have occurred in respect of periods ending in the surcharge period, as follows.

Default involving late payment of VAT in the surcharge period	Surcharge as a percentage of the VAT outstanding at the due date
First	2%
Second	5%
Third	10%
Fourth or more	15%

Surcharges at the 2% and 5% rates are not normally demanded unless the amount due would be at least £400 but for surcharges calculated using the 10% or 15% rates there is a minimum amount of £30 payable.

If a substantial trader is late with more than one payment (on account or final) for a return period, this only counts as one default. The total VAT paid late is the total of late payments on account plus the late final payment.

Question   Default surcharge

Peter Popper has an annual turnover of around £300,000. His VAT return for the quarter to 31.12.05 is late. He then submits returns for the quarters to 30.9.06 and 31.3.07 late as well as making late payment of the tax due of £12,000 and £500 respectively.

Peter's VAT return to 31.3.08 is also late and the VAT due of £1,100 is also paid late. All other VAT returns and VAT payments are made on time. Outline Peter Popper's exposure to default surcharge.

Answer

A surcharge liability notice will be issued after the late filing on the 31.12.05 return outlining a surcharge period extending to 31.12.06.

The late 30.9.06 return is in the surcharge period so the period is extended to 30.9.07. The late VAT payment triggers a 2% penalty. 2% × £12,000 = £240. Since £240 is less than the £400 de minimis limit it is not collected by Customs.

The late 31.3.07 return is in the surcharge period so the period is now extended to 31.3.08. The late payment triggers a 5% penalty. 5% × £500 = £25. Since £25 is less than the £400 de minimis limit it is not collected by Customs.

The late 31.03.08 return is in the surcharge period. The period is extended to 31.03.09. The late payment triggers a 10% penalty 10% × £1,100 = £110. This is collected by Customs since the £400 de minimis does not apply to penalties calculated at the 10% (and 15%) rate.

Peter will have to submit all four quarterly VAT returns to 31.3.09 on time and pay the VAT on time to 'escape' the default surcharge regime.

A trader must submit one year's returns on time and pay the VAT shown on them on time in order to break out of the surcharge liability period and the escalation of surcharge percentages.

A default will be ignored for all default surcharge purposes if the trader can show that the return or payment was sent at such a time, and in such a manner, that it was reasonable to expect that Customs would receive it by the due date. Posting the return and payment first class the day before the due date is generally accepted as meeting this requirement. A default will also be ignored if the trader can demonstrate a reasonable excuse (see above) for the late submission or payment.

The application of the default surcharge regime to small businesses is modified. **A small business is one with a turnover below £150,000**. When a small business is late submitting a VAT return or paying VAT it will receive a letter from Customs offering help. No penalty will be charged. Four such letters will be issued without penalty. However, on the issue of a fifth letter a 10% penalty will apply which increases to 15% on the issue of a sixth or subsequent letter.

8.2 The misdeclaration penalty: very large errors

The making of a return which understates a person's true liability or overstates the repayment due to him incurs a penalty of 15% of the VAT which would have been lost if the return had been accepted as correct. The same penalty applies when Customs issue an assessment which is too low and the trader fails to notify the error within 30 days from the issue of the assessment.

These penalties apply only where the VAT which would have been lost equals or exceeds the lower of

(a)   **£1,000,000 or**

(b)   **30% of the sum of the true input tax and the true output tax**. This sum is known as the gross amount of tax (GAT). In the case of an incorrect assessment 30% of the true amount of tax (TAT), the VAT actually due from the trader, is used instead of 30% of the GAT.

The penalty may be mitigated.

Question   Misdeclaration penalty - GAT

A trader declares output tax of £100,000 and claims input tax of £30,000 on the VAT return for the quarter ended 31 March 2006. It is subsequently discovered that output tax is understated by £28,000.

Does a misdeclaration penalty arise?

Answer

The test for misdeclaration penalty is the lower of:

- 30% of GAT (Gross Amount of Tax)
  30% × £(100,000 + 28,000 + 30,000)
  = £47,400

- £1,000,000

ie £47,400

Since the error of £28,000 is less than £47,400 the error is not 'large' and hence no penalty arises.

Question   Misdeclaration penalty - TAT

A trader fails to submit a VAT return for the quarter to 30 June 2005. On 31 August 2005 Customs issue an assessment showing VAT due of £200,000.

The true VAT liability for the quarter is:

	£
Output tax	370,000
Input tax	(80,000)
Net VAT due	290,000

The trader pays the £200,000 of VAT assessed but does not bring the correct position to Customs' attention.

The true position is discovered during a control visit in December 2006.

Will a misdeclaration penalty apply?

Answer

The under-assessment of £90,000 will attract a penalty if it exceeds the lower of:

- 30% of TAT (True Amount of Tax)
  30% × £290,000
  = £87,000

- £1,000,000

ie £87,000.

The £90,000 under-assessment exceeds £87,000, thus a misdeclaration penalty will be charged at £90,000 × 15% = £13,500.

The trader will have to pay the additional £90,000 due as well as the £13,500 penalty.

Errors on a VAT return of up to £2,000 (net: underdeclaration minus overdeclaration) may be corrected on the next return without giving rise to a misdeclaration penalty or interest (see below for details on interest).

This penalty does not apply if the trader can show reasonable excuse (see above) for his conduct, or if he made a full disclosure when he had no reason to suppose that Customs were enquiring into his affairs.

If his conduct leads to a conviction for fraud, or to a penalty for conduct involving dishonesty, it cannot also lead to a misdeclaration penalty.

8.3 Default interest

Interest (not deductible in computing taxable profits) **is charged on VAT which is the subject of an assessment** (where returns were not made or were incorrect), **or which could have been the subject of an assessment but was paid before the assessment was raised. It runs from the reckonable date until the date of payment.** This interest is sometimes called 'default interest'.

The reckonable date is when the VAT should have been paid (one month from the end of the return period), or in the case of VAT repayments, seven days from the issue of the repayment order. However, where VAT is charged by an assessment, interest does not run from more than three years before the date of the assessment; and where the VAT was paid before an assessment was raised, interest does not run for more than three years before the date of payment.

In practice, interest is only charged when there would otherwise be a loss to the Exchequer. It is not, for example, charged when a company failed to charge VAT but if it had done so another company would have been able to recover the VAT.

8.4 Repayment supplement

Where a person is entitled to a repayment of VAT and the original return was rendered on time but Customs do not issue a written instruction for the repayment to be made within 30 days of the receipt of the return, then the person will receive a supplement of the greater of £50 and 5% of the amount due.

If the return states a refund due which differs from the correct refund due by more than the greater of 5% of the correct refund and £250, no supplement is added.

Days spent in raising and answering reasonable enquiries in relation to the return do not count towards the 30 days allowed to Customs to issue an instruction to make the repayment. The earliest date on which the 30 days can start is the day following the end of the prescribed accounting period.

8.5 Interest on overpayments due to official errors

If VAT is overpaid or a credit for input tax is not claimed because of an error by Customs, then the trader may claim interest on the amount eventually refunded, running from the date on which he paid the excessive VAT (or from the date on which Customs might reasonably be expected to have authorised a VAT repayment) **to the date on which Customs authorise a repayment.**

Interest must be claimed within three years of the date on which the trader discovered the error or could with reasonable diligence have discovered it. Interest is not available where a repayment supplement is available. Interest does not run for periods relating to reasonable enquiries by Customs into the matter in question.

Chapter roundup

- VAT is charged on turnover at each stage in a production process, but in such a way that the burden is borne by the final consumer.

- VAT is chargeable on taxable supplies made by a taxable person. Supplies may be of goods or services.

- A trader becomes liable to register for VAT if the value of taxable supplies in any period up to 12 months exceeds £60,000 or if there are reasonable grounds for believing that the value of the taxable supplies will exceed £60,000 in the next 30 days. A trader may also register voluntarily.

- VAT is accounted for on regular returns. Extensive records must be kept.

- The tax point is the deemed date of supply. The basic tax point is the date on which goods are removed or made available to the customer, or the date on which services are completed. If a VAT invoice is issued or payment is received before the basic tax point, the earlier of these dates becomes the tax point. If the earlier date rule does not apply, and the VAT invoice is issued within 14 days of the basic tax point, the invoice date becomes the actual tax point.

- A taxable person making a taxable supply to another registered person must supply a VAT invoice within 30 days.

- In order to ascertain the amount of VAT on a supply, the supply must be valued. If a discount is offered for prompt payment, VAT is chargeable on the net amount even if the discount is not taken up.

- VAT is administered by HMRC, and the RCPO hears appeals.

- A default occurs when a trader either submits his VAT return late, or submits the return on time but pays the VAT late. A default surcharge is applied if there is a default during a default surcharge period.

Quick quiz

1   On what transactions will VAT be charged?
2   What is a taxable person?
3   When may a taxable person be exempt from registration?
4   When may a person choose to be deregistered?
5   What is the time limit in respect of claiming pre-registration input tax on goods?
6   Within what time limit must an appeal to a tribunal be lodged?
7   What is a default?

Answers to quick quiz

1. VAT is charged on taxable supplies of goods and services made in the UK by a taxable person in the course or furtherance of any business carried on by him.

2. Any 'person' whose taxable turnover exceeds the registration limit. The term 'person' includes individuals, partnerships, companies, clubs, associations and charities.

3. If a taxable person makes only zero-rated supplies he may request exemption from registration.

4. A person is eligible for voluntary deregistration if Customs are satisfied that the value of his taxable supplies in the following year will not exceed £58,000.

5. The VAT must have been incurred in the three years prior to the effective date of registration.

6. Within 30 days of the date of the decision by Customs.

7. A default occurs when a trader either submits his VAT return late or submits the return on time but pays the VAT late.

Now try the question below from the Exam Question Bank

Number	Level	Marks	Time
Q13	Examination	15	27 mins

11

Value added tax 2

Topic list	Syllabus references
1 Zero-rated and exempt supplies	1(i), 2(e)
2 The deduction of input tax	1(i), 2(e)
3 Special schemes	1(i), 2(e)

Introduction

This chapter concentrates on matters which do not apply to every trader. We start this chapter by looking at zero-rated and exempt supplies.

Finally, we look at three special VAT schemes.

1 Zero-rated and exempt supplies

Some supplies are taxable (either standard-rated, reduced-rated or zero-rated). Others are exempt.

1.1 Types of supply

Zero-rated supplies are taxable at 0%. A taxable supplier whose outputs are zero-rated but whose inputs are standard-rated will obtain repayments of the VAT paid on purchases.

Exempt supplies are not so advantageous. In exactly the same way as for a non-registered person, a **person making exempt supplies is unable to recover VAT on inputs**.

The exempt supplier thus has to shoulder the burden of VAT. Of course, he may increase his prices to pass on the charge, but he cannot issue a VAT invoice which would enable a taxable customer to obtain a credit for VAT, since no VAT is chargeable on his supplies.

1.2 Example: standard-rated, zero-rated and exempt supplies

Here are figures for three traders, the first with standard-rated outputs, the second with zero-rated outputs and the third with exempt outputs. All their inputs are standard-rated.

	Standard-rated £	Zero-rated £	Exempt £
Inputs	20,000	20,000	20,000
VAT	3,500	3,500	3,500
	23,500	23,500	23,500
Outputs	30,000	30,000	30,000
VAT	5,250	0	0
	35,250	30,000	30,000
Pay/(reclaim)	1,750	(3,500)	0
Net profit	10,000	10,000	6,500

VAT legislation lists zero-rated, lower rate and exempt supplies. There is no list of standard-rated supplies.

If a trader makes a supply you need to categorise that supply for VAT as follows:

Step 1 Look at the zero-rated list to see if it is zero-rated. If not:

Step 2 Look at the exempt list to see if it is exempt. If not:

Step 3 Look at the lower rate list to see if the reduced rate of VAT applies. If not:

Step 4 The supply is standard rated.

1.3 Zero-rated supplies

The following are items on the **zero-rated list**.

    (a) Human and animal food

    (b) Sewerage services and water

    (c) Printed matter used for reading (eg books, newspapers)

    (d) Construction work on new homes or the sale of the freehold of (or a lease over 21 years (at least 20 years in Scotland) of) new homes by builders

    (e) Sales of substantially reconstructed listed buildings, and alterations to such buildings, where such buildings are to be used for residential or charitable purposes

(f) Services relating to ships and aircraft, and the transport of goods and passengers

(g) The hire or sale of houseboats and caravans used as homes

(h) Gold supplied between central banks and members of the London Gold market

(i) Bank notes

(j) Drugs and medicines on prescription or provided in private hospitals

(k) Exports of goods to outside the EU

(l) Specialised equipment used by rescue/first aid services.

(m) Sales or hire by a charity

(n) Clothing and footwear for young children and certain protective clothing eg motor cyclists' crash helmets

(o) Certain supplies (eg advertising services) to charitable institutions

1.4 Exempt supplies

The following are items on the **exempt** list.

(a) Sales of freeholds of buildings (other than commercial buildings within three years from completion) and leaseholds of land and buildings of any age including a surrender of a lease.

(b) Financial services

(c) Insurance

(d) Postal services provided by the Post Office

(e) Betting and gaming

(f) Certain education and vocational training

(g) Health services

(h) Burial and cremation services

(i) Supplies to members by trade unions and professional bodies if in consideration only for a membership subscription

(j) Entry fees to non-profit making sports competitions

(k) Disposals of works of art and other items to public bodies in lieu of capital taxes

(l) Welfare services supplied by charities

(m) Supplies by charities, philanthropic bodies, trade unions, professional associations and non-profit making sports bodies in connection with fund raising events

(n) Residential care services

(o) Admission charges to certain cultural events or places

(p) Supplies of training, retraining and work experience paid for using further education funding council funds

(q) Investment gold

(r) The supply of goods on which input tax was irrecoverable on purchase

1.5 Lower rate of VAT

Certain supplies are charged at **5%. The supplies are still taxable supplies**.

The main supplies are:

- supplies of fuel for domestic use;

- supplies of the services of installing energy saving materials to homes;

- supplies of installing central heating or security equipment in the homes of people over the age of 60.

Note that energy saving materials themselves are standard-rated – if you pay someone to install them for you, they will recover 17.5% input tax on the purchase of the materials, and charge you 5% output tax on a composite supply of the fitting work.

The 5% rate also applies to a range of building work (which would not qualify for zero-rating or exemption), including:

- renovation of dwellings which have been empty for at least 3 years;
- conversion of residential property into a different number of dwellings;
- conversion of a non-residential property into a dwelling or a number of dwellings;
- conversion of a dwelling into a care home or into a house in multiple occupation.

1.6 Exceptions to the general rule

The zero-rated, exempt and lower rate lists outline general categories of goods or services which are either zero-rated or exempt or charged at a lower rate of 5%. However, the VAT legislation then goes into great detail to outline exceptions to the general rule.

For example the zero-rated list states human food is zero-rated. However, the legislation then states that food supplied in the course of catering (eg restaurant meals, hot takeaways) is not zero-rated. Luxury items of food (eg crisps, peanuts, chocolate covered biscuits) are also not zero-rated.

In the exempt list we are told that financial services are exempt. However the legislation then goes on to state that credit management and processing services are not exempt. Investment advice is also not exempt.

Thus great care must be taken when categorising goods or services as zero-rated, exempt or standard-rated. It is not as straightforward as it may first appear.

1.7 Standard-rated supplies

As mentioned previously, there is no list of standard-rated supplies. If a supply is not zero-rated and is not exempt then it is treated as standard-rated. Standard-rated supplies normally have a 17.5% VAT charge.

1.8 Land and buildings

The construction of new dwellings or buildings to be used for residential or charitable purposes is zero-rated. The sale of new residential accommodation created by the conversion of non-residential buildings is also zero-rated when sold by the person who does the converting (The conversion work itself is standard-rated unless the reduced rate applies). Zero-rating extends to the construction of homes for children, the elderly, students and the armed forces, but not to hospitals, prisons or hotels, to which the standard-rate applies. The sale of the freehold of a 'new' commercial building is standard-rated. The definition of 'new' is less than three years old. The construction of commercial buildings is also standard-rated.

Other sales and also grants, variations and surrenders of leases (including reverse surrenders, when the tenant pays the landlord) are exempt. The provision of holiday accommodation is standard-rated.

2 The deduction of input tax

2.1 Input tax recovery

Not all input VAT is deductible, eg VAT on most motor cars.

For input tax to be deductible, the payer must be a taxable person, with the supply being to him in the course of his business. In addition a VAT invoice must be held (except for payments of up to £25 including VAT which are for telephone calls or car park fees or which are made through cash operated machines).

Input tax recovery can be denied to any business that does not hold a valid VAT invoice and cannot provide alternative evidence to prove the supply took place.

In addition, for businesses that operate in trade sectors dealing in computers, telephones, alcohol products and oils used as road fuel, Customs expect to see evidence of the bona fide nature of the transaction where there is no valid VAT invoice.

2.2 Capital items

The distinction between capital and revenue which is important in other areas of tax **does not apply to VAT**. Thus a manufacturer buying plant subject to VAT will be able to obtain a credit for all the VAT immediately. The plant must of course be used to make taxable supplies, and if it is only partly so used only part of the VAT can be reclaimed. Conversely, if plant is sold secondhand then VAT should be charged on the sale and is output tax in the normal way.

2.3 Non-deductible input tax

The following input tax is not deductible even for a taxable person with taxable outputs.

(a) **VAT on motor cars** not used wholly for business purposes. VAT on cars is never reclaimable unless the car is acquired new for resale or is acquired for use in or leasing to a taxi business, a self-drive car hire business or a driving school. Private use by a proprietor **or an employee** is non-business use (regardless of any charge under the benefits code) unless the user pays a full commercial hire charge (not just a reimbursement of costs). However, VAT on accessories such as car radios is deductible if ordered on a separate purchase order and fitted after delivery of the car. The VAT charged when a car is hired for business purposes is reclaimable, but if there is some non-business use and the hire company has reclaimed VAT on the original purchase of the car, only 50% of the VAT on hire charges can be reclaimed by the hirer. A hiring for five days or less is assumed to be for wholly business use.

VAT need not be charged on the sale of a used car except on any profit element (which, of course, is rare), unless input tax on the original purchase of the car was recoverable.

(b) **VAT on business entertaining** where the cost of the entertaining is not a tax deductible trading expense. If the items bought are used partly for such entertaining and partly for other purposes, the proportion of the VAT relating to the entertainment is non-deductible.

In *Ernst & Young v CCE* the Tribunal held that staff entertaining was wholly for business purposes and a full input tax recovery was allowed. Customs accept this decision in respect of staff entertainment but maintain that following the case *KPMG v CCE* input tax on entertaining guests at a staff party is non-deductible.

(c) **VAT on expenses incurred on domestic accommodation for directors;**

(d) **VAT on non-business items passed through the business accounts.** However, when goods are bought partly for business use, the purchaser may:

(i) Deduct all the input tax, and account for output tax in respect of the private use, or
(ii) Deduct only the business proportion of the input tax.

Where services are bought partly for business use, only method (ii) may be used. If services are initially bought for business use but the use then changes, a fair proportion of the input tax (relating to the private use) is reclaimed by Customs by making the trader account for output tax.

A business that provides employees with mobile phones for business use can, regardless of any private use, deduct all the VAT incurred on purchase and on standing charges provided the charges do not contain any element for calls.

If a business allows its employees to make private calls without charge, then it must apportion the VAT incurred on the call charges. Any method of apportionment may be used, eg a sample of bills over a reasonable time, providing the method produces a fair and reasonable result. Apportionment must be made where the phone package allows the business to make a certain volume of calls for a fixed monthly payment and there is no standing payment, or where the contract is for the purchase of the phone and the advance payment of a set amount of call time for a single charge.

If a business imposes clear rules prohibiting private calls, and enforces them, Customs allow a deduction of all of the VAT incurred on the call charges. Similarly, if a business tolerates only a small amount of calls, Customs allow all of the input tax incurred to be deducted.

(e) **VAT which does not relate to the** making of supplies by the buyer in the course of a **business**.

2.4 Irrecoverable VAT

Where all (as with many cars) or some (as with partially exempt traders) of the input tax on a purchase is not deductible, the **non-deductible VAT is included in the cost for income tax, corporation tax, capital allowance or capital gains purposes. Deductible VAT is omitted from costs, so that only net amounts are included in accounts. Similarly, sales** (and proceeds in chargeable gains computations) **are shown net of VAT**, because the VAT is paid over to Customs.

2.5 Motoring expenses

2.5.1 Cars

The VAT incurred on the purchase of a car not used wholly for business purposes is not recoverable (except as in Paragraph 2.2(a) above). If accessories are fitted after the original purchase and a separate invoice is raised then the VAT on the accessories can be treated as input tax so long as the accessories are for business use.

If a car is used wholly for business purposes (including leasing, so long as the charges are at the open market rate), the input tax is recoverable but the buyer must account for VAT when he sells the car. **If a car is leased, the lessor recovered the input tax when the car was purchased and the lessee makes some private use of the car** (for example private use by employees)**, the lessee can only recover 50% of the input tax on the lease charges.**

If a car is used for business purposes then any VAT charged on repair and maintenance costs can be treated as input tax. No apportionment has to be made for private use.

If an employee accepts a reduced salary in exchange for being allowed to use his employer's car privately, or pays his employer for that use, there is no supply, so VAT is not due on the salary reduction. However, VAT is due on charges for running costs. VAT is also due on charges for employee use in the rare cases where the charge is a full commercial rate so that the employer has recovered input tax on the cost or on leasing charges in full.

2.5.2 Fuel for business use

The VAT incurred on fuel used for business purposes is fully deductible as input tax. If the fuel is bought by employees who are reimbursed for the actual cost or by a mileage allowance, the employer may deduct the input tax.

2.5.3 Fuel for private use

If fuel is supplied for private purposes all input VAT incurred on the fuel is allowed but the business must account for output VAT using a set of scale charges.

When fuel is supplied for an individual's private use at less than the cost of that fuel to the business, all input tax incurred on the fuel is allowed, but the business must account for output tax using set scale charges per VAT return period, based on the cylinder capacity of the car's engine. The scale figures will be stated in the exam if required. However, take care to note whether the examiner has given you the VAT inclusive or the VAT exclusive scale figure. The VAT inclusive scale charges are reproduced in the tax rates and allowances tables in this text. The output tax is the VAT inclusive scale charge × 7/47 or the VAT exclusive scale charge × 17.5%.

If the employee has to pay the full cost of fuel (or more than its cost) to the employer, the employer must account for VAT on the amount paid, rather than on the scale charge.

Question	VAT and private use fuel

Iain is an employee of ABC Ltd. He has the use of a 1000 cc car for one month and an 1800 cc car for two months during the quarter ended 31 March 2006.

ABC Ltd pay all the petrol costs in respect of both cars without requiring Iain to make any reimbursement in respect of private fuel. Total petrol costs for the quarter amount to £300 (including VAT).

What is the VAT effect of the above on ABC Ltd?

VAT Scale rates (VAT inclusive)

	Quarterly	
	Petrol	Diesel
	£	£
Up to 1400cc	246	236
1401 to 2000cc	311	236
Over 2000cc	457	300

Answer

Value for the quarter:

	£
Car 1	
Up to 1400 cc £246 × 1/3 =	82.00
Car 2	
1401-2000 cc £311 × 2/3 =	207.33
	289.33
Output tax:	
7/47 × £289	£43.04
Input tax	
7/47 × £300	£44.68

2.6 Relief for bad debts

FAST FORWARD

Relief for VAT on bad debts is available if the debt is over six months old (measured from when the payment is due) and has been written off in the trader's accounts.

Where a supplier of goods or services has accounted for VAT on the supply and the customer does not pay, the supplier may claim a refund of VAT on the amount unpaid. **Relief is available for VAT on bad debts if the debt is over six months old (measured from when payment is due) and has been written off in the creditor's accounts.** Where payments on account have been received, they are attributed to debts in chronological order. If the debtor later pays all or part of the amount owed, a corresponding part of the VAT repaid must be paid back to Customs.

Bad debt relief claims must be made within three years of the time the debt became eligible for relief. The creditor must have a copy of the VAT invoice, and records to show that the VAT in question has been accounted for and that the debt has been written off. The VAT is reclaimed on the creditor's VAT return.

A business which has claimed input tax on a supply, but which has not paid the supplier of the goods or services within six months of date of supply (or the date on which the payment is due, if later), must repay the input tax, irrespective of whether the supplier has made a claim for bad debt relief. The input tax will be repaid by making an adjustment to the input tax on the VAT return for the accounting period in which the end of the six months falls.

2.7 Self-supply

A person making exempt supplies cannot reclaim input tax relating to those supplies. Also, there are certain supplies on which input tax cannot be recovered at all (eg the purchase of a motor car where there is an element of personal use). This could lead to a distortion of competition where a person produces for himself goods or services which, if purchased externally, would result in restricted or no input tax recovery. The Treasury can deal with such distortions by making regulations taxing self-supplies.

The effect is that the trader is treated as supplying the goods or services to himself (in general, at market value). **Output tax is due to Customs, but input tax can only be recovered to the extent that it related to taxable supplies made by the business or that it is deductible under the normal rules eg cars.** Thus the business suffers a VAT cost.

The amount of the self-supply is excluded from both the numerator and the denominator of the fraction used in the partial exemption calculation.

Examples of self-supply include construction services provided in-house and motor cars where input tax has been recovered and the car is subsequently put to a use which would not qualify for such credit.

3 Special schemes

Special schemes include the cash accounting scheme, the annual accounting scheme and the optional flat rate scheme. These schemes make VAT accounting easier for certain types of trader.

3.1 The cash accounting scheme

The cash accounting scheme enables businesses to account for VAT on the basis of cash paid and received. That is, the date of payment or receipt determines the return in which the transaction is dealt with. **The scheme can only be used by a trader whose annual taxable turnover (exclusive of VAT) does not exceed £660,000.** A trader can join the scheme only if all returns and VAT payments are up to date (or arrangements have been made to pay outstanding VAT by instalments).

If the value of taxable supplies exceeds £825,000 in the 12 months to the end of a VAT period a trader must leave the cash accounting scheme immediately.

Businesses which leave the scheme (either voluntarily or because they have breached the £825,000 limit) can account for any outstanding VAT due under the scheme on a cash basis for a further six months.

3.2 The annual accounting scheme

The annual accounting scheme is only available to traders who regularly pay VAT to Customs, not to traders who normally receive repayments. It is available for traders **whose taxable turnover (exclusive of VAT) for the 12 months starting on their application to join the scheme is not expected to exceed £660,000.** Traders cannot apply to join until they have been registered for at least 12 months.

The 12-month qualifying period does not apply to businesses with a taxable turnover of up to £150,000. Such businesses can join the scheme as soon as they are registered.

Under the annual accounting scheme traders file annual VAT returns but throughout the year they must make payments on account of their VAT liability by direct debit. The year for which each return is made may end at the end of any calendar month. Unless Customs agree otherwise, the trader must pay 90% of the previous year's net VAT liability during the year by means of nine monthly payments commencing at the end of the fourth month of the year. The balance of the year's VAT is then paid with the annual return. There is an option for businesses to pay three larger interim instalments.

Late payment of instalments is not a default for the purposes of the default surcharge.

An annual VAT return must be submitted to Customs along with any balancing payment due within two months of the end of the year.

It is not possible to use the annual accounting scheme if input tax exceeded output tax in the year prior to application. In addition, all returns must have been made up to date. Annual accounting is not available where VAT registration is in the name of a VAT group or a division.

If the expected value of a trader's taxable supplies exceeds £825,000 notice must be given to Customs within 30 days and he may then be required to leave the scheme. If the £825,000 limit is in fact exceeded, the trader must leave the scheme.

If a trader fails to make the regular payments required by the scheme or the final payment for a year, or has not paid all VAT shown on returns made before joining the scheme, he may be expelled from the scheme. Customs can also prevent a trader using the scheme 'if they consider it necessary to do so for the protection of the revenue'.

Advantages of annual accounting:

- Only one VAT return each year so fewer occasions to trigger a default surcharge

- Ability to manage cash flow more accurately

- Avoids need for quarterly calculations for partial exemption purposes and input tax recovery

Disadvantages of annual accounting:

- Need to monitor future taxable supplies to ensure turnover limit not exceeded

- Timing of payments have less correlation to turnover (and hence cash received) by business

- Payments based on previous year's turnover may not reflect current year turnover which may be a problem if the scale of activities has reduced

3.3 Flat Rate Scheme

The optional flat rate scheme enables businesses to calculate VAT due simply by applying a flat rate percentage to their turnover.

Under the scheme, businesses calculate VAT by applying a fixed percentage to their tax inclusive turnover, i.e. the total turnover, including all reduced rate, zero-rated and exempt income. The percentage depends upon the trade sector into which a business falls. It ranges from 2% for retailing food, confectionery or newspapers to 13.5% for construction services. The percentage for accountancy and book-keeping is 13%, for financial services is 11.5%, for hotels 9.5% and for catering 12%. A 1% reduction off the flat rate % can be made by businesses in their first year of VAT registration.

Exam focus point

> The flat rate percentage to use will be given to you in your examination.

Businesses using the scheme must issue VAT invoices to their VAT registered customers but they do not have to record all the details of the invoices issued or purchase invoices received to calculate the VAT due. Invoices issued will show VAT at the normal rate rather than the flat rate.

To join the flat rate scheme businesses must have:

- **a tax exclusive annual taxable turnover of up to £150,000**; and

- **a tax exclusive annual total turnover, including the value of exempt and/or other non-taxable income, of up to £187,500.**

3.4 Example

An accountant undertakes work for individuals and for business clients. In a VAT year, the business client work amounts to £35,000 and the accountant will issue VAT invoices totalling £41,125 (£35,000 plus VAT at 17.5%). Turnover from work for individuals totals £18,000, including VAT. Total gross sales are therefore £59,125. The flat rate percentage for an accountancy businesses is 13%.

VAT due to Customs will be 13% × £59,125 = £7,686.25

Under the normal VAT rules the output tax due would be:

	£
£35,000 x 17.5%	6,125.00
£18,000 x 7/47	2,680.85
	8,805.85

Whether the accountant is better off under the scheme depends on the amount of input tax incurred as this would be offset, under normal rules, from output tax due.

Chapter roundup

- Some supplies are taxable (either standard-rated, reduced-rated or zero-rated). Others are exempt.

- Not all input VAT is deductible, eg VAT on most motor cars.

- If fuel is supplied for private purposes all input VAT incurred on the fuel is allowed but the business must account for output VAT using a set of scale charges.

- Relief for VAT on bad debts is available if the debt is over six months old (measured from when the payment is due) and has been written off in the trader's accounts.

- Special schemes include the cash accounting scheme, the annual accounting scheme and the optional flat rate scheme. These schemes make VAT accounting easier for certain types of trader.

Quick quiz

1   What input tax is never deductible?

2   What relief is available for bad debts?

3   What are the turnover limits for the annual accounting and cash accounting schemes?

4   What is the optional flat rate scheme?

Answers to quick quiz

1   VAT on:

- motor cars
- business entertaining
- expenses incurred on domestic accommodation for directors
- non-business items passed through the accounts
- items which do not relate to making business supplies

2   Where a supplier has accounted for VAT on a supply and the customer fails to pay, then the supplier may claim a refund of the VAT accounted for to Customs but never actually collected from the customer.

3   Turnover not exceeding £660,000 to join the schemes. Once turnover exceeds £825,000 must leave the schemes.

4   The optional flat rate scheme enables businesses to calculate VAT simply by applying a percentage to their tax-inclusive turnover. Under the scheme, businesses calculate VAT due by applying a flat rate percentage to their tax inclusive turnover, i.e. the total turnover generated, including all reduced-rate, zero-rated and exempt income. The percentage depends upon the trade sector into which a business falls.

Now try the questions below from the Exam Question Bank

Number	Level	Marks	Time
Q14	Introductory	10	18 mins
Q15	Examination	15	27 mins

BPP
PROFESSIONAL EDUCATION

Part B
Unincorporated businesses

12

An outline of income tax

Topic list	Syllabus reference
1 The aggregation of income	2(a)
2 Various types of income	2(a)
3 Charges on income	2(a)
4 Personal allowance	2(a)
5 The personal tax computation	2(a)

Introduction

We look here at income tax, which is a tax on what individuals make from their jobs, their businesses and their savings. We see how to collect together all of an individual's income in a personal tax computation, and then work out the tax on that income.

In later chapters, we look at particular types of income in more detail.

1 The aggregation of income

In a personal income tax computation, we bring together income from all sources, splitting the sources into non-savings, savings (excl. dividend) and dividend income.

An individual's income from all sources is brought together in a personal tax computation. Three columns are needed. Here is an example. All items are explained later in this text.

RICHARD: INCOME TAX COMPUTATION 2005/06

	Non-savings income £	Savings (excl dividend) income £	Dividend income £	Total £
Income from employment	40,000			
Building society interest		1,320		
UK dividends			1,000	
	40,000	1,320	1,000	
Less charges on income	(2,000)			
Statutory total income (STI)	38,000	1,320	1,000	40,320
Less personal allowance	(4,895)			
Taxable income	33,105	1,320	1,000	35,425

Income tax

	£	£
Non savings income		
£2,090 × 10%		209
£30,310 × 22%		6,668
£705 × 40%		282
		7,159
Savings (excl. dividend) income		
£1,320 × 40%		528
Dividend income		
£1,000 × 32.5%		325
		8,012
Add basic rate tax withheld on charges paid net £2,000 × 22%		440
Tax liability		8,452
Less tax suffered		
Tax credit on dividend income	100	
PAYE tax on salary (say)	5,650	
Tax on building society interest	264	
		(6,014)
Tax payable		2,438

Key terms

Statutory total income (STI) is all income before deducting the personal allowance. The **tax liability** is the amount which must be accounted for to the Revenue. **Tax payable** is the balance of the liability still to be settled in cash.

Income tax is charged on **'taxable income'**. Non-savings income is dealt with first, then savings (excl. dividend) income and then dividend income.

For non-savings income, the first £2,090 (the starting rate band) is taxed at the starting rate (10%), the next £30,310 (the basic rate band) is taxed at the basic rate (22%) and the rest at the higher rate (40%). We will look at the taxation of the other types of income later in this chapter.

The remainder of this chapter gives more details of the income tax computation.

2 Various types of income

FAST FORWARD >>

An individual may receive interest net of 20% tax suffered at source. The amount received must be grossed up by multiplying by 100/80 and must be included gross in the income tax computation. Similarly dividends, which are received net of a 10% tax credit, must be grossed up for inclusion in the tax computation.

2.1 Classification of income

The main types of income for individuals relevant for Paper 2.3 are:

- Profits of trades, professions and vocations
- Income from employment and pensions
- Savings and investment income, including interest and dividends

2.2 Savings income received net of 20% tax

The following savings income is **received net of 20% tax**.

(a) Interest paid to individuals by UK companies on debentures and loan notes/stock
(b) Bank and building society interest paid to individuals
(c) The income portion of a purchased annuity

The amount received is grossed up by multiplying by 100/80 and included gross in the income tax computation. The tax deducted at source is deducted in computing tax payable and may be repaid.

Exam focus point

In examinations you may be given either the net or the gross amount of such income: read the question carefully. If you are given the net amount (the amount received or credited), you should gross up the figure at the rate of 20%. For example, net building society interest of £160 is equivalent to gross income of £160 × 100/80 = £200 on which tax of £40 (20% of £200) has been suffered.

2.3 Dividends on UK shares

Dividends on UK shares are received net of a 10% tax credit. This means a dividend of £90 has a £10 tax credit, giving gross income of £100 to include in the income tax computation. The tax credit can be deducted in computing tax payable but it cannot be repaid.

2.4 Exempt income

Some income is exempt from income tax. Several of these exemptions are mentioned at places in this text where the types of income are described in detail, but you should note the following types of exempt income now.

(a) Scholarships (exempt as income of the scholar. If paid by a parent's employer, a scholarship may be taxable income of the parent)

(b) Betting and gaming winnings, including **premium bond prizes**

(c) Interest or terminal bonus on **National Savings Certificates**

(d) Certain social security benefits

(e) Gifts

 151

(f)   Damages and payments for personal injury. The exemption applies to lump sum and periodical payments, including payments made via trusts and payments made by buying annuities. Payments under annuities are made gross (unlike most annuities)

(g)   Certain payments under insurance policies to compensate for loss of income on illness or disability (permanent health insurance) or while out of work (eg policies to pay interest on mortgages).

(h)   The amount by which a pension awarded on a retirement due to a disability caused at work, by a work related illness or by war wounds exceeds the pension that would have been payable if the retirement had been on ordinary ill health grounds. This exemption only applies to pensions paid under non-approved pension schemes.

(i)   Interest on amounts repaid to borrowers under the income contingent student loans scheme

(j)   Payments made under the 'new deal 50 plus' scheme and payments made under the employment zones programme.

(k)   Income on investments made through individual savings accounts (ISAs)

Exam focus point

Learn the different types of exempt income. They are popular items in the exam. Always state on your exam script that such income is exempt (do not ignore it) to gain an easy half mark.

3 Charges on income

FAST FORWARD

Deduct charges from total income. They are deducted firstly from non savings income, then from savings (excl. dividend) and finally from dividend income.

3.1 Types of charges

Charges on income are deducted in computing taxable income.

Key term

A **charge on income** is a payment by the taxpayer which income tax law allows as a deduction.

Examples of **charges on income for individuals** are:

(a)   Eligible interest
(b)   Patent royalties
(c)   Copyright royalties

Charges on income paid in money fall into two categories: those from which basic rate (22%) income tax is first deducted by the payer (charges paid net) and those which are paid gross (without any tax deduction). Always deduct the gross figure in the payer's tax computation.

Patent royalties are the only examinable example of a charge on income which individuals pay net. Eligible interest and copyright royalties are paid gross.

In the personal tax computation of someone who *receives* such income, for example the owner of a patent who receives royalties from someone who exploits the patent you should:

(a)   Include the **gross** amount under non-savings income. If the charge was paid gross, the gross amount is the amount received. If it was paid net, ie it was a patent royalty, the gross amount is the amount received × 100/78.

(b) If the charge was received net, ie it was a patent royalty, then under the heading 'less tax suffered' (between tax liability and tax payable) include the tax deducted. This is the gross amount $\times$ 22%.

3.2 Eligible interest

Interest qualifies for tax relief as a charge if the loan concerned is used for a qualifying purpose:

(a) **The purchase of an interest in a partnership, or contribution to the partnership of capital or a loan**. The borrower must be a partner (other than a limited partner), and relief ceases when he ceases to be one.

(b) **The purchase of ordinary shares in, or the loan of money to, a close trading company.** When the interest is paid the individual must either have (with any associates) a material (more than 5%) interest in the company, or he must hold (ignoring associates) **some** ordinary share capital and work full time as a manager or director of the company. A close company is (broadly) a company controlled by its shareholder-directors or by five or fewer shareholders.

(c) **Investment in a co-operative**. This provision applies to investment in shares or through loans to the co-operative. The borrower must work for the greater part of his time in the co-operative.

(d) **The purchase of shares in an employee-controlled company**. The company must be an unquoted trading company resident in the UK with at least 50% of the voting shares held by employees.

(e) **The purchase by a partner of plant or machinery used in the business**. Interest is allowed for three years from the end of the tax year in which the loan was taken out. If the plant is used partly for private purposes, then the allowable interest is apportioned.

(f) **The purchase by an employee of plant or machinery used by him in the performance of his duties**. The interest is allowable for three years from the end of the tax year in which the loan was taken out.

(g) The replacement of other loans qualifying under (a) to (f) above.

Interest on a loan within (a) to (d) above continues to be allowable if a partnership is succeeded by a new partnership or is incorporated into a close company, a co-operative or an employee controlled company, or if shares in a company of one of these kinds are exchanged for shares in a company of another of these kinds, provided that interest on a new loan (to make the loan to or buy the shares in the new entity) would have qualified.

Interest is never allowed if it is payable under a scheme or arrangement of which the expected sole or main benefit was tax relief on the interest. Interest on an overdraft or on a credit card debt does not qualify. Relief under (a) to (d) above is reduced or withdrawn if capital is withdrawn from the business.

3.3 Business interest

A taxpayer paying interest wholly and exclusively for business purposes can deduct such interest in computing his trading profits, instead of as a charge. The interest need not fall into any of the categories outlined above, and it may be on an overdraft or a credit card debt.

If interest is allowable as a deduction in computing trading profits, the amount payable (on an accruals basis) is deducted. Only interest paid in the tax year may be set against total income as a charge.

3.4 Charges in personal tax computations

The gross amount of any charge is deducted from the taxpayer's income to arrive at STI. Deduct charges from non-savings income, then from savings (excl dividend) income and lastly from dividend income.

If a charge has been paid net, the basic rate income tax deducted (22% of the gross charge) is added to any tax liability. The taxpayer obtained tax relief because the charge reduced his income: he cannot keep the basic rate tax as well, but must pay it to the Revenue.

If charges paid net exceed total income (ignoring charges paid net) **minus allowances deductible from STI, the payer of the charge must, under s 350 ICTA 1988, pay the Revenue the tax withheld when the excess charge was paid**. In other words, the Revenue ensure that you do not get tax relief for charges if you are not a payer of tax.

3.5 Example

Three taxpayers have the following trading profits and allowances for 2005/06. Taxpayers A and B pay a patent royalty of £176 (net). Taxpayer C pays a patent royalty of £1,248 (net).

	A	B	C
	£	£	£
Trading profits	6,000	4,000	39,795
Less: charge on income (× 100/78)	(226)	(226)	(1,600)
	5,774	3,774	38,195
Less: personal allowance	(4,895)	(4,895)	(4,895)
Taxable income	879	–	33,300
Income tax			
10% on £1,879/-/£2,090	88	–	209
22% on -/-/£30,310			6,668
40% on -/-/£900			360
	88	–	7,237
Add: 22% tax retained on charge	50	50	352
Tax payable	138	50	7,589

4 Personal allowance

> All persons are entitled to a personal allowance. It is deducted from statutory total income, first against non savings income, then against savings (excluding dividend) income and lastly against dividend income.

Once taxable income from all sources has been aggregated and any charges on income deducted, the remainder is the taxpayer's statutory total income (STI). An allowance, the personal allowance is deducted from STI. Like charges, it comes off non savings income first, then off savings (excl. dividend) income and lastly off dividend income.

All persons (including children) are entitled to the personal allowance of £4,895.

Question   Calculation of taxable income

Susan has an annual salary of £37,000. She has a loan of £7,000 at 10% interest to buy shares in her employee-controlled company, and another loan of £5,000 at 12% interest to buy double glazing for her house. She receives building society interest of £2,000 a year. What is her taxable income for 2005/06?

Answer

	Non-savings £	Savings (excl dividend) £	Total £
Salary	37,000		
Building society interest £2,000 × 100/80		2,500	
	37,000	2,500	
Less charge £7,000 × 10%	(700)		
STI	36,300	2,500	38,800
Less personal allowance	(4,895)		
Taxable income	31,405	2,500	33,905

5 The personal tax computation

FAST FORWARD

Work out income tax on the taxable income, and take account of tax retained on charges. Deduct the tax credit on dividend income and any income tax suffered at source to arrive at tax payable. The tax credit on dividend income cannot be repaid if it exceeds the tax liability so far calculated. Other tax suffered at source can be repaid.

5.1 Steps in the personal tax computation

Step 1 **The first step in preparing a personal tax computation is to set up three columns**
One column for non-savings income, one for savings (excl. dividend) income and one for dividend income.

Step 2 **Deal with non-savings income first**
Income of up to £2,090 is taxed at 10%. Next any income in the basic rate band is taxed at 22%, and finally income above the basic rate threshold is taxed at 40%.

Step 3 **Now deal with savings (excl dividend) income**
If any of the starting or basic rate bands remain **after taxing non savings income**, they can be used here. Savings (excl) dividend income is taxed at 10% in the starting rate band. If savings (excl. dividend) income falls within the basic rate band it is taxed at 20% (not 22%). Once income is above the higher rate threshold, it is taxed at 40%.

Step 4 **Lastly, tax dividend income**
If dividend income falls within the starting or basic rate bands, it is taxed at 10% (never 20% or 22%). If, however, the dividend income exceeds the basic rate threshold of £32,400, it is taxable at 32.5%.

Step 5 **Next, deduct the tax credit on dividends**
Although deductible this tax credit cannot be repaid if it exceeds the tax liability calculated so far.

Step 6 **Finally deduct the tax deducted at source from savings (excluding dividend) income and any PAYE**
These amounts can be repaid to the extent that they exceed the income tax liability.

5.2 Examples: personal tax computations

(a)   Kathe has a salary of £10,000 and receives dividends of £4,500.

	Non-savings	Dividends	Total
	£	£	£
Earnings	10,000		
Dividends £4,500 × 100/90		5,000	
STI	10,000	5,000	15,000
Less personal allowance	(4,895)		
Taxable income	5,105	5,000	10,105

	£
Income tax	
Non savings income	
£2,090 × 10%	209
£3,015 × 22%	663
Dividend income	
£5,000 × 10%	500
Tax liability	1,372
Less tax credit on dividend	(500)
Tax payable	872

Some of the tax payable has probably already been paid on the salary under PAYE (see later in this Text).

The dividend income falls within the basic rate band so it is taxed at 10% (*not* 22%).

(b)   Jules has a salary of £20,000, trade profits of £30,000, net dividends of £6,750 and building society interest of £3,000 net. He pays gross charges of £2,000.

	Non-savings	Savings (excl dividend)	Dividend	Total
	£	£	£	£
Trade profits	30,000			
Earnings	20,000			
Dividends £6,750 × 100/90			7,500	
Building society interest £3,000 × 100/80	-	3,750	-	
	50,000	3,750	7,500	
Less charges	(2,000)			
STI	48,000	3,750	7,500	59,250
Less personal allowance	(4,895)			
Taxable income	43,105	3,750	7,500	54,355

	£
Income tax	
Non savings income	
£2,090 × 10%	209
£30,310 × 22%	6,668
£10,705 × 40%	4,282
	11,159
Savings (excl. dividend) income	
£3,750 × 40%	1,500
Dividend income	
£7,500 × 32.5%	2,438
Less tax credit on dividend income	(750)
Less tax suffered on building society interest	(750)
Tax payable	13,597

Savings (excl. dividend) income and dividend income fall above the basic rate threshold so they are taxed at 40% and 32.5% respectively.

(c)   Jim does not work. He receives net bank interest of £38,000. He pays gross charges of £2,000.

	Savings (excl dividend) £	Total £
Bank interest × 100/80	47,500	
Less charges	(2,000)	
STI	45,500	45,500
Less personal allowance	(4,895)	
	40,605	40,605

	£
Savings (excluding dividend) income	
£2,090 × 10%	209
£30,310 × 20%	6,062
£8,205 × 40%	3,282
Tax liability	9,553
Less tax suffered	(9,500)
Tax payable	53

Savings (excl. dividend) income within the basic rate band is taxed at 20% (*not* 22%).

5.3 Savings income

'Savings income' does not include everything you might expect it to. Here are lists of savings and non-savings income.

Savings income

(a)   **Interest** (includes interest from banks, buildings societies, gilts and debentures and under the accrued income scheme)

(b)   **Dividends**

(c)   **The income part of a purchased life annuity**. This is an annuity which lasts for a period depending on someone's lifespan, and which is bought for a lump sum. Part of each payment is treated as income and is paid net of 20% tax, while the rest is treated as a return of capital and is tax-free (see later in this text).

Non-savings income

(a)   Income from a job
(b)   Income from running a business (alone or as a partner)
(c)   Rental income
(d)   Charges **received** (other than interest)

5.4 The complete proforma

Here is a complete proforma computation of taxable income. It is probably too much for you to absorb at this stage, but refer back to it as you come to the chapters dealing with the types of income shown.

	Non-savings £	Savings (excl dividend) £	Dividend £	Total £
Business profits	X			
Less losses set against business profits	(X)			
	X			
Wages less occupational pension contributions	X			
Other non-savings (as many lines as necessary)	X			
Building society interest (gross)		X		
Other savings (excl. dividends) (gross) (as many lines as necessary)		X		
Dividends (gross)			X	
	X	X	X	
Less charges (gross)	(X)	(X)	(X)	
	X	X	X	
Less losses set against general income	(X)	(X)	(X)	
STI	X	X	X	X
Less personal allowance	(X)	(X)	(X)	
Taxable income	X	X	X	X

Chapter roundup

- In a personal income tax computation, we bring together income from all sources, splitting the sources into non-savings, savings (excl. dividend) and dividend income.

- An individual may receive interest net of 20% tax suffered at source. The amount received must be grossed up by multiplying by 100/80 and must be included gross in the income tax computation. Similarly dividends which are received net of a 10% tax credit must be grossed up for inclusion in the tax computation.

- Deduct charges from total income. They are deducted firstly from non savings income, then from savings (excl. dividend) and finally from dividend income.

- All persons are entitled to a personal allowance. It is deducted from statutory total income, first against non savings income, then against savings (excluding dividend) income and lastly against dividend income.

- Work out income tax on the taxable income, and take account of tax retained on charges. Deduct the tax credit on dividend income and any income tax suffered at source to arrive at tax payable. The tax credit on dividend income cannot be repaid if it exceeds the tax liability so far calculated. Other tax suffered at source can be repaid.

Quick quiz

1   At what rates is income tax charged on non-savings income?

2   List three types of savings income that is received by individuals net of 20% tax.

3   Give an example of a charge on income paid net by individuals.

4   How is dividend income taxed?

Answers to quick quiz

1   10%, 22% and 40%.

2   Interest paid by UK companies on UK debentures and loan stock, bank and building society interest, the income portion of a purchased annuity.

3   Patent royalties

4   Dividend income in the starting and basic rate band is taxed at 10%. Dividend income in excess of the higher rate threshold is taxed at 32.5%

Now try the questions below from the Exam Question Bank

Number	Level	Marks	Time
Q16	Introductory	7	13 mins
Q17	Examination	15	27 mins

13

Trading income

Topic list	Syllabus reference
1 The badges of trade	2(c)(i)
2 The computation of trading income	2(c)(ii)
3 Basis periods	2(c)(iii)
4 Change of accounting date	2(c)(iv)
5 Capital allowances for unincorporated businesses	2(c)(v)

Introduction

We are now going to look at the computation and taxation of profits of unincorporated businesses. We work out a business's profit as if it were a separate entity (the separate entity concept familiar to you from basic bookkeeping) but as an unincorporated business has no legal existence apart from its proprietor, we cannot tax it separately. We have to feed its profit into the proprietor's personal tax computation.

1 The badges of trade

FAST FORWARD

> The badges of trade can be used to decide whether or not a trade exists. If one does exist, the accounting profits need to be adjusted in order to establish the taxable profits.

Key term

> A trade is defined in the legislation only in an unhelpful manner as including every trade, manufacture, adventure or concern in the nature of a trade. It has therefore been left to the courts to provide guidance. This guidance is often summarised in a collection of principles known as the **'badges of trade'**. These are set out below. They apply to both corporate businesses and unincorporated businesses.

1.1 The subject matter

Whether a person is trading or not may sometimes be decided by examining the subject matter of the transaction. Some assets are commonly held as investments for their intrinsic value: an individual buying some shares or a painting may do so in order to enjoy the income from the shares or to enjoy the work of art. A subsequent disposal may produce a gain of a capital nature rather than a trading profit. But **where the subject matter of a transaction is such as would not be held as an investment** (for example 34,000,000 yards of aircraft linen (*Martin v Lowry 1927*) or 1,000,000 rolls of toilet paper (*Rutledge v CIR 1929*)), **it is presumed that any profit on resale is a trading profit.**

1.2 The frequency of transactions

Transactions which may, in isolation, be of a capital nature will be interpreted as trading transactions where their **frequency indicates the carrying on of a trade**. It was decided that whereas normally the purchase of a mill-owning company and the subsequent stripping of its assets might be a capital transaction, where the taxpayer was embarking on the same exercise for the fourth time he must be carrying on a trade (*Pickford v Quirke 1927*).

1.3 The length of ownership

The courts may infer adventures in the nature of **trade where items purchased are sold soon afterwards.**

1.4 Supplementary work and marketing

When work is done to make an asset more marketable, or steps are taken to find purchasers, the courts will be more ready to ascribe a trading motive. When a group of accountants bought, blended and recasked a quantity of brandy they were held to be taxable on a trading profit when the brandy was later sold (*Cape Brandy Syndicate v CIR 1921*).

1.5 A profit motive

The absence of a profit motive will not necessarily mean that someone is not trading, but its presence is a strong indication that a person is trading. The purchase and resale of £20,000 worth of silver bullion by the comedian Norman Wisdom, as a hedge against devaluation, was held to be a trading transaction (*Wisdom v Chamberlain 1969*).

1.6 The way in which the asset sold was acquired

If goods are acquired deliberately, trading may be indicated. If goods are acquired unintentionally, for example by gift or inheritance, their later sale is unlikely to be trading.

1.7 The taxpayer's intentions

Where a transaction is clearly trading on objective criteria, **the taxpayer's intentions are irrelevant**. If, however, a transaction has (objectively) a dual purpose, the taxpayer's intentions may be taken into account. An example of a transaction with a dual purpose is the acquisition of a site partly as premises from which to conduct another trade, and partly with a view to the possible development and resale of the site.

This test is not one of the traditional badges of trade, but it may be just as important.

2 The computation of trading income

The adjustments needed to the accounting profits for unincorporated businesses are similar to those needed for companies. However, one difference is that the private use proportion of any expenditure is disallowed for unincorporated businesses.

2.1 The adjustment of profits

As for companies, although the net profit before taxation shown in the accounts is the starting point in computing the taxable trading profit, many adjustments may be required to find the trading income subject to tax. The same rules apply to profits of a profession or vocation, and we will just refer to trading profits from now on. Many of the same rules apply to both corporate and unincorporated businesses even though the rules relating to unincorporated business have been rewritten in the Income Tax (Trading and Other Income) Act 2005. Where appropriate, reference is made to the appropriate parts of Chapter 2.

2.2 Accounting policies

The fundamental concept is that the profits of the business must be calculated in accordance with generally accepted accounting practice. The profit is subject to any adjusted specifically required for income tax purposes.

2.3 Rounding

Where an individual or a partnership has an annual turnover of at least £5,000,000 and prepares its accounts with figures rounded to at least the nearest £1,000, figures in computations of adjusted profits may generally be rounded to the nearest £1,000.

2.4 Deductible and non-deductible expenditure

2.4.1 Payments contrary to public policy and illegal payments

Fines and penalties are not deductible. However, the Revenue usually allow employees' parking fines incurred in parking their employer's cars while on their employer's business. Fines relating to proprietors, however, are never allowed.

A payment is (by statute) not deductible if making it constitutes an offence by the payer. This covers protection money paid to terrorists, and also bribes. Statute also prevents any deduction for payments made in response to blackmail or extortion.

2.4.2 Capital expenditure

The principles in Chapter 2 Section 2.2 also apply to unincorporated businesses.

Two exceptions to the 'capital' rule are worth noting.

(a)   The costs of **registering patents and trade marks** are deductible.

(b)   **Incidental costs of obtaining loan finance**, or of attempting to obtain or redeeming it, are deductible other than a discount on issue or a premium on redemption (which are really alternatives to paying interest).

2.4.3 Appropriations

Salary or interest on capital paid to a proprietor, and also depreciation, amortisation and general provisions are not deductible. A specific provision against a particular trade debt is deductible if it is a reasonable estimate of the likely loss.

The private proportion of payments for motoring expenses, rent, heat and light and telephone expenses of a proprietor is not deductible. Where the payments are to or on behalf of employees, the full amounts are deductible but the employees are taxed as benefits for income tax.

2.4.4 Charges

Charges (such as royalties) are dealt with in the personal tax computation. They can not also be deducted in computing trading profits.

2.4.5 Entertaining and gifts

The principles in Chapter 2 Section 2.4 also apply to unincorporated businesses.

2.4.6 Expenditure not wholly and exclusively for the purposes of the trade

Expenditure is not deductible if it is not for trade purposes (the remoteness test), or if it reflects more than one purpose (the duality test). If an exact apportionment is possible (as with motor expenses) relief is given on the business element. The cases in Chapter 2 Section 2.6 also apply to unincorporated businesses.

However, the cost of overnight accommodation when on a business trip may be deductible and reasonable expenditure on an evening meal and breakfast in conjunction with such accommodation is then also deductible.

2.4.7 Subscriptions and donations

The general 'wholly and exclusively' rule determines the deductibility of expenses. Subscriptions and donations are not deductible unless the expenditure is for the benefit of the trade. The following are the main types of subscriptions and donations you may meet and their correct treatments.

- Trade subscriptions (such as to a professional or trade association) are generally deductible.

- Charitable donations are deductible only if they are small and to local charities.

- Political subscriptions and donations are generally not deductible.

- When a business makes a gift of equipment manufactured, sold or used in the course of its trade to an educational establishment or for a charitable purpose, nothing need be brought into account as a trading receipt or (if capital allowances had been obtained on the asset) as disposal proceeds, so full relief is obtained for the cost. The donor must claim the relief. The time limit for the claim for unincorporated businesses is the 31 January which is 22 months after the end of the tax year in whose basis period the gift is made. The value of any benefit to the donor from the gift is taxable on him.

- Where a donation represents the most effective commercial way of disposing of stock (for example, where it would not be commercially effective to sell surplus perishable food), the donation can be treated as for the benefit of the trade and the disposal proceeds taken as £Nil. In other cases, the amount credited to the accounts in respect of a donation of stock should be its market value.

2.4.8 Legal and professional charges/irrecoverable and doubtful debts

The principles in Chapter 2 Section 2.8 also apply to unincorporated businesses.

2.4.9 Interest

Interest paid by an individual on borrowings for trade purposes is deductible as a trading expense on an accruals basis, so no adjustment to the accounts figure is needed.

Individuals cannot deduct interest on overdue tax.

2.4.10 Pre-trading expenditure and other miscellaneous deductions

The principles in Chapter 2 Section 2.11 also apply to unincorporated businesses.

2.4.11 Miscellaneous deductions

Here is a list of various other items that you may meet.

Item	Treatment	Comment
Educational courses for staff	Allow	
Educational courses for proprietor	Allow	If to update existing knowledge or skills, not if to acquire new knowledge or skills
Removal expenses (to new business premises)	Allow	Only if not an expansionary move
Travelling expenses to the trader's place of business	Disallow	*Ricketts v Colquhoun 1925*: unless an itinerant trader (*Horton v Young 1971*)
Contribution to expenses of agents under the payroll deduction scheme	Allow	
Redundancy pay in excess of the statutory amount	Allow	If the trade ceases, the limit on allowability is 3 × the statutory amount (in addition to the statutory amount)
Compensation for loss of office and ex gratia payments	Allow	If for benefit of trade: *Mitchell v B W Noble Ltd 1927*
Counselling services for employees leaving employment	Allow	If qualify for exemption from employment income charge on employees
Contributions to any of: local enterprise agencies; training and enterprise councils; local enterprise companies; business link organisations;	Allow	
Pension contributions (to schemes for employees and company directors)	Allow	If paid, not if only provided for; special contributions may be spread over the year of payment and future years

Item	Treatment	Comment

Premiums for insurance:
 	
  against an employee's death or illness
 	
  to cover locum costs or fixed overheads whilst the policyholder is ill
	Allow	Receipts are taxable

Payments to employees for restrictive undertakings	Allow	Taxable on employee
Damages paid	Allow	If not too remote from trade: *Strong and Co v Woodifield 1906*
Preparation and restoration of waste disposal sites	Allow	Spread preparation expenditure over period of use of site. Pre-trading expenditure is treated as incurred on the first day of trading. Allow restoration expenditure in period of expenditure
Improving an individual's personal security	Allow	Provision of a car, ship or dwelling is excluded

2.5 Income taxable as trading income but excluded from the accounts

The usual example is when a proprietor takes goods for his own use. In such circumstances the normal selling price of the goods is added to the accounting profit. In other words, the proprietor is treated for tax purposes as having made a sale to himself (*Sharkey v Wernher 1955*). This rule does not apply to supplies of services, which are treated as sold for the amount (if any) actually paid (but the cost of services to the trader or his household is not deductible).

2.6 Accounting profits not taxable as trading income

The principles in Chapter 2 Section 3 also apply to unincorporated businesses.

2.7 Deductible expenditure not charged in the accounts

The principles in Chapter 2 Section 4 also apply to unincorporated businesses.

2.8 The cessation of trades

2.8.1 Taxation of post cessation receipts

Post-cessation receipts (including any releases of debts incurred by the trader) **are taxable** as miscellaneous income. If they are received in the tax year of cessation or the next six tax years, the trader can elect that they be treated as received on the day of cessation. The time limit for electing is the 31 January which is 22 months after the end of the tax year of receipt.

Post-cessation expenses can be deducted so long as they would have been deductible had the trade continued, and they did not arise as a result of the cessation. Capital allowances which the trader was entitled to immediately before the discontinuance but which remain unrelieved can also be deducted.

2.8.2 Post-cessation expenses set against total income

If an individual trader or a partner incurs expenses within the seven years after ceasing to trade and no deduction from post-cessation receipts is possible, he can claim to **deduct them from his total income for the year of payment**. The deduction should be made in the personal tax computation after deductions for charges and post-employment expenses, and before deductions for trading losses set against income as a whole. The trader cannot, of course, claim to the extent that an accrual for the expenses was allowed in computing his trading profits.

This relief is only available for the following expenses.

(a)   Certain costs incurred in connection with defects. Any corresponding amounts received, for example under an insurance policy, are treated as taxable post-cessation receipts for the later of the tax year of receipt and the tax year of the corresponding payment.

(b)   Insurance against the above costs. Any sum received under the insurance policy or as a return of premiums is treated as a taxable post-cessation receipt for the later of the tax year of receipt and the tax year of the corresponding payment.

(c)   The cost of collecting a debt which was taken into account in computing the profits of the former trade. Any sum recovered for the cost of collection is treated as a taxable post-cessation receipt for the later of the tax year of receipt and the tax year of the corresponding payment.

(d)   The amount of a debt which was taken into account in computing the profits of the former trade, but which later proves to be bad or is released under a voluntary arrangement under the Insolvency Act 1986 or a compromise or arrangement under section 425 of the Companies Act 1985. If any amount is later received in respect of such a debt, it is treated as a taxable post-cessation receipt.

The relief is only available for expenses which cannot be set against post-cessation receipts. Expenses which do not fall within the categories in the above paragraph are set against those receipts first. The remaining expenses are eligible for relief against total income.

This relief must be claimed. A claim may be made or not made for each payment separately, but any one payment must be claimed in full or not at all. The time limit for claims is the 31 January which is nearly two years from the end of the tax year of payment (so 31 January 2008 for payments in 2005/06).

If the payments deductible in a tax year exceed total income, the excess cannot be carried back or forward to any other year. However, the ex-trader can claim to set the excess against his chargeable gains for the year. The gains against which the excess is set are the gains for the year minus the losses for the year, ignoring losses brought forward, the annual exempt amount and any relief for trading losses against capital gains. Payments may be claimed or not claimed individually, but any one payment must be claimed in full or not at all.

2.8.3 Valuing trading stock on cessation

When a trade ceases, the closing stock must be valued. The higher the value, the higher the profit for the final period of trading will be.

If the stock is sold to a UK trader who will deduct its cost in computing his taxable profits, it is valued under the following rules.

(a)   If the seller and the buyer are unconnected, take the actual price.

(b)   If the seller and the buyer are connected, take what would have been the price in an arm's length sale.

(c)   However, if the seller and the buyer are connected, the arm's length price exceeds both the original cost of the stock and the actual transfer price, and both the seller and the buyer make an election, then take the greater of the original cost of the stock and the transfer price. The time limit for election for unincorporated business is the 31 January which is 22 months after the end of the tax year of cessation.

In all cases covered above, the value used for the seller's computation of profit is also used as the buyer's cost.

Key term

> An individual is **connected** (connected person) with his spouse, with the relatives (brothers, sisters, ancestors and lineal descendants) of himself and his spouse, and with the spouses of those relatives. He is also connected with his partners (except in relation to bona fide commercial arrangements for the disposal of partnership assets), with their spouses and relatives and with a company he controls. Partners are connected with their partnerships, two partnerships are connected if they have any member in common.

If the stock is not transferred to a UK trader who will be able to deduct its cost in computing his profits, then it is valued at its open market value as at the cessation of trade.

3 Basis periods

FAST FORWARD

> Basis periods are used to link periods of account to tax years. Broadly, the profits of a period of account ending in a tax year are taxed in that year. In the first tax year of trade actual profits of the tax year are taxed. In the second tax year, the basis period is either the first 12 months, the 12 months to the accounting date ending in year two or the actual profits from April to April. Profits of the twelve months to the accounting date are taxed in year three.

3.1 Basis periods and tax years

A tax year runs from 6 April to 5 April, but most businesses do not have periods of account ending on 5 April. **Thus there must be a link between a period of account of a business and a tax year.** The procedure is to **find a period to act as the basis period for a tax year. The profits for a basis period are taxed in the corresponding tax year**. If a basis period is not identical to a period of account, the profits of periods of account are time-apportioned as required. We will assume that profits accrue evenly over a period of account. We will also apportion to the nearest month.

We will now look at the basis period rules that apply in the opening, continuing and closing years of a business when there is no change of accounting date. Special rules are needed when the trader changes his accounting date. We will look at these rules in the next section.

The first tax year is the year during which the trade commences. For example, if a trade commences on 1 June 2005 the first tax year is 2005/06.

3.2 The first tax year

The **basis period for the first tax year runs from the date the trade starts to the next 5 April** (or to the date of cessation if the trade does not last until the end of the tax year).

3.3 The second tax year

If the accounting date falling in the second tax year is at least 12 months after the start of trading, the basis period is the 12 months to that accounting date.

If the accounting date falling in the second tax year is less than 12 months after the start of trading, the basis period is the first 12 months of trading.

If there is no accounting date falling in the second tax year, because the first period of account is a very long one which does not end until a date in the third tax year, **the basis period for the second tax year is the tax year itself (from 6 April to 5 April).**

The following flowchart may help you determine the basis period for the second tax year.

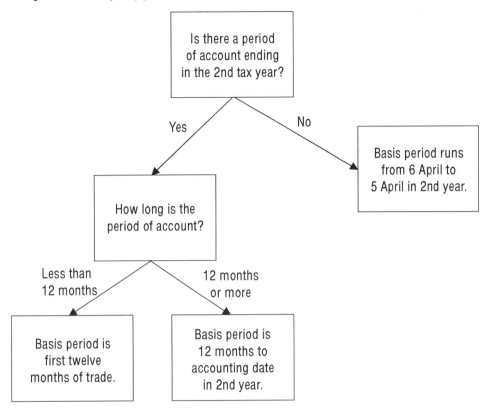

3.4 The third tax year

If there is an accounting date falling in the second tax year, the basis period for the third tax year is the period of account ending in the third tax year.

If there is no accounting date falling in the second tax year, the basis period for the third tax year is the 12 months down to the accounting date falling in the third tax year.

3.5 Later tax years

For later tax years, except the year in which the trade ceases, **the basis period is the period of account ending in the tax year.** This is known as the **current year basis of assessment** (CYB).

3.6 The final year

If a trade starts and ceases in the same tax year, the basis period for that year is the whole lifespan of the trade.

If the final year is the second year, the basis period runs from 6 April at the start of the second year to the date of cessation. This rule overrides the rules that normally apply for the second year.

If the final year is the third year or a later year, **the basis period runs from the end of the basis period for the previous year to the date of cessation.** This rule overrides the rules that normally apply in the third and later years.

3.7 Overlap profits

Key term

Profits which have been taxed more than once are called **overlap profits**.

When a business starts, some profits may be taxed twice because the basis period for the second year includes some or all of the period of trading in the first year or because the basis period for the third year overlaps with that for the second year.

Overlap profits may be deducted on a change of accounting date (see below). Any overlap profits unrelieved when the trade ceases are deducted from the final year's taxable profits. Any deduction of overlap profits may create or increase a loss. The usual loss reliefs (covered later in this text) are then available.

3.8 Example: accounting date in 2nd year at least 12 months

Jenny trades from 1 July 2000 to 31 December 2005, with the following results.

Period	Profit £
1.7.00 – 31.8.01	7,000
1.9.01 – 31.8.02	12,000
1.9.02 – 31.8.03	15,000
1.9.03 – 31.8.04	21,000
1.9.04 – 31.8.05	18,000
1.9.05 – 31.12.05	5,600
	78,600

The profits to be taxed in each tax year from 2000/01 to 2005/06, and the total of these taxable profits are calculated as follows.

Year	Basis period	Working	Taxable profit £
2000/01	1.7.00 – 5.4.01	£7,000 × 9/14	4,500
2001/02	1.9.00 – 31.8.01	£7,000 × 12/14	6,000
2002/03	1.9.01 – 31.8.02		12,000
2003/04	1.9.02 – 31.8.03		15,000
2004/05	1.9.03 – 31.8.04		21,000
2005/06	1.9.04 – 31.12.05	£(18,000 + 5,600 – 3,500)	20,100
			78,600

The overlap profits are those in the period 1 September 2000 to 5 April 2001, a period of seven months. They are £7,000 × 7/14 = £3,500. Overlap profits are either relieved on a change of accounting date (see below) or are deducted from the final year's taxable profit when the business ceases. In this case the overlap profits are deducted when the business ceases. Over the life of the business, the total taxable profits equal the total actual profits.

 Question — Calculation of taxable profits for six tax years

Peter trades from 1 September 2000 to 30 June 2005, with the following results.

Period	Profit £
1.9.00 – 30.4.01	8,000
1.5.01 – 30.4.02	15,000
1.5.02 – 30.4.03	9,000
1.5.03 – 30.4.04	10,500
1.5.04 – 30.4.05	16,000
1.5.05 – 30.6.05	950
	59,450

Show the profits to be taxed in each year from 2000/01 to 2005/06, the total of these taxable profits and the overlap profits.

Answer

Year	Basis period	Working	Taxable profits £
2000/01	1.9.00 – 5.4.01	£8,000 × 7/8	7,000
2001/02	1.9.00 – 31.8.01	£8,000 + (£15,000 × 4/12)	13,000
2002/03	1.5.01 – 30.4.02		15,000
2003/04	1.5.02 – 30.4.03		9,000
2004/05	1.5.03 – 30.4.04		10,500
2005/06	1.5.04 – 30.6.05	£(16,000 + 950 – 12,000)	4,950
			59,450

The overlap profits are the profits from 1 September 2000 to 5 April 2001 (taxed in 2000/01 and in 2001/02) and those from 1 May 2001 to 31 August 2001 (taxed in 2001/02 and 2002/03).

	£
1.9.00 – 5.4.01 £8,000 × 7/8	7,000
1.5.01 – 31.8.01 £15,000 × 4/12	5,000
Total overlap profits	12,000

3.9 Example: no accounting date in the second year

Thelma starts to trade on 1 March 2004. Her first accounts, covering the 16 months to 30 June 2005, show a profit of £36,000. The taxable profits for the first three tax years and the overlap profits are as follows.

Year	Basis period	Working	Taxable profits £
2003/04	1.3.04 – 5.4.04	£36,000 × 1/16	2,250
2004/05	6.4.04 – 5.4.05	£36,000 × 12/16	27,000
2005/06	1.7.04 – 30.6.05	£36,000 × 12/16	27,000

The overlap profits are the profits from 1 July 2004 to 5 April 2005: £36,000 × 9/16 = £20,250.

3.10 The choice of an accounting date

A new trader should consider which accounting date would be best. There are **three factors to consider** from the point of view of taxation.

- **If profits are expected to rise, a date early in the tax year** (such as 30 April) will delay the time when rising accounts profits feed through into rising taxable profits, whereas a date late in the tax year (such as 31 March) will accelerate the taxation of rising profits. This is because with an accounting date of 30 April, the taxable profits for each tax year are mainly the profits earned in the previous tax year. With an accounting date of 31 March the taxable profits are almost entirely profits earned in the current year.

- If the accounting date in the second tax year is less than 12 months after the start of trading, the taxable profits for that year will be the profits earned in the first 12 months. If the accounting date is at least 12 months from the start of trading, they will be the profits earned in the 12 months to that date. **Different profits may thus be taxed twice (the overlap profits)**, and if profits are fluctuating this can make a considerable difference to the taxable profits in the first few years. **It may be many years before relief for the overlap profits is obtained.**

- The choice of an accounting date affects the profits shown in each set of accounts, and this may affect the taxable profits.

Question

The choice of an accounting date

Christine starts to trade on 1 December 2003. Her monthly profits are £1,000 for the first seven months, and £2,000 thereafter. Show the taxable profits for the first three tax years with each of the following accounting dates (in all cases starting with a period of account of less than 12 months).

(a)   31 March
(b)   30 April
(c)   31 December

Answer

(a)   *31 March*

Period of account	Working	Profits £
1.12.03 – 31.3.04	£1000 × 4	4,000
1.4.04 – 31.3.05	£1,000 × 3 + £2,000 × 9	21,000
1.4.05 – 31.3.06	£2,000 × 12	24,000

Year	Basis period		Taxable profits £
2003/04	1.12.03 – 5.4.04		4,000
2004/05	1.4.04 – 31.3.05		21,000
2005/06	1.4.05 – 31.3.06		24,000

(b)   *30 April*

Period of account	Working	Profits £
1.12.03 – 30.4.04	£1,000 × 5	5,000
1.5.04 – 30.4.05	£1,000 × 2 + £2,000 ×10	22,000

Year	Basis period	Working	Taxable profits £
2003/04	1.12.03 – 5.4.04	£5,000 × 4/5	4,000
2004/05	1.12.03 – 30.11.04	£5,000 + £22,000 × 7/12	17,833
2005/06	1.5.04 – 30.4.05		22,000

(c)   *31 December*

Period of account	Working	Profits £
1.12.03 – 31.12.03	£1,000 × 1	1,000
1.1.04 – 31.12.04	£1,000 × 6 + £2,000 × 6	18,000
1.1.05 – 31.12.05	£2,000 × 12	24,000

Year	Basis period	Working	Taxable profits £
2003/04	1.12.03 – 5.4.04	£1,000 + £18,000 × 3/12	5,500
2004/05	1.1.04 – 31.12.04		18,000
2005/06	1.1.05 – 31.12.05		24,000

4 Change of accounting date

On a change of accounting date, special rules may apply for fixing basis periods. Overlap profits may either be created or relieved on a change of accounting date. Overlap profits may be relieved if more than 12 months worth of profits would otherwise be taxed in a year following a change of accounting date. On cessation any remaining overlap profits are relieved.

4.1 Need for special rules

A trader may change the date to which he prepares his annual accounts for a variety of reasons. For example, he may wish to move to a calendar year end or to fit in with seasonal variations of his trade. Special rules normally apply for fixing basis periods when a trader changes his accounting date.

On a change of accounting date there may be

- One set of accounts covering a period of less than twelve months, or
- One set of accounts covering a period of more than twelve months, or
- No accounts, or
- Two sets of accounts

ending in a tax year. In each case, the basis period for the year relates to the new accounting date. We will look at each of the cases in turn.

4.2 One short period of account

When a change of accounting date results in one short period of account ending in a tax year, the basis period for that year is always the 12 months to the new accounting date.

4.3 Example

Sue prepares accounts to 31 December each year until she changes her accounting date to 30 June by preparing accounts for the six months to 30 June 2005.

There is one short period of account ending during 2005/06. This means the basis period for 2005/06 is the twelve months to 30 June 2005.

Sue's basis period for 2004/05 was the twelve months to 31 December 2004. This means the profits of the six months to 31 December 2004 are overlap profits that have been taxed twice. These overlap profits must be added to any overlap profits that arose when the business began. The total is either relieved when the business ceases or it is relieved on a subsequent change of accounting date.

4.4 One long period of account

When a change of accounting date results in one long period of account ending in a tax year, the basis period for that year ends on the new accounting date. It begins immediately after the basis period for the previous year ends. This means the basis period will exceed 12 months.

No overlap profits arise in this situation. However, more than twelve months worth of profits are taxed in one income tax year and to compensate for this, relief is available for brought forward overlap profits. The overlap relief cannot reduce the number of months worth of profits taxed in the year to below twelve. So, if you have a fourteen month basis period you can give relief for up to two months worth of overlap profits.

4.5 Example

Zoe started trading on 1 October 2002 and prepared accounts to 30 September until she changed her accounting date by preparing accounts for the fifteen months to 31 December 2005. Her results were as follows

Year to 30 September 2003	£24,000
Year to 30 September 2004	£48,000
Fifteen months to 31 December 2005	£75,000

Profits for the first three tax years of the business are:

2002/03 (1.10.02 – 5.4.03)	
6/12 × £24,000	£12,000
2003/04 (1.10.02 – 30.9.03)	£24,000
2004/05 (1.10.03 – 30.9.04)	£48,000

Overlap profits are £12,000. These arose in the six months to 5.4.03.

The change in accounting date results in one long period of account ending during 2005/06 which means the basis period for 2005/06 is the fifteen months to 31 December 2005. Three months worth of the brought forward overlap profits can be relieved.

	£
2005/06 (1.10.04 – 31.12.05)	75,000
Less: Overlap profits 3/6 × £12,000	(6,000)
	69,000

The unrelieved overlap profits of £6,000 (£12,000 – £6,000) are carried forward for relief either when the business ceases or on a further change of accounting date.

4.6 No accounting date ending in the year

If a change of accounting date results in there being no period of account ending in a tax year there is a potential problem because basis periods usually end on an accounting date. To get round this problem **you must manufacture a basis period by taking the new accounting date and deducting one year. The basis period is then the twelve months to this date**.

4.7 Example

Anne had always prepared accounts to 31 March. She then changed her accounting date by preparing accounts for the thirteen months to 30 April 2006.

There is no period of account ending during 2005/06 so the basis period for this year is the manufactured basis period of the twelve months to 30 April 2005.

You've probably spotted that this produces an overlap with the previous basis period. The overlap period is 1 May 2004 to 31 March 2005. The overlap profits arising in this period are added to any other unrelieved overlap profits and are carried forward for future relief.

4.8 Two accounting dates ending in the year

When two periods of account end in a tax year, the basis period for the year ends on the new accounting date. It begins immediately following the previous basis period. This means that the basis period will exceed 12 months and overlap relief can be allowed to ensure that only twelve months worth of profits are assessed in the tax year.

4.9 Example

Elizabeth prepared accounts to 30 September until 2006 when she changed her accounting date by preparing accounts for the six months to 31 March 2006.

The new accounting date is 31 March 2006. This is the end of the basis period for 2005/06. The basis period for 2004/05 ended on 30 September 2004. The 2005/06 basis period is therefore the eighteen month period 1 October 2004 to 31 March 2006. Six months worth of overlap profits can be relieved in this year.

4.10 Conditions

The above changes in basis period automatically occur if the trader changes his accounting date during the first three tax years of his business.

In other cases **the following conditions must be met before a change in basis periods can occur**:

- The trader must notify the Revenue of the change by the 31 January, following the tax year in which the change is made. (By 31 January 2007 for a change made during 2005/06.)

- The period of account resulting from the change must not exceed 18 months.

- In general, there must have been no previous change of accounting date in the last 5 tax years. However, a second change can be made within this period if the later change is for genuine commercial reasons. If the Revenue do not respond to a notification of a change of accounting date within 60 days of receiving it, the trader can assume that they are satisfied that the reasons for making the change are genuine commercial ones.

If the above conditions are not satisfied because the first period of account ending on the new date exceeds 18 months or the change of accounting date was not notified in time, but the 'five year gap or commercial reasons' condition is satisfied, then the basis period for the year of change is the 12 months to the *old* accounting date in the year of change. The basis period for the next year is then found using rules above as if it were the year of change.

If the 'five year gap or commercial reasons' test is not satisfied, the old accounting date remains in force for tax purposes (with the profits of accounts made up to the new date being time-apportioned as necessary) until there have been five consecutive tax years which were not years of change. The sixth tax year is then treated as the year of change to the new accounting date, and the rules above apply.

5 Capital allowances for unincorporated businesses

Capital allowances apply to unincorporated businesses with some special rules. In particular, allowances on privately used assets are restricted to reflect the proportion of private use.

5.1 Introduction

Many of the rules are similar, or identical, to those for companies but we recap them here.

Capital expenditure is not in itself an allowable deduction for computing trading profits, but it *may* attract capital allowances. Capital allowances are treated as a trading expense and are deducted in arriving at taxable trading profits. Balancing charges, effectively negative allowances, are added in arriving at those profits.

For capital expenditure to qualify for capital allowances it must fall into one of the following categories:

- plant and machinery
- industrial buildings

For unincorporated businesses, capital allowances are calculated for periods of account. These are simply the periods for which the trader chooses to make up accounts.

The definition of plant is the same for both corporate and unincorporated businesses (see Chapter 3 Section 2).

5.2 Writing down allowances

Allowances are claimed in the tax return. Any business can claim less than the full allowances. This may be to its advantage, if, for example, the trader wants to avoid making such a large loss claim as to lose the benefit of the personal allowance. Higher capital allowances will then be available in later years because the WDV carried forward will be higher.

When plant is sold the proceeds (but limited to a maximum of the original cost) are taken out of the pool of qualifying expenditure. Provided that the trade is still being carried on, the balance remaining is written down in the future by writing down allowances, even if there are no assets left.

Writing down allowances are 25% × months/12 for unincorporated businesses where the period of account is longer or shorter than 12 months.

Expenditure on plant and machinery by a person about to begin a trade is treated as incurred on the first day of trading. Assets previously owned by a trader and then brought into the trade (at the start of trading or later) are treated as bought for their market values at the times when they are brought in.

5.3 First year allowances

5.3.1 Spending by medium sized enterprises

Expenditure incurred on plant and machinery (other than leased assets, cars, sea going ships, railway assets or long life assets) on or after 2 July 1998 **by medium sized enterprises qualifies for a first year allowance** (FYA) of 40%.

Exam focus point

The rates of FYAs will be given to you on the exam paper.

Key term

A **medium sized enterprise,** is an individual or partnership that either satisfies at least two of the following conditions in the chargeable period in which the expenditure is incurred. (a)   **Turnover not more than £22.8 million** (b)   **Assets not more than £11.4 million** (c)   **Not more than 250 employees** or which was medium sized in the previous year. A company must not be a member of a large group when the expenditure is incurred.

5.3.2 Spending by small sized enterprises

Expenditure incurred on plant and machinery after 1 July 1998 by small sized enterprises qualifies for a FYA of 40% in the same way as for medium sized enterprises. **This rate was increased from 40% to 50% for expenditure on or after 6 April 2004 (for unincorporated businesses) for one year.**

A **small enterprise** is an individual or partnership, which satisfies at least two of the following conditions in the chargeable period in which the expenditure is incurred:

(a)   **Turnover not more than £5.6 million**

(b)   **Assets not more than £2.8 million**

(c)   **Not more than 50 employees**

or which was small in the previous year.

5.3.3 100% FYAs

A 100% FYA is available to all businesses for expenditure incurred on designated energy saving technologies and on plant to refuel vehicles with compressed natural gas or hydrogen (in this case on expenditure between 17 April 2002 and 31 March 2008). The equipment must be used in the person's business.

A car registered between 16 April 2002 and 31 March 2008 qualifies for 100% FYAs if it either:

- emits not more than 120 gm/km CO_2 ; or
- it is electrically propelled

In addition, the special rules for expensive cars (see below), which restrict the availability of capital allowances and the deductibility of lease rental payments, do not apply to low emission cars.

Equipment acquired for leasing does not normally qualify for the 100% FYA. Exceptionally, leased low emission and electric cars, natural gas/hydrogen refuelling equipment and certain energy saving equipment all do qualify for FYAs.

In exam questions you should only treat motor cars as low emission cars if they are specifically described as such. You are not expected to know the 120g/km limit.

5.3.4 Calculation

For FYA purposes, the provisions which treat capital expenditure incurred prior to the commencement of trading as incurred on the first day of trading do not apply.

First year allowances are given in the place of writing down allowances. For subsequent years a WDA is given on the balance of expenditure at the normal rate. You should therefore transfer the balance of the expenditure to the pool at the end of the first period.

FYAs are given for incurring expenditure. It is irrelevant whether the basis period of expenditure is twelve months or not. FYAs are never scaled up or down by reference to the length of the period.

Question   Calculation of taxable profits

Walton starts a trade on 1 March 2002, and has the following results (before capital allowances).

Period of account	Profits
	£
1.3.02 - 31.7.03	42,500
1.8.03 - 31.7.04	36,800
1.8.04 - 31.7.05	32,000

Plant (none of which is eligible for 100% FYAs) is bought as follows.

Date	Cost
	£
1.3.02	13,000
1.6.02	9,603
1.2.04	5,000
31.12.04	1,600

On 1 May 2004, plant which cost £7,000 is sold for £4,000.

Walton's business is a small sized enterprise for FYA purposes.

Show the taxable trading profits arising in the above periods of account.

Answer

The capital allowances are as follows.

	FYA	Pool	Allowances
	£	£	£
1.3.02 – 31.7.03			
Additions	22,603		
FYA 40%	(9,041)		9,041
		13,562	
1.8.03 – 31.7.04			
Disposals		(4,000)	
		9,562	
WDA 25%		(2,391)	2,391
		7,171	
Addition (1.2.04)	5,000		
FYA 40%	(2,000)		2,000
		3,000	4,391
		10,171	
1.8.04 – 31.7.05			
WDA 25%		(2,543)	2,543
		7,628	
Addition (31.12.04)	1,600		
FYA 50%	(800)		800
		800	
TWDV c/f		8,428	
			3,343

Note: **First year allowances are not pro-rated in a long period of account.**

The profits of the first three periods of account are as follows.

Period of account	Working	Profits
		£
1.3.02 – 31.7.03	£(42,500 – 9,041)	33,459
1.8.03 – 31.7.04	£(36,800 – 4,391)	32,409
1.8.04 – 31.7.05	£(32,000 – 3,343)	28,657

5.4 Long life assets

The rules in Chapter 3 Section 3.7 also apply to unincorporated businesses. **Individuals and partnerships spending less than £100,000 a year are also excluded** from the long life asset rules provided the individual, or at least half of the partners, works full time in the business.

5.5 Assets which are not pooled

Some items are not pooled. A separate record of allowances and WDV must be kept for each such asset and when it is sold a balancing allowance or charge emerges. The items are:

(a)   **assets** not wholly used for business purposes (such as cars **with private use by the proprietor**);

(b)   **motor cars costing more than £12,000**, where the maximum WDA is £3,000 a year. The limit is £3,000 × months/12 for short or long periods of account of unincorporated businesses.

(c)   **short-life assets** for which an election has been made.

5.6 Assets not wholly used for business purposes

Where an asset (for example, a car) is used partly for private purposes by a sole trader or a partner, make all calculations on the full cost but claim only the business use proportion of the allowances. An asset with some private use by an employee (not a proprietor), however, suffers no such restriction. The employee may be taxed on the private use element as a benefit for income tax so the business gets capital allowances on the full cost of the asset.

Question	Capital allowances on a car

A trader started to trade on 1 July 2002, making up accounts to 31 December 2002 and each 31 December thereafter. On 1 August 2002 he bought a car for £15,500. The private use proportion is 10%. The car was sold in July 2005 for £4,000. What are the capital allowances?

Answer

	Car	Allowances 90%
	£	£
1.7.02 – 31.12.02		
Purchase price	15,500	
WDA 25% × 6/12 of £15,500 = £1,938,		
Limited to £3,000 × 6/12 = £1,500	(1,500)	1,350
	14,000	
1.1.03 – 31.12.03		
WDA 25% of £14,000 = £3,500,		
Limited to £3,000	(3,000)	2,700
	11,000	
1.1.04 – 31.12.04		
WDA 25% of £11,000	(2,750)	2,475
	8,250	
1.1.05 – 31.12.05		
Proceeds	(4,000)	
Balancing allowance	4,250	3,825

5.7 Employees' capital allowances

An employee who provides plant and machinery necessarily for use in the performance of his duties may claim the same allowances as a sole trader, to set against his earnings from employment income. Capital allowances are not available on cars or bicycles.

5.8 The cessation of a trade

When a business ceases to trade no FYAs or WDAs are given in the final period of account. Each asset is deemed to be disposed of on the date the trade ceased (usually at the then market value). Additions in the relevant period are brought in and then the disposal proceeds (limited to cost) are deducted from the balance of qualifying expenditure. If the proceeds exceed the balance then a balancing charge arises. If the balance of qualifying expenditure exceeds the proceeds then a balancing allowance is given.

5.9 Short life assets

The rules in Chapter 3 Section 4 also apply to unincorporated businesses.

Connected persons for individuals are defined above.

5.10 Hire purchase and leasing

The rules in Chapter 3 Section 5 also apply to unincorporated businesses.

5.11 Successions

Balancing adjustments arise on the cessation of a business. No writing down allowances are given, but the final proceeds (limited to cost) on sales of plant are compared with the tax WDV to calculate balancing allowances or charges.

Balancing charges may be avoided where the trade passes from one connected person to another. If a succession occurs both parties must elect if the avoidance of the balancing adjustments is required. **An election will result in the plant being transferred at its tax written down value for capital allowances purposes.** The predecessor can write down the plant for the period prior to cessation and the successor can write it down from the date of commencement. The election must be made within two years of the date of the succession.

If no election is made on a transfer of business to a connected person, assets are deemed to be sold at their market values.

Where a person succeeds to a business under a will or on intestacy, then even if he was not connected with the deceased he may elect to take over the assets at the lower of their market value and their tax written down value.

For both connected persons transfers and transfers on death, where the elections are made, the limit on proceeds to be brought into account on a later sale of an asset is the original cost of the asset, not the deemed transfer price.

5.12 Industrial buildings allowance

The principles in Chapter 3 Sections 7 and 8 also apply to unincorporated businesses. The allowance is only available to traders with trading income from a trade (not to those unincorporated businesses which are professions or vocations) and landlords who let qualifying buildings to traders. The building must be in use on the last day of the basis period for a WDA to be given. The WDA is 4% (or 2%) × months/12 if the basis period is not 12 months long.

Chapter roundup

- The badges of trade can be used to decide whether or not a trade exists. If one does exist, the accounts profits need to be adjusted in order to establish the taxable profits.

- The adjustments needed to the accounting profits for unincorporated businesses are similar to those needed for companies. However, one difference is that the private use proportion of any expenditure is disallowed for unincorporated businesses.

- Basis periods are used to link periods of account to tax years. Broadly, the profits of a period of account ending in a tax year are taxed in that year. In the first tax year of trade actual profits of the tax year are taxed. In the second tax year, the basis period is either the first 12 months, the 12 months to the accounting date ending in year two or the actual profits from April to April. Profits of the twelve months to the accounting date are taxed in year three.

- On a change of accounting date, special rules may apply for fixing basis periods. Overlap profits may either be created or relieved on a change of accounting date. Overlap profits may be relieved if more than 12 months worth of profits would otherwise be taxed in a year following a change of accounting date. On cessation any remaining overlap profits are relieved.

- Capital allowances apply to unincorporated businesses with some special rules. In particular, allowances on private use assets are restricted to reflect the proportion of private use.

Quick quiz

1   List the traditional badges of trade.

2   What is the basis period for the tax year in which a trade commences?

3   On what two occasions can overlap profits potentially be relieved?

4   How is an asset with private use by the proprietor of a business dealt with for capital allowances?

Answers to quick quiz

1   The subject matter
    The frequency of transactions
    The length of ownership
    Supplementary work and marketing
    A profit motive
    The way in which the goods were acquired

2   Date of commencement to 5 April in that year ie the actual tax year.

3   On a change of accounting date where a basis period resulting from the change exceeds 12 months or on the cessation of a business.

4   Calculations of allowances based on full cost but only the business use proportion allowable.

Now try the questions below from the Exam Question Bank

Number	Level	Marks	Time
Q18	Examination	15	27 mins
Q19	Examination	15	27 mins

14

Trading losses

Topic list	Syllabus references
1 Losses	2(c)(vi)
2 Relief for trading losses by carry forward: s 385 ICTA 1988	2(c)(vi)
3 Setting trading losses against total income: s 380 ICTA 1988	2(c)(vi)
4 Losses when business transferred to a company: s 386 ICTA 1988	2(c)(vi)
5 Trade charges: s 387 ICTA 1988	2(c)(vi)
6 Losses in the early years of a trade: s 381 ICTA 1988	2(c)(vi)
7 Losses on the cessation of a trade: s 388 ICTA 1988	2(c)(vi)

Introduction

Traders sometimes make losses rather than profits. In this chapter we consider the reliefs available for losses. A loss does not in itself lead to getting tax back from the Revenue. Relief is obtained by setting a loss against trading profits, against other income or against capital gains, so that tax need not be paid on them. An important consideration is the choice between different reliefs. The aim is to use a loss to save as much tax as possible, as quickly as possible.

1 Losses

Trade losses may be relieved against future profits of the same trade, against total income or against capital gains.

When computing taxable trade profits, profits may turn out to be negative, that is a loss has been made in the basis period. **A loss is computed in exactly the same way as a profit**, making the same adjustments to the accounts profit or loss.

If there is a loss in a basis period, the taxable trade profits for the tax year based on that basis period are nil.

This chapter considers how losses are calculated and how a loss-suffering taxpayer can use a loss to reduce his tax liability. Most of the chapter concerns the trade losses in respect of trades, professions and vocations.

The rules in this chapter apply only to individuals, trading alone or in partnership. Loss reliefs for companies are completely different and were covered earlier in this text.

Losses of one spouse cannot be relieved against income of the other spouse.

2 Relief for trading losses by carry forward: s 385 ICTA 1988

Under s 385 ICTA 1988 trading losses may be relieved against future profits of the same trade. The relief is against the first available profits of the same trade.

2.1 The relief

A trade loss not relieved in any other way may be **carried forward to set against the first available trade profits of the same trade**. Losses may be carried forward for any number of years.

2.2 Example: carrying forward losses

B has the following results.

Year ending	£
31 December 2003	(6,000)
31 December 2004	5,000
31 December 2005	11,000

B's taxable profits, assuming that he claims loss relief only under s 385 are:

	2003/04 £		2004/05 £		2005/06 £
Trade profits	0		5,000		11,000
Less s 385 relief	(0)	(i)	(5,000)	(ii)	(1,000)
Profits	0		0		10,000

Loss memorandum		£
Trading loss, y/e 31.12.03		6,000
Less: claim in y/e 31.12.04	(i)	(5,000)
claim in y/e 31.12.05 (balance of loss)	(ii)	(1,000)
		0

3 Setting trading losses against total income: s 380 ICTA 1988

Under s 380 ICTA 1988 a trading loss may be set against STI in the year of the loss and/or the preceding year. Personal allowances may be lost as a result of a s 380 ICTA 1988 claim. Once a s 380 claim has been made in any year, the remaining loss can be set against net chargeable gains.

3.1 The relief

Instead of carrying a trade loss forward against future trade profits, it may be relieved against current income of all types.

3.2 The computation of the loss

The trade loss for a tax year is the trade loss in the basis period for that tax year. However, **if basis periods overlap then a loss in the overlap period is a trade loss for the earlier tax year only**. There is no such thing as overlap losses.

3.3 Example

Here is an example of a trader who starts to trade on 1 July 2005 and makes losses in opening years.

Period of account			Loss £
1.7.05 – 31.12.05			9,000
1.1.06 – 31.12.06			24,000

Tax year	Basis period	Working	Trade loss for the tax year £
2005/06	1.7.05 – 5.4.06	£9,000 + (£24,000 × 3/12)	15,000
2006/07	1.1.06 – 31.12.06	£24,000 – (£24,000 × 3/12)	18,000

3.4 Example

The same rule against using losses twice applies when losses are netted off against profits in the same basis period. Here is an example, again with a commencement on 1 July 2005 but with a different accounting date.

Period of account			(Loss)/profit £
1.7.05 – 30.4.06			(10,000)
1.5.06 – 30.4.07			24,000

Tax year	Basis period	Working	Trade (Loss)/Profit £
2005/06	1.7.05 – 5.4.06	£(10,000) × 9/10	(9,000)
2006/07	1.7.05 – 30.6.06	£24,000 × 2/12 + £(10,000) × 1/10	3,000

3.5 Relieving the loss

Relief under s 380 **is against the income of the tax year in which the loss arose. In addition or instead,** relief may be claimed **against the income of the preceding year**.

If there are losses in two successive years, and relief is claimed against the first year's income both for the first year's loss and for the second year's loss, relief is given for the first year's loss before the second year's loss.

A claim for a loss must be made by the 31 January which is 22 months after the end of the tax year of the loss: thus by 31 January 2008 for a loss in 2005/06.

The taxpayer cannot choose the amount of loss to relieve: thus the loss may have to be set against income part of which would have been covered by the personal allowance. However, the taxpayer can choose whether to claim full relief in the current year and then relief in the preceding year for any remaining loss, or the other way round.

Set the loss against non-savings income then against savings (excluding dividend) income and finally against dividend income.

Relief is available by carry forward under s 385 for any loss not relieved under s 380.

Question
s 380 relief

Janet has a loss in her period of account ending 31 December 2005 of £25,000. Her other income is £18,000 rental income a year, and she wishes to claim loss relief for the year of loss and then for the preceding year. Show her taxable income for each year, and comment on the effectiveness of the loss relief. Assume that tax rates and allowances for 2005/06 have always applied.

Answer

The loss-making period ends in 2005/06, so the year of the loss is 2005/06.

	2004/05 £	2005/06 £
Income	18,000	18,000
Less s 380 relief	(7,000)	(18,000)
STI	11,000	0
Less personal allowance	(4,895)	(4,895)
Taxable income	6,105	0

In 2005/06, £4,895 of the loss has been wasted because that amount of income would have been covered by the personal allowance. If Janet claims s 380 relief, there is nothing she can do about this waste of loss relief.

3.6 Capital allowances

The trader may adjust the size of the total s 380 claim by not claiming all the capital allowances he is entitled to: a reduced claim will increase the balance carried forward to the next year's capital allowances computation. This may be a useful **tax planning point where the effective rate of relief for capital allowances in future periods will be greater than the rate of tax relief for the s 380 loss**.

3.7 Trading losses relieved against capital gains

Where relief is claimed against total income of a given year, the taxpayer may include **a further claim to set the loss against his chargeable gains for the year** less any allowable capital losses for the same year or for previous years. This amount of net gains is computed ignoring taper relief and the annual exempt amount (see later in this text).

The trading loss is first set against total income of the year of the claim, and only any excess of loss is set against capital gains. The taxpayer cannot specify the amount to be set against capital gains, so the annual exempt amount may be wasted. We include an example here for completeness. You will study chargeable gains later in this text and we suggest that you come back to this example at that point.

Question — Loss relief against income and gains

Sibyl had the following results for 2005/06.

	£
Loss available for relief under s 380	27,000
Income	19,500
Capital gains less current year capital losses	10,000
Annual exemption for capital gains tax purposes	8,500
Capital losses brought forward	4,000

Assume no taper relief is due.

Show how the loss would be relieved against income and gains.

Answer

	£
Income	19,500
Less loss relief	(19,500)
STI	0
Capital gains	10,000
Less loss relief: lower of £(27,000 – 19,500) = £7,500 (note 1) and £(10,000 – 4,000) = £6,000 (note 2)	(6,000)
	4,000
Less annual exemption (restricted)	(4,000)
	0

Note 1 This equals the loss left after the S380 claim
Note 2 This equals the gains left after losses b/fwd but ignoring taper relief and the annual exemption.

A trading loss of £(7,500 – 6,000) = £1,500 is carried forward. Sibyl's personal allowance and £(8,500 – 4,000) = £4,500 of her capital gains tax annual exemption are wasted. Her capital losses brought forward of £4,000 are carried forward to 2006/07. Although we deducted this £4,000 in working out how much trading loss we were allowed to use in the claim, we do not actually use any of the £4,000 unless there are gains remaining after the annual exemption.

3.8 Restrictions on s 380 relief

Relief cannot be claimed under s 380 unless a business is conducted on a commercial basis with a view to the realisation of profits; this condition applies to all types of business.

3.9 The choice between loss reliefs

FAST FORWARD

It is important for a trader to choose the right loss relief, so as to save tax at the highest possible rate and so as to obtain relief reasonably quickly.

When a trader has a choice between loss reliefs, he should aim to obtain relief both quickly and at the highest possible tax rate. However, do consider that losses relieved against income which would otherwise be covered by the personal allowance are wasted.

Another consideration is that a trading loss cannot be set against the capital gains of a year unless relief is first claimed under s 380 against income of the same year. It may be worth making the claim against income and wasting the personal allowance in order to avoid a CGT liability.

Question	The choice between loss reliefs

Felicity's trading results are as follows.

Year ended 30 September	Trading profit/(loss)
	£
2003	1,900
2004	(21,000)
2005	13,000

Her other income (all non-savings income) is as follows.

	£
2003/04	2,200
2004/05	25,895
2005/06	12,000

Show the most efficient use of Felicity's trading loss. Assume that the personal allowance has been £4,895 throughout.

Answer

Relief could be claimed under s 380 for 2003/04 and/or 2004/05, with any unused loss being carried forward under s 385. Relief in 2003/04 would be against total income of £(1,900 + 2,200) = £4,100, all of which would be covered by the personal allowance anyway, so this claim should not be made. A s 380 claim should be made for 2004/05 as this saves tax quicker than a s 385 claim in 2005/06 would. The final results will be as follows:

	2003/04	2004/05	2005/06
	£	£	£
Trading income	1,900	0	13,000
Less s 385 relief	(0)	(0)	(0)
	1,900	0	13,000
Other income	2,200	25,895	12,000
	4,100	25,895	25,000
Less s 380 relief	(0)	(21,000)	(0)
STI	4,100	4,895	25,000
Less personal allowance	(4,895)	(4,895)	(4,895)
Taxable income	0	0	20,105

Exam focus point

Before recommending s 380 loss relief consider whether it will result in the waste of the personal allowance and any tax reducers. Such waste is to be avoided if at all possible.

4 Losses when business transferred to a company: s 386 ICTA 1988

Where a business is transferred to a company, loss relief is available for the existing loss of the unincorporated business against income received from the company.

Although the set-off under s 385 is restricted to future profits of the same business, this is extended to cover income received from a company to which the business is sold; under s 386.

The amount carried forward is the total unrelieved trading losses of the business. The set-off must be made against the first available income from the company. The order of set-off is:

(a) Against **salary** derived from the company by the former proprietor of the business; **then**
(b) Against **interest and dividends** from the company

The consideration for the sale must be wholly or mainly shares, which must be retained by the vendor throughout any tax year in which the loss is relieved; the Revenue treat this condition as being satisfied if 80% or more of the consideration consists of shares.

5 Trade charges: s 387 ICTA 1988

Excess trade charges can be set against future profits in the same way as losses under s.385.

5.1 The relief

Annual charges such as patent royalties, although they may be paid out wholly and exclusively for business purposes, are nevertheless not deducted in arriving at the adjusted trade profits or losses.

But it is possible to suffer a 'loss' if STI is reduced to zero by such a charge because the Revenue will collect the tax withheld from the charge under s 350 ICTA 1988. **Excess trade charges can be carried forward against future profits from the same trade** in the same way as losses under s 385. Non-trade charges, however cannot be relieved in this way.

5.2 Example: excess trade charges

A taxpayer has the following results for 2005/06.

	£
Trading profits	4,000
Other income	1,000
	5,000
Less patent royalty	(7,000)
STI	0

Basic rate tax would be due on the unrelieved £2,000, so that the taxpayer accounted for 22% × £2,000 = £440, but the taxpayer could then carry forward the £2,000 against future profits from the trade.

6 Losses in the early years of a trade: s 381 ICTA 1988

In opening years, a special relief involving the carry back of losses against total income is available. Losses arising in the first four tax years of a trade may be set against total income in the three years preceding the loss making year, taking the earliest year first.

S 381 relief is available for **trading losses incurred in the first four tax years of a trade**.

Relief is obtained by **setting the allowable loss against total income in the three years preceding the year of loss**, applying the loss to the earliest year first. Thus a loss arising in 2005/06 may be set off against income in 2002/03, 2003/04 and 2004/05 in that order.

A claim under s 381 applies to all three years automatically, provided that the loss is large enough. The taxpayer cannot choose to relieve the loss against just one or two of the years, or to relieve only part of the loss. However, the taxpayer could reduce the size of the loss by not claiming the full capital allowances available to him. This will result in higher capital allowances in future years.

Do not double-count a loss. If basis periods overlap, a loss in the overlap period is treated as a loss for the earlier tax year only. This is the same rule as applies for s 380 purposes.

Claims for the relief must be made by the 31 January which is nearly two years after the end of the tax year in which the loss is incurred.

The 'commercial basis' test is stricter for loss relief under s 381 than under s 380. The trade must be carried on in such a way that profits could reasonably have been expected to be realised in the period of the loss or within a reasonable time thereafter.

> **Question**   s 381 loss relief
>
> Mr A is employed as a dustman until 1 January 2004. On that date he starts up his own business as a scrap metal merchant, making up his accounts to 30 June each year. His earnings as a dustman are:

	£
2000/01	5,000
2001/02	6,000
2002/03	7,000
2003/04 (nine months)	6,000

His trading results as a scrap metal merchant are:

	Profit/(Loss)
	£
Six months to 30 June 2004	(3,000)
Year to 30 June 2005	(1,500)
Year to 30 June 2006	(1,200)
Year to 30 June 2007	0

Assuming that loss relief is claimed as early as possible, show the final taxable income before personal allowances for each of the years 2000/01 to 2006/07 inclusive.

Answer

Since reliefs are to be claimed as early as possible, s 381 ICTA 1988 is applied. The losses available for relief are as follows.

	£	£	Years against which relief is available
2003/04 (basis period 1.1.04 – 5.4.04)			
3 months to 5.4.04 £(3,000) × 3/6		(1,500)	2000/01 to 2002/03
2004/05 (basis period 1.1.04 – 31.12.04)			
3 months to 30.6.04			
(omit 1.1.04 – 5.4.04: overlap) £(3,000) × 3/6	(1,500)		
6 months to 31.12.04 £(1,500) × 6/12	(750)		
		(2,250)	2001/02 to 2003/04
2005/06 (basis period 1.7.04 – 30.6.05)			
6 months to 30.6.05			
(omit 1.7.04 – 31.12.04: overlap) £(1,500) × 6/12		(750)	2002/03 to 2004/05
2006/07 (basis period 1.7.05 – 30.6.06)			
12 months to 30.6.06		(1,200)	2003/04 to 2005/06

The revised taxable income before personal allowances is as follows.

	£	£
2000/01		
Original	5,000	
Less 2003/04 loss	(1,500)	
		3,500
2001/02		
Original	6,000	
Less 2004/05 loss	(2,250)	
		3,750
2002/03		
Original	7,000	
Less 2005/06 loss	(750)	
		6,250
2003/04		
Original	6,000	
Less 2006/07 loss	(1,200)	
		4,800

The taxable trade profits for 2003/04 to 2006/07 are zero. There were losses in the basis periods.

7 Losses on the cessation of a trade: s 388 ICTA 1988

FAST FORWARD

On the cessation of trade, a loss arising in the last 12 months of trading may be set against trade profits of the tax year of cessation and the previous 3 years, taking the last year first.

7.1 The relief

S 380 relief will often be insufficient on its own to deal with a loss incurred in the last months of trading. For this reason there is a special relief, **terminal loss relief, which allows a loss on cessation to be carried back for relief in previous years.**

7.2 Computing the terminal loss

A terminal loss under s 388 is **the loss of the last 12 months of trading**.

It is built up as follows.

			£
(a)	The actual trade loss for the tax year of cessation (calculated from 6 April to the date of cessation)		X
(b)	The actual trade loss for the period from 12 months before cessation until the end of the penultimate tax year		X
(c)	Any excess trade charges for the tax year of cessation		X
(d)	A proportion of any excess trade charges for the penultimate tax year		X
	Total terminal loss		X

If either (a) or (b) above yields a profit as opposed to a loss, the profit is regarded as zero for this purpose.

The terminal loss cannot include any amounts for which relief has already been given. Make sure that computations exclude any amounts claimed under s 380 and also any losses which have been set off in computing the taxable profits for the final tax year.

The proportion mentioned in (d) above is needed to ensure that only trade charges of the last 12 months are included. The figure included in the terminal loss is limited to the total trade charges multiplied by:

$$\frac{\text{number of months in item (b) in the computation}}{12}$$

Any unrelieved overlap profits may be deducted in the tax year of cessation and should, therefore, be included within (a) above.

7.3 Relieving the terminal loss

The income against which the terminal loss can be set in any one year is computed as follows.

	£
Taxable trade profits	X
Less the excess of the gross amount of charges paid net of tax over other income *	(X)
Available for s 388 relief	X

*   This amount also comes off the terminal loss available for relief in earlier years to the extent that it is charges which are non-trade *and* do not give rise to a s 350 charge.

Relief is given in the tax year of cessation and the three preceding years, later years first.

Question	Terminal loss relief

Set out below are the results of a business up to its cessation on 30 September 2005.

	Profit/(loss) £
Year to 31 December 2002	2,000
Year to 31 December 2003	400
Year to 31 December 2004	300
Nine months to 30 September 2005	(1,950)

Overlap profits on commencement were £450. These were all unrelieved on cessation.

Show the available terminal loss relief, and suggest an alternative claim if the trader had had other non-savings income of £10,000 in each of 2004/05 and 2005/06. Assume that 2005/06 tax rates and allowances apply to all years.

Answer

The terminal loss comes in the last 12 months, the period 1 October 2004 to 30 September 2005. This period is split as follows.

2004/05	Six months to 5 April 2005
2005/06	Six months to 30 September 2005

The terminal loss is made up as follows.

Unrelieved trading losses		£	£
2004/05			
3 months to 31.12.04	£300 × 3/12	75	
3 months to 5.4.05	£(1,950) × 3/9	(650)	
			(575)
2005/06			
6 months to 30.9.05	£(1,950) × 6/9		(1,300)
Overlap relief	£(450)		(450)
			(2,325)

Taxable trade profits will be as follows.

Year	Basis period	Profits £	Terminal loss relief £	Final taxable profits £
2002/03	Y/e 31.12.02	2,000	1,625	375
2003/04	Y/e 31.12.03	400	400	0
2004/05	Y/e 31.12.04	300	300	0
2005/06	1.1.05 – 30.9.05	0	0	0
			2,325	

If the trader had had £10,000 of other income in 2004/05 and 2005/06, we would have had to consider s380 claims for these two years, using the loss of £(1,950 + 450) = £2,400 for 2005/06.

The final results would be as follows. (We could alternatively claim loss relief in 2004/05.)

	2002/03 £	2003/04 £	2004/05 £	2005/06 £
Trade profits	2,000	400	300	0
Other income	0	0	10,000	10,000
	2,000	400	10,300	10,000
Less s 380 claims	0	0	0	(2,400)
STI	2,000	400	10,300	7,600

Chapter roundup

- Trade losses may be relieved against future profits of the same trade, against total income and against capital gains.

- Under s 385 ICTA 1988 trading losses may be relieved against future profits of the same trade. The relief is against the first available profits of the same trade.

- Under s 380 ICTA 1988 a trading loss may be set against STI in the year of the loss and/or the preceding year. Personal allowances may be lost as a result of a s 380 ICTA 1988 claim. Once a s 380 claim has been made in any year, the remaining loss can be set against net chargeable gains.

- It is important for a trader to choose the right loss relief, so as to save tax at the highest possible rate and so as to obtain relief reasonably quickly.

- Where a business is transferred to a company, loss relief is available for the existing loss of the unincorporated business against income received from the company.

- Excess trade charges can be set against future profits in the same way as losses under s.385.

- In opening years, a special relief involving the carry back of losses against total income is available. Losses arising in the first four tax years of a trade may be set against total income in the three years preceding the loss making year, taking the earliest year first.

- On the cessation of trade, a loss arising in the last 12 months of trading may be set against trade profits of the tax year of cessation and the previous 3 years, taking the last year first.

Quick quiz

1   Against what income trade losses carried forward be set off?

2   When a loss is to be relieved against total income, how are losses linked to particular tax years?

3   Against which years' total income may a loss be relieved under s 380 ICTA 1988?

4   For which losses is s 381 relief available?

5   In which years may relief for a terminal loss be given?

Answers to quick quiz

1   Against trade profits from the same trade.

2   The loss for a tax year is the loss in the basis period for that tax year. However, if basis periods overlap, a loss in the overlap period is a loss of the earlier tax year only.

3   The year in which the loss arose and/or the preceding year.

4   Losses incurred in the first four years of a trade.

5   In the year of cessation and then in the three preceding years, later years first.

Now try the question below from the Exam Question Bank			
Number	**Level**	**Marks**	**Time**
Q20	Examination	15	27 mins

15

Partnerships

Topic list	Syllabus references
1 Partnerships	2(c)(vii)
2 Limited liability partnerships	2(c)(vii)

Introduction

We now see how the income tax rules for traders are adapted to deal with business partnerships. On the one hand, a partnership is a single trading entity, making profits as a whole. On the other hand, each partner has a personal tax computation, so the profits must be apportioned to the partners. The general approach is to work out the profits of the partnership, then tax each partner as if he were a sole trader running a business equal to his slice of the partnership (for example 25% of the partnership).

1 Partnerships

A partnership is simply treated as a source of profits and losses for trades being carried on by the individual partners. Divide profits or losses between the partners according to the profit sharing ratio in the period of account concerned. If any of the partners are entitled to a salary or interest on capital, apportion this first, not forgetting to pro-rate in periods of less than 12 months.

1.1 Basis of assessment

A business partnership is treated like a sole trader for the purposes of computing its profits. (As usual, 'trade' in this chapter includes professions and vocations.) Partners' salaries and interest on capital are not deductible expenses and must be added back in computing profits, because they are a form of drawings.

Once the partnership's profits for a period of account have been computed, they are shared between the partners according to the profit sharing arrangements for that period of account.

1.2 The tax positions of individual partners

Each partner is taxed like a sole trader who runs a business which:

- Starts when he joins the partnership

- Finishes when he leaves the partnership

- Has the same periods of account as the partnership (except that a partner who joins or leaves during a period will have a period which starts or ends part way through the partnership's period)

- Makes profits or losses equal to the partner's share of the partnership's profits or losses

1.3 Changes in membership

Commencement and cessation rules apply to partners individually when they join or leave.

When a trade continues but partners join or leave (including cases when a sole trader takes in partners or a partnership breaks up leaving only one partner as a sole trader), **the special rules for basis periods in opening and closing years do not apply to the people who were carrying on the trade both before and after the change. They carry on using the period of account ending in each tax year as the basis period for the tax year. The commencement rules only affect joiners, and the cessation rules only affect leavers.**

However, when no-one carries on the trade both before and after the change, as when a partnership transfers its trade to a completely new owner or set of owners, the cessation rules apply to the old owners and the commencement rules apply to the new owners.

1.4 Loss reliefs

There are restrictions on loss reliefs for non-active partners in the first four years of trading.

Partners are entitled to the same loss reliefs as sole traders. A partner is entitled to s 381 relief for losses in the four tax years starting with the year in which he is treated as starting to trade and he is entitled to terminal loss relief when he is treated as ceasing to trade. This is so even if the partnership trades for many years before the partner joins or after he leaves. Loss relief under s 380 and s 385 is also available to partners. Different partners may claim loss reliefs in different ways.

There is a restriction for loss relief for a partner who does not spend a significant amount of time (less than 10 hours a week) in running the trade of the partnership. Such a partner can only use loss relief under s 380 and s 381 ICTA 1988 or against capital gains **up to an amount equal to the amount that he contributes to the partnership.** These rules apply in any of the first four years in which the partner carries on a trade.

1.5 Example: loss relief restriction

Laura, Mark and Norman form a partnership and each contribute £10,000. Laura and Mark run the trade full time. Norman is employed elsewhere and plays little part in running the trade. Profits and losses are to be shared 45: 35: 20 to L:M:N. The partnership makes a loss of £60,000 of which £12,000 is allocated to Norman.

Norman may only use £10,000 of loss under s 380 (plus against capital gains) or s 381. £2,000 is carried forward, for example to be relieved against future profits under s 385.

When a partnership business is transferred to a company, each partner can carry forward his share of any unrelieved losses against income from the company under s 386 ICTA 1988.

1.6 Assets owned individually

Where the partners own assets (such as their cars) individually, a capital allowances computation must be prepared for each partner in respect of the assets he owns (not forgetting any adjustment for private use). **The capital allowances must go into the partnership's tax computation.**

1.7 Example: a partnership

Alice and Bertrand start a partnership on 1 July 2002, making up accounts to 31 December each year. On 1 May 2004, Charles joins the partnership. On 1 November 2005, Charles leaves. On 1 January 2006, Deborah joins. The profit sharing arrangements are as follows.

	Alice	Bertrand	Charles	Deborah
1.7.02 – 31.1.03				
Salaries (per annum)	£3,000	£4,500		
Balance	3/5	2/5		
1.2.03 – 30.4.04				
Salaries (per annum)	£3,000	£6,000		
Balance	4/5	1/5		
1.5.04 – 31.10.05				
Salaries (per annum)	£2,400	£3,600	£1,800	
Balance	2/5	2/5	1/5	
1.11.05 – 31.12.05				
Salaries (per annum)	£1,500	£2,700		
Balance	3/5	2/5		
1.1.06 onwards				
Salaries (per annum)	£1,500	£2,700		£600
Balance	3/5	1/5		1/5

Profits and losses as adjusted for tax purposes are as follows.

Period	Profit(loss)
	£
1.7.02 – 31.12.02	22,000
1.1.03 – 31.12.03	51,000
1.1.04 – 31.12.04	39,000
1.1.05 – 31.12.05	15,000
1.1.06 – 31.12.06	(18,000)

Show the taxable trade profits for each partner for 2002/03 to 2005/06, and outline the loss reliefs available to the partners in respect of the loss in the year ending 31 December 2006. All the partners work full time in the partnership. Assume that the partnership will continue to trade with the same partners until 2015.

Solution

We must first share the trade profits and losses for the periods of account between the partners, remembering to adjust the salaries for periods of less than a year.

	Total £	Alice £	Bertrand £	Charles £	Deborah £
1.7.02 – 31.12.02					
Salaries	3,750	1,500	2,250		
Balance	18,250	10,950	7,300		
Total (P/e 31.12.02)	22,000	12,450	9,550		
1.1.03 – 31.12.03					
January					
Salaries	625	250	375		
Balance	3,625	2,175	1,450		
Total	4,250	2,425	1,825		
February to December					
Salaries	8,250	2,750	5,500		
Balance	38,500	30,800	7,700		
Total	46,750	33,550	13,200		
Total for y/e 31.12.03	51,000	35,975	15,025		
1.1.04 – 31.12.04					
January to April					
Salaries	3,000	1,000	2,000		
Balance	10,000	8,000	2,000		
Total	13,000	9,000	4,000		
May to December					
Salaries	5,200	1,600	2,400	1,200	
Balance	20,800	8,320	8,320	4,160	
Total	26,000	9,920	10,720	5,360	
Total for y/e 31.12.04	39,000	18,920	14,720	5,360	

	Total £	Alice £	Bertrand £	Charles £	Deborah £
1.1.05 – 31.12.05					
January to October					
Salaries	6,500	2,000	3,000	1,500	
Balance	6,000	2,400	2,400	1,200	
Total	12,500	4,400	5,400	2,700	
November and December					
Salaries	700	250	450		
Balance	1,800	1,080	720		
Total	2,500	1,330	1,170		
Total for y/e 31.12.05	15,000	5,730	6,570	2,700	
1.1.06 – 31.12.06					
Salaries	4,800	1,500	2,700		600
Balance	(22,800)	(13,680)	(4,560)		(4,560)
Total loss for y/e 31.12.06	(18,000)	(12,180)	(1,860)		(3,960)

The next stage is to work out the basis periods and hence the taxable trade profits for the partners. All of them are treated as making up accounts to 31 December, but Alice and Bertrand are treated as starting to trade on 1 July 2002, Charles as trading only from 1 May 2004 to 31 October 2005 and Deborah as starting to trade on 1 January 2006. Applying the usual rules gives the following basis periods and taxable profits.

Alice

Year	Basis period	Working	Taxable profits £
2002/03	1.7.02 – 5.4.03	£12,450 + (£35,975 × 3/12)	21,444
2003/04	1.1.03 – 31.12.03		35,975
2004/05	1.1.04 – 31.12.04		18,920
2005/06	1.1.05 – 31.12.05		5,730

Note that for 2002/03 we take Alice's total for the year ended 2003 and apportion that, because the partnership's period of account runs from 1 January to 31 December 2003. Alice's profits for 2002/03 are *not* £12,450 + £2,425 + (£33,550 × 2/11) = £20,975.

Alice will have overlap profits for the period 1 January to 5 April 2003 (£35,975 × 3/12 = £8,994) to deduct when she ceases to trade.

Bertrand

Year	Basis period	Working	Taxable profits £
2002/03	1.7.02 – 5.4.03	£9,550 + (£15,025 × 3/12)	13,306
2003/04	1.1.03 – 31.12.03		15,025
2004/05	1.1.04 – 31.12.04		14,720
2005/06	1.1.05 – 31.12.05		6,570

Bertrand's overlap profits are £15,025 × 3/12 = £3,756.

Charles

Year	Basis period	Working	Taxable profits £
2004/05	1.5.04 – 5.4.05	£5,360 + (£2,700 × 3/10)	6,170
2005/06	6.4.05 – 31.10.05	£2,700 × 7/10	1,890

Because Charles ceased to trade in his second tax year of trading, his basis period for the second year starts on 6 April and he has no overlap profits.

Deborah

Year	Basis period	Working	Taxable profits £
2005/06	1.1.06 – 5.4.06	A loss arises	0

Finally, we must look at the loss reliefs available to Alice, Bertrand and Deborah. Charles is not entitled to any loss relief, because he left the firm before any loss arose.

Alice and Bertrand

For 2006/07, Alice has a loss of £12,180 and Bertrand has a loss of £1,860. They may claim relief under s 380 or under s 385.

Deborah

Deborah's losses are as follows, remembering that a loss which falls in the basis periods for two tax years is only taken into account in the earlier year.

Year	Basis period	Working	Loss £
2005/06	1.1.06 – 5.4.06	£3,960 × 3/12	990
2006/07	1.1.06 – 31.12.06	£3,960 – £990 (used in 2005/06)	2,970

Deborah may claim relief for these losses under s 380, s 381 (because she has just started to trade) or s 385.

<table>
<tr><td>

Exam focus point

</td><td>

Partners are effectively taxed in the same way as sole traders with just one difference. Before you tax the partner you need to take each set of accounts (as adjusted for tax purposes) and divide the trade profit (or loss) between each partner.

Then carry on as normal for a sole trader – each partner is that sole trader in respect of his trade profits for each accounting period.

</td></tr>
</table>

2 Limited liability partnerships

FAST FORWARD

Limited liability partnerships are taxed on virtually the same basis as normal partnerships but loss relief is restricted for all partners.

It is possible to form a limited liability partnership. The difference between a limited liability partnership (LLP) and a normal partnership is that **in a LLP the liability of the partners is limited to the capital they contributed.**

The partners of a LLP are taxed on virtually the same basis as the partners of a normal partnership (see above). However, the amount of loss relief that a partner can claim under s 380 and s 381 ICTA 1988 when the claim is against non-partnership income is restricted to the capital he contributed. This rule is not restricted to the first four years of trading and the rules apply to all partners whether or not involved in the running of the trade.

Chapter roundup

- A partnership is simply treated as a source of profits and losses for trades being carried on by the individual partners. Divide profits or losses between the partners according to the profit sharing ratio in the period of account concerned. If any of the partners are entitled to a salary or interest on capital, apportion this first, not forgetting to pro-rate in periods of less than 12 months.

- Commencement and cessation rules apply to partners individually when they join or leave.

- There are restrictions on loss reliefs for non-active partners in the first four years of trading.

- Limited liability partnerships are taxed on virtually the same basis as normal partnerships but loss relief is restricted for all partners.

Quick quiz

1   How are partnership trading profits divided between the individual partners?

2   What loss reliefs are partners entitled to?

Answers to quick quiz

1   Profits are divided in accordance with the profit sharing ratio that existed during the period of account in which the profits arose.

2   Partners are entitled to the same loss reliefs as sole traders. This means that partners may claim relief for their share or a loss under s 380, s 381, s 385, s 388 or s 386 as appropriate.

Now try the questions below from the Exam Question Bank

Number	Level	Marks	Time
Q21	Examination	15	27 mins
Q22	Examination	15	27 mins

Personal pensions. NICs for the self employed

16

Topic list	Syllabus reference
1 Personal pension schemes	2(c)(viii)
2 National insurance contributions (NICs) for the self employed	2(f)

Introduction

Employees may be provided with pensions under an occupational pension scheme (dealt with in Chapter 21) or under a personal pension scheme. Tax relief is given for contributions to either type of pension scheme.

Self-employed individuals must make provision under a personal pension scheme.

The self-employed are required to make national insurance contributions in two ways: a flat rate contribution (Class 2) and a contribution based on profits (Class 4).

1 Personal pension schemes

Key term

> **Personal pension schemes (PPSs)** are a means of providing pensions for the self-employed, employees who are not in an employer's occupational scheme and also those who are not in work.

1.1 Introduction

FAST FORWARD

> Anyone can contribute to a personal pension scheme, even if they are not earning, subject to the contributions threshold of £3,600 (gross). A stakeholder pension is a type of personal pension scheme.

Stakeholder pensions are a type of personal pension scheme. The rules for personal pension schemes discussed below apply to both personal pension and stakeholder schemes.

Exam focus point

> There are certain non-tax advantages to stakeholder pensions but these are not examinable.

1.2 Eligibility

An individual who is below the age of 75 may contribute to a personal pension scheme in a tax year if he satisfies one of the following conditions:

(a)   he has **no actual net relevant earnings** (see below) in the year and is not in an occupational pension scheme, but is **resident and ordinarily resident in the UK at some time in the tax year**. An individual may also continue contributing to pension arrangements made whilst he was resident and ordinarily resident in the UK for up to five tax years after he ceases to satisfy the residency condition, or

(b)   **he is in an occupational pension scheme** and is entitled to join a personal pension scheme under **'concurrent membership'** (see further below), or

(c)   he has **actual net relevant earnings** in the year.

It is possible for a personal pension scheme to accept payments from a person other than the scheme member where that member satisfies condition (a). Thus a parent may make contributions for his child (even under the age of 18) or a working spouse could contribute on behalf of a housewife/husband. **If a scheme member is employed (ie falls under condition (b) or (c)), his employer may make contributions to the personal pension scheme.**

Concurrent membership (ie. membership of both an occupational scheme and a personal pension scheme) is available to an individual who satisfies the following conditions:

(a)   **the individual is not a controlling director** of a company at any time in the tax year or in any tax year in the last five tax years, and

(b)   **in at least one out of the last five tax years his earnings were below the remuneration limit.** This is set as £30,000 for 2005/06.

(c)   he is resident and ordinarily resident in the UK at sometime in the tax year (or was so resident and ordinarily resident at the time the arrangements were made and at some time in the last five tax years).

A 'controlling director' is broadly an individual who owns or controls (by himself or with his family or business associates) more than 20% of the company which employs him.

1.3 Limits

1.3.1 Time of retirement

Normal Retirement Age can be at any time between 50 and 75. Unplanned retirement - early retirement - can take place before age 50, but only on the grounds of serious ill health. However, some occupations, eg sportsmen, are allowed to have normal retirement ages earlier than 50.

1.3.2 Benefits

There are **no limits** on the amount of the pension allowable. At retirement the fund can be used to buy the highest annuity available at the time and there will be no restriction on the amounts.

It is also possible to take out a **tax-free cash lump sum** on retirement. There is **no restriction** on the **amount** of tax-free cash but it is limited to 25% of the size of the fund at the time. The individual effectively takes a reduced pension in order to obtain the tax free cash simply because only the balance (75%) of the fund remains for an annuity purchase (ie buying an annual pension).

1.3.3 Contributions

FAST FORWARD

> The maximum contributions that can be made by earners to personal pension plans are a certain specified percentage of net relevant earnings of the basis year. The percentage depends on the taxpayer's age at the start of the year. The basis year for contributions may be the current tax year or any of the previous five tax years.

Although benefits are not limited, there is a restriction placed on **contributions**.

For individuals within 1.2(a) and (b) above (ie those with no net relevant earnings or with concurrent membership), **annual contributions (by the scheme member and anyone else, eg employer, parent) to the personal pension scheme cannot in total exceed the contributions threshold**. The contributions threshold is fixed at £3,600 for 2005/06. This figure includes tax relief at the basic rate. Therefore, net payments of £2,808 can be made into the scheme. This would be increased by tax relief of £792 (at 22%) given by the Revenue to the pension provider to make up the total of £3,600 (see further below for more details on tax relief).

For individuals within 1.2(c) (those with net relevant earnings), **annual contributions (by the scheme member and anyone else, eg employer) to the personal pension scheme cannot in total exceed the greater of**:

    (a)   the **contributions threshold**, and
    (b)   the **relevant percentage of net relevant earnings of the basis year** (see further below).

Again, the amount determined under this test includes tax relief at basic rate. For example, if the permitted contributions were £5,000, a net payment of £3,900 could be made on which tax relief of £1,100 would be given by the Revenue to the pension provider, resulting in a total payment of £5,000 into the personal pension fund.

Net relevant earnings in a tax year cannot exceed the earnings cap (£105,600 for 2005/06).

Net relevant earnings (NRE) is calculated thus.

	£	£
Taxable trade profits		X
Earnings not providing occupational pension scheme rights		X
Income from furnished holiday lettings		X
		X
Less: the excess of trade charges over other income	X	
loss relief*	X	
deductions from earnings	X	
		(X)
Net relevant earnings		X

* If, in any tax year for which an individual claims relief for a premium payment, a deduction for loss relief is made from income *other* than relevant earnings but that loss relates to activities any income from which *would* be relevant earnings, then the individual's NRE for the *next* tax year are treated as reduced by the loss. Any balance is carried forward to the third year and so on.

Non-trading charges are not deducted in arriving at NRE even if there is insufficient other income to deduct them from.

In any tax year in which he has actual net relevant earnings, an individual may choose a basis year for his deemed net relevant earnings on which contributions are based. This can be the **current tax year or one of the previous five tax years**. Therefore, for 2005/06 the basis year may be any year from 2000/01 to 2005/06. If a basis year is not chosen, only contributions up to the contributions threshold can be made.

The basis year need not be a tax year in which the individual was a member of the personal pension scheme. Evidence of net relevant earnings in the basis year (eg. P60 for employees, letter from accountant for those who are self-employed) must be given to the scheme provider by the individual.

Once a basis year has been chosen, the level of net relevant earnings will be presumed to be the same in the basis year and the next five tax years. Therefore, if 2000/01 had been chosen to be the basis year, the level of NRE will be deemed to be the same for the years 2000/01 to 2005/06 inclusive and no further evidence of earnings needs to given (new rules will apply for 2006/07, which are not examinable until the June 2007 examination). However, it is also possible to choose a new basis year with higher earnings within this time if the individual wishes to make increased contributions.

Even if the basis year is not the year the contribution is made, it is the earnings cap for the year of the contribution (and not that of the basis year) **which applies**.

Having determined the basis year, the next stage is to determine the relevant percentage for the tax year of the contribution. The maximum contributions are:

Age at start of tax year of contribution	% of NRE of the basis year
Up to 35	17.5
36 - 45	20
46 - 50	25
51 - 55	30
56 - 60	35
61 - 74	40

Question   Basis years and relevant percentages

An individual (born 13 January 1959) first has net relevant earnings for 2004/05 and wishes to make maximum personal pension contributions for that year and all following years. He expects to have the following net relevant earnings:

2004/05	£30,000
2005/06	£25,000
2006/07	£20,000
2007/08	£28,000
2008/09	£27,500
2009/10	£24,000
2010/11	£20,000
2011/12	£34,000

Show the maximum amount of pension contributions he can pay for 2004/05 up to 2011/12, assuming the rules in 2005/06 stay the same in later years.

Answer

Tax year	Age at start of yr	% of NRE	Basis year	Maximum contribution
2004/05	45	20	2004/05(N1)	£30,000 × 20% = £6,000
2005/06	46	25(N2)	2004/05	£30,000 × 25% = £7,500
2006/07	47	25	2004/05	£30,000 × 25% = £7,500
2007/08	48	25	2004/05	£30,000 × 25% = £7,500
2008/09	49	25	2004/05	£30,000 × 25% = £7,500
2009/10	50	25	2004/05	£30,000 × 25% = £7,500
2010/11	51	30	2007/08(N3)	£28,000 × 30% = £8,400
2011/12	52	30	2011/12(N4)	£34,000 × 30% = £10,200

Notes

1. The basis year for 2004/05 will apply for 2004/05 to 2009/10 (maximum).

2. The relevant percentage is determined by the age of the individual at the start of the *contribution* year. The basis year used is irrelevant.

3. In 2010/11, any year from 2005/06 to 2010/11 inclusive can be chosen as the basis year. 2007/08 has been chosen as it gives the highest NRE. This does not affect the contributions made in 2007/08 to 2009/10 because the basis year for those years (2004/05) has higher NRE.

4. In 2011/12, any year from 2006/07 to 2011/12 inclusive can be chosen as the basis year. 2011/12 has been chosen as it gives the highest NRE.

There are also special rules where an individual ceases to have net relevant earnings which allow contributions to continue to be made above the contributions threshold, in the five years following the cessation.

The first year in which the individual has no net relevant earnings is known as **'the break year'**. The year in which net relevant earnings ceased is known as the **'cessation year'**. The cessation year and the five previous years are known as the 'reference years'.

The individual may continue to make contributions based on NRE in the five tax years following the cessation year or, if earlier, until the individual has net relevant earnings again or becomes a member of an occupational pension scheme. Such contributions may be made out of any source of income or capital.

In determining the basis year for such contributions, **the individual may nominate any one of the reference years to be the basis year.**

Question | Cessation

Sharon (born 7 March 1973) gives up work on 7 August 2004, prior to the birth of her first child. She intends to take a career break to stay at home with her small child(ren). Her NRE is:

1999/00	£40,000
2000/01	£38,000
2001/02	£35,000
2002/03	£37,000
2003/04	£30,000
2004/05	£10,000

What are the maximum contributions that Sharon may make for 2004/05 to 2010/11 inclusive? What would be the effect if Sharon returned to work in January 2007 and earns £8,000 in the tax year to 5 April 2007?

Assume the rules for 2005/06 also apply in later years.

Answer

Tax year	Age at start of yr	% of NRE	Basis year	Maximum contribution
2004/05	31	17.5	1999/00 (N1)	£40,000 × 17.5% = £7,000
2005/06	32	17.5	1999/00 (N2)	£40,000 × 17.5% = £7,000
2006/07	33	17.5	1999/00 (N2)	£40,000 × 17.5% = £7,000
2007/08	34	17.5	1999/00 (N2)	£40,000 × 17.5% = £7,000
2008/09	35	17.5	1999/00 (N2)	£40,000 × 17.5% = £7,000
2009/10	36	20	1999/00 (N2)	£40,000 × 20% = £8,000
2010/11	37	20	n/a (N3)	£3,600 (contributions threshold)

Notes

1. 2004/05 is the cessation year. Sharon can make 1999/00 her basis year for 2004/05 under the normal rules.

2. 2005/06 is the break year. The reference years are the preceding six tax years ie. 1999/00 to 2004/05. Therefore, Sharon can again chose 1999/00 as her basis years for post cessation contributions. These can be made for 2005/06 to 2009/10 inclusive.

3. No contributions can be made above the contributions threshold in 2010/11.

If Sharon goes back to work in 2006/07, the post cessation rules cease to apply for that year. Sharon can then chose a new basis year between 2001/02 and 2004/05 (she had no NRE in 2005/06 so this cannot be a basis year). She should choose 2002/03 to give a maximum contribution of £37,000 × 17.5% = £6,475.

Some of the premium paid can be used to secure a lump sum or an annuity for a spouse or dependants in the event of death prior to retirement age. The limit (which forms part of the overall limit) for such premiums is 10% of the total contribution.

1.3.4 Carrying back premiums

It is possible in certain circumstances to treat a contribution as if it had been paid in the previous tax year. This is especially useful to self employed people who wish to maximise their contributions, but cannot determine their net relevant earnings until after the end of the tax year.

An irrevocable election must be made at or before the time the contribution is made for the carry back to take effect. The contribution must be made by 31 January following the end of the tax year in which the contribution is to be treated has having been paid. So, if a contribution is to be treated as paid in 2004/05 it must be paid by 31 January 2006. Note that contributions paid on or after 6 April 2006 will be dealt with under the new rules (see beyond) and cannot be treated as paid in 2005/06.

1.3.5 Excess contributions

Any contributions in excess of the amount eligible for relief must be repaid to the taxpayer.

1.4 Tax treatment of contributions

FAST FORWARD

Personal pension contributions are paid net of basic rate tax. Additional tax relief is given to higher rate tax payers by extending the individual's basic rate band by the gross amount of the pension contribution.

All contributions to a personal pension scheme are treated as amounts paid net of basic rate tax. This applies whether the member is an employee, self employed or not employed at all. The Revenue then pays the basic rate tax to the pension provider.

Further tax relief is given if the scheme member is a higher rate taxpayer. The relief is given by increasing the basic rate limit for the year by the gross amount of contributions for which he is entitled to relief.

Question   Higher rate relief

Joe has earnings of £50,000 in 2005/06. He pays a personal pension contribution of £7,020 (net). He has no other taxable income.

Show Joe's tax liability for 2005/06.

Answer

	Non savings income £
Earnings/STI	50,000
Less: PA	(4,895)
Taxable income	45,105

Tax	£
£2,090 × 10%	209
£30,310 × 22%	6,668
£9,000 (7,020 × 100/78) × 22%	1,980
£3,705 × 40%	1,482
45,105	10,339

2 National insurance contributions (NICS) for the self employed

FAST FORWARD

The self employed pay Class 2 and Class 4 NICs. Class 2 NICs are paid at a flat weekly rate. Class 4 NICs are based on the level of the individual's profits.

2.1 Classes of NICs

Four classes of national insurance contribution (NIC) exist, as set out below.

(a)   **Class 1**. This is divided into:

     (i)   **Primary**, paid by employees

     (ii)   **Secondary**, **Class 1A and Class 1B** paid by employers

(b)   **Class 2**. Paid by the self-employed

(c)   **Class 3**. Voluntary contributions (paid to maintain rights to certain state benefits)

(d)   **Class 4**. Paid by the self-employed

National insurance contributions for employees are considered later in this text.

Exam focus point

> Class 1B and Class 3 contributions are outside the scope of your syllabus.

The National Insurance Contributions Office (NICO), which is part of HM Revenue and Customs, examines employers' records and procedures to ensure that the correct amounts of NICs are collected.

2.2 National insurance contributions (NICs) for the self employed

The self employed (sole traders and partners) **pay NICs in two ways. Class 2 contributions are payable at a flat rate**. It is possible, however, to be excepted from payment of Class 2 contributions (or to get contributions already paid repaid) if annual profits are less than £4,345. **The Class 2 rate for 2005/06 is £2.10 a week.**

Self employed people must register with the Revenue for Class 2 contributions within three months of the end of the month in which they start self employment. People who fail to register may incur a £100 penalty.

Additionally, **the self employed pay Class 4 NICs, based on the level of the individual's business profits**.

Main rate Class 4 NICs are calculated by applying a fixed percentage (8% for 2005/06) to the individual's profits between the lower limit (£4,895 for 2005/06) and the upper limit (£32,760 for 2005/06). Additional rate contributions are 1% (for 2005/06) on profits above that limit.

2.3 Example: Class 4 contributions

If a sole trader had profits of £14,080 for 2005/06 his Class 4 NIC liability would be as follows.

	£
Profits	14,080
Less lower limit	(4,895)
	9,185

Class 4 NICs = 8% × £9,185 = £734.80 (main only)

2.4 Example: additional class 4 contributions

If an individual's profits were £35,000, additional Class 4 NICs are due on the excess over the upper limit. Thus the amount payable in 2005/06 is as follows.

	£
Profits (upper limit)	32,760
Less lower limit	(4,895)
	27,865

Main rate Class 4 NICs 8% × £27,865	2,229
Additional rate class 4 NICs £(35,000 – 32,760) = £2,240 × 1%	22
	2,251

For Class 4 NIC purposes, profits are the trade profits taxable for income tax purposes, less:

(a) **Trading losses**

(b) **Trade charges on income**

There is no deduction for personal pension premiums.

Class 4 NICs are collected by the Revenue. They are paid **at the same time as the associated income tax liability**. Interest is charged on overdue contributions.

Chapter roundup

- Anyone can contribute to a personal pension scheme, even if they are not earning, subject to the contributions threshold of £3,600 (gross). A stakeholder pension is a type of personal pension scheme.

- The maximum contributions that can be made by earners to personal pension plans are a certain specified percentage of net relevant earnings of the basis year. The percentage depends on the taxpayer's age at the start of the year. The basis year for contributions may be the current tax year or any of the previous five tax years.

- Personal pension contributions are paid net of basic rate tax. Additional tax relief is given to higher rate tax payers by extending the individual's basic rate band by the gross amount of the pension contribution.

- The self employed pay Class 2 and Class 4 NICs. Class 2 NICs are paid at a flat weekly rate. Class 4 NICs are based on the level of the individual's profits.

Quick quiz

1   When can a member of a personal pension plan retire?

2   How are stakeholder pensions treated for tax purposes?

3   How are Class 4 NICs calculated?

Answers to quick quiz

1   Retirement age under a personal pension scheme is between 50 and 75, unless retirement is because of ill-health or some occupations (eg footballers).

2   Stakeholder pension schemes are treated in the same way a personal pension schemes for tax purposes.

3   The main rate is a fixed percentage of an individual's profits between an upper limit and lower limit. The additional rate applies above the upper limit.

Now try the question below from the Exam Question Bank

Number	Level	Marks	Time
Q23	Examination	15	27 mins

17

Capital gains tax

Topic list	Syllabus reference
1 Chargeability of individuals to CGT	2(d)(i)
2 Connected persons	2(d)(i)
3 Calculating CGT	2(d)(i), 2(d)(ii)
4 Shares and securities	2(d)(ii)
5 Gift relief ('holdover' relief)	2(d)(iii)
6 Incorporation relief	2(d)(iii)
7 Rollover relief	2(d)(iii)

Introduction

In this chapter we see what gains are taxed on individuals and how to work out
the tax on an individual's taxable gains. We also look at the rules on shares and
securities and three deferral reliefs.

1 Chargeability of individuals to CGT

Individuals pay capital gains tax (CGT) on their capital gains.

Individuals are chargeable persons and are charged to capital gains tax on their gains arising from investments and from assets used in an unincorporated business. Partners are chargeable on their share of gains of partnership assets (but details of partnership capital gains are not in your syllabus).

CGT was introduced for individuals in 1965. The base date for taxing gains was generally moved from 1965 to 1982 in 1988. You will not be asked to deal with gains or losses on assets acquired before 31 March 1982.

For individuals, indexation allowance was abolished from April 1998 and a new relief, taper relief, was introduced. This is dealt with later in this chapter.

The rules on shares and securities held by individuals was also changed from April 1998 as the result of the introduction of taper relief. Again, these rules are dealt with later in this chapter.

The rules about chargeable assets and disposals are broadly the same for companies and individuals, so you should look again at Chapter 5 section 2.

The rules on transfers of trading stock in Chapter 5 Section 2.3 apply to individuals. The time limit for the election to have no chargeable gains or allowable loss is the 31 January which is 22 months after the end of the tax year which included the end of the period of account of appropriation.

The following are exempt assets with particular reference to individuals:

- motor vehicles suitable for private use
- national savings certificates and premium bonds
- foreign currency for private use
- decorations for valour unless acquired by purchase
- damages for personal or professional injury
- life assurance policies (only exempt in the hands of the original beneficial owner)
- certain chattels
- debts (except debts on a security)
- pension and annuity rights

Transfers of assets on death are not chargeable to capital gains tax. The heirs of the estate inherit assets as if they bought them at death for the then market values.

2 Connected persons

Disposals to connected persons are deemed to take place at market value.

A transaction between 'connected persons' is treated as one between parties to a transaction otherwise than by way of a bargain made at arm's length. This means that the acquisition and disposal are deemed to take place for a consideration equal to the market value of the asset, rather than the actual price paid. In addition, if a loss results, it can be set only against gains arising in the same or future years from disposals to the same connected person and the loss can only be set off if he or she is still connected with the person sustaining the loss.

Key term

> **Connected person.** An individual is connected with:
>
> - His spouse
> - His relatives (brothers, sisters, ancestors and lineal descendants)
> - The relatives of his spouse
> - The spouses of his and his spouse's relatives

3 Calculating CGT

Individuals pay CGT on their taxable gains. Taxable gains are arrived at after deducting taper relief and the annual exemption.

3.1 Basis of assessment

Individuals are generally liable to CGT on the disposal of assets situated anywhere in the world.

An individual pays CGT on any taxable gains arising in the tax year. **Taxable gains are the net chargeable gains (gains minus losses) of the tax year reduced by unrelieved losses brought forward from previous years, taper relief and the annual exemption.**

There is an annual exemption for each tax year. For 2005/06 it is £8,500. It is the last deduction to be made in the calculation of taxable gains.

3.2 Calculating CGT

Taxable gains are chargeable to capital gains tax as if the gains were an extra slice of savings (excl dividend) income for the year of assessment concerned. This means that CGT may be due at 10%, 20% or 40%.

The rate bands are used first to cover income and then gains.

Question	Rates of CGT

In 2005/06, Carol, a single woman, has the following income, gains and losses. Find the CGT payable.

	£
Salary	35,010
Chargeable gains (not eligible for taper relief - see later)	26,700
Allowable capital losses	8,000

Answer

(a) Carol's taxable income is as follows.

	£
Salary	35,010
Less personal allowance	(4,895)
Taxable income	30,115

(b)   The gains to be taxed are as follows.

	£
Gains	26,700
Less losses	(8,000)
	18,700
Less annual exemption	(8,500)
Taxable gains	10,200

(c)   The tax bands are allocated as follows.

	Total	Income	Gains
Starting rate	2,090	2,090	0
Basic rate	30,310	28,025	2,285
Higher rate	7,915	0	7,915
		30,115	10,200

(d)   The CGT payable is as follows.

	£
£2,285 × 20%	457
£7,915 × 40%	3,166
Total CGT payable	3,623

3.3 Allowable losses

Deduct allowable capital losses from chargeable gains in the tax year in which they arise. Any loss which cannot be set off is carried forward to set against future chargeable gains. Losses must be used as soon as possible (subject to the following paragraph). Losses may not normally be set against income.

Allowable losses brought forward are only set off to reduce current year chargeable gains less current year allowable losses to the annual exempt amount. No set-off is made if net chargeable gains for the current year do not exceed the annual exempt amount.

3.4 Example: the use of losses

(a)   George has chargeable gains for 2005/06 of £10,000 and allowable losses of £6,000. As the losses are *current year losses* they must be fully relieved against the £10,000 of gains to produce net gains of £4,000, despite the fact that net gains are below the annual exemption.

(b)   Bob has gains of £12,400 for 2005/06 and allowable losses brought forward of £6,000. Bob restricts his loss relief to £3,900 so as to leave net gains of £(12,400 − 3,900) = £8,500, which will be exactly covered by his annual exemption for 2005/06. The remaining £2,100 of losses will be carried forward to 2006/07.

(c)   Tom has chargeable gains of £5,000 for 2005/06 and losses brought forward from 2004/05 of £4,000. He will leapfrog 2004/05 and carry forward all of his losses to 2006/07. His gains of £5,000 are covered by his annual exemption for 2005/06.

3.5 Taper relief

FAST FORWARD

The amount of taper relief depends on the number of complete years for which an asset has been held and whether the asset is a business or a non business asset. Non business assets held before 17.3.98 are treated as held for one additional year for taper relief purposes.

Taper relief may be available to reduce gains realised after 5 April 1998 by individuals. It replaced indexation allowance which was frozen at April 1998.

You will not be expected to calculate indexation allowance for individuals to April 1998. You will either be given a base cost at April 1998 or the actual amount of indexation that is available.

Taper relief reduces the percentage of the gain chargeable according to how many complete years the asset had been held since acquisition or 6 April 1998 if later. Taper relief is more generous for business assets than for non-business assets.

The percentages of gains which remain chargeable after taper relief for disposals after 5 April 2002 are set out below.

Complete years after 5.4.98 for which asset held	Gains on business assets	Gains on non business assets
1	50%	100%
2	25%	100%
3	25%	95%
4	25%	90%
5	25%	85%
6	25%	80%
7	25%	75%
8	25%	70%
9	25%	65%
10	25%	60%

You will be given the above taper relief table in your exam.

Non-business assets acquired before 17 March 1998 qualify for an addition of 1 year (a 'bonus year') to the period for which they are actually held after 5 April 1998. For disposals of non-business assets during 2005/06, taper relief will be based on eight complete years of ownership where the asset was owned prior to 17 March 1998. Only 70% of the gain will be chargeable.

3.6 Example: complete years held for taper relief

Peter buys a non business asset on 1 January 1998 and sells it on 1 July 2005. For the purposes of the taper Peter is treated as if he had held the asset for 8 complete years (seven complete years after 5 April 1998 plus one additional year).

If the asset had been a business asset, Peter holds the asset for seven years only but in any case has maximum taper relief after two years ownership.

FAST FORWARD   Losses are set off before taper relief against gains of the same year or of future years.

Taper relief is applied to net chargeable gains after the deduction of current year and brought forward losses. The annual exemption is then deducted from the tapered gains.

3.7 Example: use of losses and taper relief

Ruby sold a business asset in July 2005 which she had purchased in January 2004. She realised a chargeable gain (before taper relief) of £18,000. She also sold a painting in 2005/06 realising a capital loss of £6,000. She has a capital loss brought forward from 2004/05 of £10,000.

Losses are dealt with **before** taper relief. However losses brought forward are only deducted from net current gains to the extent that the gains exceed the CGT annual exemption:

	£
Gain	18,000
Loss	(6,000)
Current net gains	12,000
Less: brought forward loss	(3,500)
Gains before taper relief	8,500
Gains after taper relief (1 year ownership) £8,500 × 50%	4,250
Less: annual exemption	(8,500)
Taxable gains	Nil

Note that the benefit of the taper relief is effectively wasted since the brought forward loss reduces the gain down to the annual exemption amount but the taper is then applied to that amount reducing it further.

The loss carried forward is £6,500 (£10,000 – £3,500).

Allocate losses to gains in the way that produces the lowest tax charge. Losses should therefore be deducted from the gains attracting the lowest rate of taper (ie where the highest percentage of the gain remains chargeable).

3.8 Example: allocation of losses to gains

Alastair made the following capital losses and gains in 2005/2006:

	£
Loss	10,000
Gains (before taper relief)	
Asset A (non-business asset)	25,000
Asset B (business asset)	18,000

Asset A was purchased in December 1997 and sold in January 2006. Taper relief reduces the gain to 70% of the original gain (8 years including additional year; non-business asset). Asset B was purchased on 5 November 2002 and sold on 17 December 2005. Taper relief reduces the gain to 25% of the original gain (3 years; business asset).

The best use of the loss is to offset it against the gain on the non-business asset:

	£	£
Gain – Asset A	25,000	
Less loss	(10,000)	
Net gain before taper relief	15,000	
Gain after taper relief (£15,000 × 70%)		10,500
Gain – Asset B	18,000	
Gain after taper relief £18,000 × 25%		4,500
Gains after taper relief		15,000
Less annual exemption		(8,500)
Taxable gains		6,500

Where gains have been relieved under a provision which reduces the cost of the asset in the hands of a new owner (such as gift relief, see later in this text) the taper will operate by reference to the holding period of the new owner.

3.9 Definition of business asset

A business asset is:

- An asset **used for the purposes of a trade** carried on by any individual or partnership (whether or not the owner of the asset is involved in carrying on the trade concerned) or by a qualifying company.

- An asset **held for the purposes of any office or employment** held by the individual owner with a person carrying on a trade.

- **Shares in a qualifying company** held by an individual.

A qualifying company is a **trading company** (or holding company of a trading group) where:

(a) The company is **not listed** on a recognised stock exchange nor is a 51% subsidiary of a listed company (companies listed on the Alternative Investment Market (AIM) are unlisted for this purpose), or

(b) The individual is an **officer or employee** of the company or of a company with a **relevant connection**, or

(c) The individual holds at least **5% of the voting rights** in the company.

A company is also a qualifying company if it is a **non-trading company** (or holding company of a non-trading group) where:

(a) The individual is an **officer or employee** of the company or a company with a relevant connection, and

(b) The individual did not have a **material interest** in the company or in any other company which at that time had control of the company.

A **material interest** is defined as possession or the ability to control more than 10% of the issued shares in the company, or more than 10% of the voting rights in the company, or an entitlement to more than 10% of the income of the company or more than 10% of the assets of the company available for distribution. For this purpose, an individual is treated as having a material interest if he, together with one or more connected persons (see next chapter) has a material interest. For example, if A holds 5% of the voting rights in the company and his brother B (a connected person) has 15% of the voting rights, A will have a material interest in the company as between them A and B hold more than 10% of the voting rights.

A company has a **relevant connection** with another company if:

(a) The companies are both members of a 51% group, or

(b) The companies are under common control and they carry on a complementary business which can reasonably be regarded as one composite undertaking, or

(c) One company (X Ltd) is a joint enterprise company in which 75% or more of the ordinary shares capital is held by five or fewer persons and the other company (Y Ltd) holds 10% or more of the ordinary share capital in X Ltd.

If an asset qualifies as a business asset for part of the time of ownership, and part not, the business part and the non-business part are treated as separate assets calculated by time apportionment over the period of ownership of the asset (not just complete years). Taper relief applies to each gain separately but the period of ownership for calculating the taper relief percentage is taken to be the *whole* number of years of ownership of the asset.

Question

Mixed asset

Robert bought a warehouse on 5 August 1999. He used the whole of the building for his trade until 4 April 2003. The building was then let out to a quoted company until it was sold on 4 December 2005. The gain on sale was £140,000.

Show Robert's gain after taper relief.

Answer

	Business use	Non business use
Period between 5.8.99 - 4.4.03	44 months	
Period between 5.4.03 - 4.12.05		32 months

Number of complete years ownership is 5.8.99 – 4.8.05 = 6 years

Gain on business asset after taper relief is:

£140,000 × 44/76 × 25% (6 years) = £20,263

Gain on non-business asset after taper relief is:

£140,000 × 32/76 × 80% (6 years) = £47,158

Total gain 20,263 + 47,158 = £67,421

If the asset was acquired before 6 April 1998, only use on or after that date is taken into account. If the asset is owned for more than ten years after 5 April 1998, only the use in the **last ten years** of ownership is taken into account.

4 Shares and securities

FAST FORWARD

Shares and securities are not pooled for individuals after 5 April 1998. Each acquisition is treated separately.

4.1 Matching rules for individuals

Up to 6 April 1998, the matching rules for shares and securities for companies and individuals were identical. **For individuals the pooling of shares ceased on 5 April 1998. This allows the time of each post April 1998 acquisition to be recorded so that the length of ownership of each share can be calculated for taper relief purposes.**

For individuals, share disposals are matched with acquisitions in the following order.

(a)   Same day acquisitions.

(b)   Acquisitions within the following 30 days (known as the 'bed and breakfast rule').

(c)   Previous acquisitions after 5 April 1998 identifying the most recent acquisition first (a LIFO basis).

(d)   Any shares in the FA 1985 pool at 5 April 1998 (the FA 1985 pool runs from 6 April 1982 (instead of 1 April 1982) to 5 April 1998 for individuals).

The 'bed and breakfast' rule stops shares being sold to crystallise a capital gain or loss and then being repurchased a day or so later. Without the rule a gain or loss would arise on the sale since it would be 'matched' to the original acquisition.

For all FA 1985 pools held by an individual at 5 April 1998 indexation allowance to April 1998 is calculated for the first disposal after 5 April 1998. No further indexation then applies.

Exam focus point

The examiner will state the value of the FA 1985 indexed pool at 5 April 1998 (including indexation to that date).

4.2 Example: Post April 1998 disposals for individuals

Ron acquired the following shares in First plc:

Date of acquisition	No of shares	Cost
9.11.90	15,000	25,000
4.8.04	5,000	19,400
15.7.05	5,000	19,000

He disposed of 20,000 of the shares on 10 July 2005 for £80,000. The shares are not business assets for the purposes of taper relief. Calculate the chargeable gain arising. The indexation allowance arising in the FA 1985 pool from November 1990 to April 1998 is £6,269.

Solution

Matching of shares

(a) Acquisition in 30 days after disposal:

	£
Proceeds $\frac{5,000}{20,000} \times £80,000$	20,000
Less cost (15.7.05)	(19,000)
Gain	1,000

(b) Post 5.4.98 acquisitions

	£
Proceeds $\frac{5,000}{20,000} \times £80,000$	20,000
Less cost (4.8.04)	(19,400)
Gain	600

Note. No taper relief is due against this gain since the period of ownership was only 11 months.

(c) FA 1985 pool

	Number of shares	Cost £	Indexed cost £
11.90 Acquisition	15,000	25,000	25,000
Indexation to April 1998			6,269
Pool at 5.4.98	15,000	25,000	31,269
10.7.05 sale (× 10/15)	(10,000)	(16,667)	(20,846)
	5,000	8,333	10,423

Gain

	£
Proceeds $\frac{10,000}{20,000} \times £80,000$	40,000
Less cost	(16,667)
	23,333
Less indexation from FA 1985 pool £(20,846 – 16,667)	(4,179)
Gain before taper relief	19,154

Gain after taper relief (6.4.98 – 5.4.05 = 7 years plus additional year = 8 years)

70% × £19,154	£13,408
Total gains £(1,000 + 600 + 13,408)	£15,008

Bonus and rights issues are dealt with in the same way as for companies (see Chapter 5 sections 7.1 and 7.2).

Question   Rights issue

Simon had the following transactions in S Ltd.

1.10.95	Bought 10,000 shares (10%) holding for £15,000
11.9.04	Bought 2,000 shares for £5,000
1.2.05	Took up rights issue 1 for 2 at £2.75 per share
14.10.05	Sold 5,000 shares for £15,000

Compute the gain arising in October 2005, after taper relief (if applicable). The shares have always been a business asset for taper relief purposes.

The indexation allowance arising in the Finance Act 1985 pool from October 1995 to April 1998 is £1,282.

Answer

(a)   *Post 5.4.98 holding*

	Number	Cost
		£
Shares acquired 11.9.04	2,000	5,000
Shares acquired 1.2.05 (rights) 1:2 @ £2.75	1,000	2,750
	3,000	7,750

Gain

	£
Proceeds $\dfrac{3,000}{5,000} \times £15,000$	9,000
Less: cost	(7,750)
Gain	1,250

Taper relief (based on ownership of original holding 11.9.04 – 10.9.05)

50% (One year: business asset) × £1,250	£625

(b)   *FA 1985 pool*

	Number	Cost	Indexed cost
		£	£
1.10.95	10,000	15,000	15,000
IA to 4.98			1,282
Pool at 5.4.98	10,000	15,000	16,282
Rights issue 1.2.05	5,000	13,750	13,750
	15,000	28,750	30,032
14.10.05 Sale	(2,000)	(3,833)	(4,004)
c/F	13,000	24,917	26,028

Gain

	£
Proceeds $\dfrac{2,000}{5,000} \times £15,000$	6,000
Less: cost	(3,833)
Unindexed gain	2,167
Less: indexation £(4,004 – 3,833)	(171)
Indexed gain	1,996

Taper relief (based on original holding 6.4.98 – 5.4.05)

25% (Seven years: business asset) × £1,996	£499

BPP
PROFESSIONAL EDUCATION

(c)   Total gains (after taper relief)

£(625 + 499)   £1,124

The rules on reorganisations and takeovers in Chapter 5 Section 7.3 also apply to individuals.

5 Gift relief ('holdover' relief)

FAST FORWARD   Gift relief can be claimed on gifts of business assets.

5.1 The relief

If an individual gives away a qualifying asset, the transferor and the transferee can jointly elect by the 31 January which is nearly six years after the end of the tax year of the transfer, **that the transferor's gain be reduced to nil. The transferee is then deemed to acquire the asset for market value at the date of transfer less the transferor's deferred gain** (no taper relief given). The transferee will qualify for further indexation allowance (if available) on that reduced base cost from the date of the transfer. The transferee will start a new period for taper relief from the date of his acquisition.

If a disposal involves actual consideration rather than being a pure gift but is still not a bargain made at arm's length (so that the proceeds are deemed to be the market value of the asset), **then any excess of actual consideration over allowable costs** (excluding indexation allowance) **is chargeable immediately and only the balance of the gain is deferred**. Of course, the amount chargeable immediately is limited to the full gain after indexation allowance.

5.2 Qualifying assets

Gift relief can be claimed on gifts or sales at undervalue on transfers of **business assets** as described below. Note that the definition of what is a business asset for gift relief is not the same as for taper relief.

Transfers of business assets are transfers of assets:

    (a)   Used in a trade, profession or vocation carried on:

        (1)   by the donor

        (2)   if the donor is an individual, by his personal company or a member of a 51% trading group of which the holding company is his personal company (a personal company is one of which he holds at least 5% of voting rights)

        If the asset was used for the purposes of the trade, profession or vocation for only part of its period of ownership, the gain to be held over is the gain otherwise eligible × period of such use/total period of ownership.

        If the asset was a building or structure only partly used for trade, professional or vocational purposes, only the **part of the gain attributable to the part so used is eligible for gift relief.**

    (b)   **Shares and securities in trading companies**, or holding companies of 51% trading groups, where:

        (1)   the shares or securities are **not listed on a recognised stock exchange** (but they may be on the AIM); or

223

(2)   if the donor is an individual, the company concerned is his **personal company** (defined as above);

If the company has chargeable non-business assets at the time of the gift, and (2) applied at any time in the last 12 months, **the gain to be held over is the gain otherwise chargeable × the value of the chargeable business assets/the value of the chargeable assets of the company**.

Question   Gift relief

On 6 December 2005 Angelo sold to his son Michael a freehold shop valued at £200,000 for £50,000, and claimed gift relief. Angelo had originally purchased the shop from which he had run his business in July 2001 for £30,000. Michael continued to run a business from the shop premises but decided to sell the shop in May 2007 for £195,000. Compute any chargeable gains arising. Assume the rules of CGT in 2005/06 continue to apply in May 2007.

Answer

(a)   *Angelo's CGT position (2005/06)*

	£
Proceeds	200,000
Less cost	(30,000)
Gain	170,000
Less gain deferred £170,000 – £(50,000 – 30,000)	(150,000)
Gain left in charge	20,000
Gain after taper relief (note)	£5,000

(b)   *Michael's CGT position (2007/08)*

	£
Proceeds	195,000
Less cost £(200,000 – 150,000)	(50,000)
Gain	145,000
Chargeable gain after taper relief (50%)	£72,500

Note. Taper relief is available for Angelo since the asset disposed of in December 2005 is a 'business asset'. The period of ownership is four complete years. Thus only 25% of the gain will be taxable.

Michael acquired the asset on 6 December 2005 and sold it in May 2007. He therefore owned the asset for one complete year. 50% of the gain is taxable.

6 Incorporation relief

FAST FORWARD

A gain arising on the incorporation of a business can be deferred into the base cost of the shares acquired by incorporation relief. However, an individual can elect not to receive incorporation relief.

If a person transfers his business to a company then he makes a disposal of the business assets for CGT purposes and realises net chargeable gains (chargeable gains less allowable losses) on those assets. (Note that the individual assets are disposed of. Contrast this with a sale of shares, when shares are disposed of but business assets remain the property of the company which issued the shares, and are not disposed of.) It is, however, clearly undesirable to discourage entrepreneurs from incorporating their businesses and so a relief is available.

The relief (sometimes called Incorporation Relief) is **automatic** (so no claim need be made). **All or some of the gains are held over if all the following conditions are met**.

(a) The **business is transferred as a going concern**.

(b) **All its assets** (or all its assets other than cash) **are transferred** (but see below for a claim to disapply the relief).

(c) **The consideration is wholly or partly in shares**.

The amount held over is found by applying the fraction:

$$\frac{\text{Value of shares received from the company}}{\text{Total value of consideration from the company}}$$

to the indexed gain. This amount is then deducted from the base cost of the shares received. The company is deemed to acquire assets transferred at their market values.

Incorporation relief applies to the chargeable gain calculated before taper relief.

Question	Incorporation relief

Mr P transferred his business to a company in May 2005, realising a gain after indexation allowance but before taper relief of £24,000 on the only business asset transferred (a factory). The consideration comprised cash of £15,000 and shares at a market value of £75,000.

(a) What is the gain on the transfer before taper relief?
(b) What is the base cost of the shares for any future disposal?

Answer

(a)

	£
Gain	24,000
Less held over $\dfrac{75,000}{15,000+75,000} \times £24,000$	(20,000)
Chargeable gain before taper relief	4,000

(b)

	£
Market value	75,000
Less gain held over	(20,000)
Base cost of shares	55,000

An individual can elect not to receive incorporation relief. He might do this, for example, to keep his entitlement to taper relief on the gain arising on incorporation. The election must in general be made by 31 January, nearly three years after the end of the tax year of disposal. This long time limit is to allow shareholders to see whether they want to elect to disapply incorporation relief depending on whether they have built up two years (the maximum) taper relief on shares between incorporation and disposal. For example if a business was incorporated on 1 April 2006 (2005/06) the shares will need to be held at least to 1 April 2008 (tax year 2007/08) to see whether they have got full taper relief. In this case an election need not be made until 31 January 2009.

7 Rollover relief

FAST FORWARD

> Reliefs for the replacement of business assets are available to unincorporated businesses which reinvest in qualifying assets in the period commencing one year before and ending 36 months after the disposal concerned.

The reliefs on the replacement of business assets apply to sole traders and partners. The conditions for the reliefs to apply are the same as for companies, as set out in Chapter 5 section 8. However, there are two additional categories of asset which qualify for relief for unincorporated businesses:

(i)   goodwill
(ii)   milk, potato, ewe and suckler cow premium, and fish quotas.

Rollover relief applies to the untapered gain. Any gain left in charge will then be eligible for taper relief. When the replacement asset is sold taper relief on that sale will only be given by reference to the holding period for that asset (assuming further rollover relief is not claimed on this disposal). **Effectively, taper relief on the rolled over gain, for the period of ownership of the original asset, is lost.**

Question
Rollover relief and taper relief interaction

Karen is a sole trader who bought a business asset for £170,625 on 5 November 1991 and sold it on 31 December 2005 for £491,400. A replacement business asset was acquired on 1 November 2005 at a cost of £546,000. The new asset was sold on 3 September 2007 for £914,550. Karen made a claim for rollover relief on the first asset sale but not on the second asset sale.

Calculate the taxable gains for each asset disposal. The indexation factor from November 1991 to April 1998 is 0.199.

Answer

31 December 2005 disposal

	£
Sale proceeds	491,400
Cost (5.11.1991)	(170,625)
	320,775
Less: indexation allowance to April 1998	
0.199 x £170,625	(33,954)
Chargeable gain before taper relief	286,821

Since the asset was sold for £491,400 and within the required time period a replacement asset was purchased for £546,000 there was a full reinvestment of the sale proceeds. Thus the full gain before taper relief of £286,821 is rolled over against the cost of the new asset.

3 September 2007 disposal

	£	£
Sale proceeds		914,550
Cost (1 November 2005)	546,000	
Less: rollover relief	(286,821)	
		(259,179)
Gain		655,371

	£	£

Ownership period is 1 November 2005 to 3 September 2007
= 1 complete year of ownership
Gain after taper relief
Taxable gain (50%) for Karen   £327,686

Where the replacement asset is a depreciating asset, the gain is not rolled over by reducing the cost of the replacement asset. Rather it is 'frozen' until it crystallises on the earliest of:

(a)   The disposal of the replacement asset.

(b)   Ten years after the acquisition of the replacement asset.

(c)   The date the replacement asset ceases to be used in the trade (but the gain does not crystallise on the taxpayer's death).

Key term

> An asset is a **depreciating asset** if it is, or within the next ten years will become, a wasting asset. Thus, any asset with an expected life of 60 years or less is covered by this definition. Plant and machinery (including ships, aircraft, hovercraft, satellites, space stations and spacecraft) is always treated as depreciating unless it becomes part of a building: in that case, it will only be depreciating if the building is held on a lease with 60 years or less to run.

Taper relief is applied to the original gain *before* it is deferred, in relation to the ownership of the original asset. No further relief is given for the time that the gain is deferred. Taper relief applies on the depreciating asset from the date of purchase in the normal way.

Question   Frozen gain on investment into depreciating asset

Norma bought a freehold shop for use in her business in June 2004 for £125,000. She sold it for £140,000 on 1 August 2005. On 10 July 2005, Norma bought some fixed plant and machinery to use in her business, costing £150,000. She then sells the plant and machinery for £167,000 on 19 November 2007. Show Norma's CGT position.

Answer

Gain frozen

	£
Proceeds of shop	140,000
Less cost	(125,000)
Gain	15,000

Gain after taper relief (1 year)
  50% x £15,000   £7,500

This gain is frozen due to the purchase of the plant and machinery.

Sale of plant and machinery

	£
Proceeds	167,000
Less cost	(150,000)
Gain	17,000

Gain on plant and machinery after taper relief (2 years)

  £17,000 × 25%   £4,250

Total gain chargeable on sale (gain on plant and machinery plus frozen gain)

£(4,250 + 7,500)   £11,750

Where a gain on disposal is deferred against a replacement depreciating asset it is possible to transfer the frozen gain to a non-depreciating asset provided the non-depreciating asset is bought before the deferred gain has crystallised.

Chapter roundup

- Individuals pay capital gains tax (CGT) on their capital gains.

- Disposals to connected persons are deemed to take place at market value.

- Individuals pay CGT on their taxable gains. Taxable gains are arrived at after deducting taper relief and the annual exemption.

- The amount of taper relief depends on the number of complete years for which an asset has been held and whether the asset is a business or a non business asset. Non business assets held before 17.3.98 are treated as held for one additional year for taper relief purposes.

- Losses are set off before taper relief against gains of the same year or of future years.

- Shares and securities are not pooled for individuals after 5 April 1998. Each acquisition is treated separately.

- Gift relief can be claimed on gifts of business assets.

- A gain arising on the incorporation of a business can be deferred into the base cost of the shares acquired by incorporation relief. However, an individual can elect not to receive incorporation relief.

- Reliefs for the replacement of business assets are available to unincorporated businesses which reinvest in qualifying assets in the period commencing one year before and ending 36 months after the disposal concerned.

Quick quiz

1   At what rate or rates do individuals pay CGT?

2   To what extent must allowable losses be set against chargeable gains?

3   What is a qualifying company for taper relief?

4   In what order are acquisitions of shares matched with disposals for individuals?

5   An individual acquired 1,000 shares in January 1993 and January 2005 in X plc. He sells 1,500 shares in January 2006. How are the shares matched on sale?

6   Sharon acquired 10,000 share in Z plc in 1986. She takes up a 1 for 2 rights offer in 2005. How are the rights issue shares dealt with?

7   Which disposals of shares qualify for gift relief?

8   What are the conditions for deferring gains on the incorporation of a business?

Answers to quick quiz

1   10%, 20% and 40%

2   Current year losses must be set off against gains in full, even if this reduces gains below annual exemption
     Losses brought forward are set off to bring down untapered gains to the level of annual exemption.

3   A trading company (or holding company of trading group) which is unlisted or of which the individual is
     an officer or employee or of which the individual holds at least 5% voting rights.

     A non-trading company (or holding company of a non-trading group) of which the individual is an officer
     or employee and in which the individual does not have a material interest.

4   (a)   Same day acquisitions
     (b)   Acquisitions in following 30 days
     (c)   Previous acquisitions after 5 April 1998 on LIFO basis
     (d)   Shares in FA 1985 pool

5   January 2005 1,000 shares
     January 1993 (FA 1985 pool) 500 shares

6   The rights issue shares are added to the FA 1985 pool holding (1986 acquisition).

7   Shares which qualify for gift relief are those in trading companies

     -    which are not listed on a recognised stock exchange, or

     -    where the donor is an individual, which are in that individual's personal company.

8   The conditions for incorporation relief are:

     -    the business is transferred as a going concern
     -    all of its assets (or all assets other than cash) are transferred
     -    the consideration is wholly or partly in shares

Now try the question below from the Exam Question Bank

Number	Level	Marks	Time
Q30	Examination	15	27 mins

This was a pilot paper question. It has been analysed to give you guidance on how to approach paper 2.3 exam questions.

Self assessment for individuals and partnerships

Topic list	Syllabus references
1 Notification of liability to income tax and CGT	2(b)
2 Tax returns and keeping records	2(b)
3 Self-assessment and claims	2(b)
4 Payment of income tax and capital gains tax	2(b)
5 Enquiries, determinations and discovery assessments	2(b)

Introduction

In this chapter we see how individuals (including partners) must 'self assess' their liability to income tax and capital gains tax.

1 Notification of liability to income tax and CGT

Individuals who do not receive a tax return must notify their chargeability to income tax or CGT.

Individuals and trustees who are chargeable to income tax or CGT for any tax year and who have not received a notice to file a return are required to give notice of chargeability to an Officer of Revenue and Customs within six months from the end of the year ie by 5 October 2006 for 2005/06.

A person who has no chargeable gains and who is not liable to higher rate tax does not have to give notice of chargeability if all his income:

    (a)   Is taken into account under PAYE
    (b)   Is from a source of income not subject to tax under a self-assessment
    (c)   Has had (or is treated as having had) income tax deducted at source, or
    (d)   Is a UK dividend.

The maximum mitigable penalty where notice of chargeability is not given is 100% of the tax assessed which is not paid on or before 31 January following the tax year.

2 Tax returns and keeping records

Tax returns must usually be filed by 31 January following the end of the tax year. There are penalties for late filing. Returns may be filed online.

2.1 Tax returns

The tax return comprises a Tax Form, together with supplementary pages for particular sources of income. Taxpayers are sent a Tax Form and a number of supplementary pages depending on their known sources of income, together with a Tax Return Guide and various notes relating to the supplementary pages. Taxpayers with new sources of income may have to ask the orderline for further supplementary pages.

If a return for the previous year was filed electronically, or a computer generated substitute form used, the taxpayer may be sent a notice to file a return, rather than the official Revenue form.

Taxpayers with simple tax affairs may be asked to complete a Short four page Tax Return. Short Tax Returns may be sent to employees (not directors) with taxable benefits, sole traders with three line accounts (see later in this text) and pensioners who have pensions and simple investment income. The Revenue process these returns using an automated data capture facility. Taxpayers can also choose to file the return online.

Notice to make a trust tax return may be given to any one relevant trustee, or to all the relevant trustees, or to some of the relevant trustees, as the officer of the Board thinks fit.

Partnerships must file a separate return which includes 'a partnership statement' showing the firm's profits, losses, proceeds from the sale of assets, tax suffered, tax credits, charges on income and the division of all these amounts between partners. The partnership return must normally be made by the senior partner (or whoever else may be nominated by the partnership), but the Revenue have power to require any, all, or some of the partners (or their nominated successors) to submit the return.

A partnership return must include a declaration of the name, residence and tax reference of each partner, as well as the usual declaration that the return is correct and complete to the best of the signatory's knowledge.

Each partner must then include his share of partnership profits on his personal tax return.

2.2 Time limit for submission of tax returns

Key term

The **filing due date for filing a tax return is the later of:**

* **31 January following the end of the tax year which the return covers.**
* **Three months after the notice to file the return was issued.**

If an individual wishes for the Revenue to prepare the self-assessment on their behalf, **earlier deadlines apply. The filing date is then the later of:**

* **30 September following the tax year; eg for 2005/06, by 30 September 2006.**
* **Two months after notice to file the return was issued.**

Since a partnership return does not include a self-assessment these revised deadlines do not apply to partnership returns. This may, of course, create problems if one of the partners wishes the Revenue to complete his personal self-assessment.

2.3 Penalties for late filing

2.3.1 Individual and trustees returns

The maximum penalties for delivering a tax return after the filing due date are:

(a)	**Return up to 6 months late:**	**£100**
(b)	**Return more than 6 months but not more than 12 months late:**	**£200**
(c)	**Return more than 12 months late:**	**£200 + 100% of the tax liability**

In addition, the General or Special Commissioners can direct that a maximum penalty of £60 per day be imposed where failure to deliver a tax return continues after notice of the direction has been given to the taxpayer. In this case the additional £100 penalty, imposed under (b) if the return is more than six months late, is not charged.

The fixed penalties of £100/£200 can be set aside by the Commissioners if they are satisfied that the taxpayer had a reasonable excuse for not delivering the return. If the tax liability shown on the return is less than the fixed penalties, the fixed penalty is reduced to the amount of the tax liability. The tax geared penalty is mitigable by the Revenue or the Commissioners.

2.3.2 Partnership returns

The maximum penalties for late delivery of a partnership tax return are as shown above, save that there is no tax-geared penalty if the return is more than 12 months late. The penalties apply separately to each partner.

2.3.3 Reasonable excuse

A taxpayer only has a reasonable excuse for a late filing if a default occurred because of a factor outside his control. This might be non-receipt of the return by the taxpayer, an industrial dispute in the post office after the return was posted, serious illness of the taxpayer or a close relative, or destruction of records through fire and flood. Illness etc is only accepted as a reasonable excuse if the taxpayer was taking timeous steps to complete the return, and if the return is filed as soon as possible after the illness etc.

2.3.4 Returns rejected as incomplete

If a return, filed before the filing date, is rejected by the Revenue as incomplete later than 14 days before the filing deadline of 31 January, a late filing penalty will not be charged if the return is completed and returned within 14 days of the rejection. This only applies if the omission from the return was a genuine error. It does not apply if a return was deliberately filed as incomplete in the hope of extending the time limit.

2.4 Electronic lodgement of tax returns

The electronic lodgement of tax returns and other documents is possible if:

    (a)   The information is transferred by persons approved by the Revenue.

    (b)   The information is transmitted using approved hardware and software.

    (c)   A hard copy of the information (signed by the taxpayer etc) was made before the information is transmitted electronically and the fact that this has been done is signified as part of the transmission.

    (d)   The information is accepted by the Revenue's computer.

Where a return is filed electronically, supporting documents may be sent separately (eg. by post). Provided they are submitted within one month of the return and have been referred to in the return the Revenue accept that they 'accompany' the return.

2.5 Standard accounting information

'Three line' accounts (ie income less expenses equals profit) only need be included on the tax return of businesses with a turnover (or gross rents from property) of less than £15,000 pa. This is not as helpful as it might appear, as underlying records must still be kept for tax purposes (disallowable items etc) when producing three line accounts.

Large businesses with a turnover of at least £5 million which have used figures rounded to the nearest £1,000 in producing their published accounts can compute their profits to the nearest £1,000 for tax purposes.

The tax return requires trading results to be presented in a standard format. Although there is no requirement to submit accounts with the return, accounts may be filed. If accounts accompany the return, the Revenue's power to raise a discovery assessment (see below) is restricted.

2.6 Keeping of records

All taxpayers must keep and retain all records required to enable them to make and deliver a correct tax return.

Records must be retained until the later of:

    (a)   (i)   **5 years after the 31 January following the tax year where the taxpayer is in business** (as a sole trader or partner or letting property), or

          (ii)   **1 year after the 31 January following the tax year otherwise,** or

    (b)   Provided notice to deliver a return is given before the date in (a):

          (i)   **The time after which enquiries by the Revenue into the return can no longer be commenced,** or

          (ii)   **The date any such enquiries have been completed.**

Where a person receives a notice to deliver a tax return after the normal record keeping period has expired, he must keep all records in his possession at that time until no enquiries can be raised in respect of the return or until such enquiries have been completed.

The maximum (mitigable) penalty for each failure to keep and retain records is £3,000 per tax year/accounting period.

The duty to preserve records can generally be satisfied by retaining copies of original documents except that for documents which show domestic or foreign tax deducted or creditable, the originals (eg. dividend certificates) must be kept.

Record keeping failures are taken into account in considering the mitigation of other penalties. Where the record keeping failure is taken into account in this way, a penalty will normally only be sought in serious and exceptional cases where, for example, records have been destroyed deliberately to obstruct an enquiry or there has been a history of serious record keeping failures.

3 Self-assessment and claims

FAST FORWARD

Although taxpayers must normally self assess their income tax, Class 4 NIC and CGT liabilities the Revenue will calculate the tax on their behalf if they file their tax return by 30 September following the end of the tax year.

3.1 Self assessment

Every full personal tax return must be accompanied by a self-assessment.

Key term

> **A self-assessment** is a calculation of the amount of taxable income and gains after deducting reliefs and allowances, and a calculation of the income tax and CGT payable after taking into account tax deducted at source and tax credits.

Although Tax Calculation Working Sheets are provided with the tax return there is no requirement for the taxpayer to use these in computing his self-assessment. It is sufficient to enter the appropriate figures on the tax return.

The self-assessment calculation may either be made by the taxpayer or the Revenue. If a return is filed within certain time limits (normally, 30 September following the tax year to which it relates, see above) an Officer of Revenue and Customs must make a self-assessment on the taxpayer's behalf on the basis of the information contained in the return. He must send a copy of the assessment to the taxpayer. These assessments, even though raised by the Revenue, are treated as self-assessments.

If the taxpayer files a return after the above deadline but without completing the self-assessment, the Revenue will not normally reject the return as incomplete. However the Revenue are not then bound to complete the self-assessment in time to notify the taxpayer of the tax falling due on the normal due date (generally the following 31 January), and it is the taxpayer's responsibility to estimate and pay his tax on time.

Within nine months of receiving a tax return, the Revenue can amend a taxpayer's self-assessment to correct any obvious errors or mistakes; whether errors of principle, arithmetical mistakes or otherwise. The taxpayer does have the right to reject any corrections of obvious errors made by the Revenue.

Within 12 months of the due filing date (*not* the actual filing date), the taxpayer can give notice to an officer to amend his tax return and self-assessment. Such amendments by taxpayers are not confined to the correction of obvious errors. An amendment may be made whilst the Revenue are making enquiries into the return, but will not take effect until the end of the enquiry.

The same rules apply to corrections and amendments of partnership statements and stand alone claims (see below).

The Short Tax Return form does not have the facility for the taxpayer to complete a self-assessment although if needed there is a two-page simple calculation to give people a rough idea of their tax liability. The Revenue calculate the tax for such returns. Therefore the Revenue encourage taxpayers to file the return by 30 September following the tax year. However, the latest date for filing is 31 January.

3.2 Claims

All claims and elections which can be made in a tax return must be made in this manner if a return has been issued. A claim for any relief, allowance or repayment of tax must be quantified at the time it is made. These rules do not apply to claims involving two or more years.

Certain claims have a time limit that is longer than the time limit for filing or amending a tax return. A claim may therefore be made after the time limit for amending the tax return has expired. Claims not made on the tax return are referred to as **'stand alone' claims**.

Claims made on a tax return are subject to the administrative rules governing returns, for the making of corrections, enquiries etc.

3.2.1 Stand alone claims

Claims and elections not made in a tax return are governed by provisions which are similar to the rules governing the treatment of tax returns. The rules cover:

(a)   Keeping supporting records. Records must be kept until enquiries may no longer be made into the claim, or until any enquiries which are made have been completed

(b)   Amending the claim. The Revenue's nine month time limit is unchanged, but the taxpayer has twelve months from the date the claim was made (see below)

(c)   Giving effect to the claim (ie repaying the tax)

(d)   Enquiring into the claim and making any necessary amendments (see below)

3.2.2 Claims involving more than one year

Self-assessment is intended to avoid the need to reopen earlier years, so relief should be given for the year of the claim. This rule can best be explained by considering a claim to carry back a trade loss to an earlier year of assessment:

(a)   The claim for relief is treated as made in relation to the year in which the loss was actually incurred

(b)   The amount of any tax repayment due is calculated in terms of tax of the earlier year to which the loss is being carried back, and

(c)   Any tax repayment etc is treated as relating to the later year in which the loss was actually incurred. A repayment supplement may accrue from the later year.

These rules apply not only to trading losses, but also to pension premiums carried back (see later in this text) and to the carry back of post cessation receipts.

3.2.3 Time limits

The time limit for making a claim is 5 years from 31 January following the tax year, unless a different limit is specifically set for the claim. Many reliefs have a shorter time limit specifically set – of one year from the 31 January following the end of the tax year. These time limits are mentioned, where relevant, throughout this text.

Since a taxpayer needs to be able to calculate his tax liability under self-assessment a certain amount of formality in the claims procedure is needed. For example, capital losses are only allowable if notified to an officer of the Board and such notification is treated as a claim for relief for the year in which the loss accrues. Therefore, notification of such losses has to be made within 5 years from 31 January following the tax year in which they accrue.

3.2.4 Error or mistake claims

An error or mistake claim may be made for errors in a return or partnership statement where tax would otherwise be overcharged. The claim may not be made where the tax liability was computed in accordance with practice prevailing at the time the return or statement was made.

An error or mistake claim may not be made in respect of a claim. If a taxpayer makes an error or mistake in a claim, he may make a supplementary claim within the time limits allowed for the original claim.

The taxpayer may appeal to the Special Commissioners against any refusal of an error or mistake claim.

4 Payment of income tax and capital gains tax

FAST FORWARD

> Two payments on account and a final balancing payment of income tax and Class 4 NICs may be due. All capital gains tax is due on 31 January following the end of the tax year.

4.1 Payments on account and final payment

The self-assessment system may result in the taxpayer making three payments of income tax and Class 4 NICs.

Date	Payment
31 January in the tax year	1st payment on account
31 July after the tax year	2nd payment on account
31 January after the tax	Final payment to settle the remaining liability

The Revenue issue payslips/demand notes in a credit card type 'Statement of Account' format, but there is no statutory obligation for it to do so and **the onus is on the taxpayer to pay the correct amount of tax on the due date.**

Key term

> **Payments on account** are usually required where the income tax and Class 4 NICs due in the previous year exceeded the amount of income tax deducted at source; this excess is known as **'the relevant amount'**. Income tax deducted at source includes tax suffered, PAYE deductions and tax credits on dividends.

The payments on account are each equal to 50% of the relevant amount for the previous year.

Question   **Payments on account**

Sue is a self employed writer who paid tax for 2005/06 as follows:

		£
Total amount of income tax charged		9,200
This included:	Tax deducted on savings income	3,200
She also paid:	Class 4 NIC	1,900
	Class 2 NIC	109
	Capital gains tax	4,800

How much are the payments on account for 2006/07?

Answer

	£
Income tax:	
Total income tax charged for 2005/06	9,200
Less: tax deducted for 2005/06	(3,200)
	6,000
Class 4 NIC	1,900
'Relevant amount'	7,900
Payments on account for 2006/07:	
31 January 2007 £7,900 × ½	3,950
31 July 2007 As before	3,950

There is no requirement to make payments on account of capital gains tax nor Class 2 NIC.

Payments on account are not required if the relevant amount falls below a de minimis limit of £500. Also, payments on account are not required from taxpayers who paid 80% or more of their tax liability for the previous year through PAYE or other deduction at source arrangements.

If the previous year's liability increases following an amendment to a self-assessment, or the raising of a discovery assessment, an adjustment is made to the payments on account due.

Payments on account are normally fixed by reference to the previous year's tax liability but if a taxpayer expects his liability to be lower than this **he may claim to reduce his payments on account to:**

(a)   **A stated amount**, or
(b)   **Nil**.

The claim must state the reason why he believes his tax liability will be lower, or nil.

If the taxpayer's eventual liability is higher than he estimated he will have reduced the payments on account too far. Although the payments on account will not be adjusted, the taxpayer will suffer an interest charge on late payment.

A penalty of the difference between the reduced payment on account and the correct payment on account may be levied if the reduction was claimed fraudulently or negligently.

The balance of any income tax and Class 4 NICs together with all CGT due for a year, is normally payable on or before the 31 January following the year.

 Question

Payments of tax

Giles made payments on account for 2005/06 of £6,500 each on 31 January 2005 and 31 July 2005, based on his 2004/05 liability. He then calculates his total income tax and Class 4 NIC liability for 2005/06 at £18,000 of which £2,750 was deducted at source. In addition he calculated that his CGT liability for disposals in 2005/06 is £5,120.

What is the final payment due for 2005/06?

Answer

Income tax and Class 4 NIC: £18,000 − £2,750 − £6,500 − £6,500 = £2,250. CGT = £5,120.
Final payment due on 31 January 2007 for 2005/2006 £2,250 + £5,120 = £7,370

In one case the due date for the final payment is later than 31 January following the end of the year. **If a taxpayer has notified chargeability by 5 October but the notice to file a tax return is not issued before 31 October, then the due date for the payment is three months after the issue of the notice.**

Tax charged in an amended self-assessment is usually payable on the later of:

(a)   The normal due date, generally 31 January following the end of the tax year, and

(b)   The day following 30 days after the making of the revised self-assessment.

Tax charged on a discovery assessment is due thirty days after the issue of the assessment.

FAST FORWARD

> Self assessment is enforced through a system of automatic surcharges, penalties and interest.

4.2 Surcharges

Key term

> **Surcharges** are normally imposed in respect of amounts paid late:
>
> | Paid | Surcharge |
> |------|-----------|
> | (a) Within 28 days of due date: | none |
> | (b) More than 28 days but not more than six months after the due date: | 5% |
> | (c) More than six months after the due date: | 10% |

Surcharges apply to:

(a)   Balancing payments of income tax and Class 4 NICs and any CGT under self-assessment or a determination

(b)   Tax due on the amendment of a self-assessment

(c)   Tax due on a discovery assessment

The surcharge rules do not apply to late payments on account.

No surcharge will be applied where the late paid tax liability has attracted a tax-geared penalty on the failure to notify chargeability to tax, or the failure to submit a return, or on the making of an incorrect return (including a partnership return).

4.3 Interest

Interest is chargeable on late payment of both payments on account and balancing payments. In both cases interest runs from the due date until the day before the actual date of payment.

Interest is charged from 31 January following the tax year (or the normal due date for the balancing payment, in the rare event that this is later), even if this is before the due date for payment on:

(a)   Tax payable following an amendment to a self-assessment

(b)   Tax payable in a discovery assessment, and

(c)   Tax postponed under an appeal which becomes payable.

Since a determination (see below) is treated as if it were a self-assessment, interest runs from 31 January following the tax year.

If a taxpayer claims to reduce his payments on account and there is still a final payment to be made, interest is normally charged on the payments on account as if each of those payments had been the lower of:

(a)   the reduced amount, plus 50% of the final income tax liability; and

(b)   the amount which would have been payable had no claim for reduction been made.

Question   Interest

Herbert's payments on account for 2005/06 based on his income tax liability for 2004/05 were £4,500 each. However when he submitted his 2004/05 income tax return in January 2005 he made a claim to reduce the payments on account for 2005/06 to £3,500 each. The first payment on account was made on 29 January 2006, and the second on 12 August 2006.

Herbert filed his 2005/06 tax return in December 2006. The return showed that his tax liabilities for 2005/06 (before deducting payments on account) were income tax and Class 4 NIC: £10,000, capital gains tax: £2,500. Herbert paid the balance of tax due of £5,500 on 19 February 2007.

For what periods and in respect of what amounts will Herbert be charged interest?

Answer

Herbert made an excessive claim to reduce his payments on account, and will therefore be charged interest on the reduction. The payments on account should have been £4,500 each based on the 2004/05 liability (not £5,000 each based on the 2005/06 liability). Interest will be charged as follows:

(a)   First payment on account

    (i)   On £3,500 – nil – paid on time

    (ii)   On £1,000 from due date of 31 January 2006 to day before payment, 18 February 2007

(b)   Second payment on account

    (i)   On £3,500 from due date of 31 July 2006 to day before payment, 11 August 2006

    (ii)   On £1,000 from due date of 31 July 2006 to day before payment, 18 February 2007

(c)   Balancing payment

    (i)   On £3,500 from due date of 31 January 2007 to day before payment, 18 February 2007

Where interest has been charged on late payments on account but the final balancing settlement for the year produces a repayment, all or part of the original interest is remitted.

If a taxpayer provided the Revenue in good time with the information needed to calculate the payment on account due on 31 January but did not receive a Statement of Account in time to make the correct payment by 31 January, it is Revenue practice to treat the due date for interest purposes as 30 days after the issue of the Statement.

4.4 Repayment of tax and repayment supplement

Tax is repaid when claimed unless a greater payment of tax is due in the following 30 days, in which case it is set-off against that payment.

Interest is paid on overpayments of:

    (a)   Payments on account

    (b)   Final payments of income tax and Class 4 NICs and CGT, including tax deducted at source or tax credits on dividends, and

    (c)   Penalties and surcharges.

Repayment supplement runs from the original date of payment (even if this was prior to the due date), until the day before the date the repayment is made. Income tax deducted at source and tax credits are treated as if they were paid on the 31 January following the tax year concerned.

Tax repaid is identified with tax payments in the following order:

(a) Final balancing payment

(b) Equally to the payments on account

(c) Income tax deducted at source/tax credits

(d) If it is attributable to tax paid in instalments, to a later instalment before an earlier one.

4.5 Payment of CGT by instalments

Where the consideration for a disposal of an asset is receivable in instalments over a period exceeding 18 months, the taxpayer has the option to pay the CGT arising in instalments. The Revenue then allow payment of CGT to be spread over the shorter of:

(a) The period of instalment, and

(b) Eight years.

5 Enquiries, determinations and discovery assessments

FAST FORWARD

The Revenue can enquire into tax returns but strict procedural rules govern enquiries.

5.1 Enquiries into returns

An Officer of the Revenue and Customs has a limited period within which to commence enquiries into a return or amendment. The officer must give written notice of his intention by:

(a) The **first anniversary of the due filing date (not the actual filing date)**, or

(b) **If the return is filed after the due filing date, the quarter day following the first anniversary of the actual filing date. The quarter days are 31 January, 30 April, 31 July and 31 October.**

If the taxpayer amended the return after the due filing date, the enquiry 'window' extends to the quarter day following the first anniversary of the date the amendment was filed. Where the enquiry was not raised within the limit which would have applied had no amendment been filed, the enquiry is restricted to matters contained in the amendment.

Enquiries may be made into partnership returns (or amendments) upon which a partnership statement is based within the same time limits. A notice to enquire into a partnership return is deemed to incorporate a notice, to enquire into each individual partner's return.

Enquiries may also be made into stand alone claims, provided notice is given by the Officer of Revenue and Customs by the later of:

(a) The quarter day following the first anniversary of the making or amending of the claim

(b) 31 January next but one following the tax year, if the claim relates to a tax year, or

(c) The first anniversary of the end of the period to which a claim relates if it relates to a period other than a tax year.

The procedures for enquiries into claims mirror those for enquiries into returns.

The Officer does not have to have, or give, any reason for raising an enquiry. In particular the taxpayer will not be advised whether he has been selected at random for an audit. Enquiries may be full enquiries, or may be limited to 'aspect' enquiries.

In the course of his enquiries **the Officer may require the taxpayer to produce documents, accounts or any other information required. The taxpayer can appeal to the Commissioners.**

During the course of his enquiries an Officer may amend a self-assessment if it appears that insufficient tax has been charged and an immediate amendment is necessary to prevent a loss to the Crown. This might apply if, for example, there is a possibility that the taxpayer will emigrate.

If a return is under enquiry the Revenue may postpone any repayment due as shown in the return until the enquiry is complete. The Revenue have discretion to make a provisional repayment but there is no facility to appeal if the repayment is withheld.

At any time during the course of an enquiry, the taxpayer may apply to the Commissioners to require the officer to notify the taxpayer within a specified period that the enquiries are complete, unless the officer can demonstrate that he has reasonable grounds for continuing the enquiry.

If both sides agree, disputes concerning a point of law can be resolved through litigation without having to wait until the whole enquiry is complete.

An Officer must issue a notice that the enquiries are complete, and a statement of the amount of tax that he considers should be included in the tax return, or the amounts which should be contained in the partnership statement, or the amount of the claim. The taxpayer then has thirty days to amend his self-assessment, partnership statement or claim to give effect to the Officer's conclusions. He may also make any other amendments that he could have made had the enquiry not been commenced (amendments may not be made whilst enquiries are in progress).

If the Officer is not satisfied with the taxpayer's amendment he has thirty days in which to amend the self-assessment, partnership statement or claim. Also if a claim has been disallowed, but does not affect the self-assessment, he must advise the taxpayer of the extent to which it has been disallowed.

If the taxpayer is not satisfied with the Officer's amendment he may, within 30 days, appeal to the Commissioners.

Once an enquiry is complete the Officer cannot make further enquiries. The Revenue may, in limited circumstances, raise a discovery assessment if they believe that there has been a loss of tax (see below).

5.2 Determinations

The Revenue may only raise enquiries if a return has been submitted.

If notice has been served on a taxpayer to submit a return but the return is not submitted by the due filing date, an Officer of Revenue and Customs may make a determination of the amounts liable to income tax and CGT tax and of the tax due. Such a determination must be made to the best of the officer's information and belief, and is then treated as if it were a self-assessment. This enables the officer to seek payment of tax, including payments on account for the following year and to charge interest.

The determination must be made within the period ending 5 years after 31 January following the tax year. It may be superseded by a self-assessment made within the same period or, if later, within 12 months of the date of the determination.

5.3 Discovery assessments

If an Officer of Revenue and Customs discovers that profits have been omitted from assessment, that any assessment has become insufficient, or that any relief given is, or has become excessive, an assessment may be raised to recover the tax lost.

If the tax lost results from an error in the taxpayer's return but the return was made in accordance with prevailing practice at the time, no discovery assessment may be made.

A discovery assessment may only be raised where a return has been made if:

(a)   There has been fraudulent or negligent conduct by the taxpayer or his agent, or

(b) At the time that enquiries into the return were completed, or could no longer be made, the officer did not have information to make him aware of the loss of tax.

Information is treated as available to an officer if:

(a) It is contained in the taxpayer's return for the period (or for either of the two preceding periods) or in any accompanying documents.

(b) It is contained in a claim made in respect of that period or in any accompanying documents;

(c) It is contained in any documents, produced in connection with an enquiry into a return (or claim) for the period or either of the two preceding periods;

(d) It is information, the existence and relevance of which, could reasonably be expected to be inferred by an officer from the information described above, or which was notified in writing by or on behalf of the taxpayer to an officer. The information supplied must be sufficiently detailed to draw the Revenue's attention to contentious matters, such as the use of a valuation or estimate.

These rules do not prevent the Revenue from raising assessments in cases of genuine discoveries, but prevent assessments from being raised due to the Revenue's failure to make timely use of information or to a change of opinion on information made available.

5.4 Appeals and postponement of payment of tax

A taxpayer may appeal against an amendment to a self-assessment or partnership statement, or an amendment to or disallowance of a claim, following an enquiry, or against an assessment which is not a self-assessment, such as a discovery assessment.

The appeal must normally be made within 30 days of the amendment or self-assessment.

The notice of appeal must state the **grounds** of appeal. These may be stated in general terms. At the hearing the Commissioners may allow the appellant to put forward grounds not stated in his notice if they are satisfied that his omission was not wilful or unreasonable.

In some cases it may be possible to agree the point at issue by negotiation with the Revenue, in which case the appeal may be settled by agreement. If the appeal cannot be agreed, it will be heard by the General or Special Commissioners.

An appeal does not relieve the taxpayer of liability to pay tax on the normal due date unless he obtains a 'determination' of the Commissioners or agreement of the Inspector that payment of all or some of the tax may be postponed pending determination of the appeal. The amount not postponed is due 30 days after the determination or agreement is issued, if that is later than the normal due date.

If any part of the postponed tax becomes due a notice of the amount payable is issued and the amount is payable 30 days after the issue of the notice. Interest, however, is still payable from the normal due date.

5.5 Income tax fraud

There is a statutory offence of evading income tax. The penalty may be up to seven years in prison or an unlimited fine, or both.

Chapter roundup

- Individuals who do not receive a tax return must notify their chargeability to income tax or CGT.

- Tax returns must usually be filed by 31 January following the end of the tax year. There are penalties for late filing. Returns may be filed online.

- Although taxpayers must normally self assess their income tax, Class 4 NIC and CGT liabilities the Revenue will calculate the tax on their behalf if they file their tax return by 30 September following the end of the tax year.

- Two payments on account and a final balancing payment of income tax and Class 4 NICs may be due. All capital gains tax is due on 31 January following the end of the tax year.

- Self assessment is enforced through a system of automatic surcharges, penalties and interest.

- The Revenue can enquire into tax returns but strict procedural rules govern enquiries.

Quick quiz

1   By when must a taxpayer who has not received a tax return give notice of his chargeability to capital gains tax due in 2005/06?

2   By when must a taxpayer, who intends to calculate his own tax, file a tax return for 2005/06?

3   What are the normal payment dates for income tax?

4   What surcharges are due in respect of income tax payments on account that are paid two months after the due date?

Answers to quick quiz

1   Within six months of the end of the year, ie by 5 October 2006.

2   By 31 January 2007 or, if later, 3 months after a notice to file the return was issued.

3   Two payments on account of income tax are due on 31 January in the tax year and on the 31 July following. A final balancing payment is due on 31 January following the tax year.

4   None. Surcharges do not apply to late payment of payments on account.

Now try the question below from the Exam Question Bank

Number	Level	Marks	Time
Q24	Introductory	8	15 mins

Part C
Employees

Employment income and PAYE

Introduction

Most people have jobs, which pay them wages or salaries. This chapter starts by looking at the way in which employment income is taxed.

Sometimes, the income for tax purposes is less than the total received from the employer. This may be because the employee can deduct some expenses. We look at the rules in Section 2.

The Revenue require employers to deduct tax at source from wages under the PAYE system. This system ensures that the Revenue get their money. We look at it in Section 3.

In the next chapter we look at how benefits received as a result of employment are taxed.

1 Employment income

1.1 Outline of the charge

Employment income includes income arising from an employment under a contract of service (see below) and the income of office holders, such as directors. The term 'employee' is used in this text to mean anyone who receives employment income (ie both employees and directors).

There are two types of employment income:

- **General earnings**, and
- **Specific employment income**.

General earnings are an employees' earnings (see key term below) plus the 'cash equivalent' of any taxable non-monetary benefits.

Key term

> **'Earnings'** means any salary, wage or fee, any gratuity or other profit or incidental benefit obtained by the employee if it is money or money's worth (something of direct monetary value or convertible into direct monetary value) or anything else which constitutes an emolument of the employment.

'Specific employment income' includes payments on termination of employment and share related income. These types of income are not examinable in Paper 2.3.

Taxable earnings from an employment in a tax year are the general earnings received in that tax year.

1.2 When are earnings received?

FAST FORWARD

> General earnings are taxed in the year of receipt. Money earnings are generally received on the earlier of the time payment is made and the time entitlement to payment arises.

General earnings consisting of money are treated as received at the earlier of:

- **The time when payment is made**
- **The time when a person becomes entitled to payment of the earnings.**

If the employee is a director of a company, earnings from the company are received on the earliest of:

- The earlier of the two alternatives given in the general rule (above)
- The time when the amount is credited in the company's accounting records
- The end of the company's period of account (if the amount was determined by then)
- The time the amount is determined (if after the end of the company's period of account).

Taxable benefits are generally treated as received when they are provided to the employee.

The receipts basis does not apply to pension income. Pensions are taxed on the amount accruing in the tax year, whether or not it has actually been received in that year.

1.3 Net taxable earnings

Total taxable earnings less total allowable deductions (see below) **are net taxable earnings of a tax year. Deductions cannot usually create a loss: they can only reduce the net taxable earnings to nil.** If there is more than one employment in the tax year, separate calculations are required for each employment.

1.4 Person liable for tax on employment income

The person liable to tax on employment income is generally the **person to whose employment the earnings relate**. However, if the tax relates to general earnings received after the death of the person to whose employment the earnings relate, the person's personal representatives are liable for the tax. The tax is a liability of the estate.

1.5 Employment and self employment

FAST FORWARD

Employment involves a contract of service whereas self employment involves a contract for services. The distinction between employment and self employment is decided by looking at all the facts of a case.

The distinction between employment (receipts taxable as earnings) and self employment (receipts taxable as trading income) is a fine one. Employment involves a contract of service, whereas self employment involves a contract for services. Taxpayers tend to prefer self employment, because the rules on deductions for expenses are more generous.

Factors which may be of importance include:

- The degree of control exercised over the person doing the work
- Whether he must accept further work
- Whether the other party must provide further work
- Whether he provides his own equipment
- Whether he hires his own helpers
- What degree of financial risk he takes
- What degree of responsibility for investment and management he has
- Whether he can profit from sound management
- Whether he can work when he chooses
- The wording used in any agreement between the parties.

Relevant cases include:

(a) *Edwards v Clinch 1981*

A civil engineer acted occasionally as an inspector on temporary ad hoc appointments.

Held: there was no ongoing office which could be vacated by one person and held by another so the fees received were from self employment not employment.

(b) *Hall v Lorimer 1994*

A vision mixer was engaged under a series of short-term contracts.

Held: the vision mixer was self employed, not because of any one detail of the case but because the overall picture was one of self-employment.

(c) *Carmichael and Anor v National Power plc 1999*

Individuals engaged as visitor guides on a casual 'as required' basis were not employees. An exchange of correspondence between the company and the individuals was not a contract of employment as there was no provision as to the frequency of work and there was flexibility to accept work or turn it down as it arose. Sickness, holiday and pension arrangements did not apply and neither did grievance and disciplinary procedures.

A worker's status also affects national insurance contributions. The self-employed generally pay less than employees.

2 Allowable deductions

> Deductions for expenses are extremely limited. Relief is available for the costs that an employee is obliged to incur in travelling in the performance of his duties or in travelling to the place he has to attend in performance of his duties. Relief is not available for normal commuting costs.

2.1 General rules

Certain expenditure is specifically deductible in computing net taxable earnings:

(a) **Contributions** (within certain limits) **to approved occupational pension schemes**

(b) **Subscriptions to professional bodies** on the list of bodies issued by the Revenue (which includes most UK professional bodies), if relevant to the duties of the employment

(c) Payments for certain liabilities relating to the employment and for insurance against them (see below)

(d) Payments to charity made under the payroll deduction scheme operated by an employer

(e) Mileage allowance relief (see next chapter).

Otherwise, **allowable deductions are notoriously hard to obtain. They are limited to**:

- **Qualifying travel expenses** (see below)

- **Other expenses the employee is obliged to incur and pay as holder of the employment which are incurred wholly, exclusively and necessarily in the performance of the duties of the employment**

- **Capital allowances on plant and machinery (other than cars or other vehicles) necessarily provided for use in the performance of those duties.**

2.2 Liabilities and insurance

If a director or employee incurs a liability related to his employment or pays for insurance against such a liability, the cost is a deductible expense. If the employer pays such amounts, there is no taxable benefit.

A liability relating to employment is one which is imposed in respect of the employee's acts or omissions as employee. Thus, for example, liability for negligence would be covered. Related costs, for example the costs of legal proceedings, are included.

For insurance premiums to qualify, the insurance policy must:

(a) Cover only liabilities relating to employment, vicarious liability in respect of liabilities of another person's employment, related costs and payments to the employee's own employees in respect of their employment liabilities relating to employment and related costs, and

(b) It must not last for more than two years (although it may be renewed for up to two years at a time), and the insured person must not be not required to renew it.

2.3 Travel expenses

Tax relief is not available for an employee's normal commuting costs. This means relief is not available for any costs an employee incurs in getting from home to his normal place of work. However **employees are entitled to relief for travel expenses which basically are the full costs that they are obliged to incur and pay as holder of the employment in travelling in the performance of their duties or travelling to or**

from a place which they have to attend in the performance of their duties (other than a permanent workplace).

2.4 Example: travel in the performance of duties

Judi is an accountant. She often travels to meetings at the firm's offices in the North of England returning to her office in Leeds after the meetings. Relief is available for the full cost of these journeys as the travel is undertaken in the performance of her duties.

Question	Relief for travelling costs

Zoe lives in Wycombe and normally works in Chiswick. Occasionally she visits a client in Wimbledon and travels direct from home. Distances are shown in the diagram below:

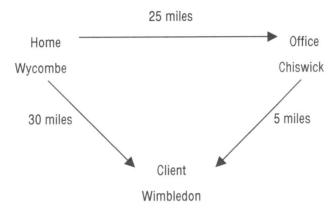

What tax relief is available for Zoe's travel costs?

Answer

Zoe is not entitled to tax relief for the costs incurred in travelling between Wycombe and Chiswick since these are normal commuting costs. However, relief is available for all costs that Zoe incurs when she travels from Wycombe to Wimbledon to visit her client.

To prevent manipulation of the basic rule normal commuting will not become a business journey just because the employee stops en-route to perform a business task (eg make a 'phone call'). Nor will relief be available if the journey is essentially the same as the employee's normal journey to work.

2.5 Example: normal commuting

Judi is based at her office in Leeds City Centre. One day she is required to attend a 9.00 am meeting with a client whose premises are around the corner from her Leeds office. Judi travels from home directly to the meeting. As the journey is substantially the same as her ordinary journey to work relief is not available.

Site based employees (eg construction workers, management consultants etc) **who do not have a permanent workplace, are entitled to relief for the costs of all journeys made from home to wherever they are working**. This is because these employees do not have an ordinary commuting journey or any normal commuting costs. However there is a caveat that the employee does not spend more than 24 months of continuous work at any one site.

Tax relief is available for travel, accommodation and subsistence expenses incurred by an employee who is working at a temporary workplace on a secondment expected to last up to 24 months. If a secondment is initially expected not to exceed 24 months, but it is extended, relief ceases to be due from the date the employee becomes aware of the change. When looking at how long a secondment is expected to last, the Revenue will consider not only the terms of the written contract but also any verbal agreement by the employer and other factors such as whether the employee buys a house etc.

Question   Temporary workplace

Philip works for Vastbank at its Newcastle City Centre branch. Philip is sent to work full-time at another branch in Morpeth for 20 months at the end of which he will return to the Newcastle branch. Morpeth is about 20 miles north of Newcastle.

What travel costs is Philip entitled to claim as a deduction?

Answer

Although Philip is spending all of his time at the Morpeth branch it will not be treated as his normal work place because his period of attendance will be less than 24 months. Thus Philip can claim relief in full for the costs of travel from his home to the Morpeth branch.

2.6 Other expenses

The word 'exclusively' strictly implies that the expenditure must give no private benefit at all. If it does, none of it is deductible. In practice inspectors may ignore a small element of private benefit or make an apportionment between business and private use.

Whether an expense is 'necessary' is not determined by what the employer requires. The test is whether the duties of the employment could not be performed without the outlay.

- *Sanderson v Durbridge 1955*

  The cost of evening meals taken when attending late meetings was not deductible because it was not incurred in the performance of the duties.

- *Blackwell v Mills 1945*

  As a condition of his employment, an employee was required to attend evening classes. The cost of his textbooks and travel was not deductible because it was not incurred in the performance of the duties.

- *Lupton v Potts 1969*

  Examination fees incurred by a solicitor's articled clerk were not deductible because they were incurred neither wholly nor exclusively in the performance of the duties, but in furthering the clerk's ambition to become a solicitor.

- *Brown v Bullock 1961*

  The expense of joining a club that was virtually a requisite of an employment was not deductible because it would have been possible to carry on the employment without the club membership, so the expense was not necessary.

- *Elwood v Utitz 1965*

  A managing director's subscriptions to two residential London clubs were claimed by him as an expense on the grounds that they were cheaper than hotels.

  The expenditure was deductible as it was necessary in that it would be impossible for the employee to carry out his London duties without being provided with first class accommodation. The residential facilities (which were cheaper than hotel accommodation) were given to club members only.

- *Lucas v Cattell 1972*

  The cost of business telephone calls on a private telephone is deductible, but **no part of the line or** telephone **rental charges is deductible**.

- *Fitzpatrick v IRC 1994; Smith v Abbott 1994*

  Journalists cannot claim a deduction for the cost of buying newspapers which they read to keep themselves informed, since they are merely preparing themselves to perform their duties.

The cost of clothes for work is not deductible, except that for certain trades requiring protective clothing there are annual deductions on a set scale.

An employee required to work at home may be able to claim a deduction for an appropriate proportion of his or her expenditure on lighting, heating and (if a room is used exclusively for work purposes) **the council tax.** Employers can pay up to £2 per week without the need for supporting evidence of the costs incurred by the employee. Payments above the £2 limit require evidence of the employee's actual costs.

3 The PAYE system

Most tax in respect of income is deducted under the PAYE system. The objective of the PAYE system is to collect the correct amount of tax over the year. An employee's PAYE code is designed to ensure that allowances etc are given evenly over the year.

3.1 Introduction

3.1.1 Cash payments

The objective of the PAYE system is to deduct the correct amount of tax over the year. Its scope is very wide. It applies to most cash payments, other than reimbursed business expenses, and to certain non cash payments.

In addition to wages and salaries, PAYE applies to round sum expense allowances and payments instead of benefits. It also applies to any readily convertible asset.

A readily convertible asset is any asset which can effectively be exchanged for cash. The amount subject to PAYE is the amount that would be taxed as employment income. This is usually the cost to the employer of providing the asset.

Tips paid direct to an employee are normally outside the PAYE system (although still assessable as employment income). An exception may apply in the catering trades where tips are often pooled. Here the PAYE position depends on whether a 'tronc', administered other than by the employer, exists.

It is the employer's duty to deduct income tax from the pay of his employees, whether or not he has been directed to do so by the Revenue. **If he fails to do this he** (or sometimes the employee) **must pay over the tax which he should have deducted and the employer may be subject to penalties.** Interest will also run from 14 days after the end of the tax year concerned on any underpaid PAYE. Officers of the Revenue and Customs can inspect employer's records in order to satisfy themselves that the correct amounts of tax are being deducted and paid over to the Revenue.

3.1.2 Benefits

PAYE is not normally operated on benefits; instead the employee's PAYE code is restricted (see below).

However, PAYE must be applied to remuneration in the form of a taxable non-cash voucher if at the time it is provided:

(a) the voucher is capable of being exchanged for readily convertible assets; or

(b) the voucher can itself be sold, realised or traded.

PAYE must be normally operated on cash vouchers and on each occasion when a director/employee uses a credit-token (eg a credit card) to obtain money or goods which are readily convertible assets. However, a cash voucher or credit token which is used to defray expenses is not subject to PAYE.

3.2 How PAYE works

3.2.1 Operation of PAYE

To operate PAYE the employer needs:

(a) deductions working sheets

(b) codes for employees that reflect the tax allowances to which the employees are entitled

(c) tax tables

The employer works out the amount of PAYE tax to deduct on any particular pay day by using the employees code number (see below) in conjunction with the PAYE tables. The tables are designed so that tax is normally worked out on a cumulative basis. This means that with each payment of earnings the running total of tax paid is compared with tax due on total earnings to that date. The difference between the tax due and the tax paid is the tax to be deducted on that particular payday.

National insurance tables are used to work out the national insurance due on any payday.

Although PAYE is normally operated on a cumulative basis, an employee may have a week 1/month 1 code (see below). In this case the figures for pay and tax deducted are not cumulated, and the tax on each payday is worked out on the pay on that payday as if it were the first payday in the tax year (using week1/month 1 table).

If a K code applies there is a restriction on the amount of tax that can be deducted (see below). On a cumulative basis, this restriction will be recouped on a later payday (subject to the overriding limit on the later pay day). On a week 1/month 1 basis the restriction cannot be recouped, and will be dealt with by the Revenue after the end of the tax year.

3.2.2 Records

The employer must keep records of each employee's pay and tax at each pay day. The records must also contain details of National Insurance. The employer has a choice of three ways of recording and returning these figures:

(a) he may use the official deductions working sheet (P11)

(b) he may incorporate the figures in his own pay records using a substitute document

(c) he may retain the figures on a computer

These records will be used to make a return at the end of the tax year.

3.3 Payment under the PAYE system

Under PAYE income tax and national insurance is normally paid over to the Inland Revenue monthly, 14 days after the end of each tax month.

If an employer's average monthly payments under the PAYE system are less than £1,500, the employer may choose to pay quarterly, within 14 days of the end of each tax quarter. Tax quarters end on 5 July, 5 October, 5 January and 5 April. Payments can continue to be made quarterly during a tax year even if the monthly average reaches or exceeds £1,500, but a new estimate must be made and a new decision taken to pay quarterly at the start of each tax year. Average monthly payments are the average net monthly payments due to the Revenue for income tax and NICs.

3.4 PAYE codes

An employee is normally entitled to various allowances. Under the PAYE system an amount reflecting the effect of a proportion of these allowances is set against his pay each pay day. To determine the amount to set against his pay the allowances are expressed in the form of a code which is used in conjunction with the Pay Adjustment Table (Table A).

An employee's code may be any one of the following:

L   tax code with basic personal allowance

K   prefix when allowances are less than benefits.

The codes BR, DO and OT are generally used where there is a second source of income and all allowances have been used in a tax code which is applied to the main source of income.

Generally, a tax code number is arrived at by deleting the last digit in the sum representing the employee's tax free allowances. Every individual is entitled to a personal tax free allowance of £4,895. The code number for an individual who is entitled to this but no other allowance is 489L.

The code number may also reflect other items. For example, it will be restricted to reflect benefits, small amounts of untaxed income and unpaid tax on income from earlier years. If an amount of tax is in point, it is necessary to gross up the tax in the code using the taxpayer's estimated marginal rate of income tax.

Question	PAYE codes

Adrian is a 40 year old single man (suffix letter L) who earns £15,000 pa. He has benefits of £560 and his unpaid tax for 2003/04 was £57.50. Adrian is entitled to a tax free personal allowance of £4,895 in 2005/06.

Adrian pays income tax at the marginal rate of 22%.

What is Adrian's PAYE code for 2005/06?

Answer

	£
Personal allowance	4,895
Benefits	(560)
Unpaid tax £57.50 × 100/22	(261)
Available allowances	4,074

Adrian's PAYE code is 407L

Codes are determined and amended by the Revenue. They are normally notified to the employer on a code list. The employer must act on the code notified to him until amended instructions are received from the Revenue, even if the employee has appealed against the code.

By using the code number in conjunction with the tax tables, an employee is generally given 1/52nd or 1/12th of his tax free allowances against each week's/month's pay. However because of the cumulative nature of PAYE, if an employee is first paid in, say, September, that month he will receive six months' allowances against his gross pay. In cases where the employee's previous PAYE history is not known, this could lead to under-deduction of tax. To avoid this, codes for the employees concerned have to be operated on a 'week 1/month1' basis, so that only 1/52nd or 1/12th of the employee's allowances are available each week/month.

'K' codes increase taxable pay instead of reducing it. This means benefits exceed allowances. The PAYE deducted under a K code could remove all of an employee's actual remuneration for a pay period. As this could cause hardship, **the PAYE deduced on any payday is not to exceed 50% of the amount of actual remuneration on that pay day**. (This overriding limit does not restrict the tax on non cash payments).

3.5 Employer's responsibilities: year end returns and employees leaving or joining

FAST FORWARD

Employers must complete forms P60, P14, P35, P9D, P11D and P45 as appropriate. A P45 is needed when an employee leaves. Forms P9D and P11D record details of benefits. Forms P60, P14 and P35 are year end returns.

At the end of each tax year, the employer must provide each employee with a form P60. This shows total taxable earnings for the year, tax deducted, code number, NI number and the employer's name and address. **The P60 must be provided by 31 May following the year of assessment.**

Following the end of each tax year, the employer must send the Revenue:

(a) **by 19 May**:

    (i) **End of year Returns P14** (showing the same details as the P60);
    (ii) **Form P35** (summary of tax and NI deducted).

(b) **by 6 July**:

    (i) **Forms P11D** (benefits etc for directors and employees paid £8,500+ pa);
    (ii) **Forms P11D(b)** (return of Class 1A NICs (see below));
    (iii) **Forms P9D** (benefits etc for other employees).

A copy of the form P11D (or P9D) must also be provided to the employee by 6 July. The details shown on the P11D include the full cash equivalent of all benefits, so that the employee may enter the details on his self-assessment tax return. Specific reference numbers for the entries on the P11D are also used on the employee's self assessment tax return.

When an employee leaves, a certificate on form P45 (particulars of Employee Leaving) must be prepared. This form shows the employee's code and details of his income and tax paid to date and is a four part form. One part is sent to the Revenue, and three parts handed to the employee. One of the parts (part 1A) is the employee's personal copy. If the employee takes up a new employment, he must hand the other two parts of the form P45 to the new employer. The new employer will fill in details of the new employment and send one part to the Revenue, retaining the other. The details on the form are used by the new employer to calculate the PAYE due on the next payday. If the employee dies a P45 should be completed, and the whole form sent to the Revenue.

If an employee joins with a form P45, the new employer can operate PAYE. If there is no P45 the employer still needs to operate PAYE. The employee is required to complete a form P46. If he declares that the employment is his first job since leaving education, or his only or main job and that he not in receipt of a pension, the emergency code (489L for 2005/06) applies, on a cumulative basis or week 1/month 1 basis respectively. Otherwise the employer must use code BR. The P46 is sent to the Revenue, unless the pay is below the PAYE and NIC thresholds, and the emergency code applies. In this case no PAYE is deductible until the pay exceeds the threshold.

3.6 Penalties

A form P35 is due on 19 May after the end of the tax year. In practice, a 7 day extension to the due date of 19 May is allowed.

Where a form P35 is late, a penalty of £100 per month per 50 employees may be imposed. This penalty cannot be mitigated. **This penalty ceases 12 months after the due date and a further penalty of up to 100% of the tax (and NIC) for the year which remains unpaid** at 19 April may be imposed. This penalty can be mitigated. The Revenue automatically reduce the penalty by concession to the greater of £100 and the total PAYE/NIC which should be reported on the return.

Where a person has fraudulently or negligently submitted an incorrect form P35 the penalty is 100% of the tax (and NIC) attributable to the error. This penalty can be mitigated.

3.7 PAYE settlement agreements

PAYE settlement agreements (PSAs) are arrangements under which employers can make single payments to settle their employees' income tax liabilities on expense payments and certain benefits. Benefits may be included in a PSA if the Revenue consider them to be minor (eg small gifts), irregular (eg, relocation payments of over £8,000) or benefits in respect of which it is impractical to apply PAYE or identify the amount attributable to a particular employee (eg free dental care). Items covered by a PSA do not have to be included on either Forms P9D or P11D or on the employee's tax return.

PSAs cannot be used to settle tax on:

    (a)   cash payments of salaries, wages or bonuses

    (b)   major benefits provided regularly for the sole use of individual employees (for example, company cars)

    (c)   round sum allowances

Tax due under a PSA must be paid by 19 October following the end of the tax year.

3.8 Charitable donations under the payroll deduction scheme

Employees can make tax deductible donations under the payroll deduction scheme to an approved charity of their choice by asking their employer to deduct the donation from their gross earnings prior to calculating PAYE due thereon.

Chapter roundup

- General earnings are taxed in the year of receipt. Money earnings are generally received on the earlier of the time payment is made and the time entitlement to payment arises.

- Employment involves a contract of service whereas self employment involves a contract for services. The distinction between employment and self employment is decided by looking at all the facts of a case.

- Deductions for expenses are extremely limited. Relief is available for the costs that an employee is obliged to incur in travelling in the performance of his duties or in travelling to the place he has to attend in performance of his duties. Relief is not available for normal commuting costs.

- Most tax in respect of income is deducted under the PAYE system. The objective of the PAYE system is to collect the correct amount of tax over the year. An employee's PAYE code is designed to ensure that allowances etc are given evenly over the year.

- Employers must complete forms P60, P14, P35, P9D, P11D and P45 as appropriate. A P45 is needed when an employee leaves. Forms P9D and P11D record details of benefits. Forms P60, P14 and P35 are year end returns.

Quick quiz

1   On what basis are earnings taxed?

2   What are the conditions for general expenses of employment to be deductible?

3   Give an example of a PAYE code.

Answers to quick quiz

1   Earnings are taxed on a receipts basis.

2   The expenses must be incurred wholly, exclusively and necessarily in the performance of the duties of the employment.

3   489L.

Now try the question below from the Exam Question Bank

Number	Level	Marks	Time
Q25	Examination	15	27 mins

20

Taxable and exempt benefits

Topic list	Syllabus references
1 Taxable benefits	3(a)(iv)
2 Exempt benefits	3(a)(iv)

Introduction

In this chapter we look at how employees are taxed on the benefits they derive from their employment.

1 Taxable benefits

Most employees are taxed on benefits under the benefits code. 'Excluded employees' (lower paid/non-directors) are only subject to part of the provisions of the code.

1.1 Introduction

The Income Tax (Earnings and Pensions) Act 2003 (ITEPA 2003) provides comprehensive legislation covering the taxation of benefits.

The legislation generally applies to all employees. However, only certain parts of it apply to 'excluded employees'.

An excluded employee is an employee in lower paid employment who is either not a director of a company or is a director but has no material interest in the company ('material' means control of more than 5% of the ordinary share capital) **and either**:

(a)   **He is full time working director**, or

(b)   **The company is non-profit-making or is established for charitable purposes only.**

The term 'director' refers to any person who acts as a director or any person in accordance with whose instructions the directors are accustomed to act (other than a professional advisor).

Lower paid employment is one where the earnings rate for the tax year is less than £8,500. To decide whether this applies, add together the **total earnings and benefits that would be taxable, if the employee were *not* an excluded employee**.

A number of **specific deductions** must be taken into account to determine lower paid employment. These include **contributions to authorised pension schemes and payroll giving**. However, general deductions from employment income (see later in this chapter) are not taken into account.

Where a car is provided but the employee could have chosen an alternative benefit, an extra amount is added to the lower paid employment calculation. This amount is the higher of:

(a)   the cash equivalents of the car benefit and of any fuel benefit, and

(b)   the amount which might be chargeable to tax as earnings.

1.2 General business expenses

If business expenses on such items as travel or hotel stays, are reimbursed by an employer, the reimbursed amount is a taxable benefit for employees other than excluded employees. To avoid being taxed on this amount, **an employee must then make a claim to deduct it as an expense** under the rules set out below. **In practice**, however, **many such expense payments are not reported to the Inland Revenue and can be ignored because it is agreed in advance that a claim to deduct them would be possible (a P11D dispensation)**.

When an individual has to spend one or more nights away from home, his employer may reimburse expenses on items incidental to his absence (for example meals and private telephone calls). **Such incidental expenses are exempt** if:

(a)   The expenses of travelling to each place where the individual stays overnight, throughout the trip, are incurred necessarily in the performance of the duties of the employment (or would have been, if there had been any expenses).

(b)   The total (for the whole trip) of incidental expenses not deductible under the usual rules is no more than £5 for each night spent wholly in the UK and £10 for each other night. If this limit is exceeded, all of the expenses are taxable, not just the excess. The expenses include any VAT.

This incidental expenses exemption applies to expenses reimbursed, and to benefits obtained using credit tokens and non-cash vouchers.

1.3 Vouchers

If any employee (including an excluded employee):

    (a)   receives cash vouchers (vouchers exchangeable for cash)

    (b)   uses a credit token (such as a credit card) to obtain money, goods or services, or

    (c)   receives exchangeable vouchers (such as book tokens), also called non-cash vouchers

he is taxed on the cost of providing the benefit, less any amount made good.

However, the first 15p per working day of meal vouchers (eg luncheon vouchers) is not taxed.

1.4 Accommodation

FAST FORWARD

> The benefit in respect of accommodation is its annual value. There is an additional benefit if the property cost over £75,000.

The taxable value of accommodation provided to an employee (including an excluded employee) is the rent that would have been payable if the premises had been let at their annual value (taken to be their **rateable value**, despite the abolition of domestic rates). **If the premises are rented** rather than owned by the employer, then **the taxable benefit is the higher of the rent actually paid and the annual value**. If property does not have a rateable value the Revenue estimate a value.

If a property cost more than £75,000, an additional amount is chargeable as follows:

(Cost of providing the living accommodation – £75,000) × the official rate of interest at the start of the tax year.

Thus with an official rate of 5%, the total benefit for accommodation costing £90,000 and with an annual value of £2,000 would be £2,000 + £(90,000 – 75,000) × 5% = £2,750.

The 'cost of providing' the living accommodation is the aggregate of the cost of purchase and the cost of any improvements made before the start of the tax year for which the benefit is being computed. It is therefore not possible to avoid the charge by buying an inexpensive property requiring substantial repairs and improving it.

Where the property was acquired more than six years before first being provided to the employee, the market value when first so provided plus the cost of subsequent improvements is used as the cost of providing the living accommodation. However, unless the actual cost plus improvements up to the start of the tax year in question exceeds £75,000, the additional charge cannot be imposed, however high the market value.

Exam focus point

> The 'official rate' of interest will be given to you in the exam.

There is no taxable benefit in respect of job related accommodation. Accommodation is job related if:

    (a)   Residence in the accommodation **is necessary for the proper performance of the employee's duties** (as with a caretaker), or

    (b)   The accommodation is provided **for the better performance of the employee's duties** and the employment is of a kind in which it is **customary for accommodation to be provided** (as with a policeman), or

(c)   The **accommodation is provided as part of arrangements in force because of a special threat to the employee's security**.

Directors can only claim exemptions (a) or (b) if:

(a)   They have no **material interest** ('material' means over 5%) in the company, and

(b)   Either they are **full time working directors** or the company is **non-profit making or is a charity**.

Any contribution paid by the employee is deducted from the annual value of the property and then from the additional benefit.

If the employee is given a cash alternative to living accommodation, the benefits code still applies in priority to treating the cash alternative as earnings. If the cash alternative is greater than the taxable benefit, the excess is treated as earnings.

1.5 Expenses connected with living accommodation

In addition to the benefit of living accommodation itself, **employees, other than excluded employees, are taxed on related expenses paid by the employer**, such as:

(a)   **Heating, lighting or cleaning the premises**
(b)   **Repairing, maintaining or decorating the premises**
(c)   **The provision of furniture (the annual value is 20% of the cost)**

Unless the accommodation qualifies as 'job related' (as defined above) **the full cost of ancillary services** (excluding structural repairs) **is taxable. If the accommodation is 'job related'**, however, **taxable ancillary services are restricted to a maximum of 10% of the employee's 'net earnings'**. For this purpose, net earnings are all earnings from the employment (excluding the ancillary benefits (a) - (c) above) less any allowable expenses, statutory mileage allowances, contributions to approved occupational pension schemes and retirement annuity schemes (but not personal pension plans), and capital allowances. If there are ancillary benefits other than those falling within (a) - (c) above (such as a telephone) they are taxable in full.

    Question   Expenses connected with living accommodation

Mr Quinton has a gross salary in 2005/06 of £28,850. He normally lives and works in London, but he is required to live in a company house in Scotland which cost £70,000 three years ago, so that he can carry out a two year review of his company's operations in Scotland. The annual value of the house is £650. In 2005/06 the company pays an electricity bill of £550, a gas bill of £400, a gardener's bill of £750 and redecoration costs of £1,800. Mr Quinton makes a monthly contribution of £50 for his accommodation. He also pays £1,450 occupational pension contributions.

Calculate Mr Quinton's taxable employment income for 2005/06.

Answer

	£	£
Salary		28,850
Less occupational pension scheme contributions		(1,450)
Net earnings		27,400
Accommodation benefits		
Annual value: exempt (job related)		
Ancillary services		
Electricity	550	
Gas	400	
Gardener	750	
Redecorations	1,800	
	3,500	
Restricted to 10% of £27,400	2,740	
Less employee's contribution	(600)	
		2,140
Employment income		29,540

Council tax and water or sewage charges paid by the employer are taxable in full as a benefit unless the accommodation is 'job-related'.

1.6 Cars

FAST FORWARD

Employees who have a company car are taxed on a % of the car's list price which depends on the level of the car's CO_2 emissions. The same % multiplied by £14,400 determines the benefit where private fuel is also provided. Authorised mileage allowances can be paid tax free to employees who use their own vehicle for business journeys.

A car provided by reason of the employment to an employee or member of his family or household for private use gives rise to a taxable benefit. This does not apply to excluded employees. **'Private use' includes home to work travel.**

(a) A tax charge arises whether the car is provided by the employer or by some other person. The benefit is computed as shown below, even if the car is taken as an alternative to another benefit of a different value.

(b) The starting point for calculating a car benefit is the list price of the car (plus accessories). **The percentage of the list price that is taxable depends on the car's CO_2 emissions**.

(c) The price of the car is the sum of the following items.

(i) The list price of the car for a single retail sale at the time of first registration, including charges for delivery and standard accessories. The manufacturer's, importer's or distributor's list price must be used, even if the retailer offered a discount. A notional list price is estimated if no list price was published.

(ii) The price (including fitting) of all optional accessories provided when the car was first provided to the employee, excluding mobile telephones and equipment needed by a disabled employee. The extra cost of adapting or manufacturing a car to run on road fuel gases is not included.

(iii) The price (including fitting) of all optional accessories fitted later and costing at least £100 each, excluding mobile telephones and equipment needed by a disabled employee. Such accessories affect the taxable benefit from and including the tax year in which they are fitted. However, accessories which are merely replacing existing accessories and are not superior to the ones replaced are ignored. Replacement accessories which *are* superior are taken into account, but the cost of the old accessory is then ignored.

(d) There is a special rule for classic cars. If the car is at least 15 years old (from the time of first registration) at the end of the tax year, and its market value at the end of the year (or, if earlier, when it ceased to be available to the employee) is over £15,000 and greater than the price found under (c), that market value is used instead of the price. The market value takes account of all accessories (except mobile telephones and equipment needed by a disabled employee).

(e) If the price or value found under (c) or (d) exceeds £80,000, then £80,000 is used instead of the price or value.

(f) Capital contributions are payments by the employee in respect of the price of the car or accessories. In any tax year, we take account of capital contributions made in that year and previous years (for the same car). The maximum deductible capital contributions is £5,000: contributions beyond that total are ignored.

(g) **For cars that emit CO_2 of 140g/km (2005/06) or less, the taxable benefit is 15% of the car's list price. This percentage increases by 1% for every 5g/km (rounded down to the nearest multiple of 5) by which CO_2 emissions exceed 140g/km up to a maximum of 35%.**

Exam focus point	The CO_2 baseline figure will be given to you in the tax rates and allowances section of the exam paper.

(h) Diesel cars have a supplement of 3% of the car's list price added to the taxable benefit. However, the benefit is discounted for cars that are particularly environmentally friendly. The maximum percentage, however, remains 35% of the list price.

(i) Cars which do not have an approved CO_2 emissions figure are taxed according to engine size.

(j) **The benefit is reduced on a time basis where a car is first made available or ceases to be made available during the tax year** or is incapable of being used for a continuous period of not less than 30 days (for example because it is being repaired).

(k) **The benefit is reduced by any payment the user must make for the private use of the car** (as distinct from a capital contribution to the cost of the car). Payments for insuring the car do not count *(IRC v Quigley 1995)*. The benefit cannot become negative to create a deduction from the employee's income.

(l) Pool cars are exempt. A car is a pool car if **all** the following conditions are satisfied.

- It is used by more than one employee and is not ordinarily used by any one of them to the exclusion of the others.

- Any private use is merely incidental to business use.

- It is not normally kept overnight at or near the residence of an employee.

There are many ancillary benefits associated with the provision of cars, such as insurance, repairs, vehicle licences and a parking space at or near work. No extra taxable benefit arises as a result of these, with the exception of the cost of providing a driver.

1.7 Fuel for cars

Where fuel is provided there is a further benefit in addition to the car benefit.

No taxable benefit arises where either

(a) **All the fuel provided was made available only for business travel**, or

(b) **The employee is required to make good, and has made good, the whole of the cost of any fuel provided for his private use**.

Unlike most benefits, a reimbursement of only part of the cost of the fuel available for private use does not reduce the benefit.

The taxable benefit is a percentage of a base figure. The base figure for 2005/06 is £14,400. The percentage is the same percentage as is used to calculate the car benefit (see above).

Exam focus point

The fuel base figure will be given to you in the tax rates and allowances section of the exam paper.

The fuel benefit is reduced in the same way as the car benefit **if the car is not available for 30 days or more**.

The fuel benefit is also reduced if private fuel is not available for part of a tax year. However, if private fuel later becomes available in the same tax year, the reduction is not made. If, for example, fuel is provided from 6 April 2005 to 30 June 2005, then the fuel benefit for 2005/06 will be restricted to just three months. This is because the provision of fuel has permanently ceased. However, if fuel is provided from 6 April 2005 to 30 June 2005, and then again from 1 September 2005 to 5 April 2006, then the fuel benefit will not be reduced since the cessation was only temporary.

Question — Car and fuel benefit

An employee was provided with a new car (2,500 cc) costing £15,000. The car emits 191g/km of CO_2. During 2005/06 the employer spent £900 on insurance, repairs and a vehicle licence. The firm paid for all petrol, costing £1,500, without reimbursement. The employee paid the firm £270 for the private use of the car. Calculate the taxable benefit.

Answer

Round CO_2 emissions figure down to the nearest 5, ie 190 g/km.

Amount by which CO_2 emissions exceed the baseline:

(190 − 140) = 50 g/km

Divide by 5 = 10

Taxable percentage = 15% + 10% = 25%

	£
Car benefit £15,000 × 25%	3,750
Fuel benefit £14,400 × 25%	3,600
	7,350
Less contribution towards use of car	(270)
	7,080

If the contribution of £270 had been towards the petrol the benefit would have been £7,350.

1.8 Vans and heavier commercial vehicles

If a van (of normal maximum laden weight up to 3,500 kg) **is made available for an employee's private use, there is an annual scale charge of £500, or £350 if the van is at least four years old at the end of the tax year**. The scale charge covers ancillary benefits such as insurance and servicing. Paragraphs 2.6 (j) and (k) above apply to vans as they do to cars.

From 6 April 2005, there is **no taxable benefit where an employee takes a van home** (ie uses the van for home to work travel) but is not allowed any other private use.

If a commercial vehicle of normal maximum laden weight over 3,500 kg is made available for an employee's private use, but the employee's use of the vehicle is not wholly or mainly private, no taxable benefit arises except in respect of the provision of a driver.

1.9 Statutory mileage allowances

A single authorised mileage allowance for business journeys in an employee's own vehicle applies to all cars and vans. There is no income tax on payments up to this allowance and employers do not have to report mileage allowances up to this amount. The allowance for 2005/06 is 40p per mile on the first 10,000 miles in the tax year with each additional mile over 10,000 miles at 25p per mile. The statutory mileage allowance for employees using their own motor cycle is 24p per mile. For employees using their own pedal cycle it is 20p per mile.

If employers pay less than the statutory allowance, employees can claim tax relief up to that level.

The statutory allowance does not prevent employers from paying higher rates, but any excess will be subject to income tax. There is a similar (but slightly different) system for NICs, covered later in this text.

Employers can make income tax and NIC free payments of up to 5p per mile for each fellow employee making the same business trip who is carried as a passenger. If the employer does not pay the employee for carrying business passengers, the employee cannot claim any tax relief.

Question   Mileage allowance

Sophie uses her own car for business travel. During 2005/06, Sophie drove 15,400 miles in the performance of her duties. Sophie's employer paid her 35p a mile. How is the mileage allowance received by Sophie treated for tax purposes?

Answer

	£
Mileage allowance received (15,400 × 35p)	5,390
Less: tax free [(10,000 × 40p) + (5,400 × 25p)]	(5,350)
Taxable benefit	40

£5,350 is tax free and the excess amount received of £40 is a taxable benefit.

1.10 Beneficial loans

FAST FORWARD

Cheap loans are charged to tax on the difference between the official rate of interest and any interest paid by the employee.

1.10.1 Basic rules

Employment related loans to employees (other than excluded employees) and their relatives give rise to a benefit equal to:

(a)   **Any amounts written off** (unless the employee has died), and

(b)   **The excess of the interest based on an official rate prescribed by the Treasury, over any interest actually charged ('taxable cheap loan')**. Interest payable during the tax year but paid after the end of the tax year is taken into account, but if the benefit is determined before such interest is paid a claim must be made to take it into account.

The following loans are normally not treated as taxable cheap loans for calculation of the interest benefits (but not for the purposes of the charge on loans written off).

(a)   A loan on normal commercial terms made in the ordinary course of the employer's money-lending business.

(b)   A loan made by an individual in the ordinary course of the lender's domestic, family or personal arrangements.

1.10.2 Calculating the interest benefit

There are two alternative methods of calculating the taxable benefit. The simpler **'average' method** automatically applies unless the taxpayer or the Revenue elect for the alternative **'strict' method**. (The Revenue normally only make the election where it appears that the 'average' method is being deliberately exploited.) In both methods, the benefit is the interest at the official rate minus the interest payable.

The 'average' method averages the balances at the beginning and end of the tax year (or the dates on which the loan was made and discharged if it was not in existence throughout the tax year) and applies the official rate of interest to this average. If the loan was not in existence throughout the tax year only the number of complete tax months (from the 6th of the month) for which it existed are taken into account.

The 'strict' method is to compute interest at the official rate on the actual amount outstanding on a daily basis.

Question	Loan benefit

At 6 April 2005 a taxable cheap loan of £30,000 was outstanding to an employee earning £12,000 a year, who repaid £20,000 on 7 December 2005. The remaining balance of £10,000 was outstanding at 5 April 2006. Interest paid during the year was £250. What was the benefit under both methods for 2005/06, assuming that the official rate of interest was 5%?

Answer

Average method

	£
$5\% \times \dfrac{30,000 + 10,000}{2}$	1,000
Less interest paid	(250)
Benefit	750

Alternative method (strict method)

	£
£30,000 × $\frac{245}{365}$ (6 April - 6 December) × 5%	1,007
£10,000 × $\frac{120}{365}$ (7 December - 5 April) × 5%	164
	1,171
Less interest paid	(250)
Benefit	921

The Revenue might opt for the alternative method.

1.10.3 The de minimis test

The benefit is not taxable if:

(a)   The **total of all taxable cheap loans to the employee did not exceed £5,000** at any time in the tax year, or

(b)   **The loan is not a qualifying loan and the total of all non-qualifying loans to the employee did not exceed £5,000** at any time in the tax year.

A qualifying loan is one on which all or part of any interest paid would qualify as a charge.

When the £5,000 threshold is exceeded, a benefit arises on interest on the whole loan, not just on the excess of the loan over £5,000.

When a loan is written off and a benefit arises, there is no £5,000 threshold: writing off a loan of £1 gives rise to a £1 benefit.

1.10.4 Qualifying loans

If the whole of the interest payable on a qualifying loan is eligible for tax relief, then no taxable benefit arises. If the interest is only partly eligible for tax relief, then the employee is treated as receiving earnings because the actual rate of interest is below the official rate. He is also treated as paying interest equal to those earnings. This **deemed interest paid may qualify as a business expense or as a charge in addition to any interest actually paid.**

Question	Beneficial loans

Anna, who is single, has an annual salary of £30,000, and two loans from her employer.

(a)   A season ticket loan of £2,300 at no interest

(b)   A loan, 90% of which was used to buy shares in her employee-controlled company of £54,000 at 3% interest

The official rate of interest is to be taken as 5%.

What is Anna's tax liability for 2005/06?

Answer

	£
Salary	30,000
Season ticket loan: not over £5,000	0
Loan to buy shares £54,000 × (5 −3 = 2%)	1,080
Earnings	31,080
Less: charge on income (£54,000 × 5%× 90%)	(2,430)
	28,650
Less personal allowance	(4,895)
Taxable income	23,755
Income tax	
£2,090 × 10%	209
£21,665 × 22%	4,766
Tax liability	4,975

1.11 Other assets made available for private use

 FAST FORWARD
> 20% of the value of assets made available for private use is taxable.

When assets are made available to employees or members of their family or household, the taxable benefit is the higher of 20% of the market value when first provided as a benefit to any employee, or on the rent paid by the employer if higher. The 20% charge is time-apportioned when the asset is provided for only part of the year. The charge after any time apportionment is reduced by any contribution made by the employee.

If the asset is a computer which is made available under arrangements to employees which do not favour directors, the liability to tax only arises in aspect of any excess charge over £500. If the asset is a bicycle provided for journeys to work, there is no charge.

If an asset made available is subsequently acquired by the employee, **the taxable benefit on the acquisition is the *greater* of:**

- The **current market value minus the price paid by the employee**.

- The **market value when first provided minus any amounts already taxed (ignoring contributions by the employee) minus the price paid by the employee**.

This rule prevents tax free benefits arising on rapidly depreciating items through the employee purchasing them at their low secondhand value.

There is an exception to this rule for computers and bicycles which have previously been provided as exempt or partly exempt benefits. The taxable benefit on acquisitions is restricted to current market value, minus the price paid by the employee. To the extent that the £500 limit for computer equipment has not been used up by the annual use charge for the tax year, the excess can be deducted from this charge.

1.12 Example: assets made available for private use

A suit costing £400 is purchased by an employer for use by an employee on 6 April 2004. On 6 April 2005 the suit is purchased by the employee for £30, its market value then being £50.

The benefit in 2004/05 is £400 × 20% £80

 269

The benefit in 2005/06 is £290, being the *greater* of:

			£
(a)	Market value at acquisition by employee		50
	Less price paid		(30)
			20
			400
(b)	Original market value		(80)
	Less taxed in respect of use		320
			(30)
	Less price paid		290

Question · Computers

Rupert is provided with a new laptop computer by his employer on 6 April 2005. The computer is available for private use. It cost the employer £1,500 when new. On 6 October 2005 the employer transfers ownership of the laptop to Rupert when it is worth £800. Rupert does not pay anything for the computer.

What is the total taxable benefit on Rupert for 2005/06 in respect of the computer?

Answer

	£
Use benefit $£1,500 \times 20\% \times \dfrac{6}{12}$	150
Less: exemption	(150)
Taxable benefit	nil
Transfer benefit (use MV at transfer to employee only)	£
MV at transfer	800
Less: balance of exemption £(500 – 150)	(350)
Taxable benefit	450

1.13 Scholarships

If scholarships are given to members an employee's family, the **employee is taxable on the cost** unless the scholarship fund's or scheme's payments by reason of people's employments are not more than 25% of its total payments.

1.14 Residual charge

FAST FORWARD

There is a residual charge for other benefits, usually equal to the cost to the employer of the benefits.

We have seen above how certain specific benefits are taxed. **A 'residual charge' is made on the taxable value of other benefits. In general, the taxable value of a benefit is the cost of the benefit less any part of that cost made good by the employee to the persons providing the benefit.**

The residual charge applies to any benefit provided for an employee or a member of his family or household, by reason of the employment. There is an exception where the employer is an individual and the provision of the benefit is made in the normal course of the employer's domestic, family or personal relationships.

This rule does not apply to taxable benefits provided to excluded employees. **These employees are taxed only on the second hand value of any benefit that could be converted into money**.

2 Exempt benefits

There are a number of exempt benefits including removal expenses, childcare, mobile phones, meal vouchers and workplace parking.

Various benefits are exempt from tax. These include:

(a) **Entertainment provided to employees by genuine third parties** (eg seats at sporting/cultural events), even if it is provided by giving the employee a voucher.

(b) **Gifts of goods** (or vouchers exchangeable for goods) from third parties (ie not provided by the employer or a person connected to the employer) if the total cost (incl. VAT) of all gifts by the same donor to the same employee in the tax year is £250 or less. If the £250 limit is exceeded, the full amount is taxable, not just the excess.

(c) **Non-cash awards for long service** if the period of service was at least 20 years, no similar award was made to the employee in the past 10 years and the cost is not more than £50 per year of service.

(d) **Awards under staff suggestion schemes if**:

   (i) There is a formal scheme, open to all employees on equal terms.

   (ii) The suggestion is outside the scope of the employee's normal duties.

   (iii) Either the award is not more than £25, or the award is only made after a decision is taken to implement the suggestion.

   (iv) Awards over £25 reflect the financial importance of the suggestion to the business, and either do not exceed 50% of the expected net financial benefit during the first year of implementation or do not exceed 10% of the expected net financial benefit over a period of up to five years.

   (v) Awards of over £25 are shared on a reasonable basis between two or more employees putting forward the same suggestion.

   If an award exceeds £5,000, the excess is always taxable.

(e) **The first £8,000 of removal expenses if:**

   (i) The employee does not already live within a reasonable daily travelling distance of his new place of employment, but will do so after moving.

   (ii) The expenses are incurred or the benefits provided by the end of the tax year following the tax year of the start of employment at the new location.

(f) The cost of running a **workplace nursery or playscheme (without limit). Otherwise up to £50 a week of childcare is tax free** if the employer contracts with an approved childcarer or provides childcare vouchers to pay an approved childcarer. The childcare must be available to all employees and the childcare must either be registered or approved home-childcare.

(g) **Sporting or recreational facilities available to employees generally and not to the general public**, unless they are provided on domestic premises, or they consist in an interest in or the use of any mechanically propelled vehicle or any overnight accommodation. Vouchers only exchangeable for such facilities are also exempt, but membership fees for sports clubs are taxable.

(h)   **Assets or services used in performing the duties of employment** provided any private use of the item concerned is insignificant. This exempts, for example, the benefit arising on the private use of employer-provided tools.

(i)   **Welfare counselling** and similar minor benefits if the benefit concerned is available to employees generally.

(j)   **Bicycles or cycling safety equipment provided to enable employees to get to and from work or to travel between one workplace and another**. The equipment must be available to the employer's employees generally. Also, it must be used mainly for the aforementioned journeys.

(k)   **Workplace parking**

(l)   **Up to £7,000 a year paid to an employee who is on a full-time course lasting at least a year**, with average full-time attendance of at least 20 weeks a year. If the £7,000 limit is exceeded, the whole amount is taxable.

(m)   **Work related training and related costs. This includes the costs of** training material and assets either made during training or incorporated into something so made.

(n)   **Air miles or car fuel coupons** obtained as a result of business expenditure but used for private purposes.

(o)   **The cost of work buses and minibuses or subsidies to public bus services**.

A works bus must have a seating capacity of 12 or more and a works minibus a seating capacity of 9 or more but not more than 12 and be available generally to employees of the employer concerned. The bus or minibus must mainly be used by employees for journeys to and from work and for journeys between workplaces.

(p)   Transport/overnight costs where public transport is disrupted by industrial action, late night taxis and travel costs incurred where car sharing arrangements unavoidably breakdown.

(q)   The private use of a **mobile phone** and the **first £500 in any tax year of benefits arising in respect of the private use of computer equipment**.

(r)   **Employer provided uniforms** which employees must wear as part of their duties.

(s)   The cost of **staff parties** which are open to staff generally provided that the **cost per staff member per year (including VAT) is £150 or less**. The £150 limit may be split between several parties. If exceeded, the full amount is taxable, not just the excess over £150.

(t)   **Private medical insurance premiums paid to cover treatment when the employee is outside the UK in the performance of his duties**. Other medical insurance premiums are taxable as is the cost of medical diagnosis and treatment except for routine check ups.

(u)   **The first 15p per day of meal vouchers (eg luncheon vouchers)**.

(v)   Cheap loans **that do not exceed £5,000** at any time in the tax year (see earlier).

(w)   **Job related accommodation.**

(x)   **Employer contributions towards additional household costs incurred by an employee who works wholly or partly at home**. Payments up to £2 pw (£104 pa) may be made without supporting evidence. Payments in excess of that amount require supporting evidence that the payment is wholly in respect of additional household expenses.

(y)   **Meals or refreshments for cyclists** provided as part of official 'cycle to work' days.

Chapter roundup

- Most employees are taxed on benefits under the benefits code. 'Excluded employees' (lower paid/non-directors) are only subject to part of the provisions of the code.

- The benefit in respect of accommodation is its annual value. There is an additional benefit if the property cost over £75,000.

- Employees who have a company car are taxed on a % of the car's list price which depends on the level of the car's CO_2 emissions. The same % multiplied by £14,400 determines the benefit where private fuel is also provided. Authorised mileage allowances can be paid tax free to employees who use their own vehicle for business journeys.

- Cheap loans are charged to tax on the difference between the official rate of interest and any interest paid by the employee.

- 20% of the value of assets made available for private use is taxable.

- There is a residual charge for other benefits, usually equal to the cost to the employer of the benefits.

- There are a number of exempt benefits including removal expenses, childcare, mobile phones, meal vouchers and workplace parking.

Quick quiz

1   What accommodation does not give rise to a taxable benefit?

2   When may an employee who is provided with a fuel by his employer avoid a fuel scale charge?

3   To what extent are removal expenses paid for by an employer taxable?

Answers to quick quiz

1   Job related accommodation

2   There is no fuel scale charge if:

   (a)   All the fuel provided was made available only for business travel, or
   (b)   The full cost of any fuel provided for private use was completely reimbursed by the employee.

3   The first £8,000 of removal expenses are exempt. Any excess is taxable.

> Now try the question below from the Exam Question Bank

Number	Level	Marks	Time
Q26	Examination	15	27 mins

Occupational pension schemes. NICs for employees

Topic list	Syllabus reference
1 Occupational pension schemes	3(b)
2 NICs for employees	3(c)

Introduction

We finish our consideration of employees with two topics.

First we consider the provision of pensions for employees under an occupational pension scheme. Remember that employees may also make pension provisions through personal pensions, already considered.

Lastly we look at the national insurance contributions payable under Classes 1 and 1A in respect of employment.

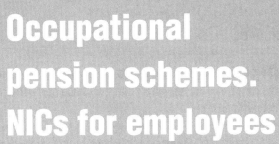

1 Occupational pension schemes

1.1 Introduction

FAST FORWARD

Employers may set up occupational pension schemes for their employees. Approved schemes have tax advantages for example contributions by both employer and employee to an approved occupational pension scheme are deductible for tax purposes.

1.1.1 Approved occupational pension schemes

Key term

Employers may set up an **occupational pension scheme**. Such schemes may either require contributions from employees or be non-contributory. The employer may use the services of an insurance company (an insured scheme) or may set up a totally self administered pension fund.

Schemes can be of two kinds: Revenue approved and unapproved. **Approved schemes have significant tax advantages** that have made them very popular.

The Revenue may withdraw approval of a scheme if approval is no longer warranted, or if the scheme is changed in a way which has not been approved, either specifically or through being on the list of changes which do not require individual approval.

If a scheme is Revenue approved:

- **contributions made by the employee are deductible from his employment income** (up to a limit of 15% of gross earnings, with gross earnings limited to the earnings cap (see below))

- **the employer's contributions actually paid** (not merely provided for) **are deductible in calculating profits** subject to tax (although deductions for large contributions above the normal level may be spread over several years)

- **the employer's contributions are not regarded as benefits for the employee** and are not earnings for NICs purposes

- **the fund of contributions, and the income and gains arising from their investment, are not, in general, liable to tax.** It is this long-term tax-free accumulation of funds that makes approved schemes so beneficial

- provision can be made for a **lump sum** to be **paid on the employee's death in service.** Provided that it does not exceed four times his final remuneration, it is **tax-free**

- **a tax-free lump sum may be paid to the employee on retirement**

The following limits apply to an approved occupational pension scheme.

- The maximum pension is normally two thirds of the individual's final remuneration, being calculated as one sixtieth for each year of service, with a maximum of 40 years.

- A scheme may provide for part of the pension to be taken as a lump sum. The maximum lump sum is 1.5 times final remuneration, being calculated as 3/80 for each year of service, with a maximum of 40 years.

The Revenue have discretion to approve schemes which do not comply with these limits. In particular, many schemes provide for a pension of two thirds of final salary after less than 40 years service.

The parties to a divorce can share pension rights without affecting the tax approved status of the pension scheme.

There is a surplus in an occupational pension scheme if the amount held in the scheme exceeds the amount needed to meet the scheme's pension liabilities plus 5%. This surplus may, subject to certain conditions, be repaid to the employer.

1.1.2 The earnings cap

There are limits on the benefits that may be provided under an occupational pension scheme. The maximum tax free lump sum is 1.5 x final remuneration. The maximum pension is 2/3 x final remuneration.

An earnings cap applies to tax-approved occupational pension schemes. The cap is £105,600 for 2005/06.

The earnings cap has two consequences.

- The maximum pension payable from an approved scheme is the cap × 2/3.
- The maximum tax-free lump sum is the cap × 1.5.

1.1.3 Additional voluntary contributions (AVCs)

An employee may be entitled, under an occupational pension scheme, to benefits which are **less than the maximum allowed by the Revenue**. There will usually be one of two reasons for this: (a) the employee has **not worked for the employer for long enough**, or (b) the level of benefits provided by the employer is **less than allowed**.

In order to deal with these two situations, an employee may make **voluntary contributions** (in **addition** to any compulsory contributions) in order to improve the his pension position. There are three ways of doing this.

(a)   Via the employer by in-house AVCs
(b)   Independently by FSAVCs (free standing AVCs)
(c)   Independently by concurrent personal pension contributions

Employers must provide AVC schemes if employees wish to contribute voluntarily.

An employee can arrange to pay voluntary contributions to a provider quite **independently of the employer**. This provider will usually be an insurance company although it may also be a bank, building society or unit trust.

Remember the limit on employee's contributions for occupational pensions. **The limit remains at 15%.** Thus if, for example, an employee was a member of a contributory scheme to which contributions of 4% were required and was voluntarily contributing an additional 5%, then the employee could contribute no more than 6% to a free standing AVC scheme to make up the total of 15%.

Notice that an employee may contribute to **both** an in house scheme **and** a free standing AVC scheme. However, **the limit on the benefits does not change**. The benefits from the main scheme, plus those from an in house AVC scheme plus those from an FSAVC scheme, must still not exceed in **total** the limits set by the Revenue, ie two-thirds of final salary as a maximum pension.

Certain individuals who are members of an occupational pension scheme may also contribute to a **personal pension scheme under the concurrent membership rules**. Such individuals are broadly those **earning £30,000 or less who are not controlling directors of the employing company**. The limit on contributions is **£3,600 for 2005/06**. This is in addition to any AVCs or FSAVCs that the individual may be paying.

1.1.4 Small self-administered schemes

All employees, including owner-directors of small companies, may join approved schemes. The creation of a self-administered pension scheme is an important part of tax planning for the smaller company. However, regulations restrict the extent to which pension schemes can invest in the companies setting them up (a common practice with smaller companies).

In addition, there is a special tax charge when a scheme with fewer than 12 members, or one with a controlling director (a director holding at least 20% of the ordinary shares) as a member, loses its Revenue approval. Tax of 40% of the value of the scheme's assets at that time must be paid. Thus such schemes must be careful not to lose their approval.

2 NICs for employees

2.1 Class 1 NICs

FAST FORWARD

Class 1 NICs are payable by employees and employers on earnings.

Both employees and employers pay Class 1 NICs related to the employee's earnings. NICs are not deductible from an employee's gross salary for income tax purposes. However, employers' contributions are deductible trading expenses.

Employer's Class 1 NICs at 12.8% (2005/06) **are due on earnings in excess of the earnings threshold** of £4,895 per year.

Employee Class 1 NICs at 11% (2005/06) are due on **earnings between the earnings threshold** of £4,895 **and the upper limit** of £32,760 per year. They also pay additional primary contributions of 1% on earnings above the upper earnings limit. Employee contributions are not allowable deductions for income tax purposes.

'Earnings' for class 1 purposes are **gross earnings paid in money** including

- wages, salary, bonuses and commission
- non-cash vouchers

An employer's contribution to an employee's approved personal pension or an approved occupational pension scheme is excluded from the definition of 'earnings'.

In general income tax and NIC exemptions mirror one another. For example, payment of personal incidental expenses covered by the £5/£10 a night income tax de minimis exemption are excluded from NIC earnings. Relocation expenses of a type exempt from income tax are also excluded from NIC earnings but without the income tax £8,000 upper limit (although expenses exceeding £8,000 are subject to class 1A NICs as described below).

An expense with a business purpose is not treated as earnings. For example, if an employee is reimbursed for business travel or for staying in a hotel on the employer's business this is not normally 'earnings'.

In general, non cash vouchers are subject to NICs. However, the following are exempt.

- Childcare vouchers up to £50 per week
- Vouchers for the use of sports and recreational facilities (where tax exempt)
- Vouchers for meals on the employer's premises
- Other luncheon vouchers to a maximum of 15p per day
- Transport vouchers where the employee earns less than £8,500 a year.

Class 1 contributions are not due in respect of people aged under 16 or people employed outside the UK. An employee who continues to work after attaining the pensionable age (65 for a man, 60 for a woman) has no liability for primary Class 1 NICs. The employer is still liable for full secondary contributions.

2.2 Example

Anne is paid £10,550 per annum and Zoe is paid £52,000 per annum.

Calculate the Class 1 contributions due.

Solution

	£
Anne	
Employee's Class 1 NIC	
(£10,550 – £4,895) × 11% =	622.05
Employer's Class 1 NIC	
(£10,550 – £4,895) × 12.8%	723.84
	1,345.89
Zoe	£
Employee's Class 1 NIC	
(£32,760 – £4,895) × 11% (main)	3,065.15
(£52,000 – £32,760) × 1% (additional)	192.40
Employer's Class 1 NIC	
(£52,000 – £4,895) × 12.8%	6,029.44
	9,286.99

2.3 Class 1A NICs

FAST FORWARD

> Class 1A NICs are payable by employers on benefits provided for employees.

Employers must pay Class 1A NIC at 12.8% in respect of most taxable benefits. Taxable benefits are calculated in accordance with income tax rules. There is no Class 1A in respect of any benefits already treated as earnings for Class 1 purposes (eg non cash vouchers).

No contributions are levied when an employee is earning less than £8,500 a year. In addition, **childcare provision in kind is usually wholly or partly exempt from Class 1A NICs which mirrors the income tax treatment of such provision.** Therefore provision in an **employer provided nursery or playscheme is usually exempt** from Class 1A NICs. **Provision of other childcare, for example where an employer contracts directly for places in a commercial nursery is exempt up to £50 per week.** However, if an employer provides cash to meet or reimburse childcare expenses the cash is 'earnings' for employer and employee Class 1 NIC purposes.

2.4 Example

James has the following benefits for income tax purposes

	£
Company car	5,200
Living accommodation	10,000
Medical insurance	800

Calculate the Class 1A NICs that the employer will have to pay.

Class 1A NICs:

12.8% × £16,000 = £2,048

2.5 Miscellaneous points

Employee contributions are not charged on benefits but employees may agree to pay employer's contributions.

Class 1A contributions are collected annually in arrears, and are due by 19 July following the tax year.

The provision by an employer of fuel for use in an employee's own car does not lead to a Class 1A charge. However, mileage allowances in excess of the Statutory Mileage Rates leads to Class 1 (primary and secondary) contributions on the excess (subject to the usual upper limit for primary contributions).

If Class 1 contributions for a year are not paid to the Revenue by 19 April following the year, or Class 1A contributions due in a year are not paid over by 19 July following the year, interest is charged from that date onwards. Interest is paid to employers on excessive payments refunded to them, but only from the end of the year of payment and never from earlier than 12 months after the end of the year for which the contributions were paid.

Chapter roundup

- Employers may set up occupational pension schemes for their employees. Approved schemes have tax advantages. For example, contributions by both employer and employee to an approved occupational pension scheme are deductible for tax purposes

- There are limits on the benefits that may be provided under an occupational pension scheme. The maximum tax free lump sum is 1.5 x final remuneration. The maximum pension is 2/3 x final remuneration.

- Class 1 NICs are payable by employees and employers on earnings.

- Class 1A NICs are payable by employers on benefits provided for employees.

Quick quiz

1   What is the maximum pension available under an occupational pension scheme?

2   What is the limit on employee contributions to an occupational pension scheme?

3   What national insurance contributions are payable by employers and employees?

Answers to quick quiz

1   2/3rd of the employee's remuneration at retirement.

2   15% of earnings.

3   Employees -   Class 1 primary contributions

      Employers -   Class 1 secondary contributions
                         Class 1A contributions

Now try the question below from the Exam Question Bank			
Number	**Level**	**Marks**	**Time**
Q27	Examination	25	45 mins

Part D

Tax planning

Tax planning

Topic list	Syllabus reference
1 Employment and self-employment	4(a)
2 Remuneration packages	4(b)
3 The choice of a business medium	4(c)
4 The incorporation of a business	4(d)
5 Disposal of a business	4(e)
6 Directors and shareholders	4(f)

Introduction

In this final chapter, we will bring together several different topics by considering some typical tax planning problems.

1 Employment and self-employment

FAST FORWARD ⟩⟩ As a general rule, self-employment leads to lower overall tax and NIC burdens than employment.

A taxpayer who has a choice between being employed and being self-employed, on similar gross incomes, should consider the following points.

(a) An employee must pay **income tax and NICs as salary is received, under the PAYE system** and on a current year basis. A self-employed person pays **Class 2 NICs during the year, but income tax and Class 4 NICs are at least partly payable after all of the profits concerned have been earned**. There is thus a cash flow advantage in self-employment.

(b) **An employee is likely to suffer significantly higher NICs in total than a self-employed person**, although the employee's entitlement to state benefits will also be higher. In particular, note that the self-employed earn no entitlement to the State Second Pension.

(c) An **employee may receive benefits as well as salary**. Taxable values of benefits may be less than their actual value to the employee and benefits do not attract employee NICs (this is however only relevant if salary does not exceed the upper NIC limit). Most benefits attract Employer's Class 1A NIC.

(d) The **rules on the deductibility of expenses are much stricter for employees** (incurred wholly, exclusively and necessarily in the performance of duties) than for the self-employed (normally incurred wholly and exclusively for the purposes of the trade).

2 Remuneration packages

FAST FORWARD ⟩⟩ If someone is to be an employee, the tax effects of the remuneration package should be taken into account.

2.1 Income tax considerations

An employee will usually be rewarded largely by salary, but several other elements can be included in a remuneration package. Some of them bring tax benefits to the employee only, and some will also benefit the employer.

Bonuses are treated like salary, except that if a bonus is accrued in the employer's accounts but is paid more than nine months after the end of the period of account, its deductibility tax purposes will be delayed.

The general position for benefits is that they are subject to income tax and employer Class 1A NICs. The cost of providing benefits is generally deductible in computing trading profit for the employer (but if a car costing over £12,000 is provided, the employer's capital allowances (or deductions for lease payments) are restricted).

However, there are a large number of tax and NI free benefits and there is a great deal of planning that can be done to ensure a tax and NIC efficient benefits package for directors and employees. The optimum is to ensure that the employer receives a tax deduction for the expenditure whilst creating tax and NI free remuneration for employees. The main tax free benefits are:

(a) Growth in value and exercise in shares in approved share option schemes
(b) Free car parking at/near place of work
(c) Contributions to approved occupational or personal pension scheme (see later in this Text)
(d) Mileage paid at statutory rates

(e)   Training courses provided (day release, block release, sandwich courses etc)
(f)   Air miles obtained through business travel
(g)   Beneficial loans under £5,000
(h)   Long service awards (20 years, max £50 pa)
(i)   Staff suggestion schemes
(j)   Free or subsidised canteens available to all staff
(k)   Sports facilities provided on the employer's premises
(l)   Workplace nursery or playscheme provision
(m)   Staff uniforms
(n)   Provision of goods or services at marginal cost only
(o)   Gifts from third parties up to £250 per source
(p)   Removal expenses up to £8,000
(q)   Health checks, screening and eye tests
(r)   Mobile phones
(s)   Computer equipment worth less than £2,500
(t)   The first £30,000 of an ex gratia termination payment

For further details of taxable and exempt benefits see earlier in this text.

Question — Comparison of two remuneration packages

Employee A receives a salary of £20,000.

Employee B receives a salary of £15,000, the use of a new video camera which cost £800 on 6.4.05 and the use of a car which cost £17,732 on 1.1.05. The taxable benefit for this car is £4,433. No fuel is supplied.

Employee B is also in a pension scheme (not contracted out) to which he contributes 5% of his gross salary (excluding benefits) and his employer company contributes 10% of his gross salary (excluding benefits). (We will look at pensions later in this text but for the purposes of this example you need to know that employee B can deduct his own contributions, the employer contributions are not a taxable benefit for employee B and the employer can deduct the contributions as a trading expense.)

A and B are both single and have no other income.

Show the tax and the NIC effects of the two remuneration packages on both the employees and their employers. Assume the employer company does not meet the definition of "small" or "medium" sized. Use 2005/06 tax rates and allowances and assume that the employer prepares accounts to 31 March each year.

Answer

A's income tax and NIC computations are as follows.

	£
Earnings	20,000
Less personal allowance	(4,895)
Taxable income	15,105

Income tax
£2,090 × 10%	209
£13,015 × 22%	2,863
	3,072

NICs
£(20,000 − 4,895) × 11%	£1,662

A's employer must pay NICs of £20,000 – £4,895 × 12.8% = £1,933, and can deduct £(20,000 + 1,933) = £21,933 in computing trading profits.

B's income tax and NIC computations are as follows.

	£
Salary	15,000
Use of video camera £800 × 20%	160
Car	4,433
	19,593
Less pension contribution £15,000 × 5%	(750)
Earnings	18,843
Less personal allowance	(4,895)
Taxable income	13,948

Income tax	£
£2,090 × 10%	209
£11,858 × 22%	2,609
	2,818
NICs	
£(15,000 – 4,895) × 11%	1,112

B's employer must pay NICs as follows.

	£
Class 1 NICs	
£(15,000 – £4,895) × 12.8%	1,293
Class 1A NICs	
£(4,433 + 160) × 12.8%	588
	1,881

B's employer will have the following deductions in computing profits.

	£	£
Salary		15,000
Pension contribution £15,000 × 10%		1,500
NICs		1,881
Capital allowances		
Car (WDV restricted)	3,000	
Video camera £800 × 25%	200	
		3,200
		21,581

2.2 NIC planning for employment situations

NIC is payable on 'earnings' which is defined as 'any remuneration or profit derived from employment'. Remuneration packages structured to include the following items which are not 'earnings' would reduce the NIC burden.

(a)   **Dividends** – director/shareholders could take remuneration in the form of dividends. Dividend waivers and adjustments to bonuses would probably be required. There are CT implications as salary and NIC costs are allowable business expenses whereas dividends are not. However, the impact of the minimum 19% rate of CT on dividends must be considered.

Dividends are an efficient way of avoiding NICs. However dividend income is not earnings for pension purposes (see later in this text). There is also a cash flow impact since PAYE does not apply to dividends.

(b)   **Rents –** a director owning a property used by a company could be paid rent instead of remuneration. This will not impact business asset taper relief (if available) on the subsequent sale of the property. The rental expense is a deductible business expense for the company and the income is not earnings for pension contribution purposes for the individual.

3 The choice of a business medium

FAST FORWARD

An entrepreneur must choose between trading as a sole trader and trading through a company. The choice, and if a company is chosen, the choice between dividends and remuneration, can significantly affect the overall tax and NIC burden. Cashflow is also an important consideration.

3.1 Introduction

When starting in business the first decision must be whether to trade as a company (with the entrepreneur as a director taxable on earnings) or as an unincorporated business, either as a sole trader or a partnership. Certain professions may not be practised through a limited company (although unlimited companies and limited liability partnerships are often allowed).

The attraction of incorporation lies in the fact that a sole trader or a partner is liable for business debts to the full extent of his personal assets. A limited company's shareholder's liability is limited to the amount, if any, unpaid on his shares. However, limited liability is often reduced by the demands of bankers or landlords for personal guarantees from company directors. In addition, compliance with the statutory obligations (eg annual returns, audits etc) that apply to a company can be costly.

A company often finds raising finance easier than an unincorporated business. This is partly because of the misguided view that a company has greater reliability and permanence. A company can obtain equity finance through venture capital institutions and can borrow by giving a floating charge over its assets as security whereas a sole trader or partnership cannot do this.

A business may be seen as more reputable or creditworthy if conducted through the medium of a company. Companies, however, have to comply with disclosure requirements and this may be unattractive to proprietors who wish to keep information from employees, potential competitors etc. This could be avoided by using an unlimited company but in that case any advantage of limited status is lost. The disclosure requirements could be reduced by filing abbreviated accounts.

3.2 The effect of marginal tax rates and national insurance

A trader's profits whether retained or withdrawn are taxed at a marginal rate of 40% on taxable income in excess of £32,400. In addition Class 2 and Class 4 national insurance contributions are payable.

A controlling director/shareholder can decide whether profits are to be paid out as remuneration or dividends, or retained in the company.

3.3 Maximum distribution

If profits are paid out as dividends, the effect of the 19% minimum CT rate on distributions must be considered. The maximum dividend that can be paid out can be found by using the following formula.

$$\frac{100 - \text{rate of tax if no distribution}}{119 - \text{rate of tax if no distribution}} \times \text{PCTCT}$$

3.4 Example

X Ltd has PCTCT of £10,000 in 12 months to 31.03.06

What is the maximum dividend that can be paid out?

Solution

If there was no distribution the rate of CT would be 0%.

The maximum dividend that can be paid out is therefore:

$$\frac{100-0}{119-0} \times £10,000 = £8,403$$

CT on distribution is £8,403 × 19% = £1,597

Check £8,403 + £1,597 = £10,000

3.5 Example

Y Ltd has PCTCT of £20,000 in 12 months to 31.03.06.

What is the maximum dividend that can be paid out?

Solution

First compute CT as if there was no distribution:

	£
£20,000 × 19%	3,800
Less marginal relief £(50,000-20,000)×19/400	(1,425)
CT	2,375

Rate of CT is:

$$\frac{2,375}{20,000} \times 100 = 11.875\%$$

Maximum dividend is therefore:

$$\frac{100-11.875}{119-11.875} = \frac{88.125}{107.125} \times £20,000 = £16,453$$

	£
CT on £16,453 @ 19%	3,126
CT on £(20,000 − 16,453) × 11.875%	421
Total CT due	3,547

Check £(16,453 + 3,547) = £20,000

3.6 Miscellaneous considerations

If profits are retained, the consequent growth in asset values will increase the potential capital gain when shares are sold (although taper relief may reduce the amount of the taxable gain). Where remuneration is paid the total national insurance liability is greater than for the proprietor of an unincorporated business.

Where a spouse is employed his or her salary must be justifiable as 'wholly and exclusively for the purposes of the trade': the Revenue may seek to disallow excessive salary cost. On the other hand, a spouse as active partner can take any share in profits, provided that he or she is personally active in the business and there is evidence of a bona fide partnership. Thus the spouse's personal allowance and starting and basic rate bands can be used.

In choosing a business medium, we should also remember that a sole trader will be denied the enhanced state benefits that are available to an employee who pays Class 1 national insurance contributions. In particular, note that the self-employed do not build an entitlement to the State Second Pension.

Question

Alan, who is single, expects to make annual profits of £30,000 before tax and national insurance. Consider the fiscal effects of his choosing to trade as a sole trader or, alternatively, through a company, paying him a salary of £15,000 and then the largest possible dividend not giving rise to a loss of capital. Assume that accounting profits equal taxable trade profits. Use 2005/06 tax rates.

Answer

As a sole trader

	£
Profits	30,000
Less personal allowance	(4,895)
Taxable income	25,105
Tax thereon at 10%/22%	5,272
National Insurance Classes 2 (52 × £2.10) and 4 (£(30,000 − 4,895) × 8%)	2,118
	7,390
Net income £(30,000 − 7,390)	22,610

Through a company

	£	£
Profits		30,000
Less: salary		(15,000)
employer's NI 12.8% (£15,000 − £4,895)		(1,293)
Taxable profits		13,707
19% × £13,707	2,604	
Less starting rate marginal relief £ (50,000 − 13,707) × 19/400	(1,724)	
Less: corporation tax (before distribution)		(880)
Net profits		12,827

The maximum distribution is calculated as follows:

Rate of CT if no distribution $\dfrac{880}{13,707}$ = 6.42%

Maximum distribution is $13,707 \times \dfrac{(100 - 6.42)}{(119 - 6.42)}$ = £11,394

CT @ 19% on £11,394	=	£2,165
CT @ 6.42% on £(13,707-11,394)	=	£148
Total CT £(2,165 + 148)	=	£2,313
Dividend and CT (ie equal to taxable profits)	=	£13,707

A dividend of £11,394 can be paid without loss of capital.

	Non-savings £	Dividends £	Total £
Earnings	15,000		
Dividends £11,394 × 100/90		12,660	
STI	15,000	12,660	27,660
Less personal allowance	(4,895)		
Taxable income	10,105	12,660	22,765
Non-savings income			
£2,090 × 10%			209
£8,015 × 22%			1,763
Dividend income			
£12,660 × 10%			1,266
			3,238
Less tax suffered £12,660 × 10%			(1,266)
Income tax payable			1,972

Net income	£	£
Salary		15,000
Dividends		11,394
		26,394
Less: income tax	1,972	
Employee's NIC (£15,000 − £4,895) × 11%	1,112	
		(3,084)
		23,310

Trading as a sole trader would give annual net income of £(22,610 − 23,310) = £700 less than trading through a company.

Question   Small business as sole trader versus company

Let's say we have a business earning profits of £14,895.

Compare the retained profit for the business owner if he operates the business as a sole trader with a year ended 31 March 2006 to that of a company with the same year end but paying out £4,895 as a salary and the remaining post-tax profits as a dividend.

Answer

Sole Trader

Trading profits of £14,895 in 2005/2006

Year ended 31 March 2006

Income Tax		£
£(14,895 − 4,895) = £10,000		
£2,090 @ 10%		209
£7,910 @ 22%		1,740
		1,949
National Insurance		
Class 2		109
Class 4		
£(14,895 − 4,895) × 8%		800
Total Income Tax and NIC		2,858
Net income		
£(14,895 − 2,858)		£12,037

Company

Year ended 31 March 2006
PCTCT = (14,895-4,895) = £10,000
Corporation Tax
£10,000 @ 0% before distribution

£Nil

Maximum distribution is £10,000 × $\frac{100-0}{119-0}$ = £8,403

Pay dividend of £8,403
CT on distribution £8,403 × 19%

£1,597

Income Tax
Salary covered by PA
Gross dividend income = £9,337

£

£9,337 @ 10%

934

Less: Tax credit

(934)

Nil

Class 1 NIC

Nil

Net income £(4,895 + 8,403)

£13,298

As a sole-tradership the business would typically pay £2,858 in the 2005/2006 tax year as income tax and National Insurance Contributions. The same business operating as a limited company for the same year would have a tax bill of £1,597.

3.7 Benefits and expenses

The restrictions on deducting expenses against earnings may make self-employment rather more attractive than employment as a company director. Although the same expense deduction rules apply to a company and a sole trader, the company's deductible business expenses may give rise to taxable benefits as earnings for directors.

On the other hand, the provision of fringe benefits can be an advantage of incorporation. Tax exempt benefits can be used to maximise directors' net spendable income, although care is required because not all benefits are tax-efficient.

3.8 Opening Years

Companies have no equivalent to the opening year rules that apply for income tax purposes. For a sole trader or partnership, profits earned when basis periods overlap are taxed twice. Relief is available for such overlap profits but that may not take place for many years, by which time inflation may have reduced the value of the relief for overlap profits.

If a partnership is envisaged it may be worthwhile to commence trading with the prospective partner as a salaried employee for a year or so, thereby obtaining tax relief twice on his salary during the overlap period.

3.9 Losses

Losses in the first four years of an unincorporated business can be used to obtain tax repayments (using s 381 claims). In these and later years a s 380 claim permits **relief for trading losses against other income** (and capital gains) of either or both of two tax years.

With corporation tax, although there is considerable flexibility for the company itself, **a company's losses are not available to reduce shareholders' taxable incomes.**

3.10 Capital gains tax

One difference between companies and individuals is that **companies do not benefit from an exemption from tax on the first £8,500 of total gains** (for 2005/06).

Chargeable gains of an individual are charged to capital gains tax at 10%, 20% or 40%. By contrast, companies' gains are charged at normal corporation tax rates (30% full rate, 19% small companies rate, 32.75% effective marginal rate or 0% starting rate with an effective marginal rate of 23.75%).

The principal disadvantage of incorporation is the double charge to tax which arises when a company sells a chargeable asset. Firstly, the company may pay corporation tax on the chargeable gain. Secondly, the shareholders may be taxed when they attempt to realise those proceeds, either in the form of dividends or when the shares are sold, incurring a further charge on capital gains.

If there are no tax advantages in the company owning an asset, the asset should be held outside the company, perhaps being leased to the company. The lesser may receive rent without restricting CGT business asset reliefs.

3.11 Tax cashflows

A sole trader/partner is assessable to income tax and NIC (Class 4) on a current year basis but will use a prior year basis to calculate two payments on account due on 31 January in and 31 July directly following the tax year. The balance of tax is due on 31 January following the tax year. Thus tax on profits earned in the year to 30 April 2005 (assessable 2005/06) will not be payable in full until 31 January 2007 and will be used to calculate payments on account due 31 January 2007 and 31 July 2007. **Where profits are rising this lag gives a considerable benefit**. A sole trader's/partner's drawings do not of themselves attract or accelerate a tax charge.

A company pays CT nine months after the end of its accounts period. Companies paying tax at the full rate are required to make **quarterly payments on account** based on the current year's estimated liability. As an employer it will have to account for **PAYE and NIC 14 days after the end of each tax month** in which the pay date falls.

Generally therefore a business held by a company will bear tax earlier than a business held by a sole trader or partnership.

3.12 What if things go wrong?

Sound tax planning should always take account of possible changes in circumstances. A successful business may fail or a struggling concern may eventually become profitable.

Running down an unincorporated business does not normally give rise to serious problems. The proprietor may be able to cover any balancing charges with loss relief.

Taking a business out of a company (disincorporation), or winding up a corporate trade altogether is more complex and involves both tax and legal issues. Consider the following:

- No subsequent relief is available for a company's unused losses once the trade ceases.
- Liquidation costs may be considerable.
- A double charge on capital gains may arise.

4 The incorporation of a business

> The incorporation of a business should be carefully planned, taking account of consequent tax liabilities. There are both advantages and disadvantages to incorporating a business. A disposal of shares can also have several tax consequences.

4.1 Why incorporate a business?

4.1.1 Advantages

(a) Retained profits subject only to corporation tax not income tax or NIC

(b) Easier to dispose of shares in a company than interest in a business – thus advantage for raising equity and selling to outside investors

(c) More generous pension provision can be made by employer (the company) for employees (eg directors) than under the personal pensions scheme rules (see later in this text)

(d) Benefits for employees can be more tax efficient

(e) Loan finance easier to arrange as lender can take out charge on company assets

(f) Limited liability

(g) A company arguably has a more respectable image than a sole trader or partnership

(h) Incorporation is a means of converting the value of a business into shares which could be brought to the AIM or even achieve a full stock market quote. This provides for succession of ownership and can make the original proprietors very wealthy

4.1.2 Disadvantages

(a) Potential double capital gains charge on assets (see above)

(b) Trading losses restricted to set-off against corporate profits

(c) No carry back of trading losses in opening years (ie no s 381 equivalent)

(d) Partner's share of profit not openly challenged by Revenue provided the recipient is a genuine partner. Conversely excessive remuneration to employee/director can be challenged

(e) NIC for employer company and employee will generally exceed the contributions required of a self-employed person

(f) Paydays for tax on a company and its employees (CT, PAYE and NIC) are generally well in advance of paydays for self-employed

(g) There may be statutory requirement of audit, keeping books, filing accounts etc

(h) Disclosure requirements of published accounts may give information to employees/ competitors that business owners would not have willingly disclosed

4.2 Income tax

4.2.1 The choice of a date

When an unincorporated trade is transferred to a company the **trade is treated as discontinued for tax purposes and the cessation rules apply**. Careful consideration of the level of profit and date of transfer is required to avoid large taxable profits in one year from a basis period of more than 12 months. For example a trader with a 30 June year end will be assessed on 21 months of profit in his final year if he incorporates on 31 March whereas only 10 months of profit will be taxed in that final year if he delays incorporation to 30 April.

4.2.2 Capital allowances

On the transfer of a trade to a company **a balancing charge will usually arise as plant and machinery are treated as being sold at market value**. However, where the company is controlled by the transferor, **the two are connected and an election may be made** so as not to treat the transfer as a permanent discontinuance for capital allowances purposes. **Fixed assets are then transferred at their tax written down values**.

4.2.3 Trading losses

Unrelieved trading losses cannot be carried forward to a company as such, but **may be set against any income derived from the company** by way of dividends, remuneration and so on, provided the business is exchanged for shares and those shares are still held at the time the loss is set off. Terminal loss relief may also be available for the loss of the last twelve months of trading.

4.3 Capital gains tax

When the transfer takes place the **chargeable assets are deemed to be disposed of to the company at their open market values**. Capital gains tax liabilities are likely to arise, particularly on land and buildings and on goodwill. The gains will be reduced by business assets taper relief.

If the whole business (or the whole business other than cash) **is transferred to the company as a going concern in exchange for shares in the company, any chargeable gains (before taper relief) are rolled over**, reducing the base cost of the shares on a subsequent disposal. This relief is known as incorporation relief. As no capital gains tax arises on death, the tax liability may never arise.

Individuals who incorporate a business can elect that incorporation relief should not apply. This election must be made within two years of 31 January following the end of the tax year in which the business was incorporated. A shorter time limit will apply when all the shares received on the transfer are disposed of in the tax year of transfer, or in the following tax year. Making the election could be advantageous for taper relief purposes where the shares are disposed of soon after incorporation.

It may not be desirable for all the assets comprised in the business to be transferred to the company. **As an alternative**, an individual can **use gift relief** to transfer chargeable business assets to a company and **defer any gains by deducting them from the base costs of the assets** to the company.

4.4 Value added tax

The transfer of assets will not be treated as a supply for VAT purposes (called the Transfer of Going Concern (TOGC) relief) if all of the following conditions are satisfied.

(a)   The assets are to be used by the company in the same kind of business (whether or not as part of an existing business) as that carried on by the transferor, the business being transferred as a going concern.

(b)   If only part of the business is transferred, that part is capable of separate operation.

(c)   If the transferor is a taxable person, the company is a taxable person when the transfer takes place or immediately becomes one as a result of the transfer.

An application may be made for the company to take over the existing VAT registration number. In this case the company will take over all the debts and liabilities of the business but it will be able to claim VAT bad debt relief in respect of supplies made before the transfer.

If the above conditions cannot be satisfied VAT will be charged on the transfer, but this will only represent a cash flow problem in most cases.

Customs should be notified of the incorporation within 30 days.

4.5 Stamp duty land tax

The transfer of land will be subject to Stamp Duty Land Tax as a transfer at market value. The use of the gift relief route should be considered so that land can be retained outside the company.

5 Disposal of a business

FAST FORWARD

Structuring the sale/purchase of a business correctly can have major tax saving opportunities.

5.1 Assets versus shares

A purchaser could acquire the business of a **'target'** company by either acquiring the 'target' company's assets or by acquiring the 'target' company's shares. The advantages/ disadvantages of each method of acquiring a business are listed below. If an unincorporated business is bought/sold, this must be done by a sale of assets.

Advantages of buying assets

(a)   The purchaser can **choose which assets to acquire** rather than take the entire business

(b)   The expenditure on plant and certain buildings will attract **capital allowances**

(c)   The **capital gains base cost of the assets is the price paid** on acquisition. If shares are acquired the assets retain their original base cost

(d)   There is some latitude to apportion the consideration over the assets acquired to best tax effect. For example plant could attract FYAs at 40% or 100% or WDA at 25% but industrial buildings only 4% WDA and no FYA.

(e)   For the purchaser who is already trading it might be possible to **argue that it is not a separate trade which is acquired but an extension of the existing trade. This is important where losses are being carried forward**

(f)   **By acquiring assets, the liabilities** (including tax liabilities) whether known or unknown are **left behind** in the vendor company thus minimising the need for tax warranties and indemnities

Advantages of buying shares

(a)   The **business continues uninterrupted**

(b)   The 'target' company does not have to provide for tax on the profit from asset sales

(c)   **Unused tax reliefs** of the 'target' company **are potentially available** for the 'target' company

(d)   The **sale consideration is paid to the vendor shareholders** and not, as in the case of an asset sale, to the target company. The need to extract proceeds through a dividend or liquidation is thereby avoided

(e)   **If the purchaser is a company**, a share purchase opens up the **group** tax advantages although it also increases the number of associated companies in the group by one

(f)   The vendors would be able to **defer capital gains tax if the deal was paper-for-paper**

The choice of the best method of sale is partly determined by:

(a)   The **vendor might be prepared to accept a sale of assets by the target company if it can shelter the resulting gains and balancing charges with capital losses and trading losses** brought forward respectively. Alternatively can the gains be sheltered by group-wide roll-over or group capital losses?

(b)   **If the purchaser cannot recover (or fully recover) VAT paid on acquiring the assets this may be unattractive**. VAT may not actually apply provided the business is transferred as a going concern and the assets are used by the transferee in the same kind of business as before. If only some of the assets are transferred the 'going concern' point may be uncertain and will result in problems between the parties.

5.2 Reorganisation prior to sale

The target company may pay a dividend out of distributable profits prior to sale. Individual vendors normally bear less tax if their consideration is in the form of dividends (25% of the net dividend) rather than capital (40% of the gain). A corporate shareholder pays no tax on a dividend but may pay up to 32.75% on a gain. Of course a gain may be reduced by indexation.

5.3 Consideration for the disposal

The **date of disposal is normally the date of exchange of contract**, except that, where there is a condition in the contract, it is the date the contract becomes unconditional.

Any shares element in the consideration will result in deferral of the gain if:

(a)   The vendor is selling shares

(b)   The purchaser is a company who issues shares or debentures to the vendor

(c)   The purchaser owns or will own over 25% of ordinary share capital in the 'target' company, or there is a general offer to all shareholders in the 'target' company

(d)   The exchange is for bona fide commercial reasons and not with the object of tax avoidance

In this case the vendor's base cost of the 'new' paper is cost of the original shares with indexation running as though the new shares has been acquired when the original shares were acquired.

5.4 Losses and other reliefs

If the 'target' company has trading losses or capital losses it is important where possible not to waste them.

The trading losses of the 'target' company can only be carried forward if the trade in which they arose continues. This carry forward is however denied if:

(a)   Within a three year period there is both a change in ownership of the company and a major change in the nature of conduct of the company's trade

(b)   There is a change in ownership of the company after the scale of activities has become small or negligible before it revives

Capital losses of the target can be carried forward even if there is a change in ownership of the company.

The trading losses of the 'target' company are not automatically transferred with the trade.

Capital allowances will be available on plant at 25% WDA on consideration or possibly 40% or 100% if FYAs apply to the acquiring business. Industrial buildings allowances may be available on industrial buildings acquired.

5.5 Tax warranties and indemnities

Tax warranties and indemnities are only really necessary on a purchase of shares. **Warranties** are express undertakings that the company and in certain circumstances the vendor have fulfilled or will fulfil specific conditions. **Indemnities** are covenants by the vendor indemnifying the purchaser against depletion of the net assets, in consequence of specific claims against the company

6 Directors and shareholders

For director/shareholders the decision whether to pay dividends or remuneration is a major planning consideration.

6.1 The decision whether to pay dividends or remuneration

Director/shareholders may wish to consider either extracting profits as dividend or remuneration. Payments of dividends or remuneration will reduce a company's retained profits which means a reduction in net asset value and hence the value of the shares, ultimately reducing any chargeable gain on the disposal of those shares. However, the immediate tax cost of paying dividends or remuneration must be weighed against this advantage. In addition, up to 19% Corporation Tax may be payable on the amount of dividend payments made.

Remuneration and the cost of benefits will be allowed as deductions in computing the company's profits chargeable to corporation tax. The decision whether or not to make such payments could affect the rate of corporation tax by reducing the level of profits. However, **the national insurance cost must also be borne in mind**. A combination of dividends and remuneration may give the best result.

Question   Dividends and remuneration

A Ltd makes a profit before remuneration of £15,000 in the year to 31 March 2006. The shareholder/ director is entitled to only the personal allowance. Consider the director's disposable income available by paying out the profit entirely as salary (of £13,853) or by paying it out as a mixture of salary (at £4,800, so that no national insurance contributions are payable but preserving the director's entitlement to state benefits) and a dividend of £8,572.

Answer

		Salary only £	Salary and dividend £
(a)	**The company's tax position**		
	Profits	15,000	15,000
	Less: salary	(13,853)	(4,800)
	employer's national insurance	(1,147)	
	Taxable profits	0	10,200
	Corporation tax at 0% (ignoring distribution)	£Nil	£Nil
	Corporation tax at 19% on distribution (£8,572)		£1,628
	Cash dividend		£8,572
	CT plus dividend		£10,200

(b)   The director's tax position

	Non-savings £	Dividend £	Total £
Salary only			
Earnings	13,853		
Less personal allowance	(4,895)		
Taxable income	8,958		8,958
Salary and dividends			
Earnings	4,800		
Dividends (× 100/90)		9,524	
Less personal allowance	(4,800)	(95)	
	–	9,429	9,429

	Salary only £	Salary and dividend £
Non-savings income		
£2,090 × 10%	209	
£6,868 × 22%	1,511	
Dividend income £9,429 × 10%		943
Less tax credit on dividend (restricted)		(943)
Tax payable	1,720	–
Disposable income		
Salary	13,853	4,800
Less employee's national insurance		
(13,853 − 4,895) × 11%	(985)	
Dividend		8,572
Less tax payable	(1,720)	
	11,148	13,372

The overall saving through paying a dividend is £(13,372 − 11,148) = £2,224.

Remuneration and benefits give rise to an entitlement to pay personal pension premiums, whereas dividends do not.

6.2 The timing of dividend payments

If dividends are paid, timing can be important.

(a) The tax year in which a dividend is paid affects the due date for any additional tax, and if a shareholder's other income fluctuates it may determine whether or not there is any additional tax to pay.

(b) The tax credit attaching to dividends is 10%. However the different rates of tax to apply to dividend income for individual shareholders will ensure such people will not pay more tax on such income compared with other forms of savings income. However, the tax credit attaching to dividends cannot be repaid. Thus taxpayers with no or low income will not have the tax credit refunded to them from dividend income.

Chapter roundup

- As a general rule, self-employment leads to lower overall tax and NIC burdens than employment.

- If someone is to be an employee, the tax effects of the remuneration package should be taken into account.

- An entrepreneur must choose between trading as a sole trader and trading through a company. The choice, and if a company is chosen, the choice between dividends and remuneration, can significantly affect the overall tax and NIC burden. Cashflow is also an important consideration.

- The incorporation of a business should be carefully planned, taking account of consequent tax liabilities. There are both advantages and disadvantages to incorporating a business. A disposal of shares can also have several tax consequences.

- Structuring the sale/purchase of a business correctly can have major tax saving opportunities.

- For director/shareholders the decision whether to pay dividends or remuneration is a major planning consideration.

Quick quiz

1 What are the main NIC differences between the tax positions of employees and the self employed?

2 What is a major attraction of incorporation?

3 Why might a newly commencing trader employ a prospective partner at first, before forming a partnership?

4 What is the major disadvantage for an individual shareholder of an incorporated business where losses are anticipated?

Answers to quick quiz

1   Employees suffer Class 1 NIC. Their employers suffer Class 1 and Class 1A NIC too.

   The self employed pay Class 2 and Class 4 NIC. The rates of NIC due under these classes are smaller than Class 1 and Class 1A NIC.

2   The attraction of incorporation is limited liability. A sole trader or partner is liable for business debts to the full extent of his personal wealth. A limited company's shareholder is liable to the amount, if any, unpaid on his shares.

3   Commencing trade with a prospective partner as a salaried employee for a year or two initially obtains tax relief twice on his salary during any overlap period

4   A company's losses are not available to reduce shareholders' taxable incomes (unlike losses of an unincorporated business which can reduce the sole trade/partners incomes).

Now try the question below from the Exam Question Bank

Number	Level	Marks	Time
Q28	Examination	15	27 mins

Exam question bank

1 Tree Ltd

27 mins

(a) Tree Ltd, a company with no associated companies, had the following results for the eighteen months to 31 December 2005:

	£
Trading profits	180,000
Chargeable gain - realised 1.6.05	172,000
Gift aid donation - paid 30.9.05	5,000
Gift aid donation - paid 30.9.04	22,000
Bank interest	36,000
Dividend received 30.3.05	27,000

The bank interest accrued evenly over the period. No dividends were paid by the company.

Required

Compute the corporation tax liability in respect of the profits arising in the eighteen months to 31 December 2005. (10 marks)

(b) Dealers plc had profits chargeable to corporation tax of £420,000 for its year ended 31 December 2005. There were no dividends received or paid during the year.

Required

Compute Dealers plc's mainstream corporation tax liability for the year. (3 marks)

(c) Springer Ltd had profits chargeable to corporation tax of £6,200 in the year to 31 March 2006. There were no dividends received or paid during the year.

Required

Calculate Springer Ltd's mainstream corporation tax liability for the year. (2 marks)

(15 marks)

2 Traders Ltd

27 mins

Traders Ltd's profit and loss account for the year to 31 March 2006 was as follows.

	£		£
General expenses	73,611	Gross trading profit	246,250
Repairs and renewals	15,000	Irrecoverable debts recovered	
Legal and accountancy charges	1,200	(previously written off)	373
Subscriptions and donations	7,000	Commissions	800
Irrecoverable debts written off	500	Profit on sale of investment	5,265
Directors' remuneration	20,000	Building society interest (gross)	1,100
Salaries and wages	18,000		
Depreciation	15,000		
Rent and rates	1,500		
Net profit	101,977		
	253,788		253,788

Notes

(i) *General expenses include the following.*

	£
Travelling expenses of staff, including directors	1,000
Entertaining suppliers	600

(ii)   *Repairs and renewals include the following.*

	£
Redecorating existing premises	300
Renovations to new premises to remedy wear and tear of previous owner (the premises were usable before these renovations)	500

(iii)   *Legal and accountancy charges are made up as follows.*

	£
Debt collection service	200
Staff service agreements	50
Tax consultant's fees for special advice	30
45 year lease on new premises	100
Audit and accountancy	820
	1,200

(iv)   *Subscriptions and donations include the following.*

	£
Donations under the gift aid scheme	5,200
Donation to a political party	500
Sports facilities for staff	500
Contribution to a local enterprise agency	200

(v)   The commissions received were not incidental to the trade.

(vi)   The chargeable gain arising on the sale of investments was £770.

(vii)   All interest received was on investments made for non-trading purposes. The amounts received were the same as the amounts accrued in the year.

Required

Compute Traders Ltd's profits chargeable to corporation tax for the accounting period to 31 March 2006, and the corporation tax liability thereon. **(15 marks)**

3 Hardy Ltd   27 mins

Hardy Ltd, makes accounts to 30 June. Despite substantial investment in new equipment, business has been indifferent and the company will cease trading on 31 December 2008. Its last accounts will be prepared for the six months to 31 December 2008.

The tax written down value of fixed assets at 1 July 2004 was as follows.

Pool	£
General	32,000

Fixed asset additions and disposals have been as follows.

		£
20.9.04	Plant cost	1,917
25.9.04	Computer cost	4,400
15.7.05	Car for managing director's use cost	13,400
14.7.07	Plant sold for	340
10.5.08	Computer sold for	2,200

An election to depool the computer was made when it was acquired in 2004. Private use of the managing director's car was agreed at 20% for all years.

At the end of 2008, the plant would be worth £24,000 and the managing director's car £10,600.

The company has always been a medium sized enterprise for FYA purposes.

Required

Calculate the capital allowances for the periods from 1 July 2004 to 31 December 2008, assuming FY05 rates and allowances continue to apply in the future. **(15 marks)**

4 Cuckold Ltd   27 mins

(a)   Cuckold Ltd makes up accounts to 31 March each year. It is considering the purchase of an additional, secondhand factory on 1 April 2006. It has decided to spend £150,000 and the following details refer to four possible factories which could each be acquired for that sum. All are equally suitable for Cuckold Ltd's purposes and all have been used for qualifying industrial purposes throughout their lives.

	Original cost to first owner £	Date of first use
(i)	100,000	31 March 1982
(ii)	80,000	31 March 1981
(iii)	160,000	31 March 2004
(iv)	120,000	31 March 1998

Required

Advise Cuckold Ltd of the amount of industrial buildings allowances which would be available as a result of purchasing each of the above factories, indicating the periods for which the allowances would be available. Which building would you advise it to purchase?   **(10 marks)**

(b)   Having acquired a factory Cuckold Ltd intends to incur further capital expenditure on the following items.

(i)   Installation of display lighting in a showroom where customers will view his products
(ii)   Thermal insulation of the factory
(iii)   Construction of a canteen, within the factory premises, for the use of the workforce

Required

Advise Cuckold Ltd of the extent to which capital allowances would be available in respect of the above items of expenditure. Cuckold Ltd is a medium sized enterprise for FYA purposes.

(5 marks)

(15 marks)

5 Property income   20 mins

P Ltd starts to let out property on 1 July 2005. The company has the following transactions.

(a)   On 1 July 2005, it lets an office block which it has owned for several years. The tenant is required to pay an initial premium of £20,000 for a 30 year lease, and then to pay annual rent of £4,000, quarterly in advance. The office is let unfurnished.

(b)   On 1 October 2005 it buys a badly dilapidated office block for £37,000. During October, it spends £8,000 on making the office habitable. It lets it furnished for £600 a month from 1 November 2005, but the tenant leaves on 31 January 2006. A new tenant moves in on 1 March 2006, paying £2,100 a quarter in arrears. Water rates are £390 a year, payable by P Ltd. P Ltd also pays buildings insurance of £440 for the period from 1 October 2005 to 31 August 2006. P Ltd financed the purchase (but not the repairs) with a bank loan at 15% interest. P Ltd decides to claim the renewals

305

basis. It replaces some furniture on 1 May 2006, at a cost of £350. The tenant is responsible for all repair costs and council tax.

Required

Compute P Ltd's property business income for the year to 31.3.06. **(11 marks)**

6 Gains and losses

9 mins

E Ltd disposed of assets as follows.

(a)   On 1 January 2005 it sold a car which had been used by a company director at a loss of £10,700.
(b)   On 28 February 2005 it sold some shares at a loss of £16,400.
(c)   On 1 May 2005 it sold some shares and realised a gain of £17,700.
(d)   On 1 October 2005 it sold some shares at a loss of £6,000.
(e)   On 1 December 2005 it sold a picture to a collector for £50,000, making a gain of £3,000.

Required

What loss, if any, is available to be carried forward at the end of its year ended 31 March 2006? **(5 marks)**

7 Hardup Ltd

27 mins

Hardup Ltd made the following disposals in the year ended 31 March 2006.

(a)   On 31 May 2005 it sold an office block for £120,000. The company had bought the offices for £65,000 on 1 July 1991. The company had invested £100,000 in another office block on 1 May 2004.

(b)   On 18 June 2005 it sold a plot of land for £69,000. It had bought it for £20,000 on 1 April 1984 and had spent £4,000 on defending its title to the land in July 1988.

(c)   On 25 June 2005 the company exchanged contracts for the sale of a workshop for £173,000. Completion took place on 24 July 2005. It had bought the workshop for £65,000 on 16 October 1986.

Required

Compute Hardup Ltd's capital gains for the year end 31.3.05. **(15 marks)**

Assume retail prices index

May 2005 = 189.7	July 1991 = 133.8
June 2005 = 188.9	July 1988 = 106.7
July 2005 = 190.1	October 1986 = 98.45
	April 1984 = 88.64

8 Ferraro Ltd

27 mins

Ferraro Ltd has the following results.

	y/e 31.12.02 £	y/e 31.12.03 £	9m to 30.9.04 £	y/e 30.9.05 £
Trading profit (loss)	34,480	6,200	4,320	(100,000)
Bank deposit interest accrued	200	80	240	260
Rents receivable	1,200	1,420	1,440	1,600
Capital gain			12,680	
Allowable capital loss	5,000			9,423
Gift Aid donation paid (gross)	1,000	0	1,000	1,500

Required

Compute all profits chargeable to corporation tax, claiming loss reliefs as early as possible. State any amounts carried forward as at 30 September 2005. **(15 marks)**

9 P Ltd

27 mins

P Ltd owns the following holdings in ordinary shares in other companies, which are all UK resident.

Q Ltd	83%
R Ltd	77%
S Ltd	67%
M Ltd	80%

The ordinary shares of P Ltd are owned to the extent of 62% by Mr C, who also owns 70% of the ordinary shares of T Ltd, another UK resident company. In each case, the other conditions for claiming group relief, where appropriate, are satisfied.

The following are the results of the above companies for the year ended 31 March 2006.

	M Ltd £	P Ltd £	Q Ltd £	R Ltd £	S Ltd £	T Ltd £
Income						
Trading profit	20,000	0	64,000	260,000	0	70,000
Trading loss	0	223,000	0	0	8,000	0
Property business income	0	6,000	4,000	0	0	0
Charges paid						
Gift aid donation	4,000	4,500	2,000	5,000	0	0

Required

(a) Compute the MCT payable for the above accounting period by each of the above companies, assuming group relief is claimed, where appropriate, in the most efficient manner.

(b) Advise the board of P Ltd of the advantages of increasing its holding in S Ltd, a company likely to sustain trading losses for the next two years before becoming profitable.

(15 marks)

10 Apple Ltd (pilot paper)   27 mins

Apple Ltd owns 100% of the ordinary share capital of Banana Ltd and Cherry Ltd. The results of each company for the year ended 31 March 2006 are as follows:

	Apple Ltd £	Banana Ltd £	Cherry Ltd £
Tax adjusted trading profit/(loss)	(125,000)	650,000	130,000
Capital gain/(loss)	188,000	(8,000)	-

Apple Ltd's capital gain arose from the sale of a freehold warehouse on 15 April 2005 for £418,000. Cherry Ltd purchased a freehold office building for £290,000 on 10 January 2006.

Required

(a) Explain the group relationship that must exist in order that group relief can be claimed. (3 marks)

(b) Explain how group relief should be allocated between the respective claimant companies in order to maximise the potential benefit obtained from the relief. (4 marks)

(c) Assuming that reliefs are claimed in the most favourable manner, calculate the corporation tax liabilities of Apple Ltd, Banana Ltd and Cherry Ltd for the year ended 31 March 2006. (8 marks)

(15 marks)

11 M Ltd   27 mins

M Ltd is a UK resident company which owns controlling interests in two other UK resident companies and in two non-resident companies.

It also has the following interests in three non-resident companies:

Company	Shareholding	Rate of Withholding tax	Profits post tax y/e 31.03.05	Foreign tax paid
	%	%	£	£
A Inc	6	15	400,000	80,000
B P G	8	25	900,000	300,000
C S A	12	20	800,000	200,000

M Ltd had experienced a prolonged period of poor trading and, as a result of losses brought forward from earlier years, its chargeable trading profits for the year ended 31 March 2006 are only £20,000.

During the year, a gift aid donation of £75,000 had been paid to charity and this had been added back in arriving at the adjusted taxable trading profits.

The only other income received by M Ltd during the year consisted of dividends from the above three companies, each of which had substantial undistributed profits. The figures (net of withholding tax) were:

	£	Date received
A Inc	170,000	1.6.05
B P G	150,000	10.9.05
C S A	120,000	31.12.05

Required

Compute the MCT payable by M Ltd in respect of the year ended 31 March 2006. Your answer should show clearly your treatment of the gift aid payment and of the foreign taxes suffered. You should explain why you are dealing with items in a particular way and you should use a columnar layout.

(15 marks)

12 Hogg Ltd   18 mins

(a)   Hogg Ltd prepares accounts for the year to 31 December 2005. Its profits chargeable to corporation tax for the year will be £1,750,000. The company has always paid corporation tax at the full rate.

Required

State the amounts and due dates for the payment of corporation tax by Hogg Ltd in respect of the year to 31 December 2005.   (4 marks)

(b)   In 2007 Hogg Ltd changes its accounting date to 31 October 2007. Assume that the liability for the ten months to 31 October 2007 is expected to be £600,000.

Required

State the due dates for and the amount of instalments of corporation tax that Hogg Ltd will be required to pay in respect of this period.   (6 marks)

(10 marks)

13 Invoices, the tax point and returns   27 mins

Write brief notes on:

(a)   VAT invoices   (5 marks)
(b)   The tax point   (5 marks)
(c)   VAT returns.   (5 marks)

(15 marks)

14 Justin   18 mins

Justin has the following transactions in the quarter ended 30 September 2005. All amounts exclude any VAT.

	£
Purchases	
Furniture for resale	275,000
Computer for use in the business	2,400
Restaurant bills: entertaining customers	1,900
Petrol for cars owned by Justin and used only by his employees	2,800
Sales	
Furniture	490,000
Books on interior design	2,400

Only one employee's car has petrol for private motoring provided by Justin. That car's cylinder capacity is 2,400 cc.

Required

Calculate the amount of VAT which Justin must pay to HM Revenue & Customs for the quarter.

(10 marks)

15 Newcomer Ltd, Ongoing Ltd and Au Revoir Ltd (pilot paper)

27 mins

(a)   Newcomer Ltd commenced trading on 1 October 2005. Its forecast sales are as follows.

		£
2005	October	11,500
	November	14,200
	December	21,400
2006	January	13,300
	February	14,700
	March	15,200

The company's sales are all standard rated, and the above figures are exclusive of VAT.

Required

Explain when Newcomer Ltd will be required to compulsorily register for VAT.   (4 marks)

(b)   Ongoing Ltd is registered for VAT, and its sales are all standard rated. The following information relates to the company's VAT return for the quarter ended 30 September 2005:

    (1)   Standard rated sales amounted to £120,000. Ongoing Ltd offers its customers a 5% discount for prompt payment, and this discount is taken by half of the customers.

    (2)   Standard rated purchases and expenses amounted to £35,640. This figure includes £480 for entertaining customers.

    (3)   On 15 September 2005 the company wrote off bad debts of £2,000 and £840 in respect of invoices due for payment on 10 February and 5 May 2005 respectively.

    (4)   On 30 September 2005 the company purchased a motor car at a cost of £16,450 for the use of a salesperson, and machinery at a cost of £21,150. Both these figures are inclusive of VAT. The motor car is used for both business and private mileage.

Unless stated otherwise, all of the above figures are exclusive of VAT. Ongoing Ltd does not operate the cash accounting scheme.

Required

Calculate the amount of VAT payable by Ongoing Ltd for the quarter ended 30 September 2005.

(8 marks)

(c)   Au Revoir Ltd has been registered for VAT since 1995, and its sales are all standard rated. The company has recently seen a downturn in its business activities, and sales for the years ended 31 October 2005 and 2006 are forecast to be £55,000 and £47,500 respectively. Both of these figures are exclusive of VAT.

Required

Explain why Au Revoir Ltd will be permitted to voluntarily deregister for VAT, and from what date deregistration will be effective.   (3 marks)

(15 marks)

16 Income tax

13 mins

Mary, a single 24 year old, has business profits of £14,000. She also receives building society interest of £6,400 net, dividends of £1,800 (net), and pays a charge of £2,500 (gross) each year. How much cash will she have available to spend in 2005/06? Ignore national insurance.   **(7 marks)**

17 Mr and Mrs Lowrie

27 mins

John Lowrie and Helen Lowrie who are both in their thirties are a married couple. They have no children. Mr and Mrs Lowrie received the following income in 2005/06.

	Mr Lowrie £	Mrs Lowrie £
Salary (gross)	36,000	20,000
PAYE tax deducted	6,000	2,611
Dividends (amount received)	1,090	2,538
Bank deposit interest (amount received)	600	76
Building society interest (amount received)	592	420

Required

Compute the net tax payable by Mr Lowrie and by Mrs Lowrie for 2005/06. **(15 marks)**

18 Mr Cobbler

27 mins

Mr Cobbler starts a business as a sole trader on 1 January 2006.

His business plan shows that his monthly profits are likely to be as follows.

January 2006 to June 2006 (inclusive)	£800	a month
July 2006 to December 2006 (inclusive)	£1,200	a month
Thereafter	£2,000	a month

Mr Cobbler is considering two alternative accounting dates, 31 March and 30 April, in each case commencing with a period ending in 2006.

Required

Show the taxable trading profits which will arise for each of the first four tax years under each of the two alternative accounting dates, and recommend an accounting date. **(15 marks)**

19 Miss Farrington

27 mins

Miss Farrington started to trade as a baker on 1 January 2003 and made up her first accounts to 30 April 2004. Adjusted profits before capital allowances are as follows.

	£
Period to 30 April 2004	20,710
Year to 30 April 2005	15,125

Miss Farrington incurred the following expenditure on plant and machinery.

Date	Item	£
4.1.03	General plant	3,835
1.3.03	Second-hand oven acquired from Miss Farrington's father	1,200
25.3.03	Delivery van	1,800
15.4.03	Typewriter	425
15.5.03	Car for Miss Farrington	6,600
30.1.05	General plant	1,000
30.4.05	Computer	1,945

In addition Miss Farrington brought into the business on 1 January 2003 a desk and other office furniture. The agreed value was £940.

The agreed private use of the car is 35%. Miss Farrington's business is a small enterprise for capital allowance purposes.

Required

Calculate the taxable profits for the first four tax years and the overlap profits carried forward.

(15 marks)

20 Morgan   27 mins

Morgan started to trade on 6 April 2002. His business has the following results.

Year ending 5 April		£
2003	Profit	12,000
2004	Profit	16,000
2005	Profit	18,000
2006 (projected)	Profit	15,000
2007 (projected)	Loss	(32,000)

It is expected that the business will show healthy profits thereafter. In addition to his business Morgan has gross investment income of £8,000 a year.

Required

(a)   Outline the ways in which Morgan could obtain relief for his loss.   (5 marks)

(b)   Prepare a statement showing how the loss would be relieved assuming that relief were to be claimed as soon as possible. Comment on whether this is likely to be the best relief   (5 marks)

(c)   Describe briefly how the situation would alter if Morgan were to cease trading on 5 April 2007.

(5 marks)

(15 marks)

21 Adam, Bert and Charlie   27 mins

Adam, Bert and Charlie started in partnership as secondhand car dealers on 6 April 2002, sharing profits in the ratio 2:2:1, after charging annual salaries of £1,500, £1,200 and £1,000 respectively.

On 5 July 2003 Adam retires and Bert and Charlie continue, taking the same salaries as before, but dividing the balance of the profits in the ratio 3:2.

On 5 May 2005 Dick is admitted as a partner on the terms that he received a salary of £1,800 a year, that the salaries of Bert and Charlie should be increased to £1,800 a year each and that of the balance of the profits, Dick should take one tenth and Bert and Charlie should divide the remainder in the ratio 3:2.

The profits of the partnership as adjusted for tax purposes are as follows.

Year ending 31 March	Profits
	£
2003	10,200
2004	20,800
2005	12,600
2006	18,000

Required

Show the taxable profits for each partner for 2002/2003 to 2005/06 inclusive.   **(15 marks)**

22 Partnerships (pilot paper)   27 mins

(a)   *Required*

Briefly explain the basis by which partners are assessed in respect of their share of a partnership's taxable trading profit.   (3 marks)

(b)   Anne and Betty have been in partnership since 1 January 1999 sharing profits equally. On 30 June 2005 Betty resigned as a partner, and was replaced on 1 July 2005 by Chloe. Profit continued to be shared equally. The partnership's taxable trading profits are as follows:

	£
Year ended 31 December 2005	60,000
Year ended 31 December 2006	72,000

As at 6 April 2005 Anne and Betty each have unrelieved overlap profits of £3,000.

Required

Calculate the taxable trading profits of Anne, Betty and Chloe for 2005/06.   (6 marks)

(c)   Daniel and Edward have been in partnership since 6 April 1998, making up accounts to 5 April. On 31 December 2005 Edward resigned as a partner, and was replaced on 1 January 2006 by Frank. For 2005/06 the partnership made a trading loss of £40,000, and this has been allocated between the partners as follows.

	£
Daniel	20,000
Edward	15,000
Frank	5,000

Each of the partners has investment income. None of them have any capital gains.

Required

State the possible ways in which Daniel, Edward and Frank can relieve their trading losses for 2005/06.   (6 marks)

(15 marks)

23 Denise   27 mins

Denise started in business on 6 April 2005 as a designer dressmaker, having been a housewife for many years. Her trading profits in her first year of trading were:

2005/06   £115,000

She was born on 27 March 1969 and has made no pension provision.

Required

(a)   Calculate the maximum personal pension contribution that Denise can make in respect of 2005/06, showing all your workings.   (2 marks)

(b)   Draft a letter to Denise explaining the tax treatment of any pension contributions she makes under the stakeholder pension scheme and setting out the benefits she may take on retirement.

(11 marks)

(c)   Show the Class 2 and Class 4 contributions payable by Denise in 2005/06.   (2 marks)

Assume 2005/06 tax rates and allowances apply throughout.

(15 marks)

313

24 Tim
15 mins

Tim is a medical consultant. His total tax liability for 2004/05 was £16,800. Of this £7,200 was paid under the PAYE system, £800 was withheld at source from bank interest and £200 was suffered on dividends received during the year.

Tim's total tax liability for 2005/06 was £22,000. £7,100 of this was paid under PAYE system, £900 was withheld at source from bank interest and there was a £250 tax credit on dividends.

Tim did not make any claim in respect of his payments on account for 2005/06. The Revenue issued a 2005/06 tax return to Tim on 5 May 2006.

Required

State what payments Tim was required to make in respect of his 2005/06 tax liability and the due dates for the payment of these amounts.   **(8 marks)**

25 Employment and self-employment
27 mins

Required

Discuss the factors to be taken into consideration when deciding whether a person is employed or self employed for the purposes of income tax.   **(15 marks)**

26 Cars and loans
27 mins

The following items have been provided by a UK company to employees earning more than £8,500 a year.

(a)   A loan of £16,000 at 1% a year to Mr Andrews on 6 October 2005 which has been used to improve his private residence.

(b)   A £1,000 interest free loan to Mrs Preece on 6 April 2005 which was used to finance her daughter's wedding.

(c)   The loan of a TV and video system to Mr Charles from 6 June 2005, the asset having cost the company £800 in 2003 and having had a market value of £500 in June 2005.

(d)   A long service award in December 2005 to Mrs Davies, the company secretary, comprising a gold wrist watch costing £400. Mrs Davies has been employed by the company since December 1980.

(e)   The loan of a 2,500 cc petrol engined BMW motor car to Mr Edgar from 6 April 2005. The company had acquired the car new on 1 August 2002 at a cost of £23,000 and its market value in April 2005 was estimated to be £15,000. The car emits CO_2 of 139g/km. The company pays all running costs, including fuel.

(f)   The exclusive private use of a company flat in central London, by Mr Ford, the managing director. The company acquired the flat in February 2003 for £100,000 and Mr Ford has used it since that date. The flat is fully furnished at a cost of £5,000 and the council tax paid by the company amounted to £500. The annual value is £900. The running costs of the flat amounting to £1,200 for 2005/06 were paid directly by Mr Ford.

Required

State in detail how each of the above items would be treated for 2005/06, computing the amount of any taxable benefit.   **(15 marks)**

Assume an official rate of interest of 5%.

27 Lai Chan (pilot paper)   45 mins

Until 31 December 2005 Lai Chan was employed by Put-it-Right plc as a management consultant. The following information relates to the period of employment from 6 April to 31 December 2005.

(1)   Lai was paid a gross salary of £3,250 per month.

(2)   She contributed 6% of her gross salary into Put-it-right plc's Inland Revenue approved occupational pension scheme. The company contributed a further 6%.

(3)   Put-it-Right plc provided Lai with a 2600 cc motor car with a list price of £26,400. The motor car's CO_2 emissions were 190g/km. Lai paid Put-it-Right plc £130 per month for the use of the motor car.

      Put-it-Right plc paid for the petrol in respect of all the mileage done by Lai during 2005/06. She paid the company £30 per month towards the cost of her private petrol.

      The motor car was returned to Put-it-Right plc on 31 December 2005.

(4)   Put-it-Right plc provided Lai with an interest free loan of £30,000 on 1 January 2002. She repaid £20,000 of the loan on 30 June 2005 with the balance of £10,000 being repaid on 31 December 2005. The loan was not used for a qualifying purposes.

On 1 January 2006 Lai commenced in self-employment running a music recording studio. The following information relates to the period of self-employment from 1 January to 5 April 2006.

(1)   The Trading profit for the period 1 January to 5 April 2006 is £19,900. This figure is *before* taking account of capital allowances.

(2)   Lai purchased the following assets:

      | 1 January 2006 | Recording equipment | £7,440 |
      | 15 January 2006 | Motor car | £14,800 |
      | 20 February 2006 | Motor car | £10,400 |
      | 4 March 2006 | Recording equipment | £2,080 |

      The motor car purchased on 15 January 2006 for £14,800 is used by Lai, and 40% of the mileage is for private purposes. The motor car purchased on 20 February 2006 for £10,400 is used by an employee, and 10% of the mileage is for private purposes.

      The recording equipment purchased on 4 March 2006 for £2,080 is to be treated as a short-life asset.

      Lai's business meets the definition of small enterprise for FYA purposes.

(3)   Since becoming self-employed Lai has paid £390 (net) per month into a stakeholder pension scheme. Payments are made on the 20th of each month.

(4)   Lai Chan is single and does not have any children.

Required

(a)   Calculate Lai's income tax liability for 2005/06.   (20 marks)
(b)   Briefly explain how Lai's income tax liability for 2005/06 will be paid to the Revenue.   (5 marks)

                                                                              (25 marks)

28 Sasha Shah (pilot paper)   27 mins

Sasha Shah is a computer programmer. Until 5 April 2005 she was employed by Net Computers plc, but since then has worked independently from home. Sasha's income for the year ended 5 April 2006 is

£60,000. All of this relates to work done for Net Computers plc. Her expenditure for the year ended 5 April 2006 is as follows:

(1) The business proportion of light, heat and telephone for Sasha's home is £600.

(2) Computer equipment was purchased on 6 April 2005 for £10,000.

(3) A motor car was purchased on 6 April 2005 for £10,000. Motor expenses for the year ended 5 April 2006 amount to £3,500, of which 40% relate to journeys between home and the premises of Net Computers plc. The other 60% relate to private mileage.

Required

(a) List eight factors that will indicate that a worker should be treated as an employee rather than as self-employed. (4 marks)

(b) (i) Calculate the amount of taxable trading profits if Sasha is treated as self-employed during 2005/06.

(ii) Calculate the amount of Sasha's taxable earnings if she is treated as an employee during 2005/06. (7 marks)

(c) (i) Calculate Sasha's liability to Class 2 and Class 4 NIC if she is treated as self-employed during 2005/06.

(ii) Calculate Sasha's liability to Class 1 NIC if she is treated as an employee during 2005/06. (4 marks)

(15 marks)

29 Industrial Ltd (pilot paper)   54 mins

Industrial Ltd is a UK resident company that manufactures furniture. The company's results for the year ended 31 March 2006 are summarised as follows:

	£
Trading profit (as adjusted for taxation but before taking account of capital allowances and patent royalties)	1,689,710
Income from property (note 1)	110,400
Bank interest received (note 2)	12,500
Loan interest received (note 3)	36,000
Profit on disposal of shares (note 4)	87,200
Patent royalties payable (note 5)	(12,000)
Donation to charity (note 6)	(1,500)

Note 1 – Income from property

Since 1 January 2006 Industrial Ltd has leased an office building that is surplus to requirements. On that date the company received a premium of £80,000 for the grant of a ten-year lease, and the annual rent of £30,400 which is payable in advance.

Note 2 – Bank interest received

The bank interest was received on 31 March 2006. The bank deposits are held for non-trading purposes. There were no accruals of bank interest at the beginning or end of the year.

Note 3 – Loan interest received

The loan interest was received on 31 March 2006. The loan was made for non-trading purposes to another UK company. There were no accruals of loan interest at the beginning or end of the year.

Note 4 – Profit on disposal of shares

The profit on disposal of shares is in respect of a shareholding that was sold on 15 January 2006 for £223,000. The shareholding was purchased on 1 April 2001 for £135,800. The indexation allowance from April 2001 to January 2006 is £14,278.

At 1 April 2005 Industrial Ltd had unused capital losses brought forward of £10,800.

Note 5 – Patent royalties payable

The figure for patent royalties payable is calculated as follows:

	£
Payments made	11,500
Accrued at 31 March 2006	2,000
	13,500
Accrued at 1 April 2005	(1,500)
	12,000

All patent royalties were paid to other UK companies. The amount of patent royalties charged in the accounts was the amount accrued in the year.

Note 6 – Donation to charity

The donation to charity was the amount paid under the Gift Aid Scheme.

Note 7 – Industrial building

Industrial Ltd has a new factory constructed at a cost of £400,000 that was brought into use on 30 September 2005.

	£
Land	80,000
Levelling the land	9,200
Architects fees	24,300
Heating system	12,800
Fire alarm system	7,200
Strengthened concrete floor to support machinery	16,500
General offices	62,500
Factory	187,500
	400,000

Note 8 – Plant and machinery

On 1 April 2005 the tax written down values of plant and machinery were as follows:

	£
General pool	84,600
Expensive motor car	15,400

The expensive motor car was sold on 31 August 2005 for £19,600.

In addition to any items of plant and machinery included in the cost of the industrial building (see note 7), the following assets were purchased during the year ended 31 March 2006.

		£
15 June 2005	Computer	3,400
15 August 2005	Motor car	17,200
12 October 2005	Lorry	32,000

Industrial Ltd is a medium-sized company as defined by the Companies Acts.

Note 9 – Other information

Industrial Ltd has no associated companies. For the year ended 31 March 2005 Industrial Ltd had profits chargeable to corporation tax of £1,650,000.

Required

(a) Calculate the corporation tax payable by Industrial Ltd for the year ended 31 March 2006.

(25 marks)

(b) (i) Explain why Industrial Ltd is required to make quarterly instalment payments in respect of its corporation tax liability for the year ended 31 March 2006. (2 marks)

(ii) State the relevant due dates for payment of the corporation tax liability. (3 marks)

(30 marks)

Approaching the answer

You should read through the requirement before working through and annotating the question as we have so that you know what you are looking for.

Industrial Ltd is a UK resident company that manufactures furniture. The company's results for the year ended 31 March 2006 are summarised as follows:

> ALL in FY 05

	£
Trading profit (as adjusted for taxation but before taking account of capital allowances and patent royalties)	1,689,710
Income from property (note 1)	110,400
Bank interest received (note 2)	12,500
Loan interest received (note 3)	36,000
Profit on disposal of shares (note 4)	87,200
Patent royalties payable (note 5)	(12,000)
Donation to charity (note 6)	(1,500)

Note 1 – Income from property

Since 1 January 2006 Industrial Ltd has leased an office building that is surplus to requirements. On that date the company received a premium of £80,000 for the grant of a ten-year lease, and the annual rent of £30,400 which is payable in advance.

> Prorate × ³/₁₂

> Property income charge on short leases

Note 2 – Bank interest received

The bank interest was received on 31 March 2006. The bank deposits are held for non-trading purposes.

There were no accruals of bank interest at the beginning or end of the year.

> Investment income received

Note 3 – Loan interest received

The loan interest was received on 31 March 2006. The loan was made for non-trading purposes to another UK company. There were no accruals of loan interest at the beginning or end of the year.

> Received gross from UK

> Also investment income

Note 4 – Profit on disposal of shares

The profit on disposal of shares is in respect of a shareholding that was sold on 15 January 2006 for

£223,000. The shareholding was purchased on 1 April 2001 for £135,800. The indexation allowance from

April 2001 to January 2006 is £14,278.

Set off capital loss b/f v. gain

At 1 April 2005 Industrial Ltd had unused capital losses brought forward of £10,800.

Note 5 – Patent royalties payable

Trading deduction

The figure for patent royalties payable is calculated as follows:

	£
Payments made	11,500
Accrued at 31 March 2006	2,000
	13,500
Accrued at 1 April 2005	(1,500)
	12,000

Deductible amount

All patent royalties were paid to other UK companies. The amount of patent royalties charged in the

accounts was the amount accrued in the year.

Note 6 – Donation to charity

Treat as charge on income

The donation to charity was the amount paid under the Gift Aid Scheme.

Note 7 – Industrial building

Industrial Ltd has a new factory constructed at a cost of £400,000 that was brought into use on 30

September 2005.

Not eligible for IBAs

Capital allowances items

Is it less that 25% total - if so allow for IBAs

	£
Land	80,000
Levelling the land	9,200
Architects fees	24,300
Heating system	12,800
Fire alarm system	7,200
Strengthened concrete floor to support machinery	16,500
General offices	62,500
Factory	187,500
	400,000

Note 8 – Plant and machinery

On 1 April 2005 the tax written down values of plant and machinery were as follows:

	£
General pool	84,600
Expensive motor car	15,400

The expensive motor car was sold on 31 August 2005 for £19,600.

Balancing charge

In addition to any items of plant and machinery included in the cost of the industrial building (see note 7),

the following assets were purchased during the year ended 31 March 2006.

		£
15 June 2005	Computer	3,400
15 August 2005	Motor car	17,200
12 October 2005	Lorry	32,000

Industrial Ltd is a medium-sized company as defined by the Companies Acts.

Note 9 – Other information

40% FYA available

Industrial Ltd has no associated companies. For the year ended 31 March 2005 Industrial Ltd had profits

chargeable to corporation tax of £1,650,000.

Paid CT at full rate

Required

(a) Calculate the corporation tax payable by Industrial Ltd for the year ended 31 March 2006.

(25 marks)

(b) (i) Explain why Industrial Ltd is required to make quarterly instalment payments in respect of its corporation tax liability for the year ended 31 March 2006. (2 marks)

(ii) State the relevant due dates for payment of the corporation tax liability. (3 marks)

(30 marks)

Obviously instalment dates

Answer plan

Then organise the things you have noticed and your points arising into a coherent answer plan. Work through the items in a logical order and tick them off once you have dealt with them.

(a) Set out proforma on first page with trading profit at top.
Deduct capital allowances and the patent royalties payable to give the taxable trading profit.
Add other sources of income – Property business income, investment income.
Add gains (after losses).
Deduct charge on income to give PCTCT.
Calculate tax.

Workings

IBAs

Not on land, heating system, fire alarm system.
Check % on general offices – allowable if less than 25%.

P&M

Remember to add in heating system, fire alarm system – 40% FYAs.
Lorry qualifies for 40% FYAs also.
40% FYA on computer.

Property business income

Premium on short lease.
Add in rental.

Gains

Calculate gain after indexation allowance.
Deduct loss b/f.

(b) (i) Company is large this year and last.

(ii) Full instalments required. Payable every 3 months starting in 7th month of accounting period on 14th day of the month.

30 Susan White (pilot paper)   27 mins

Susan White disposed of the following assets during 2005/06.

1   On 15 July 2005 Susan sold 20,000 £1 ordinary shares in Red Ltd for £55,000. Susan bought 25,000 shares in the company on 2 June 2004 for £37,500. She bought a further 5,000 shares on 18 July 2005 for £15,000.

2   On 25 August 2005 Susan sold 50,000 £1 ordinary shares in Blue Ltd to her son for £70,000. The market value of the shares on this date was £200,000. The shareholding was purchased on 15 April 1985 for £18,000. Take the indexation allowance from April 1985 to April 1998 to be £12,800. Susan and her son are to elect to hold over the gain as a gift of a business asset.

Red Ltd and Blue Ltd are unquoted trading companies. Susan's shareholding in each company qualifies as a business asset for the purposes of CGT taper relief.

Required

(a) Describe the types of shareholding that qualify as a business asset for the purposes of CGT taper relief.   (4 marks)

(b) Calculate the capital gains arising from Susan's disposal during 2005/06. You should ignore the annual exemption.   (11 marks)

                                                                (15 marks)

Approaching the answer

You should read through the requirement before working through and annotating the question as we have so that you know what you are looking for.

Susan White disposed of the following assets during 2005/06.

Matching rules for shares

1   On 15 July 2005 Susan sold 20,000 £1 ordinary shares in Red Ltd for £55,000. Susan bought

25,000 shares in the company on 2 June 2004 for £37,500. She bought a further 5,000 shares on

18 July 2005 for £15,000.

Post 5/4/98 acquisition

Post sale acquisition

Disposal at undervalue

2   On 25 August 2005 Susan sold 50,000 £1 ordinary shares in Blue Ltd to her son for £70,000. The

market value of the shares on this date was £200,000. The shareholding was purchased on 15 April

1985 for £18,000. Take the indexation allowance from April 1985 to April 1998 to be £12,800.

Gift relief – how
does it work

Susan and her son are to elect to hold over the gain as a gift of a business asset.

Red Ltd and Blue Ltd are unquoted trading companies. Susan's shareholding in each company qualifies as a business asset for the purposes of CGT taper relief.

> Taper relief years?

Required

> Brief description only for 4 marks

(a) Describe the types of shareholding that qualify as a business asset for the purposes of CGT taper relief. (4 marks)

(b) Calculate the capital gains arising from Susan's disposal during 2005/06. You should ignore the annual exemption. (11 marks)

> Make sure you do!

(15 marks)

Answer plan

Then organise the things you have noticed and your points arising into a coherent answer plan. Not all the points you have noticed will go into your answer – you should spend a few minutes thinking them through and prioritising them.

(a) Trading co. shares: Non trading co. shares:

   (1) unquoted – all Only employees holding 10% or less of votes.
   (2) director/employee
   (3) holds 5 % votes.

(b) **Red Ltd shares**

   Matching rules for individuals:

   (1) same day
   (2) next 30 days
   (3) post 5.4.98.

   Apportion cost/proceeds as necessary.

   Taper relief periods – none for next 30 days
   – 1 year for post 5/4/98.

   Blue Ltd shares

   Gain based on MV not cash.

   'Cash' gain (ie proceeds over cost (no IA)) remains in charge. Taper relief applies from 6.4.98 ie 7 years. Rest can be held over to son – no taper relief.

   Summary of gains.

   Set losses off v. gains with least taper relief.

1 Tree Ltd

> **Tutorial note**. Long periods of account are always split into the first 12 months and the remainder. Trading profits and investment income profits are time apportioned. Chargeable gains are allocated to the period they are realised and gift aid donations to the period in which they are paid.

(a)   Tree Ltd

	Year to 30.6.05 £	Six months to 31.12.05 £
Trading profits (12/18: 6/18)	120,000	60,000
Chargeable gain	172,000	
Investment income (12/18: 6/18)	24,000	12,000
Less: charge on income	(22,000)	(5,000)
Profits chargeable to corporation tax	294,000	67,000

Year to 30.6.05 (W1)
Corporation tax (FY04 and FY05)
£294,000 × 30%   88,200

Less 11/400 (1,500,000 − 324,000) × $\dfrac{294,000}{324,000}$ (29,346)

                                                                          58,854

Six months to 31.12.05 (W2)
£67,000 × 19%   £12,730

(b)   Dealers plc's profits for small companies' rate purposes are £420,000 so tax is payable at the small companies marginal rate.

	FY 2004 and FY 2005 £
Profits chargeable to corporation tax	420,000
'Profits'	420,000
Upper limit	1,500,000
Lower limit	300,000
Corporation tax	
£420,000 × 30%	126,000
Less small companies marginal relief	
£(1,500,000 − 420,000) × 11/400	(29,700)
	96,300

(c)   Springer Ltd's 'profits' are £6,200. This means they qualify for the starting rate:

	£
£6,200 × 0%	NIL
	NIL

> **Tutorial note**
>
> If Springer Ltd were to distribute any of its profits to non corporate shareholders, the corporation tax rate would be raised to 19% in respect of the distributed profits.
>
> *Workings*
>
> 1   The year to 30.6.05 has profits of £324,000 (ie PCTCT of £294,000 plus gross dividend received) which is between the small companies bands of £300,000 and £1,500,000. Thus small companies

marginal relief applies. This can be calculated in one step as the rates for FY04 and FY05 are identical.

2   The period to 31.12.05 is only 6 months long therefore the upper and lower limits must be time apportioned. As profits of £67,000 are above the adjusted starting rate upper limit of £25,000 and below the adjusted small companies rate lower limit of £150,000 for this period, the small companies rate applies.

2 Traders Ltd

Tutorial note. You are extremely likely to be required to adjust accounts profit in your exam to arrive at your taxable trading profits. The best way to familiarise yourself with the adjustments required is to practice plenty of questions like this.

CORPORATION TAX COMPUTATION

	£	£
Net profit per accounts		101,977
Add: entertaining	600	
tax consultancy	30	
lease on new premises	100	
gift aid donation	5,200	
political donation	500	
depreciation	15,000	
		21,430
		123,407
Less: commissions (chargeable as miscellaneous income)	800	
profit on sale of investment	5,265	
building society interest	1,100	
		(7,165)
Trading profits		116,242
Investment income		1,100
Miscellaneous income		800
Chargeable gain		770
		118,912
Less charges paid		
		(5,200)
Profits chargeable to corporation tax		113,712

The profits for small companies rate purposes are below the lower limit, so the small companies rate applies.

The corporation tax liability is £113,712 × 19%   £21,605

3 Hardy Ltd

Tutorial note. The key to being able to deal with a capital allowances computation correctly is to get the layout right. Once you have done this, the figures should fall into place.

	FYA £	Pool £	Expensive car £	Short life asset £	Allowances £
1.7.04 – 30.6.05					
Brought forward		32,000			
WDA @ 25%		(8,000)			8,000
		24,000			
Additions	1,917			4,400	
FYA @ 40%	(767)			(1,760)	2,527
		1,150		2,640	10,527
		25,150			
1.7.05 – 30.6.06					
Additions			13,400		
WDA		(6,287)	(3,000)	(660)	9,947
		18,863	10,400	1,980	
1.7.06 – 30.6.07					
WDA		(4,716)	(2,600)	(495)	7,811
		14,147	7,800	1,485	
1.7.07 – 30.6.08					
Disposals		(340)		(2,200)	
		13,807		(715)	
Balancing charge				715	(715)
WDA		(3,452)	(1,950)		5,402
		10,355	5,850		4,687
1.7.08 – 31.12.08					
Disposals		(24,000)	(10,600)		
		(13,645)	(4,750)		
Balancing charges		13,645	4,750		(18,395)

> **Tutorial note 1**. The capital allowances due to a company are not restricted as a result of the private use of an asset by an employee.
>
> **Tutorial note 2**. As the company is a medium sized enterprise, FYAs are given at 40% on acquisitions during FY04. Had the company been a small enterprise FYAs would have been available at 50% on acquisitions during FY04.

4 Cuckold Ltd

> **Tutorial note**. Consider to what extent Cuckold Ltd can claim IBAs. What is the maximum period for IBAs to be claimed?

(a)   Cuckold Ltd should acquire factory (i), as shown in the working below.

Factory (ii) is clearly unattractive since, with its tax life expired, industrial buildings allowances cannot be claimed. Factories (iii) and (iv) have greater total allowances available than factory (i) but the annual allowance is much smaller.

Working: industrial buildings allowances on alternative factories

	Factory (i)	Factory (ii)	Factory (iii)	Factory (iv)
Residue after sale*	£100,000	£80,000	£150,000	£120,000
Remaining tax life**	1 yr	0	23 yrs	17 yrs
Allowances available	£100,000	0	£150,000	£120,000
	1 yr		23 yrs	17 yrs
in y/e 31.3.2007	= £100,000		= £6,522	= £7,059

*   The residue after sale is the lower of the price paid by the new purchaser and the original cost.

**   The tax life of an industrial building begins when it is first brought into use and ends 25 years later (except for expenditure incurred before 6 November 1962, when the relevant period is 50 years rather than 25 years).

(b)   (i)   *Showroom display lighting*

Expenditure on display lighting will be eligible for plant and machinery capital allowances. The most important general test in determining whether expenditure is eligible is the 'functional test'. This asks whether the item concerned fulfils a *function* in the carrying on of the trade or merely forms part of the setting *in* which the trade is carried on.

This test was used with regard to lighting in *Cole Bros Ltd v Phillips 1982*, where lighting equipment which produced higher levels of lighting than normal and which was specialised in order to display goods to customers was held to be plant.

Expenditure on plant and machinery is eligible for a first year allowance of 40%. The balance of the expenditure is then eligible for a 25% writing down allowance in subsequent years on a reducing balance basis.

     (ii)   *Thermal insulation*

Expenditure on thermal insulation for a qualifying industrial building is specifically allowed as expenditure on plant and machinery: thus a first year allowance followed by writing down allowances will be available as described above. When the building is eventually sold, the disposal value of the thermal insulation is taken to be zero, so no balancing charge can arise in respect of it.

     (iii)   *A factory canteen*

Expenditure on a factory canteen will qualify for industrial buildings allowances. The definition of an industrial building includes any building or structure provided by the person carrying on a qualifying trade (that is, one using a building that qualifies for industrial buildings allowances) for the welfare of workers employed in the trade.

5 Property income

Tutorial notes.

1   The interest on the loan is dealt with under the loan relationship rules. It is not a property business expense.

2   Income and expenses are dealt with on the accruals basis when calculating the property business profit.

P LTD: PROPERTY BUSINESS INCOME

	£	£	£
First Property			
Premium £20,000 × [1 − 0.02 (30 − 1)]			8,400
Rent £4,000 × 9/12			3,000
			11,400
Second Property			
Rent £600 × 3		1,800	
Rent £2,100 × 1/3		700	
		2,500	
Less: water rates £390 × 6/12	195		
Insurance £440 × 6/11	240		
repairs: capital	0		
furniture: in year to 31.3.07	0		
		(435)	
			2,065
Property business income			13,465

No deduction is allowed for the replacement cost of the furniture in the year to 31 March 2006. This cost will instead be allowed as a deduction in the year to 31 March 2007.

6 Gains and losses

Tutorial note. Current year losses are dealt with before losses brought forward.

Motor cars are exempt assets, so the loss brought forward from the year ended 31 March 2005 is £16,400.

The position for the year ended 31 March 2006 is as follows.

	£
Gains	
Shares	17,700
Picture	3,000
	20,700
Less loss on shares	(6,000)
	14,700
Less loss brought forward	(14,700)
Chargeable gains	Nil

The loss carried forward at 31 March 2006 is £(16,400 − 14,700) = £1,700.

7 Hardup Ltd

Tutorial note. The date of disposal for chargeable gains purposes is the date that the disposal becomes unconditional. In this case the date of exchange, not the date of completion.

Rollover relief is not available to defer the gain arising on the sale of the office block, because the reinvestment was not made in the qualifying period, commencing one year before and ending three years after the disposal.

CAPITAL GAINS COMPUTATION

	£
Office block (W1)	27,830
Plot of land (W2)	19,300
Workshop (W3)	48,265
Taxable gains	95,395

Workings

1 *The office block*

	£
Proceeds	120,000
Less cost	(65,000)
	55,000
Less indexation allowance $\dfrac{189.7 - 133.8}{133.8}$ (0.418) × £65,000	(27,170)
Chargeable gain	27,830

Rollover relief is not available.

2 *The plot of land*

	£
Proceeds	69,000
Less: cost	(20,000)
expenditure in July 1988	(4,000)
	45,000
Less indexation allowance	
$\dfrac{188.9 - 88.64}{88.64}$ (1.131) × £20,000	(22,620)
$\dfrac{188.9 - 106.7}{106.7}$ (0.770) × £4,000	(3,080)
	19,300

3 *The workshop*

	£
Proceeds	173,000
Less cost	(65,000)
	108,000
Less indexation allowance $\dfrac{188.9 - 98.45}{98.45}$ (0.919) × £65,000	(59,735)
	48,265

8 Ferraro Ltd

Tutorial note. The pro-forma for loss relief is important. If you learn the proforma you should find that the figures just slot into place. Note that the result of a losses claim may be that, as here, gift aid donations become unrelieved.

	12m to 31.12.02 £	12m to 31.12.03 £	9m to 30.9.04 £	12m to 30.9.05 £
		Accounting periods		
Trading profits	34,480	6,200	4,320	0
Investment income	200	80	240	260
Property business income	1,200	1,420	1,440	1,600
Chargeable gain (12,680 – 5,000)	0	0	7,680	0
	35,880	7,700	13,680	1,860
Less s 393A – current	0	0	0	(1,860)
	35,880	7,700	13,680	0
Less s 393A – c/b	0	(1,925)	(13,680)	(0)
Less charges	(1,000)	(0)	(0)	(0)
PCTCT	34,880	5,775	0	0

The loss carried forward against future profits of the same trade is £100,000 – £(1,925 + 13,680 + 1,860) = £82,535.

The allowable capital loss of £9,423 during the year ended 30 September 2005 is carried forward against future chargeable gains.

The gift aid donation made in the 9 months to 30.9.04 remains unrelieved. Similarly the unrelieved gift aid donation in the year 30.9.05 remains unrelieved. Unrelieved gift aid donations cannot be carried forward.

Tutorial note. The loss is carried back to set against profits arising the previous 12 months. This means that the set off in the y/e 31.12.03 is restricted to 3/12 × £7,700 = £1,925.

9 P Ltd

Tutorial note. You are asked to use group relief in the most efficient manner. This means giving it first to companies in the small companies' marginal relief band, then to companies paying tax at the full rate and then to companies in the starting rate marginal relief band. You must recognise that T Ltd is an associated company, being under common control with the P Ltd group.

(a)   There are six associated companies, so the lower and upper limits for small companies' rate purposes are £50,000 and £250,000 respectively. The upper and lower limits for starting rate purposes are £8,333 and £1,667 respectively.

S Ltd and T Ltd are outside the P Ltd group for group relief purposes. P Ltd's loss should be surrendered first to Q Ltd, to bring its taxable profits down to £50,000, then to R Ltd to bring its taxable profits down to £50,000 and finally to M Ltd.

	M Ltd £	P Ltd £	Q Ltd £	R Ltd £	S Ltd £	T Ltd £
Trading profits	20,000	0	64,000	260,000	0	70,000
Property business income	0	6,000	4,000	0	0	0
	20,000	6,000	68,000	260,000	0	70,000
Less charges	(4,000)	(4,500)	(2,000)	(5,000)	0	0
	16,000	1,500	66,000	255,000	0	70,000
Less group relief	(2,000)	0	(16,000)	(205,000)	0	0
PCTCT	14,000	1,500	50,000	50,000	0	70,000

	M Ltd £	P Ltd £	Q Ltd £	R Ltd £	S Ltd £	T Ltd £
Corporation tax: at 0%		0				
at 19%	2,660		9,500	9,500	0	
at 30%						21,000
Less: small companies Marginal relief 11/400 (£250,000 – 70,000)						(4,950)
MCT payable	2,660	0	9,500	9,500	0	16,050

There would have been no point in P Ltd making a claim to set the loss against its own PCTCT in the year as these profits are not taxable.

(b)   If P Ltd were to acquire another 8% of the share capital of S Ltd, bringing the total holding to 75%, S Ltd's losses could be surrendered to P Ltd, Q Ltd, R Ltd or M Ltd.

10 Apple Ltd

Tutorial note. The marginal rate of tax of 32.75% is an effective tax rate only. It is never actually used in working out corporation tax.

(a)   Group relief is available within a 75% group. This is one where one company is a 75% subsidiary of another company or both are 75% subsidiaries of a third company. The holding company must have at least 75% of the ordinary share capital of the subsidiary; a right to at least 75% of the distributable income of the subsidiary; and the right to at least 75% of the net assets of the subsidiary were it to be wound up.

Two companies are in a group only if there is a 75% effective interest eg if Company A holds 90% of Company B which holds 90% of Company C, all three companies are in a group because 90% × 90% = 81%.

(b)   Losses should be allocated to the company with the highest marginal rate of tax. This is Cherry Ltd and Apple Ltd to the extent that profits exceed £100,000 since the small companies rate lower limit is £300,000 ÷ 3 = £100,000. Such profits are taxed at the marginal rate of 32.75%. Then, the remainder of the loss should be set against the profits of Banana Ltd which bears tax at 30%. The capital loss cannot be group relieved.

(c)   Rollover relief for part of Apple Ltd's gain can be claimed in respect of the investment by Cherry Ltd. The excess of amount of proceeds over the amount invested remains in charge ie £(418,000 – 290,000) = £128,000.

An election should be made so that the asset disposed of at a loss by Banana Ltd is treated as having been disposed of by Apple Ltd. Apple Ltd will then be able to offset the loss of £8,000 against the gain of £128,000, leaving £120,000 chargeable.

Apple Ltd should then make a current year loss relief claim to bring its profits down to £100,000.

	Apple Ltd £	Banana Ltd £	Cherry Ltd £
Trading profits	-	650,000	130,000
Net Capital gain	120,000	-	-
	120,000	650,000	130,000
Less: s 393A(1)	(20,000)		
group relief		(75,000)	(30,000)
PCTCT	100,000	575,000	100,000

	Apple Ltd	Banana Ltd	Cherry Ltd
	£	£	£
Tax @ 19%	19,000		19,000
Tax @ 30%		172,500	

Note that the SCR upper limit is £1,500,000 ÷ 3 = £500,000.

11 M Ltd

> **Tutorial note.** In order to maximise the set off of double tax relief, charges are allocated firstly to UK profits and then to overseas sources of income that have suffered the lowest rate of overseas tax. At paper 2.3 the only charge on income that will be examined is a gift aid donation.
>
> There are five associated companies so the full rate of corporation tax applies.
>
> In an exam question, take care to identify when relief for underlying tax is available and when it is not. If relief for underlying tax is available you will need to gross the net dividend up for both withholding and underlying tax.

Year ended 31 March 2006

	Total	UK	A Inc	B PG	C SA
	£	£	£	£	£
Trading profits	20,000	20,000			
Foreign income (W1)	587,500	-	200,000	200,000	187,500
	607,500	20,000	200,000	200,000	187,500
Less: Charge on income	(75,000)	(20,000)	(55,000)	-	-
Profits chargeable to corporation tax	532,500	-	145,000	200,000	187,500
CT @ 30%	159,750	-	43,500	60,000	56,250
Less: DTR (W2)	(136,250)	-	(30,000)	(50,000)	(56,250)
Mainstream corporation tax	23,500	-	13,500	10,000	-

Workings

1 *Dividend from C SA*

Since M Ltd's shareholding in C SA is at least 10%, relief for underlying tax is available:

	£
Dividend from C SA	120,000
Withholding tax (× 20/80)	30,000
	150,000
Underlying tax	
£150,000 × $\dfrac{200,000}{800,000}$	37,500
Gross dividend	187,500

2 *Overseas dividends*

			Net	Tax credit	Gross
			£	£	£
A	Inc	(15%)	170,000	30,000	200,000
B	PG	(25%)	150,000	50,000	200,000
C	SA	(20%)	120,000	67,500	187,500

3   *Double tax relief*

	A Inc	B pg	C Sa
	£	£	£
Lower of			
(i) UK tax	43,500	60,000	56,250
(ii) Overseas tax.	30,000	50,000	*67,500
	£30,000	£50,000	£56,250

* Underlying tax + withholding tax.

12 Hogg Ltd

> **Tutorial note**. 'Large' companies must pay their CT liabilities in quarterly instalments.

(a)   Hogg Ltd's corporation tax liability for the year is £1,750,000 × 30% = £525,000. The due dates for the payment of corporation tax by Hogg Ltd in respect of the year to 31.12.05 are:

	£
14 July 2005 1/4 × £525,000	131,250
14 October 2005 1/4 × £525,000	131,250
14 January 2006 1/4 × £525,000	131,250
14 April 2006 1/4 × £525,000	131,250
Total	525,000

(b)   The due dates for the payment of corporation tax instalments by Hogg Ltd in respect of the ten months to 31 October 2007 are:

14 July 2007	£180,000
14 October 2007	£180,000
14 January 2008	£180,000
14 February 2008 (4th month of next accounting period)	£60,000 (balance)

> **Tutorial note**. The amount of the instalments is $^{3}/n \times CT = {}^{3}/10 \times £600,000 = £180,000$.

13 Invoices, the tax point and returns

> **Tutorial note**. Question 3 in your exam paper will be on VAT. The items covered in this question are basic topics that are often examined. Ensure that you can deal with them.

(a)   A VAT invoice is necessary to reclaim input tax suffered. The issue of such an invoice usually sets the tax point for a supply. A VAT invoice must show an identifying number, the supplier's name and address and VAT number, the date, the unit price, the amount payable excluding VAT, a description of the goods and services supplied and the VAT chargeable.

(b)   The tax point determines the period in respect of which value added tax is payable or reclaimable. These periods are usually three months in length, but may be one month especially if a trader makes zero rated supplies and thus receives regular repayments of VAT. The tax point is often the invoice date; it may however be when goods are removed or when services are performed. The tax point also dictates the rate of VAT which applies: it is the rate in force on the day of the tax point.

(c)   A VAT return is sent to HM Revenue & Customs within one month of the end of each VAT period. It shows the VAT payable or repayable and total outputs and inputs for the period. Any VAT payable is sent with the return.

14 Justin

> **Tutorial note**. This question is a very basic VAT computation. Note how the input and output VAT is accounted for in respect of petrol. Note also that the VAT incurred on the entertaining is irrecoverable.

	£	£
Output VAT		
Furniture: £490,000 × 17.5%		85,750
Books: £2,400 × 0%		0
Petrol (VAT scale charge): £457 × 7/47		68
		85,818
Input VAT		
Furniture: £275,000 × 17.5%	48,125	
Computer: £2,400 × 17.5%	420	
Entertaining: irrecoverable	0	
Petrol: £2,800 × 17.5%	490	
		(49,035)
VAT to account for		36,783

15 Newcomer Ltd, Ongoing Ltd and Au Revoir Ltd

> **Tutorial notes**.
>
> 1 Where a discount is offered for prompt payment, VAT is chargeable on the net amount, regardless of whether the discount is taken up.
>
> 2 VAT on business entertaining is not recoverable where the cost of the entertaining is not a deductible trading expense.
>
> 3 Bad debt relief is only available for debts over six months old (measured from when the payment is due).
>
> 4 VAT incurred on the purchase of a car not used wholly for business purposes is not recoverable.

(a)   The registration threshold is £60,000 (from 1.4.05) during any 12 month consecutive period.

This is exceeded in January 2006:

		£
2005	October	11,500
	November	14,200
	December	21,400
2006	January	13,300
		60,400

Therefore, Newcomer Ltd must register within 30 days of the end of the period ie by 2 March 2006.

Newcomer Ltd will be registered from 1 March 2006 or an earlier date agreed between the company and HM Revenue & Customs.

(b)

	£	£
Output tax		
£120,000 × 95% = 114,000 × 17.5% (note 1)		19,950
Input tax		
£(35,640 − 480) = 35,160 × 17.5% (note 2)	6,153	
£2,000 × 17.5% (note 3)	350	
£21,150 × 7/47 (note 4)	3,150	(9,653)
VAT payable		10,297

Notes

1 VAT is calculated after the deduction of the prompt payment discount.
2 Entertaining is not an expense on which input tax can be recovered.
3 The debt must be 6 months old to claim bad debt relief.
4 Input tax on motor cars is blocked.

(c) A person is eligible for voluntary deregistration if Customs are satisfied that the rate of his taxable supplies (net of VAT) in the following one year period will not exceed £58,000 (from 1.4.05). However, voluntary deregistration will not be allowed if the reasons for the expected fall in value of taxable supplies is the cessation of taxable supplies or the suspension of taxable supplies for a period of 30 days or more in that following year. HM Revenue & Customs will cancel a person's registration from the date the request is made or an agreed later date.

16 Income tax

> **Tutorial note**. If you get into the habit of setting up your income tax computations with three columns like this you should have a good chance of getting them right. Remember that savings income in the basic rate band is taxed at 20%, *not* 22%. Dividend income within the basic rate band is taxed at 10%.

	Non-savings £	Savings (excl.dividend) £	Dividend £	Total £
Business profits	14,000			
Building society interest × 100/80		8,000		
Dividends × 100/90			2,000	
	14,000	8,000	2,000	
Less charge	(2,500)	0	0	
Statutory total income	11,500	8,000	2,000	21,500
Less personal allowance	(4,895)	0	0	
Taxable income	6,605	8,000	2,000	16,605

	£
Non-savings income	
Starting rate band £2,090 × 10%	209
Basic rate band £4,515 × 22%	993
Savings (excl dividend) income	
£8,000 × 20%	1,600
Dividend income	
£2,000 × 10%	200
	3,002
Less: tax suffered on building society interest	(1,600)
tax credit on dividend income	(200)
Balance of tax still to pay	1,202

	£	£
Profits received		14,000
Building society interest received		6,400
Dividend received		1,800
		22,200
Less: charge paid	2,500	
income tax to pay	1,202	
		(3,702)
Available to spend		18,498

17 Mr and Mrs Lowrie

> **Tutorial note**. Mr Lowrie's dividend income is above the higher rate threshold, so it is taxed at 32.5%. Mrs Lowrie's dividends, however, fall below this threshold and are consequently taxed at 10%.

	Non-savings £	Savings (excl. dividends) £	Dividends £	Total £
Mr Lowrie				
Employment income	36,000			
Dividends × 100/90			1,211	
Bank deposit interest × 100/80		750		
Building society interest × 100/80		740		
STI	36,000	1,490	1,211	38,701
Less personal allowance	(4,895)			
Taxable income	31,105	1,490	1,211	33,806

Non savings income £		£	£
2,090 × 10%			209
29,015 × 22%			6,383
Savings (excluding dividend) income			
£1,295 × 20%			259
£195 × 40%			78
Dividend income			
£1,211 × 32.5%			394
			7,323
Less: tax credit on dividend		121	
tax suffered on savings income		298	
PAYE		6,000	
			(6,419)
Tax payable			904

	Non-savings £	Savings (excl. dividends) £	Dividends £	Total £
Mrs Lowrie				
Employment income	20,000			
Dividends × 100/90			2,820	
Bank deposit interest × 100/80		95		
Building society interest × 100/80	-	525		
STI	20,000	620	2,820	23,440
Less personal allowance	(4,895)			
Taxable income	15,105	620	2,820	18,545

	£	£
Non-savings income		
£2,090 × 10%		209
£13,015 × 22%		2,863
15,105		3,072
Savings (excluding dividend) income		
£620 × 20%		124
Dividend income		
£2,820 × 10%		282
Tax liability		3,478
Less: tax credit on dividends	282	
tax suffered on savings income	124	
PAYE	2,611	
		(3,017)
Tax payable		461

18 Mr Cobbler

> **Tutorial note**. Significant cash flow advantages can be gained with a careful choice of accounting date.

THE TAXABLE PROFITS FOR THE FOUR YEARS 2005/06 TO 2008/09

The accounts profits will be as follows.

Period ending in	Working	Accounting date 31 March £	Accounting date 30 April £
2006	3 × £800	2,400	
	4 × £800		3,200
2007	3 × £800 + 6 × £1,200 + 3 × £2,000	15,600	
	2 × £800 + 6 × £1,200 + 4 × £2,000		16,800
2008	12 × £2,000	24,000	24,000
2009	12 × £2,000	24,000	24,000

The taxable profits will be as follows.

		Accounting date 31 March £	Accounting date 30 April £
2005/06	Actual basis £2,400	2,400	
	£3,200 × 3/4		2,400
2006/07	Year to 31.3.07	15,600	
	First 12 months		
	£3,200 + £16,800 × 8/12		14,400
2007/08	Year to 31.3.08	24,000	
	Year to 30.4.07		16,800
2008/09	Year to 31.3.09	24,000	
	Year to 30.4.08		24,000
		66,000	57,600

30 April is the better choice of accounting date. Although the difference between the taxable profits will be compensated for on cessation, that may not be for many years, so choosing 30 April may give a considerable cash flow advantage.

19 Miss Farrington

> **Tutorial note**. In a question like this, work out the capital allowances for each period of account before you think about allocating profits to tax years.
>
> Writing down allowances are time apportioned in a long period of account but first year allowances are not.
>
> As Miss Farrington's business is a 'small enterprise' for capital allowance purposes, 50% FYA are available for expenditure incurred in the one year period to 5.4.05.

We must first work out the capital allowances.

	FYA @ 40% £	FYA @ 50% £	Pool £	Car (65%) £	Allowances £
1.1.03 - 30.4.04					
Car				6,600	
WDA @ 25% × 16/12				(2,200)	1,430
Desk and office furniture	940				
General plant	3,835				
Secondhand oven	1,200				
Delivery van	1,800				
Typewriter	425				
	8,200				
FYA @ 40%	(3,280)				3,280
			4,920	4,400	4,710
1.5.04 – 30.4.05					
WDA @ 25%			(1,230)		1,230
				(1,100)	715
			3,690	3,300	
General plant (30.1.05)		1,000			
FYA @ 50%		(500)			500
			500		
Computer (30.4.05)	1,945				
FYA @ 40%	(778)		1,167		778
			5,357	3,300	3,223

Profits are as follows.

Period	Profit £	Capital allowances £	Adjusted profit £
1.1.03 - 30.4.04	20,710	4,710	16,000
1.5.04 - 30.4.05	15,125	3,223	11,902

The taxable profits are as follows.

Year	Basis period	Working	Taxable profit £
2002/03	1.1.03 - 5.4.03	£16,000 × 3/16	3,000
2003/04	6.4.03 - 5.4.04	£16,000 × 12/16	12,000
2004/05	1.5.03 - 30.4.04	£16,000 × 12/16	12,000
2005/06	1.5.04 - 30.4.05		11,902

The overlap profits are the profits from 1 May 2003 to 5 April 2004: £16,000 × 11/16 = £11,000.

20 Morgan

> **Tutorial note**. In a losses question take care to consider all available reliefs. When deciding on the best relief you must consider both the rate of tax saved and the timing of the relief.

(a)   Loss relief could be claimed:

(i)   under s 380 ICTA 1988, against other income of the year of loss (2006/07), the investment income of £8,000;

under s 380 ICTA 1988, against other income of the preceding year (2005/06). This would be trading profits of £15,000 plus investment income of £8,000;

under s 385 ICTA 1988, against the first available future profits of the same trade.

(b)   *The quickest claim*

The quickest way to obtain relief would be for Morgan to use s 380 ICTA 1988 in both years. The tax computations would then be as follows.

	2005/06 £	2006/07 £
Trading profits	15,000	0
Investment income	8,000	8,000
	23,000	8,000
Less s 380 loss relief	(23,000)	(8,000)
Taxable income	0	0

The balance of the loss, £1,000, would be carried forward and relieved under s 385.

Although s 380 produces loss relief quickly, it has the disadvantage of wasting Morgan's personal allowance in both years. Morgan could, if he chose, delay his relief by carrying the loss forward under s 385 ICTA 1988. The loss would then be set off only against trading income, with the investment income using his personal allowance.

(c)   On a cessation, terminal loss relief under s 388 ICTA 1988 would be available. The loss would be set against profits taxable in the tax year of cessation and the three preceding tax years, later years first. This would probably be the best claim for Morgan. The effect would be as follows.

Year	Original £	Loss relief £	Revised £
2006/07	0	0	0
2005/06	15,000	(15,000)	0
2004/05	18,000	(17,000)	1,000
2003/04	16,000	0	16,000

> **Tutorial note**. Because of Morgan's choice of accounting date, no overlap profits arose on commencement.

21 Adam, Bert and Charlie

> **Tutorial note**. Your first step with a partnership question should be to calculate profits for each period of account. Only after you have done this should you consider allocating the profits to tax years. Remember that the opening year rules apply when a partner joins to that partner. Similarly, when a partner leaves the closing year rules apply to the departing partner. All other partners are assessed on a continuing basis.

PROFESSIONAL EDUCATION

	Total £	A £	B £	C £	D £
Year ending 31 March 2003					
Salaries	3,700	1,500	1,200	1,000	
Balance	6,500	2,600	2,600	1,300	
Total	10,200	4,100	3,800	2,300	
Year ending 31 March 2004					
April to June					
Salaries	925	375	300	250	
Balance	4,275	1,710	1,710	855	
Total	5,200	2,085	2,010	1,105	
July to March					
Salaries	1,650		900	750	
Balance	13,950		8,370	5,580	
Total	15,600		9,270	6,330	
Totals for the year	20,800	2,085	11,280	7,435	
Year ending 31 March 2005					
Salaries	2,200		1,200	1,000	
Balance	10,400		6,240	4,160	
Total	12,600		7,440	5,160	
Year ending 31 March 2006					
April					
Salaries	183		100	83	
Balance	1,317		790	527	
Total	1,500		890	610	
May to March					
Salaries	4,950		1,650	1,650	1,650
Balance	11,550		6,237	4,158	1,155
Total	16,500		7,887	5,808	2,805
Totals for the year	18,000		8,777	6,418	2,805

Taxable profits are as follows.

Year	A £	B £	C £	D £
2002/03	4,100	3,800	2,300	
2003/04	2,085	11,280	7,435	
2004/05		7,440	5,160	
2005/06		8,777	6,418	2,805

22 Partnerships

Tutorial note. This was a pilot paper question, so it should give you a really good indication of the type of question that you might meet in the exam.

Overlap profits are relieved either on a change of accounting date or on a cessation. Each partner obtains relief for their own overlap profits and their own losses.

(a)   Each partner is taxed like a sole trader who runs a business which starts when he joins the partnership; finishes when he leaves the partnership; has the same periods of account as the partnership; and makes profits or losses equal to the partner's share of the partnership profits or losses.

(b)

	Total £	Anne £	Betty £	Chloe £
1.1.05 – 31.12.05				
January to June	30,000	15,000	15,000	
July to December	30,000	15,000	-	15,000
Totals	60,000	30,000	15,000	15,000
1.1.06 – 31.12.06	72,000	36,000	-	36,000

Trading profit assessments 2005/06

	Anne £	Betty £	Chloe £
Profits y/e 31.12.05	30,000		
Profits 1.1.05 – 30.6.05		15,000	
Profits 1.7.05 – 31.12.05			15,000
Profits 1.1.06 – 5.4.06			
3/12 × £36,000			9,000
	30,000	15,000	24,000
Less: overlap relief for Betty on cessation		(3,000)	
Profits assessable 2005/06	30,000	12,000	24,000

(c) (i) *Daniel*

Daniel can use his £20,000 loss:

- against total income of 2005/06 and/or of 2004/05 under s 380 ICTA 1988
- against future trading profits under s 385 ICTA 1988

(ii) *Edward*

Edward can use his £15,000 loss:

- against total income of 2005/06 and/or of 2004/05 under s 380 ICTA 1988

- if there is a terminal loss in the last 12 months of trading, against trading profits of the tax year of cessation and the three preceding years, later years first, under s 388 ICTA 1988

(iii) *Frank*

Frank can use his loss of £5,000:

- against total income of 2005/06 and/or 2004/05 under s 380 ICTA 1988
- against total income of 2002/03, 2003/04 and 2004/05 under s 381 ICTA 1988
- against future trading profits under s 385 ICTA 1988

23 Denise

Tutorial note. The letter below covers the important parts of the stakeholder pension scheme which you must ensure that you are aware of. In part (b) you were asked to write a letter so you should have ensured that you did so.

(a) The maximum contributions are:

Year	Age at start of year	NRE £	% of NRE	Gross premium £
2005/06	36	105,600 (capped)	20	21,120

The maximum gross pension contribution that Denise can make in 2005/06 is £21,120. Any amount paid will be paid net of basic rate tax at 22%.

(b) Dear Denise

Stakeholder pensions

The purpose of this letter is to set out how any contributions that you make to a stakeholder pension will be treated for tax purposes and to outline the pension benefits that will be available to you on retirement.

Benefits on retirement

You will be entitled to take retirement at any time between the ages of 50 and 75. Unplanned retirement can take place before age 50 but only on the grounds of serious ill health.

There are no limits on the amount of pension that can be paid on retirement. At retirement your accumulated pension fund can be used to buy the highest annuity available at the time. It is also possible to take a tax-free cash lump sum on retirement. There is no restriction on the amount of tax free cash, but it is limited to 25% of your pension fund on retirement. If you take tax free cash, you will receive a reduced pension because only the balance of your pension fund will remain available for annuity purchase.

Contributions

Although benefits payable under a stakeholder pension scheme are not limited, there is a restriction on contributions. Annual contributions to your scheme cannot exceed the greater of

(a) £3,600 (2005/06), and

(b) the relevant percentage of your net relevant earnings in your basis year (see below).

Your net relevant earnings (NRE) will broadly be the taxable profit of your dress making business, but these will be capped at £105,600 for 2005/06.

In any tax year in which you have actual NRE, you may choose a basis year for your deemed NRE on which contributions are based. This can be the current tax year or one of the previous five tax years. If a basis year is not chosen, only contributions up to the earnings threshold can be made. Once you have chosen a basis year, your NRE will be presumed to be the same in that year and the next five tax years. Therefore if you choose 2005/06 as your basis year, your 2005/06 to 2010/11 NRE will be deemed to be £115,000 (subject to the earnings cap for the year of contribution).

It will be possible for you to choose a new basis year with higher earnings within this time limit if you wish. This will only be relevant for you if the earnings cap rises above £115,000.

The percentage of your NRE that may be paid in pension contributions depends on your age at the start of the tax year. From ages 36 to 45, it is 20%.

I hope the above is useful. If you have any queries, please do not hesitate to contact me.

Yours sincerely,

A N Accountant

(c) *Class 2 NICs*

£2.10 × 52	£109
Class 4 NICs	£
£(32,760 − 4,895) × 8%	2,229
£(115,000 − 32,760) × 1%	822
	3,051

24 Tim

> **Tutorial note**. Three payments of income tax may need to be made in respect of a tax year. Two payments on account are normally made on 31 January in the tax year and on the following 31 July. These are based on the prior year tax liability. A final balancing payment of the income tax due for a year is normally made on the 31 January following the year.

Tim's Payments on Account for 2005/06 were based on the excess of his 2004/05 tax liability over amounts deducted under the PAYE system, amounts deducted at source and tax credits on dividends:

	£
2004/05 tax liability	16,800
Less: PAYE	(7,200)
Tax deducted at source	(800)
Tax credit on dividends	(200)
Total payments on account for 2005/06	8,600

Two equal payments on account of £4,300 (£8,600 / 2) were required. The due dates for these payments were 31 January 2006 and 31 July 2006 respectively.

The final payment in respect of Tim's 2005/06 tax liability was due on 31 January 2007 and was calculated as follows:

	£
2005/06 tax liability	22,000
Less: PAYE	(7,100)
Tax deducted at source	(900)
Tax credit on dividends	(250)
	13,750
Less: Payments on account	(8,600)
Final payment due 31.1.07	5,150

25 Employment and self-employment

> **Tutorial note**. In general, individuals prefer self employment to employment because NICs are lower and the rules on the deductibility of expenses are less onerous. The Revenue will decide any particular case of employment or self employment by looking at all the relevant facts.

The factors to consider in deciding whether someone is employed or self-employed for income tax purposes are as follows.

(a) How much control is exercised over the way work is done? The greater the control, the more likely it is that the worker is an employee.

(b) Does the worker provide his own equipment? That would indicate self-employment.

(c) If the worker hires his own helpers, that indicates self-employment.

(d)   If the worker can profit by his own sound management, or lose money through errors, that indicates self-employment.

(e)   If there is a continuing obligation to provide work for the workers, and an obligation on the worker to do whatever job is offered next, that indicates employment.

(f)   If the worker accepts work from any independent sources, that indicates self-employment.

(g)   If the worker can work whenever he chooses, that indicates self-employment.

These tests are summed up in the general rule that there is employment when there is a contract of service, and self-employment when is a contract for services.

26 Cars and loans

> **Tutorial note**. The calculation of car and loan benefits are particularly important for exam purposes. Ensure that you pro-rate the benefits if they are not available for the entire year.

(a)   A taxable benefit must be computed for Mr Andrews. The benefit will equal the difference between the interest which would have arisen at the official rate and the actual interest paid. The benefit for 2005/06 is therefore £16,000 × (5 − 1)% × 6 months/12 months = £320.

(b)   Because the loan to Mrs Preece does not exceed £5,000, the taxable benefit is zero.

(c)   Mr Charles will have a taxable benefit of the annual value of the TV and video system, which will be computed as 20% of the value of the asset when first provided as a benefit to any employee. If the system had been lent to an employee when it was bought, the benefit for 2005/06 would be £800 × 20% = £160 × 10/12 = £133. If the system was first provided as a benefit in June 2005, the benefit would be £500 × 20% = £100 × 10/12 = £83.

(d)   Long service awards of tangible property to employees with at least 20 years service are not taxed provided the cost to the employer does not exceed £50 for each year of service and no similar award has been made to the same person within the previous ten years. In Mrs Davies's case the limit on value would be £50 × 25 = £1,250, so there will be no taxable benefit.

(e)   The car benefit and fuel scale benefit will apply to the car provided for Mr Edgar. The car benefit is calculated as price of car × %. The % depends on the CO_2 emissions of the car.

(i)   Because CO_2 emissions are 139g/km the percentage is 15%. The emissions figure is rounded down to the nearest 5 below ie to 135g/km. This is below the 140g/km baseline so the percentage is 15%.

(ii)   The fuel scale benefit will be at £14,400 multiplied by the percentage used in calculating the car benefit, in this case 15%.

(iii)   The charges will not be reduced on a time basis because the car was provided for the whole of 2005/06.

The taxable benefit will therefore be as follows.

	£
Car £23,000 × 15%	3,450
Fuel £14,400 × 15%	2,160
	5,610

(f)   Mr Ford will be taxed on the annual value of the flat and of the furniture. The company's payment of his council tax will also be a taxable benefit.

The following rules will apply.

(i)   There will be a basic accommodation benefit equal to the rateable value.

(ii)   There will be an additional accommodation benefit equal to the excess of the flat's cost over £75,000, multiplied by the official rate of interest at the start of the tax year.

(iii)   There will be a benefit in respect of the use of the furniture, equal to 20% of its value when first provided as a benefit to any employee.

The taxable benefit will therefore be as follows.

		£
Flat:	annual value	900
	extra charge £(100,000 - 75,000) × 5%	1,250
		2,150
Furniture £5,000 × 20%		1,000
Council tax		500
		3,650

27 Lai Chan

Tutorial notes. This pilot paper question is a good example of the type of question that you might find in Section A of the exam.

1   For capital allowance purposes the WDA is restricted by the length of the basis period, but the FYA is not.

2   There is no capital allowance restriction in respect of the private use of an asset by an employee.

3   The basic rate band is extended by the gross amount of personal pension contributions made. Occupational pension contributions are, however, deducted in computing employment income.

4   There is no taxable benefit in respect of the company's contribution to the occupational pension scheme.

(a)   *Income tax liability*

	£	Non-savings income £
Gross salary 9 × £3,250	29,250	
Less: pension contribution (6%)	(1,755)	
	27,495	
Car benefit (W1)	3,780	
Fuel benefit (W2)	2,700	
Taxable cheap loan (W3)	625	
Employment income		34,600
Trading profit	19,900	
Less: Capital allowances (W4)	(4,908)	
Taxable trading profit		14,992
STI		49,592
Less: personal allowance		(4,895)
Taxable income		44,697

Tax

	£
£2,090 × 10%	209
£31,810 × 22%	6,998
£10,797 (44,697 − 33,900(W5)) × 40%	4,319
Tax liability	11,526

Workings

1   *Car benefit*

	£
25% × £26,400 × 9/12 (note)	4,950
Less: contribution £130 × 9	(1,170)
	3,780

Note. The % depends on the CO_2 emissions of the car.

CO_2 emissions = 190 g/km

Amount above baseline figure 190 − 140 = 50 g/km

Divide by 5 = 10 g/km

Taxable percentage = 15% + 10% = 25%

The benefit is time apportioned as the car is available for only nine months of the year.

2   *Fuel benefit*

£14,400 × 25% × 9/12   £2,700

No reduction for partial reimbursement of private fuel cost. The benefit is time apportioned as the car was available for only nine months of the year.

The taxable percentage used in calculating the fuel benefit is the same as the percentage used in calculating the car benefit.

3   *Taxable cheap loan*

Average method

$$5\% \times \frac{30,000 + 10,000}{2} \times 9/12 = £750$$

Alternative method (strict method)

	£
£30,000 × 3/12 × 5% =	375
£10,000 × 6/12 × 5% =	250
	625

Elect for strict method

4

	FYA @ 40% £	General pool £	Private car (60%) £	Short life asset £	Allowances £
Additions not qualifying for FYA					
- private car			14,800		
- employee car		10,400			
WDA @ 25% × 3/12		(650)			650
		9,750			
WDA @ £3,000 (restricted) × 3/12			(750) × 60%		450
			14,050		
Additions qualifying for FYA					
- recording equipment	7,440				
- recording equipment				2,080	
Less: FYA @ 40%	(2,976)			(832)	3,808
TWDV c/f		4,464			
Allowances		14,214	14,050	1,248	
					4,908

5   Basic rate tax band.

£32,400 + (£390 × 100/78 × 3) = £33,900

(b)   Up to 31.12.05, PAYE will have been deducted from Lai Chan's salary. It is likely that her PAYE code was adjusted to take account of her benefits. Further tax payable (or tax repayable) will be dealt with under the self-assessment system.

As Lai Chan was employed before starting in business on her own account, she is unlikely to have made any payments on account for 2005/06. Therefore, the tax on her trading profit will be collected in full on 31 January 2007 under the self assessment system.

28 Sasha Shah

> **Tutorial notes.**
>
> 1   Strictly, expenses are only deductible in calculating net taxable earnings if they are incurred wholly, necessarily and exclusively in the performance of the duties. In practice, however, the Revenue allow an apportionment between private and business use as here.
>
> 2   Capital allowances are available to an employee who provides plant and machinery necessarily for use in the performance of his duties, in the same way as a sole trader.
>
> 3   The use of the car for travel between home and work is ordinary commuting and not business use.
>
> 4   'Earnings' for Class 4 NIC purposes are trading profits. However, earnings for Class 1 NIC purposes are gross earnings before the deductions of any expenses.

(a)   Factors that will indicate that a worker should be treated as an employee rather than as self employed are:

(i)   control by employer over employee's work;

(ii)   employee must accept further work if offered (and employer must offer work);

(iii)   employee does not provide own equipment;

(iv)   employee does not hire own helpers;

(v)   employee does not take substantial financial risk;

(vi)   employee does not have responsibility for investment and management of business and cannot benefit from sound management;

(vii) employee cannot work when he chooses but when an employer tells him to work;

(viii) described as an employee in any agreement between parties.

(b)   (i)   Income assessable as Trading Profits.

Note: It is assumed that Sasha's business meets the definition of 'small business' for FYA purposes.

	£	£
Gross income		60,000
Less: business expenses on heating etc	600	
FYA @ 40% on computer	4,000	
business expenses re car (£3,500 × 40%)	1,400	
WDA @ 25% on business car		
£10,000 × 25% × 40%	1,000	(7,000)
Assessable as trading profits		53,000

(iii) Net taxable earnings

	£	£
Gross income		60,000
Less: business expenses on heating etc (note 1)	600	
FYA @ 40% on computer (note 2)	4,000	(4,600)
Net taxable earnings		55,400

(c) (i) Class 2 and Class 4 NIC

		£
Class 2	£2.10 × 52	109.20
Class 4	£(32,760 – 4,895) × 8%	2,229.20
	£(53,000 – 32,760) × 1%	202.40
Total		2,540.80

(ii) Class 1 NIC (Primary)

	£
£(32,760 – 4,895) × 11%	3,065.15
£(60,000 – 32,760) × 1%	272.40
Total	3,337.55

29 Industrial Ltd

Tutorial note. This question is a typical example of the compulsory 30 mark question that you will be faced with in Section A of your exam. Do not allow the length of the question to overwhelm you – you should break the question down into parts as you work through it.

(a) *Corporation tax payable y/e 31.3.06.*

	£	£
Trading profit	1,689,710	
Less: patent royalties	(12,000)	
Less: Capital allowances		
- on Factory (W1)	(12,000)	
- on Plant and machinery (W2)	(42,110)	
Trading profit		1,623,600
Investment income	12,500	
Loan interest received	36,000	48,500
Property business income (W3)		73,200
Capital gains (W4)		62,122
Total profits		1,807,422
Less: charges on income		
- Gift Aid paid		(1,500)
PCTCT		1,805,922

Tax

	£
£1,805,922 × 30%	541,777

Workings

1   IBA

Expenditure eligible for IBAs

	£
Levelling the land	9,200
Architect's fees	24,300
Concrete floor	16,500
Factory	187,500
General offices (less than 25% of total)	62,500
	300,000
IBA @ 4% (building in use on 31.3.06)	£12,000

2   Plant and machinery

	FYAs £	General pool £	Expensive car (1) £	Expensive car (2) £	Allowances given £
TWDV b/f		84,600	15,400		
Addition not qualifying for FYAs				17,200	
Disposal			(19,600)		
Balancing charge			4,200		(4,200)
WDA @ 25%		(21,150)		(max)	24,150
				(3,000)	
		63,450		14,200	
Additions qualifying for FYA @ 40%					
Heating system	12,800				
Fire alarm system	7,200				
Computer	3,400				
Lorry	32,000				
	55,400				
Less: FYA @ 40%	(22,160)				22,160
		33,240			
TWDV c/f		96,690	–	14,200	
Allowances given					42,110

Note. The plant does not qualify for 50% FYA as Industrial Ltd is not a 'small' enterprise.

3   Property business profit

	£	£
Premium		
Amount received	80,000	
Less: 2% × (10 − 1) × 80,000	(14,400)	
Assessable as property income		65,600
Rental (3/12 × £30,400)		7,600
Property business profit		73,200

4   Capital gain on sale of shares

	£
Proceeds	223,000
Less: cost	(135,800)
Unindexed gain	87,200
Less: indexation allowance	(14,278)
Indexed gain	72,922
Less: loss b/f	(10,800)
Net gains	62,122

(b) (i) Industrial Ltd is a 'large' company as it pays corporation tax at the full rate and did so in the previous year. Therefore it is required to make quarterly payments on account of corporation tax.

(ii) Industrial Ltd must pay its liability in four equal instalments. These are due on 14 October 2005; 14 January 2006; 14 April 2006 and 14 July 2006.

30 Susan White

> **Tutorial note**. Losses are allocated to gains before taper relief is applied. They should be allocated to the gain which attracts the lowest amount of taper relief (ie where the highest percentage of the gain remains chargeable).

(a) The following shareholdings in trading companies qualify for CGT business asset taper relief.

   (i) shares in unlisted companies;
   (ii) shares in a company of which the shareholder is an officer or employee;
   (iii) shares in a company in which the shareholder can exercise at least 5% of voting rights.

In addition, an employee of a non trading company qualifies for business asset taper relief on a disposal of his shareholding providing he (together with any connected persons) does not own more than 10 per cent of (generally) the voting rights in the company.

(b) *Capital gains*

Red Ltd

	£
5,000 shares (acquired within next 30 days)	
Proceeds $\dfrac{5,000}{20,000} \times £55,000$	13,750
Less: cost	(15,000)
Loss	(1,250)
15,000 shares (post 6.4.98 acquisition)	
Proceeds $\dfrac{15,000}{20,000} \times £55,000$	41,250
Less: cost $\dfrac{15,000}{25,000} \times 37,500$	(22,500)
Gain before taper relief	18,750

Taper relief period (2.6.04 – 1.6.05) = 1 year. 50% of any net gain will remain chargeable after taper relief.

Blue Ltd

	£
MV (sale between connected persons)	200,000
Less: cost	(18,000)
Unindexed gain	182,000
Less: indexation allowance to April 1998	(12,800)
Indexed gain	169,200
Gain not available for gift relief £(70,000 – 18,000)	£52,000
Taper relief period (6.4.98 – 5.4.05) = 7 years	
Gift relief £(169,200 – 52,000)	£117,200

Summary

	1 year taper £	7 year taper £
Gains	18,750	52,000
Less: loss (best use)	(1,250)	-
Net gains before taper relief	17,500	52,000
Gains after taper relief		
50% × £17,500	8,750	
25% × £52,000		13,000
Total gains £(8,750 + 13,000)		£21,750

Index

Note: **Key Terms** and their page references are given in **bold**.

Review Form & Free Prize Draw – Paper 2.3 Business Taxation (8/05)

All original review forms from the entire BPP range, completed with genuine comments, will be entered into one of two draws on 31 January 2006 and 31 July 2006. The names on the first four forms picked out on each occasion will be sent a cheque for £50.

Name: _____ Address: _____

_____

_____

How have you used this Interactive Text?
(Tick one box only)

☐ Home study (book only)

☐ On a course: college _____

☐ With 'correspondence' package

☐ Other _____

Why did you decide to purchase this Interactive Text? *(Tick one box only)*

☐ Have used BPP Texts in the past

☐ Recommendation by friend/colleague

☐ Recommendation by a lecturer at college

☐ Saw advertising

☐ Saw information on BPP website

☐ Other _____

During the past six months do you recall seeing/receiving any of the following?
(Tick as many boxes as are relevant)

☐ Our advertisement in *ACCA Student Accountant*

☐ Our advertisement in *Pass*

☐ Our advertisement in *PQ*

☐ Our brochure with a letter through the post

☐ Our website www.bpp.com

Which (if any) aspects of our advertising do you find useful?
(Tick as many boxes as are relevant)

☐ Prices and publication dates of new editions

☐ Information on Text content

☐ Facility to order books off-the-page

☐ None of the above

Which BPP products have you used?

Text	☑	Success CD	☐	Learn Online	☐
Kit	☐	i-Learn	☐	Home Study Package	☐
Passcard	☐	i-Pass	☐	Home Study PLUS	☐

Your ratings, comments and suggestions would be appreciated on the following areas.

	Very useful	Useful	Not useful
Introductory section (Key study steps, personal study)	☐	☐	☐
Chapter introductions	☐	☐	☐
Key terms	☐	☐	☐
Quality of explanations	☐	☐	☐
Case studies and other examples	☐	☐	☐
Exam focus points	☐	☐	☐
Questions and answers in each chapter	☐	☐	☐
Fast forwards and chapter roundups	☐	☐	☐
Quick quizzes	☐	☐	☐
Question Bank	☐	☐	☐
Answer Bank	☐	☐	☐
Index	☐	☐	☐
Icons	☐	☐	☐

Overall opinion of this Study Text	Excellent ☐	Good ☐	Adequate ☐ Poor ☐

Do you intend to continue using BPP products?   Yes ☐   No ☐

On the reverse of this page are noted particular areas of the text about which we would welcome your feedback. The BPP author of this edition can be e-mailed at: pippariley@bpp.com

Please return this form to: Nick Weller, ACCA Publishing Manager, BPP Professional Education, FREEPOST, London, W12 8BR

Review Form & Free Prize Draw (continued)

TELL US WHAT YOU THINK

Please note any further comments and suggestions/errors below

Free Prize Draw Rules

1   Closing date for 31 January 2006 draw is 31 December 2005. Closing date for 31 July 2006 draw is 30 June 2006.

2   Restricted to entries with UK and Eire addresses only. BPP employees, their families and business associates are excluded.

3   No purchase necessary. Entry forms are available upon request from BPP Professional Education. No more than one entry per title, per person. Draw restricted to persons aged 16 and over.

4   Winners will be notified by post and receive their cheques not later than 6 weeks after the relevant draw date.

5   The decision of the promoter in all matters is final and binding. No correspondence will be entered into.

ACCA Order

To BPP Professional Education, Aldine Place, London W12 8AW

Tel: 0845 0751 100 (within the UK) Fax: 020 8740 1184
Tel: +44 (0)20 8740 2211 (from overseas) Web: www.bpp.com
Order online: www.bpp.com/mybpp

Mr/Mrs/Ms (Full name)

Daytime delivery address

Postcode

Daytime Tel

Date of exam (month/year)

Scots law variant Y / N

Occasionally we may wish to email you relevant offers and information about courses and products. Please tick to opt into this service. ☐

	6/05 Texts	1/05 Kits	1/05 Passcards	Success CDs	7/05 i-Learn	7/05 i-Pass	Learn Online
PART 1							
1.1 Preparing Financial Statements (UK)	£26.00	£12.95	£9.95	£14.95	£40.00	£30.00	£100
1.2 Financial Information for Management	£26.00	£12.95	£9.95	£14.95	£40.00	£30.00	£100
1.3 Managing People	£26.00	£12.95	£9.95	£14.95	£40.00	£30.00	£100
PART 2							
2.1 Information Systems	£26.00	£12.95	£9.95	£14.95	£40.00	£30.00	£100
2.2 Corporate and Business Law (UK)**	£26.00	£12.95	£9.95	£14.95	£40.00	£30.00	£100
2.3 Business Taxation FA2004 (12/05 exams)	£24.95 (8/04)	£12.95	£9.95	£14.95	£34.95 (8/04)	£24.95 (8/04)	£100
2.3 Business Taxation FA2005	£26.00 †	£12.95	£9.95	£14.95	£40.00 (9/05)	£30.00 (9/05)	£100
2.4 Financial Management and Control	£26.00	£12.95	£9.95	£14.95	£40.00	£30.00	£100
2.5 Financial Reporting (UK)	£26.00 (7/05)	£12.95	£9.95	£14.95	£40.00	£30.00	£100
2.6 Audit and Internal Review (UK)	£26.00	£12.95	£9.95	£14.95	£40.00	£30.00	£100
PART 3						**8/04**	
3.1 Audit and Assurance Services (UK)	£26.00	£12.95	£9.95	£14.95		£30.00 (4/05)	£60
3.2 Advanced Taxation FA2004 (12/05 exams)	£24.95	£12.95	£9.95	£14.95		£24.95	£60
3.2 Advanced Taxation FA2005	£26.00 †	£12.95	£9.95	£14.95		£30.00 (9/05)	£60
3.3 Performance Management	£26.00	£12.95	£9.95	£14.95		£24.95	£60
3.4 Business Information Management	£26.00	£12.95	£9.95	£14.95		£24.95	£60
3.5 Strategic Business Planning and Devt	£26.00	£12.95	£9.95	£14.95		£24.95	£60
3.6 Advanced Corporate Reporting (UK)	£26.00 (7/05)	£12.95	£9.95	£14.95		£24.95	£60
3.7 Strategic Financial Management	£26.00	£12.95	£9.95	£14.95		£24.95	£60
INTERNATIONAL STREAM						**7/05**	
1.1 Preparing Financial Statements (Int'l)	£26.00	£12.95	£9.95		£40.00	£30.00	£100
2.2 Corporate and Business Law (Global)	£26.00	£12.95	£9.95				
2.5 Financial Reporting (Int'l)	£26.00	£12.95	£9.95		£40.00	£30.00	£100
2.6 Audit and Internal Review (Int'l)	£26.00	£12.95	£9.95		£40.00	£30.00	£100
3.1 Audit and Assurance Services (Int'l)	£26.00	£12.95	£9.95		£40.00	£30.00	£60
3.6 Advanced Corporate Reporting (Int'l)	£26.00	£12.95	£9.95		£40.00 (12/05)	£30.00	£60
Success in Your Research and Analysis							
Project - Tutorial Text (10/05)	£26.00						
Learning to Learn Accountancy (7/02)	£9.95						
Business Maths and English (6/04)	£9.95						

SUBTOTAL £ _____

† **(8/05** for 6/06 & 12/06 exams. New edition Kit, Passcard, i-Learn and i-Pass available in 2006)

POSTAGE & PACKING

Study Texts/Kits

	First	Each extra	Online
UK	£5.00	£2.00	£2.00
EU*	£6.00	£4.00	£4.00
Non EU	£20.00	£10.00	£10.00

Passcards/Success CDs/i-Learn/i-Pass

	First	Each extra	Online
UK	£2.00	£1.00	£1.00
EU*	£3.00	£2.00	£2.00
Non EU	£8.00	£8.00	£8.00

Learning to Learn Accountancy/Business Maths and English

	Each	Online
UK	£3.00	£2.00
EU*	£6.00	£4.00
Non EU	£20.00	£10.00

Grand Total (incl. Postage) £ _____

I enclose a cheque for _____
(Cheques to BPP Professional Education)

Or charge to Visa/Mastercard/Switch

Card Number

Expiry date _____ Start Date _____

Issue Number (Switch Only) _____

Signature _____

ACCA Order

To BPP Professional Education, Aldine Place, London W12 8AW

Tel: 0845 0751 100 (within the UK) Fax: 020 8740 1184

Tel: +44 (0)20 8740 2211 (from overseas) Web: www.bpp.com

Order online: www.bpp.com/mybpp

Mr/Mrs/Ms (Full name)

Daytime delivery address

Postcode

Daytime Tel

Date of exam (month/year)

Scots law variant Y / N

Occasionally we may wish to email you relevant offers and information about courses and products. Please tick to opt into this service. ☐

	Home Study Package*	Home Study PLUS*	Success CDs	7/05 i-Learn	Learn Online
PART 1					
1.1 Preparing Financial Statements UK	£115.00	£180.00	£14.95	£40.00	£100.00
1.2 Financial Information for Management	£115.00	£180.00	£14.95	£40.00	£100.00
1.3 Managing People	£115.00	£180.00	£14.95	£40.00	£100.00
PART 2					
2.1 Information Systems	£115.00	£180.00	£14.95	£40.00	£100.00
2.2 Corporate and Business Law UK***	£115.00	£180.00	£14.95	£40.00	£100.00
2.3 Business Taxation FA2004 (12/05 exams)	£115.00	£180.00	£14.95	£34.95 (8/04)	£100.00
2.3 Business Taxation FA2005 (2006 exams)	£115.00	£180.00	£14.95	£40.00 (9/05)	£100.00
2.4 Financial Management and Control	£115.00	£180.00	£14.95	£40.00	£100.00
2.5 Financial Reporting UK	£115.00	£180.00	£14.95	£40.00	£100.00
2.6 Audit and Internal Review UK	£115.00	£180.00	£14.95	£40.00	£100.00
PART 3					
3.1 Audit and Assurance Services UK	£115.00	£150.00	£14.95		£60.00
3.2 Advanced Taxation FA2004 (12/05 exams)	£115.00	£150.00	£14.95		£60.00
3.2 Advanced Taxation FA2005 (2006 exams)	£115.00	£150.00	£14.95		£60.00
3.3 Performance Management	£115.00	£150.00	£14.95		£60.00
3.4 Business Information Management	£115.00	£150.00	£14.95		£60.00
3.5 Strategic Business Planning and Development	£115.00	£150.00	£14.95		£60.00
3.6 Advanced Corporate Reporting UK	£115.00	£150.00	£14.95		£60.00
3.7 Strategic Financial Management	£115.00	£150.00	£14.95		£60.00
INTERNATIONAL STREAM					
1.1 Preparing Financial Statements (Int'l)	£115.00	£180.00		£40.00	£100.00
2.2 Corporate and Business Law (Global)	£115.00	£180.00			
2.5 Financial Reporting (Int'l)	£115.00	£180.00		£40.00	£100.00
2.6 Audit and Internal Review (Int'l)	£115.00	£180.00			£100.00
3.1 Audit and Assurance Services (Int'l)	£115.00	£150.00			£60.00
3.6 Advanced Corporate Reporting (Int'l)	£115.00	£150.00		£40.00 (12/05)	£60.00
Success in Your Research and Analysis Project - Tutorial Text (10/05)	£26.00				
Learning to Learn Accountancy (7/02)	Free/£9.95				
Business Maths and English (6/04)	Free/£9.95				
				SUBTOTAL	£

POSTAGE & PACKING

Home Study Packages

	First	Each extra	Each
UK	£6.00	£6.00	-
EU**	-	-	£15.00
Non EU	-	-	£50.00

Success CDs/i-Learn

	First	Each extra	Online
UK	£2.00	£1.00	£1.00
EU**	£3.00	£2.00	£2.00
Non EU	£8.00		£8.00

Learning to Learn Accountancy/Business Maths and English/Success in Your Research and Analysis Project

	Each	Online
UK (+£5.00 Success in Your Research and Analysis Project)	£3.00†	£2.00
EU**	£6.00	£4.00
Non EU	£20.00	£10.00

Postage and packing not charged on free copy ordered with Home Study Course.

Grand Total (incl. Postage) £

I enclose a cheque for
(Cheques to BPP Professional Education)

Or charge to Visa/Mastercard/Switch

Card Number

Expiry date Start Date

Issue Number (Switch Only)

Signature

We aim to deliver to all UK addresses inside 5 working days; a signature will be required. Orders to all EU addresses should be delivered within 6 working days. All other orders should be delivered within 8 working days. *Home Study Courses include Texts, Kits, Passcards and i-Pass (i-Pass not available for 2.2 Global and 3.1 International). You can also order one free copy of either Learning to Learn Accountancy or Business Maths and English per Home Study course, to a maximum of one of each per person. **EU includes the Republic of Ireland and the Channel Islands. ***For Scots law variant students, a free Scots Law Supplement is available with the 2.2 Text.